Who loves a garden still his Eden keeps,
Perennial pleasures plants, and wholesome harvests reaps.

AMOS BRONSON ALCOTT, 1799–1888, FROM *Tablets*

Keeping Eden

A History of Gardening in America

Massachusetts Horticultural Society

Walter T. Punch, *General Editor*

with essays by

William Howard Adams, Phyllis Andersen,

D. Keith Crotz, Gordon De Wolf, Mac Griswold, Catherine M. Howett,

Tovah Martin, Diane Kostial McGuire, Keith N. Morgan, Peggy Cornett Newcomb,

Michael Pollan, Walter T. Punch, Melanie L. Simo, David C. Streatfield,

Tamara Plakins Thornton, and Elisabeth Woodburn

A BULFINCH PRESS BOOK

Little, Brown and Company   Boston · Toronto · London

BAS-TITLE: The residence of Washington Irving, Esq., near Tarrytown, New York,
showing the Hudson River and boats to the left.

FRONTISPIECE: The variegated and deeply fringed petals of parrot tulips captivated
eighteenth- and nineteenth-century American gardeners.

FIRST EDITION

Library of Congress Cataloging-in-Publication Data appears on page 276

Bulfinch Press is an imprint and trademark of Little, Brown and Company (Inc.)
Published simultaneously in Canada by Little, Brown & Company (Canada) Limited

PRINTED IN SINGAPORE

Contents

Foreword

A QUICK LOOK at the table of contents or a scan of the text and illustrations in *Keeping Eden* will give an overriding sense of the richness of American horticulture. We have borrowed plants, landscaping ideas, and techniques from cultures around the world, adapted them to American tastes and our diverse climates, and added our own contributions to gardens and gardening.

Since 1829, the Massachusetts Horticultural Society has been a leader in educating the public about the value of horticulture and plants—to us as individuals and to our culture overall. The society's library is unsurpassed for its collection of works that comprise the written record of American horticulture. Through its publications and its classes for adults, children, and teachers, through flower shows, and through recognition of distinguished men, women, and organizations in the field of horticulture, the Massachusetts Horticultural Society has tried to highlight the ways that plants and gardening touch our lives and feed our souls.

This book is a celebration of the American spirit of inventiveness and experimentation, of creativity and adaptability. The value of the book is in assembling such a wonderful array of essays and illustrations reflecting our heritage of gardening and American culture through five centuries.

RICHARD H. DALEY
Executive Director, Denver Botanic Garden
Former Executive Director,
Massachusetts Horticultural Society

Horticultural Hall, Boston, c. 1900

Preface

THE IDEA FOR THIS BOOK was born in the library of the Massachusetts Horticultural Society. In a conversation with then Executive Director Richard Daley, I proposed that the society produce a television series on the history of gardening in America, rather like "America by Design," which concerned itself with the social history of architecture and public spaces in this country. Rick reminded me of the enormous costs in time and money that would be required and thought that, since I was not a television producer but a librarian by profession, perhaps a book would be more appropriate! Shortly thereafter, Betty Childs, then an editor at Bulfinch Press, paid a visit to the library and suggested a collaborative effort between our two organizations. She was delighted at the prospect of a book on American garden history and, since there are so few such books,

thought it would be favorably received by the general public as well as gardeners, landscape designers, architects, historians, and anyone else interested in the cultural life of this country.

Over the next several months and many meetings, Betty, Rick, and I discussed endless details and particulars. One "difficulty," if such it can be called, was selecting the topics to be covered. So rich is the history of gardening in this country, so varied and so complex, that limiting the book to a certain number of essays invariably meant leaving out some favorite areas or themes. It became clear that a judicious selection that would appeal to the widest possible readership was available. The somewhat eclectic outcome, it is hoped, will serve as catalyst and invitation to other, similar, endeavors.

The contributors to this book are among the lead-

The garden of Joseph Eck and Wayne Winterrowd, North Hill, Vermont

ing scholars and authorities on American landscape and gardening history. Some are also practitioners of historic landscape design. The reader will appreciate, therefore, any prejudices, emphases, and idiosyncratic points of view as the inevitable result of loving one's work. While each chapter may be read on its own, taken collectively the book will give a sense of the complex and interconnected story that is American gardening history. Whether looking at the sustenance gardens of the early settlers or the grand estates of the nineteenth-century gentry, one comes in contact with a process that occurs between the gardener and the gardened, doing more, in some sense, to benefit the former than the latter.

The reader will see gardens everywhere and of all kinds and descriptions. Some are on such a grand scale that the average person may be overwhelmed by their sheer magnitude and scope; others are so plain and basic that the essence of gardening is laid bare in its elementary aspect. Gardens will appear everywhere: country gardens, city gardens, gardens on paper and glass, gardens in books, gardens on the windowsill, gardens of the past, present, and future. The garden is looked at from many angles: as art, as science, as place, as idea or palette, as expression of wealth and power.

One purpose *Keeping Eden* hopes to serve is to demonstrate how intricately gardens and gardening have been involved in the general cultural life of this country from its very beginnings. The subtitle refers to five hundred years of gardening. The observation of the quincentennial of Columbus's first visit is a perfectly fine time—as fine as any other—to reflect on many things and, in this case, on the role the garden has played in the evolution of a national attitude toward the land. Implicit in these essays are assumptions made about the importance, fragility, and preciousness of the land as well as about the "opposite numbers" of these attributes.

It is fitting that this book be created under the auspices of the Massachusetts Horticultural Society. One of that organization's presidents once declared that the "history of the Massachusetts Horticultural Society is the history of horticulture in America." While this may, at first glance, seem somewhat self-serving, the society has been involved in virtually every aspect of horticulture and gardening since 1829, and its officers and members have been among the leading figures in American gardening. It is also fitting that Bulfinch Press be involved as publisher. As the illustrated-book imprint of Little, Brown and Company, Bulfinch is a part of a long tradition of publishing fine and beautiful books that began a mere eight years after the founding of the Massachusetts Horticultural Society—and in the same city.

The number of books on various aspects of gardens—other than American garden history, books about which are few and far between—being published in the last few years bespeaks a resurgence of interest that has no doubt been, in part at least, urged on by the conservation and ecology movements in this country. A serious void has been a comprehensive reference work on American gardens in all their complexity and diversity. While this book does not pretend to fill that need, it does introduce the problem by its very presence. Further, it acts, we dare hope, as a cohesive factor amidst many other admirable, more specific, works.

A trend that has been in evidence for some time is the awareness of the "American garden," much of which concerns design and plant material. For a very long time the United States took its cue in gardening, as in the larger cultural picture, from Europe and often from Great Britain. This is much less the case now. Such organizations as the regional garden history societies, the Garden Conservancy, the various symposia on American gardens, the increase in books on American conditions and appropriate plants all clearly signal a new-found self-appreciation and a found identity. There will, and needs to be, more of this without any attendant jingoistic or xenophobic reaction. It is time for a clear summons to an American garden style, or styles, and a sincere, reflective, and appreciative estimation of what the garden has meant and will continue to mean to such a large, diverse, and changing nation in the future. If this book helps to give some direction to that summons, it will have been successful.

WALTER T. PUNCH

Their rype corne

Their greene corne

Corne newly sprong.

Their sitting at meate

The place of solemne prayer.

The house wherin the Tombe of their Herounds standeth

SECOTON.

A Ceremony in their prayers with strange iesturs and songs dansing abowt posts carued on the topps lyke mens faces.

The Beginnings

Gordon De Wolf

Our knowledge of gardens in the New World at the time of Columbus's expeditions is gleaned from gardening books, accounts of early explorers, and records of gardening and horticulture situations when the first European settlers arrived on the shores of Virginia and Massachusetts.

One result of earlier explorations was that information on native plants and methods of cultivation was disseminated throughout western Europe and England, so the early settlers may very well have been acquainted with the plants grown by the local people. In any case, the necessity of survival soon allowed the colonists to know intimately the plants and farming ways of their new neighbors. Indeed, it may be argued that the native peoples kept the settlers alive and helped them to prosper, a great irony in light of what happened to those natives at the hands of later settlers.

From a horticultural perspective the early settlers were not astute, and their dependence upon the native peoples for help was great. In time, however, these enterprising and hardy settlers adopted and formed gardens that resembled those they had left behind. The letters and books in which they wrote of their travels and tribulations frequently mention various fruits, herbs, and field crops. While the hardships associated with just getting by precluded most ornamental gardening, the early colonists did bring memories of their former land with its neat rectangular gardens studded with roses and lilies. More stable times and more sophisticated social structures were required, though, for gardening for delight.

ON THIS SIDE of the Atlantic, and particularly in New England, we tend to think of the original settlers of the colonies as valiant refugees from religious, political, and juridical persecution. While it is true that the individual colonists may not have fitted gracefully into the social milieu of their home countries, it is also true that they were enabled to "escape" to the New World because people of substance had banded together into various trading companies and put up money for ships and supplies with the expectation that the settlers would send back gold, silver, and precious stones, as well as medicines, spices, and other commodities. The home governments that chartered these trading companies also hoped for raw materials—England, in particular, was desperate for a new source of masts and spars for the Royal Navy—and a population that would be dependent upon the home country for manufactured goods.

For the most part, the settlers were societal misfits, not sociopaths or criminals. They were, in many cases, people of substance or younger sons of families of substance. In the first case, they sought relief from religious or political persecution; in the second they were seeking their fortune. Much has been made of the paucity of persons with agricultural experience. This most likely was an indication of either agricultural prosperity in the home countries or the well-known conservatism of the farming class in any society. Pulling up stakes and sailing off into an indeterminate sunset is not something that farmers are apt to do. Since the early settlers had no beasts of burden, their gardening comprised a simple upscaling of the hand-powered vegetable gardening with which many were familiar. Farm experience, per se, was probably not essential.

The settlements that were founded had considerable difficulties surviving. Indeed, the first ones, on Roanoke Island, did not survive. For the first few years, raising sufficient food was a serious problem— and the alternative of purchasing a sufficient supply, either from the native Americans or from the mother country, was also extremely chancy. Another aspect of the problem was that not only were farmers in short supply but few of the colonists were artisans or skilled laborers.

Let us proceed under no delusions. For the first few years of settlement no one had the time for ornamental gardening. For the balance of the colonial period and well into the nineteenth century, only the very few wealthy families had the leisure time and could afford the labor that nonproductive pursuits required.* For most colonists, most of the time, the days were taken up with trying to provide enough food, clothing, shelter, and heat to keep body and soul together. This being the case, our look at the beginnings of American horticulture concerns only field crops and vegetables and focuses on three important issues: (1) what the colonists knew (or should have known) before their arrival about the plants of the New World; (2) what knowledge, techniques, and plants were acquired from the native Americans; (3) what they brought with them from the Old World.

The first colonies existed precariously. That some of them did survive is of inherent interest to modern Americans, making the question of why they survived of more than passing interest. It is notable that Captain John Smith figured in the establishment of both the Virginia and the Plymouth colonies and that there were people in both colonies who were able to deal diplomatically with the native Americans. But overshadowing all was the need for food, and, as it turned out, indigenous crops were the most productive.†

First, we need to situate the colonists in their place in history. The period of initial settlement began with Sir Walter Raleigh's landing on Roanoke Island in 1584 and extended to the settlement of Massachusetts Bay, a period of some forty years. There were, however, considerable preliminaries—indeed, some three hundred years of preliminaries.

OPENING ILLUSTRATION:
John White's Indian village of "Secoton" presents an idealized view, for surely the paths and fields would not have had such neat, straight edges and certainly there would not have been corn "newly sprong" and "rype" at the same time. We must remember that this picture was painted before 1590 while John White was full of enthusiasm for the idea of establishing a colony in the New World, and before he knew that he had lost his daughter and granddaughter.

*For all practical purposes, you cannot eat flowers or use them to make clothes. Aesthetics does not have a big sale when you are hungry and cold. "Pretty" things, under those circumstances, are considered nonproductive.

†It is important to remember that when it came to hay and pasture for cattle, horses, and sheep, European grasses drove the native species from the fields!

MARCO POLO (1254–1324) traveled to China during the period 1271 to 1295. His record of the riches of Cathay inspired much of the exploration that took place during the succeeding two hundred years. Since the overland routes from Europe were controlled by the Islamic nations of the Middle East, which exacted a heavy toll in taxes and transportation costs, western European nations began to consider the possibilities of a sea route to the Indies. Bartholemeu Dias (1450–1500) rounded the Cape of Good Hope in 1488. This achievement climaxed seventy years of Portuguese exploration along the west coast of Africa seeking a sea route to India and Cathay (which was finally found ten years later, in 1498, by Vasco da Gama [1460–1524]). Christopher Columbus (1451–1506), sailing for Spain in 1492, sought a different sea route to Cathay. He was, as we know, unsuccessful in his original purpose, but vastly successful in opening up a new hemisphere for European exploitation. Ferdinand Magellan (1480–1521), also sailing for Spain, left Seville in 1519 with the intent of reaching the East Indies by sailing westward around the newfound continents. The expedition was successful, but Magellan died in the Philippines. One of his ships did return to Spain in 1522, having circumnavigated the planet and thereby provided a practical demonstration that the earth was at least cylindrical.

The Spanish conquest of the New World began ninety years before Raleigh's first attempt at settlement on Roanoke Island. In that time, all of the major American food crops were introduced to Europe primarily by the Spanish, with the Portuguese and the French playing a smaller role in plant dissemination. Staples of the native Americans were maize, or Indian corn (*Zea Mays*), beans (*Phaseolus vulgaris* and *P. coccineus*), pumpkins and squashes (*Cucurbita maxima, C. moschata,* and *C. Pepo*), sweet potatoes (*Ipomoea Batatas*), and white potatoes (*Solanum tuberosum*). These plants were distributed rather quickly from Spain around the Mediterranean and into southern Europe. Their introduction into northern Europe took longer, but by 1597 they were being grown by John Gerard in London, even though only the beans had gained much favor with the general public there. The Jerusalem artichoke (*Helianthus tuberosus*), which

Türckisch korn.
CCCCLXXIII.

Sixteenth-century German doctor and professor of medicine Leonhart Fuchs provided the first European illustration of maize in 1543.

arrived in Europe at the same time, was imported from Canada, via France.

Maize was seen and commented on by Columbus, in 1492. It is said that he brought it back to Spain in that year and its cultivation there is recorded in 1525. However, it apparently was still not common as late as 1571. (The Portuguese, however, had taken it to Java by 1496!) Maize is mentioned by the German herbalists Hieronymus Bock, in 1539, and Leonhart Fuchs, in 1542; John Gerard was growing it in London in 1597.

Climbing kidney beans, or French beans, are mentioned by most of the early explorers as being found from Canada to South America. Who first brought them to Europe, and when, seems not to be recorded. They were in cultivation in Germany by 1552 and Gerard grew four sorts of them in London in 1597. Although not rare, they were still not in common cultivation when John Parkinson wrote at the end of the 1620s. Squashes and pumpkins had also reached Europe by the end of the 1500s, but though widely remarked upon, they apparently were not widely cultivated. Even today it is only the vegetable marrows (forms of what we call summer squash and zucchini) that are commonly cultivated there.

Sweet or Spanish potatoes (*Ipomoea Batatas*) were quickly adopted in southern Europe, where the warm climate favored them. By 1556 they were cultivated in Spain. Gerard had them in his garden in London in 1597. They may have been brought back to Virginia by 1610 and were an established cultivated crop there by 1650. They did not reach New England until 1764.

White or English potatoes (*Solanum tuberosum*) were initially much confused with sweet potatoes. The former were first seen in the Andes by the Spaniards in 1537. Sir Frances Drake met with them in southern Chile in 1577, and they were used as food on Spanish ships shortly thereafter. They are alleged to have been cultivated in Italy in the 1580s and to have been introduced to Ireland by Sir Walter Raleigh in 1584 or 1588. He is said to have brought them from Virginia—but since there is no sure reference to white potatoes there until much later, it is more likely that he procured them from somewhere in South America. White potatoes were rather quickly adopted as a crop in Ireland and in Lancashire. They were exported to Bermuda from England and are said to have been introduced into Virginia from Bermuda in 1621. They were not cultivated in New England, however, until 1719.

In addition to food crops, tobacco (*Nicotiana Tabacum* and *N. rustica*) was seen by Columbus in 1492, but it was not introduced into Europe until 1559, in Portugal. It was illustrated in Pierre Pena and Matthias de L'Obel's herbal *Stirpium Adversaria Nova* in 1570 and was in cultivation in England in the same year. Extensively grown in Portugal by 1586, it was well enough known and used that imports into Britain were valued at £60,000 for the year 1610. James-

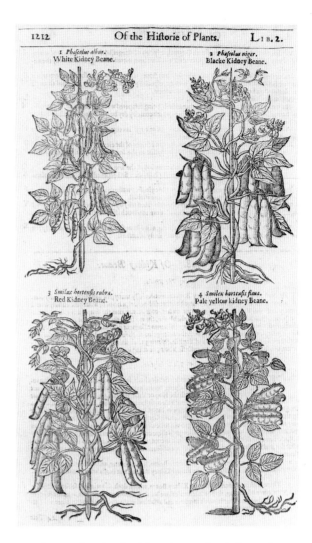

"The fruit and cods of Kidney Beanes boyled together before they be ripe, and buttered, and so eaten with their cods, are exceeding delicate meat, and doe not ingender winde as the other Pulses doe." (from John Gerard's 1633 *Herball*)

town was first settled in 1606; tobacco cultivation was introduced in 1612, supposedly by John Rolfe. From 1614 to 1615 the Virginia colony exported 105 pounds of tobacco to England. By 1618 tobacco exports had risen to 20,000 pounds, and in 1622 exports reached 60,000 pounds. Five years later exports totaled 500,000 pounds per year.[1]

In the northern colonies a little tobacco was grown by individual farmers. The Plymouth Colony traded corn and tobacco with New Netherland for needed commodities in 1629. Rhode Island and Connecticut

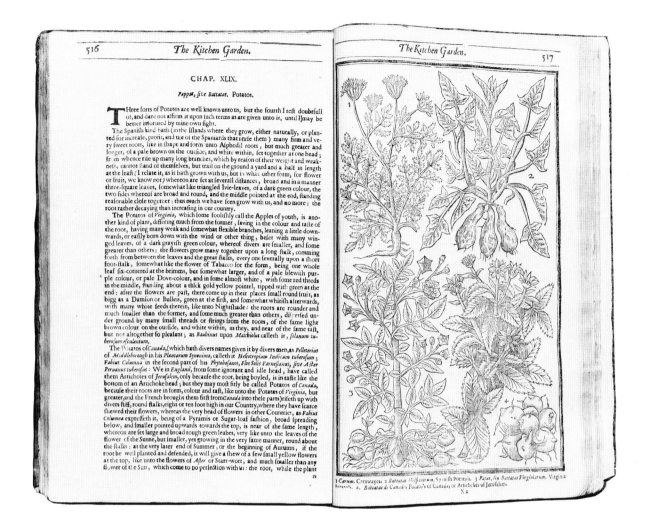

This two-page spread concerning the potato, a plant new to Europeans, appeared in John Parkinson's 1629 book *Paradisus in Sole* (*Park in Sun*).

farmers grew tobacco virtually from the beginning. However, its growth was forbidden in the Massachusetts Bay colony in 1629—though the "Old Planters" (the original settlers) were allowed to continue to grow it as had been their wont. The Rhode Island and Connecticut crops gradually increased in size throughout the eighteenth century, and the Connecticut Valley crop (Connecticut and Massachusetts) gained increasing economic importance in the nineteenth century.

So by 1606, the date of the settlement of Jamestown, the first successful colony, the staple crops native to America were reasonably well known in Europe and in Britain. The settlers at both Jamestown and Plymouth knew what "Indian" corn was, and set about obtaining it from the native Americans as soon as they came ashore. In addition, tobacco was well on the way to becoming a widely used—and lucrative—luxury item.

The first concerns of any of the original colonists were for shelter and food, and for providing both of these commodities they were ill prepared. Carpenters and sawyers, like farmers, were in short supply. Time was also in short supply. Frequently the new colonists reverted to a form of construction traditional in rural Britain—a hole in the ground:

Those in New Netherland and especially in New England, who have no means to build farm houses at first according to their wishes, dig a square pit in the ground, cellar fashion, 6 or 7 feet deep, as long and as broad as they think proper, case the earth inside with wood all round the wall, and line the wood with the bark of trees or something else to prevent the caving in of the earth; floor this cellar with plank and wainscot it overhead for a ceiling, raise a roof of spars clear up and cover the spars with bark or green sods, so that they can live dry and warm in these houses with their entire families for two, three and four years, it being understood that partitions are run through those cellars which are adapted to the size of the family. The wealthy and principal men in New England, in the beginning of the Colonies, commenced their first dwelling houses in this fashion for two reasons; firstly, in order not to waste time building and not to want food the next season; secondly, in order not to discourage poorer laboring people whom they brought over in numbers from Fatherland. In the course of 3 @ 4 years, when the country became adapted to agriculture, they built themselves handsome houses, spending on them several thousands. [2]

Civilized members of the middle classes probably had never hunted or fished in the home country. On the other hand, they undoubtedly had had experience with a domestic vegetable patch and with hens, pigs, and goats. The native American agriculture with which they were faced was vastly different from what they might have known at home—different in crops, growing techniques, and distribution. In addition, the rather aggressive expropriation of land by the Europeans did not promote a harmonious melding of the two cultures. It is a wonder that the colonists were able to learn anything.

The native Americans along the eastern coast lived in semipermanent villages surrounded by fields cultivated, mainly by the women of the tribe, by means of a slash-and-burn technique. Depletion of mineral nutrients and organic matter from the soil by repeated cropping as well as a build-up of annual and perennial

weeds in the fields reduced their yield,* and populations of insects and rodents seriously attacked the growing crops and those in winter storage. When the agricultural land became undesirable, the fields or the villages or both were abandoned.

The native Americans prepared new pieces of land for cultivation by girdling the trees and allowing them to die in place. If the area contained reasonably mature deciduous or coniferous woodland, there would be little in the way of shrubby undergrowth and virtually no herbaceous plants that could survive the increase in light intensity caused by the destruction of the tree canopy. The natives had no plows or, indeed, any beast of burden, so planting was done in "hills" prepared with hand tools—wood, stone, and bone shovels or digging sticks and hoes. Several different crops (maize, climbing beans, and squash or pumpkins) were grown on a single piece of ground simultaneously. Such a technique was blasphemously different from anything the colonists had ever encountered. Their assumptions about agriculture dictated that to grow crops the land must be cleared of all stumps and roots, dug over completely by hand or plowed and harrowed, and the seed broadcast (in the case of grains) or planted in rows so that the crops could be weeded, hoed, or cultivated throughout the growing season. However, hard labor and starvation can make the mind wondrously receptive to new ideas.

The settlers saw the natives plant corn, beans, squash, and pumpkins in hills. They witnessed the natives' girdling method of killing trees in prospective fields, and they observed the Indians' ways of storing and cooking corn, beans, and cucurbits. The colonists had the advantage of the native Americans in that they had tools of iron rather than wood, stone, bone, horn, and shells. They did not have skill in the use of their tools, and they were desperate to produce food—so they must have adopted at least

* The technique of "planting" a fish in each hill of corn indicates that the abandoned Indian fields that the Pilgrims had taken over were pretty well "run out." That is, they had been cropped until most of the available nutrients had been depleted. The decaying fish provided nitrogen for the growing crop.

774   THE SECOND BOOKE OF THE

"The pulpe of the Pompion is never eaten raw, but boiled. For so it doth more easily descend, making the belly soluble. The nourishment which commeth hereof is little, thin, moist and colde (bad, saith *Galen*) and that especially when it is not well digested: by reason whereof it maketh a man apt and readie to fall into the disease called the Cholerike passion, and of some the Felonie." (from John Gerard's 1597 *Herball*)

some of the techniques of the native Americans, which were considerably less laborious and more effective than the techniques that they brought with them.

The native Americans considered raising crops the work of women (except for tobacco, which was a man's job). What effect the sight of male colonists working in the gardens (doing women's work) had on Indian/colonial relations seems not to have been investigated. My suspicion is that it may well have had a fairly significant impact.

Raleigh's Roanoke Colony, off the coast of North Carolina, is said to have failed because of the "hostility" of the Indians. And Jamestown also is said to have suffered in the first few years from "hostile" Indians. One may assume that had the native Americans been writing the history, they would have spoken of the "hostility" or "aggressiveness" of the Europeans.

The situation in Virginia was quite different from that in New England, where the native American population had been decimated by disease some three years before the Pilgrims arrived (disease that was probably brought by European fishermen or explor-

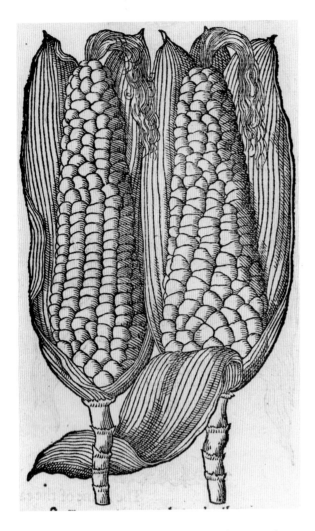

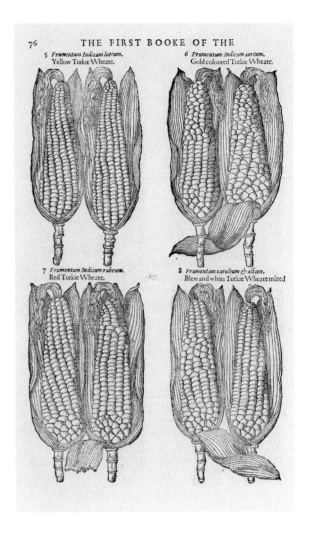

Corn, beans, and pumpkins were the staple crops of native Americans in the sixteenth century. John Gerard knew and grew these plants in England in 1597. His knowledge of plants from North America, of varying degrees of accuracy, was imparted to readers through his publications such as the *Herball*, a detail from which is shown here.

"Turky wheate [corn] doth nourish far lesse than either Wheate, Rie, Barly or Otes. The bread which is made thereof is meanly white, without bran: it is hard and drie as bisket is, and hath in it no clammines at all: for which cause it is of hard digestion, and yeeldeth to the body little or no nourishment, it slowly descendeth and bindeth the belly, as that doth which is made of Mill or Panick." (from John Gerard's 1597 *Herball*)

ers). This meant that there were large tracts of recently cultivated fields lying idle and relatively few individuals to claim or till them. Hence the new arrivals did not seem to pose an immediate threat or to push the original inhabitants from their land. In addition, the settlers were fortunate in their friendship with Samoset and Squanto, Indians who had learned to speak English and were favorably disposed toward the newcomers. Squanto is said to have ex-

plained all he could of the native way of growing crops, although the gardens were the preserve of the women of the tribe.[3]

There were 101 persons in the original party of Pilgrims that landed at Plymouth (1620), of whom 53 were men. The winter was relatively mild, but sickness was rampant. By planting time in the spring of 1621, only 54 colonists were left, of which 21 were men and 6 were grown boys. Using hand tools alone, they tilled twenty acres, which they planted to maize. An additional six acres were planted to barley and peas. The maize prospered, the barley and peas did not.

For the first twelve years all of the tillage of the land at Plymouth was done by hand, successfully enough that in 1625 enough maize was grown to stock a "small vessell" that was sent to the coast of Maine to trade with the Indians for furs. The first cattle (three heifers and a bull) arrived in March 1624. Goats were obtained from Monhegan Island in 1626.

Some fifty-eight years after the first landing, in 1678, a letter from John Winthrop, Jr.,* was published in the *Philosophical Transactions* of the Royal Society of London, in which Winthrop discussed the Indian methods of growing maize and the later colonial modification:

It is Planted between the middle of *March* and the beginning of June. But most commonly from the middle of *April* to middle of *May.* Some of the Indians take the time of the coming up of a Fish, called Aloofes, into the Rivers. Others of the budding of some Trees.

In the pure Northerly parts, they have a peculiar kind called Mohauks Corn, which though planted in *June,* will be ripe in season. The stalks of this kind are shorter, and the Ears grow nearer the bottom of the stalk, and are generally of divers colours.

The manner of Planting is in Rows, at equal distance every way, about 5. or 6. feet. They open the Earth with the Howe, taking away the surface 3. or 4. inches deep, and the bredth of the Howe, and so throw in 4. or 5. Granes, a little distant one from another, and cover them with Earth. If two or three grow, it may do well. For some of them are usually destroyed by Birds, or Mouse-Squirrels.

The Corn grown up an hands length, they cut up the weeds, and loosen the Earth, about it, with a broad Howe; repeating this labour,

as the Weeds grow. When the Stalk begins to grow high, they draw a little Earth about it: and upon the putting forth of the Eare, so much, as to make a little Hill, like Hop-Hill. After this, they have no other business about it, till Harvest. . . .

The Natives commonly Thresh it as they gather it, dry it well on Mats in the Sun, and then bestow it in holes in the Ground (which are their Barns) well lined with withered Grass and Matts, and then covered with the like, and over all with Earth: and so its kept very well, till they use it. . . .

Where the Ground is bad or worn out, the Indians used to put two or three of the forementioned Fishes, under or adjacent to each Corn-hill, whereby they had many times a Crop double to what the Ground would otherwise have produced.

The *English* have learned the like Husbandry, where these *Aloofes* come up in great plenty, or where they are near the Fishing-stages; having there the Heads and Garbage of Cod-fish in abundance, at no charge but the fetching. . . .

The Indians, and some *English* (especially in good Ground, and well fished) at every Corn-hill, plant with the Corn, a kind of *French* or *Turkey*-Beans: The Stalks of the Corn serving instead of Poles for the Beans to climb up with. And in the vacant places between the Hills they will Plant squashes and Pompions; loading the Ground with as much as it will bear. . . .

The *English* have now taken to a better way of Planting by the help of the Plough; in this manner; in the Planting time they Plough single Furrows through the whole Field, about 6 feet distant, more or less, as they see convenient. To these, they Plough others a cross at the same distance. Where these meet they throw in the Corn, and cover it either with the Howe, or by running another Furrow with the Plough. When the Weeds begin to overtop the Corn, then they Plough over the rest

*Governor of Connecticut 1657–1676, and son of John Winthrop, governor of Massachusetts Bay Colony (most of the time between) 1629–1649.

of the field between the Planted Furrows, and so turn in the Weeds. This is repeated once, when they begin to Hill the Corn with the Howe; and so the Ground is better loosened than with the Howe, and the Roots of the Corn have more liberty to spread. Where any Weeds escape the Plough, they use the Howe. [4]

So the early settlers perforce learned the agricultural methods of the native Americans—perhaps more agreeably in Plymouth than in Virginia.

What did the settlers bring with them? Roland Usher, in *The Pilgrims and Their History,* said that the Pilgrims lacked everything but virtue. [5] That is, they lacked plow, ox, and horse. They lacked agricultural experience. They lacked sufficient grain (wheat, oats, barley, rye) to feed themselves the first winter, never mind enough to sow a crop for the following year. This applied to Jamestown as well as Plymouth. By the time that Massachusetts Bay was settled, the need for provision of food and tools had been established and that colony was better supplied with food and tools and with animals, draught and otherwise.

These settlers also brought weeds. What is a weed? As Liberty Hyde Bailey defined it, a weed is a plant out of place. It is a plant that competes successfully against a plant or plants that we wish to grow. A particular species may be deliberately cultivated in one context, and a pernicious weed in another. Three European plants brought early to this country serve well as examples: Dandelion (*Taraxacum officinale*) may be a weed in one's lawn or flower garden, but it may be cultivated as a mild diuretic in the herb garden and as a salad or pot herb in the vegetable garden. Orchard grass (*Dactylis glomerata*) and timothy (*Phleum pratense*) are weeds in the vegetable or flower garden but highly desirable forage grasses in the pasture or hay field.

John Josselyn visited his brother in Maine twice, 1638/39 and 1663/71, enabling him to publish in 1672, in London, *New-Englands Rarities Discovered: In Birds, Beasts, Fishes, Serpents, and Plants of that Country,* the first "natural history" of New England. Of interest to us is the list "of such plants as have sprung

New-Englands Rarities. 85
What Cutchenele is.

The ſtalk beneath and above the knob, covered with a multitude of ſmall Bugs, about the bigneſs of a great flea, which I preſume will make good *Cutchenele,* ordered as they ſhould be before they come to have Wings: They make a perfect Scarlet Colour to Paint with, and durable.

---

4. *Of ſuch Plants as have ſprung up ſince the* Engliſh *Planted and kept Cattle in* New-England.

COuch Graſs.
Shepherds Purſe.
Dandelion.
Groundſel.
Sow Thiſtle.
Wild Arrach.
Night Shade, with the white Flower.
Nettles ſtinging, which was the firſt Plant taken notice of.
Mallowes.
                                    Plantain,

A page from John Josselyn's *New-Englands Rarities Discovered* (1672).

up since the English planted and kept cattle in New England," which is a list of weeds, and a second list "of such plants as are common with us in England," which is a list of plants that he thought were native to both England and New England. It is actually a mixture of species, some European plants that had already become naturalized, and some native species that resembled familiar European species. In any case, it indicates how quickly our common garden weeds became established.

They also brought food crops that they had deemed valuable in Europe. For example, according to U. P. Hedrick, the Spanish brought the peach to Mexico sometime during the 1500s. A fruit that requires a hot summer to mature, it was apparently readily accepted by the native Americans and was remarked upon by many of the early writers as an Indian fruit. Indeed, there was some discussion as to whether it was an indigenous plant. Thomas Ashe, in his work of 1682, *Carolina, or a Description of the Present State of that Country,* relates that "the Peach Tree in incredible numbers grows wild."

Finally, the original settlers brought disease, which killed many of them and many native Americans as well. They brought distilled liquors. They brought iron and steel, for tools and nails as well as for weapons. They brought memories of a way of life more gracious than that into which they were plunged. They brought a philosophy and various

forms of government, which, when allowed to develop three thousand miles from Europe, resulted in the declaration that "all men are created equal. . . ."

The memories of the life that they had left behind—and in particular of the plants and gardens that they had relinquished—stayed with them. Their letters were full of requests for familiar seeds and plants to be sent to them. When some of them became prosperous enough they patterned their houses and their flower gardens on the styles that they had left—or on the styles that they were persuaded were currently in vogue. But that is another story. ✍

NOTES

1. Gray, *History of Agriculture.*
2. Cornelis van Tienhoven, *Information Relative to Taking up Land in New Netherland* (1650), in E. B. O'Callaghan, ed., *Documents Relative to the Colonial History of the State of New York,* 15 vols. (Albany: Weed, Parsons, Printer, 1853–87), vol. 4, p. 31.
3. Sawyer, *History of the Pilgrims and Puritans.*
4. Furnas, *The Americans,* pp. 10–11.
5. Usher, *The Pilgrims and Their History.*

BIBLIOGRAPHY

Arber, Agnes. *Herbals, Their Origin and Evolution.* 2d ed. Cambridge: Cambridge University Press, 1938. Reprinted 1953.

Bidwell, Percy Wells, and John I. Falconer. *History of Agriculture in the Northern United States 1620–1860.* Washington, D.C.: Carnegie Institution of Washington. Publication 358, 1925.

Ewan, Joseph A., ed. *A Short History of Botany in the United States.* New York: Hafner, 1969.

Furnas, J. C. *The Americans: A Social History of the United States 1587–1914.* New York: G. P. Putnam's Sons, 1969.

Gerard, John. *The Herball or Generall Historie of Plants.* . . . London: John Norton, 1597.

————. *The Herball or Generall Historie of Plants.* . . . Edited by Thomas Johnson. London: Adam Islip, Joice Norton, and Richard Whitakers, 1633.

Goode, George Brown. "The Beginnings of Natural History in America." In *Annual Report of the Board of Regents of the Smithsonian Institution . . . 1897.* Vol. 2, 1901: 357–406 (pl. 73–85).

Gray, Lewis Cecil. *History of Agriculture in the Southern United States to 1860.* Carnegie Institution of Washington. Publication 430, 1932. Reprint. Magnolia, Mass: Peter Smith, 1941.

Hedrick, Ulysses Prentiss, ed. "Sturtevant's Notes on Edible Plants." Report of the New York Agricultural Experiment Station for the Year 1919. Vol. 2. Albany, New York: J. B. Lyon Company, State Printers, 1919.

Hedrick, Ulysses Prentiss. *A History of Horticulture in America to 1860.* New York: Oxford University Press, 1950.

Hurt, R. Douglas. *Indian Agriculture in America.* Lawrence, Kansas: University of Kansas Press, 1987.

Josselyn, John. *New-Englands Rarities Discovered: in Birds, Beasts, Fishes, Serpents, and Plants of that Country.* London: G. Widdowes, 1672.

Kerridge, Eric. *The Farmers of Old England.* London: Allen & Unwin, 1973.

Morris, Richard B., ed. *Encyclopedia of American History.* New York: Harper & Bros., 1953.

Parkinson, John, *Paradisi in Sole Paridisus Terrestris.* London: Humfrey Lownes and Robert Young, 1629.

Penrose, Boise. *Travel and Discovery in the Renaissance 1420–1620.* Cambridge, Mass.: Harvard University Press, 1955.

Russell, Howard S. *A Long, Deep Furrow: Three Centuries of Farming in New England.* Hanover, N.H.: University Press of New England, 1976.

Sawyer, Joseph Dillaway. *History of the Pilgrims and Puritans.* 3 vols. New York: Century History, 1922.

Usher, Roland G. *The Pilgrims and Their History.* New York: Macmillan, 1918.

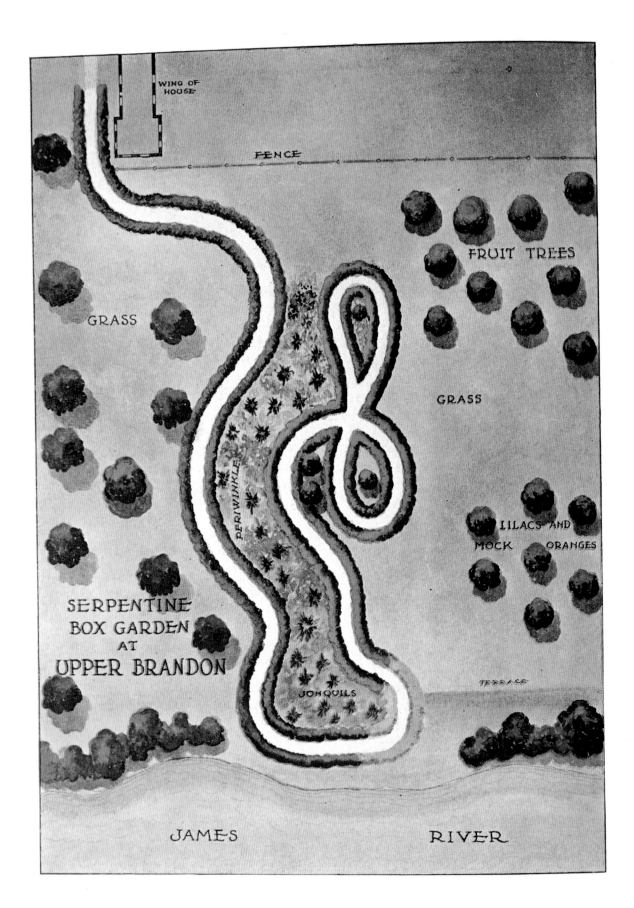

WING OF HOUSE

FENCE

FRUIT TREES

GRASS

GRASS

PERIWINKLE

LILACS AND
MOCK ORANGES

SERPENTINE
BOX GARDEN
AT
UPPER BRANDON

JONQUILS

TERRACE

JAMES   RIVER

Early Gardens Along the Atlantic Coast

Diane Kostial McGuire

As the colonies became better established and the Europe-influenced social structure more pronounced, gardens demonstrated a growing sophistication in style and planting. Within a few decades after the time with which Gordon DeWolf deals, in "The Beginnings," the colonists had begun to be more "at home" in the new lands and consequently to add English touches to their farmsteads and gardens. A clearer picture of how to impose civilization upon the wilderness was emerging.

Regional differences in approach were significant. The Southern garden was a separate space, a place of its own, whereas in the North the garden was unified with the house. This was due to the nature of the land and to the fact that in the South, as Catherine Howett points out in "Graces and Modest Majesties," the agriculturally based economy required more land, which led to the building of the great plantations. The enclosed areas of the Northern garden required less land and the crops needed less space. This also resulted in the gardens in the North being chiefly the province of women, whereas the South's plantations were the domain of men.

The progression from basic subsistence gardens in the early seventeenth century to the elegant plantations and country seats of the late eighteenth century reflected the rapidly growing and burgeoning society. Political and social transformations were radical and expansive. It is not surprising, then, that the tone in many ways was set by two of the leading political and cultural leaders of the eighteenth century: George Washington and Thomas Jefferson. Their style and inspiration led to a uniquely American style of landscape.

By the end of the Federal period, the country had begun yet another transition that led to the nineteenth century with its many changes and novel ways of looking at landscape and horticulture. Symbolically, in 1803 the country doubled in size, its expansion, as discussed by Keith Morgan in "Garden and Forest," bringing its own litany of issues.

13

IN EARLY NEW ENGLAND, the usual settlement consisted of a cluster of houses, each with a small garden and orchard at the back, a meetinghouse more or less in the middle, a graveyard and a common nearby, and one or two roads passing alongside, the whole surrounded by outlying fields. The centers of many of our New England towns still look like this today, and one can anticipate what will be found on a visit. The arrangement may vary but the structural elements are always the same.

When these towns were established in the seventeenth and eighteenth centuries, it was expected that the inhabitants would live in the towns and go out to attend to the fields during the day, returning home in the evening. However this scheme changed dramatically with the ascendancy of the overriding desire to live on one's own land, to attend to one's own livestock and plantings, and to increase one's own holdings.[1] What we actually find in much of New England is a town center, varied in shape (as it was built to fit the land), surrounded by farms with their own houses, barns, and outbuildings. In many towns only a few houses were built near the center, whereas in others, especially those with good harbors and directly facing the sea (such as Gloucester, Massachusetts, and Newport, Rhode Island), the pattern of settlement was dense. In these towns of close houses, the arrangement of gardens was exceedingly simple because there was not space for anything more elaborate. The famous dooryard gardens of Marblehead, Massachusetts, were only a few yards wide, with room for fruit trees and vegetables only at the back.

Where more space was provided, a more typical arrangement is found. At the Whipple House, directly opposite the common in Ipswich, Massachusetts, the garden is directly in front of the house, forming a forecourt through which it is necessary to pass to enter the house. The garden is surrounded by a wooden fence with a narrow gate, which protected the garden from the depredations of free-roaming livestock. Within are six beds, built in the style illustrated in early seventeenth-century English gardening books, and raised in order to make early planting in spring possible when the ground is wet. They are also boarded on the sides, with the boards pegged into the earth. These beds are extremely rustic in character; we do not know how refined their construction may have been. No illustrated records of them, or detailed written descriptions, are known to survive. It was important for these gardens to be convenient to the house because they formed part of the woman's domain. She was responsible for this essential element of colonial life. This division of labor was to be repeated many times over during the westward expansion of America.

Today the wide paths of the Whipple House garden are paved with crushed clam shells; whether they originally had bare-swept or raked earth instead is not known. Now filled with nearly one hundred sorts of plants, the densely planted beds appear as beautiful herbal bouquets, fragrant and varied in color and texture. We know the plants to be correct in the exact detail of their botanical specifications as they have been identified from letters, wills, and traveler's accounts taken from local seventeenth-century documents.[2]

Many of the plants used in these early gardens escaped into the surrounding countryside and have since become familiar as common field plants. They are so much a part of the New England countryside that we find it surprising that they all once were exotics, not part of the original landscape but introduced by settlers. Yarrow, tansy, feverfew, chicory, and butterfly weed are all familiar plants found in American meadowlands and flourishing along roadsides. They were garden plants then and today give an authentic appearance to gardens adjacent to houses built in the style of the seventeenth century.

The most useful reference for the identification of plants grown by the Puritans is John Josselyn's *New-Englands Rarities Discovered,* published in London in 1672. Josselyn, who lived in New England for ten years, differed from many early garden writers in that

OPENING ILLUSTRATION:
The serpentine, boxwood-lined path in the old garden at Brandon actually only fell back upon itself, but it still enticed the strolling visitor to see what lay beyond the next bend.

The dooryard garden of the Whipple House, densely planted in raised beds, is devoted to plants of utility for such needs as medicines, flavorings, and dyes. Reconstructed according to information found in early accounts in wills, letters, and books of the time, this is one of the most authentic colonial garden reconstructions in the United States.

he wrote directly from his own observations and not from second- and third-hand accounts. Because of its authentic voice, his book has been used as a guide in the restoration of several seventeenth-century New England gardens.

In addition to its garden, the Whipple House is of interest for its pear orchard, set out near the house diagonally to the back. This orchard has been set in the quincunx pattern, again as illustrated in seventeenth-century English garden books. This pattern is based on five trees instead of four, the fifth located in the center of a square. Such elegantly designed orchards were found in the colonies, as were beautiful cordons of fruits, graceful espaliered apples and heated walls for the growing of peaches. However, the vast majority of orchards, regardless of size, were much more utilitarian, their trees set out in simple rows. The regularity of the orchard patterns, with the organization of fencing consisting of wood or of stone walls, imposed an orderly utility on the land. From this came an expression of pastoral beauty

that has remained the dominant aesthetic in the American consciousness to the present day.

The general arrangement of the Whipple House grounds is representative of seventeenth-century gardens in New England. The garden was enclosed in front of the house and contained primarily herbs and flowers for "meate or medicine." The yards to the side and the back accommodated the vegetable garden and the orchard. The garden was as much the domain of the housewife as her kitchen and stillroom. Throughout this early period of American history the housewife had to grow her own seasonings and garnishings, her insecticides and deodorants, what was needed for syrups and cordials and waters, for the making of plasters and salves, for treating wounds, and for laying out the dead.[3]

As the settlers created these farms and towns, houses and gardens, and began to order the formlessness of their space geometrically, the order of their constructed universe contrasted vividly with the chaos and mystery of the forest that surrounded them, sep-

The plan of the garden at Tuckahoe, near Richmond, Virginia, was directly inspired by seventeenth-century English gardening books. The maze at lower right is composed of fifty-seven knots with narrow grass paths and dwarf boxwood edging. It is surprising to find designs of such intricacy in early American gardens, when maintenance in the best of times was never easy.

arated them from other towns, and divided them from the open vistas of the vast ocean and wide flowing rivers.

Our earliest commentaries, engravings, and paintings describe a scene of landscape cultivation based on old English laws of enclosure and field patterns with the divisions of the fields resembling the old hedgerows. In the beginning the English proportions were there, outlines having been decided by the charters under which the land had been granted and the boundaries put in place by the surveyor's rod. As the land was cleared and made useful agriculturally, however, a great untidiness resulted. Fields of girdled trees—some dead waiting to be taken down, some half-dead with crops growing among them—made for a mixture of dying forest and new agriculture.

What followed were open fields, the uprooted stumps forming the hedgerows, far different in aesthetic character from the neat rows of quickset hawthorns that had been left behind across the ocean but remained as part of landscape memory. A treeless field was a sign of good agricultural practice; grain could grow open to the sun and pasture land could be dry and fertile. Open, bright farmland with few trees provided a cheerful prospect, and resembled more precisely the landscape ideal of good husbandry and prosperity, an ideal the settlers had brought with them. Not every tree came down in the interest of agriculture. Great specimens were found especially in the low places, along riverbanks and near swampy ground. Primitive roads and lanes, little more than wide pathways, were made through the edges of forests. Certain specimens, especially oaks, pines and chestnuts, were admired for their great size. But all

16

trees were expendable, and many were cut down to make way for the sunlight essential to agriculture, to produce fuel for cooking and heating, to provide the lumber essential for building, for making farm implements and furniture, and to provide cash.[4]

In the south, along the edge of the eastern seaboard, the land opens up widely at the junctions of rivers and estuaries, and tributaries disperse, dividing the land into sites chosen by settlers desiring houses that would have a prospect of the river and at the same time catch the cooling breezes. The rivers were the center of plantation life, although the plantation itself might spread inland for a great distance. Houses were built near the rivers and the lands and gardens around them designed in relation to them.[5]

The plantation's inhabited spaces were exceptionally large and the distances between them exceptionally long. This geographical fact led to a concentration of community within the plantation itself, a pattern to be found throughout the rural south. With only a few important towns (Richmond, Atlanta, and New Orleans), the focus of life lay within the individual plantation or, in the case of the plain farmer, within the small farm.

In laying out plantations the interrelationships of the house, the river, and the garden were of importance from the beginning. Not only were the southern plantation gardens much larger than those in the North, they had considerably more importance in the overall arrangement of spaces as well. The relationship was one of the house *and* its garden, whereas in the North the relationship was more of the house *in* its garden or the house *near* its garden.

There were several reasons for this difference. Because the plantation economy was completely agricultural, slave labor was primarily concerned with tilling the land for growing crops of cotton, tobacco, or indigo, among others, and this land had to be wrested from the wilderness, prepared for cultivation, and then cultivated. When done on a large scale, this process involved hundreds of slaves. The larger landholdings in the mid-Atlantic colonies and in southern New England were also worked by slaves, but in far lower numbers, since the specific crops grown required fewer laborers. More significantly, on these

A boxwood hedge provides the formal edge of the flower garden at Shirley. Grown behind the hedge are old-fashioned flowers that have once again become popular—heliotrope, rose geranium, mignonette, lilies, and larkspur.

more northerly farms, gardens generally were still small and enclosed and were not important examples of garden architecture.

From the aspect of design, as one progressed from north to south, considerably more time was spent in reshaping the land, both for purposes of agriculture and for the decorative art of gardening. A great many earthworks survive in the South that resemble those in Britain. Reshaping the land in relation to the house created gardens of several acres that far surpassed the confines of the small, fenced gardens that predominated in the North.

Henry Middleton, president of the First Continental Congress and devotee of elegance, began his gardens at Middleton Place about 1741. There are

Middleton Place's beautiful "falls" of symmetrical earthworks overlooking the Butterfly Lakes are distinctive features found on riverfront properties in the South and, to a lesser extent, as far north as Newburyport, Massachusetts.

many similarities between this South Carolina garden and two in England that had been laid out several years earlier: Bramham Park and Studley Royal, both in Yorkshire. All three express a single aesthetic and all have gardens organized around water, with earthworks related to water. There is a great emphasis on modeling the ground surface and covering it with a grassy expanse. These light, cheerful, meadowlike places then contrast with high walls of foliage, shade that envelops and encloses. This simple landscape idea has in all three examples been carried through to provide a design unity, uncommon at that time and seldom found today.

Studley Royal was laid out between 1722 and 1740 by John Aislabie, who organized his garden around the River Skell. Most interesting in design are the Moon Ponds, which reflect the classical facade of the Roman-inspired Temple of Piety. The Moon Ponds at Studley and the Butterfly Lakes at Middleton are two expressions of the same inspiration. It may be that Henry Middleton knew John Aislabie and visited Studley Royal, or he may have seen plans of these waterworks. On the other hand, both gardens may have been laid out in accordance with the ideas expressed and illustrated in Dezallier d'Argenville's *La Théorie et la pratique du jardinage,* which had been published in France in 1709, but does not illustrate exact prototypes of these ponds.

The Butterfly Lakes at Middleton are especially fine in purpose because they form the foreground to the river beyond and give a controlled prospect. At Studley contrast in water is also a part of the aesthetic as the smooth, broad surface of the Moon Ponds contrasts with the swift-flowing, often turbulent,

Brandon has always been a gardener's paradise because of the remarkable variety of situations in which plants can flourish. There are areas of shade and protection from the sun alongside sunlit sections, all nurtured by excellent soil. The many years of care have resulted in an atmosphere of antiquity unusual in an American garden.

channel of the River Skell. In both instances, as at Bramham Park, the garden depends entirely on the atmospheric play of light and dark on the surfaces of water and greenswards, and on the liquidity and motion of water contrasted with the cool, static greensward surrounded by dark walls of foliage.

Middleton is also home to large formal gardens, the most important design feature of which is the strongly articulated camellia allées. These lovely allées express a close relationship between design and horticulture, which is the most impressive characteristic of many of these colonial plantation gardens.

While Middleton was only one of many Carolina low-country plantations, some very well-designed properties were also built about the same time along the James River. Of special significance are Brandon and Westover, which although not as immediately impressive as Middleton, are still intact, making the relationship between house, garden, and river immediately apparent. Brandon is conceptually a much simpler garden than Middleton as are most of the plantations along the James River between Richmond and Williamsburg: although not as grand, they are extremely dignified, having been laid out with restraint and in precise and orderly design. In fact, they are similar in many respects to contemporary northern gardens except they are often considerably larger and more finely crafted in architectural detail. This is the result of their common origin in the earlier formally intricate gardens of England, which, unlike Middleton, were not greatly influenced by French design. These gardens were laid out in the old English manner, with an axial line running from house to river. They had symmetry, orderliness, and, like the earliest gardens in New England, intimacy in character and accessibility from the house, as they were still considered to be in the woman's domain.

The garden side of the house at Brandon is the river side and the water approach and the landing rendered it the most important exposure as well. Business was transacted from this vantage point; here bales awaited shipment and visitors arrived. The visitor ascends from the river and, upon finally reaching flat land, follows a very broad grassy path through the garden, ending in a large grassy space at the house. Nothing could be simpler than this, but there are many subtleties worth noting.

The structure of the garden is found in the symmetry of the beds, the rectangularity of their design, and in the taller plants in the garden, that is, the medium-sized trees and shrubs. The absence of elaborate architectural features is very much in keeping

The magnificent elms at Westover create the space for the house, and the boxwood-lined garden walks strengthen the structural relationship between house and walls.

with the understated quality of the whole ensemble. The house and the large trees create a space away from the garden and perpendicular to the river.

Nearby, also overlooking the river, but differing from Brandon, is Westover, built by William Byrd II in the 1730s. This house is also meant to be approached from the river, but it sits on a high bluff about two hundred feet away and one surmises that this side of it was always somewhat open, both for the prospect and for the summer breezes. The hand-

some brick, two-story house, with a steep-roofed, dormered attic, is considered to be one of the finest extant examples of colonial architecture. The garden to the west is not laid out in relation to the house, although it is off to the side nearby. This is a very large, walled garden with four large parterres, each subdivided into four, so originally there may have been sixteen parterres. Dating back to ancient gardens, this design appears in Italy, France, and England and then in early American gardens. There are now fruit trees in this garden and boxwood, flowers, and vegetables, but it is not known exactly how the beds were planted when the second William Byrd lived. However, he thought highly enough of the space to locate his tomb there, giving it the additional role of memorial garden. One of the first things Mark Catesby did when he came to Virginia in 1712 was to visit Westover for three weeks, and Byrd wrote in his diary that he "directed how I should mend my garden and put it into better fashion than it is at present."

Another point of contrast with Brandon is the wrought-iron fence on the opposite side of the house from the river, which makes a forecourt for this side of the house. The fence is divided into several sections, and each pier has a carved stone finial representing a garden object—a beehive, a pinecone and so on. It was unusual to have carved stone decoration in the garden, especially in the early eighteenth century; the work might have been done by an Italian stonemason, who perhaps worked there for a brief time, or the finished sculptures may have been imported by Byrd. This decoration is reminiscent of the old gardens of Italy and the indeterminate age of the stone gives Brandon's garden an appearance of antiquity.

The garden at Berkeley, also on the James River, was fashioned about the same time as Westover and is a simple four-square garden, but with larger parterres. Again, just as at Brandon, the axial line runs directly from house to river. Here the house does not have the architectural distinction of Westover, but the grounds generally are laid out in a very fine manner, the working of the contours being especially beautiful as the garden steps down on broad terraces or falls to the river.

TODAY, THE COLONIAL plantations along the James inhabit a very fragile environment because of the invasive proximity of metropolitan Richmond. At Shirley, the James becomes busy with traffic, and beyond, up the river, one smells the fumes of industrial Richmond. In spite of this it is still possible to concentrate on the particular facets of the gardens

The broad, beautiful walk through the magnolia gardens of Drayton Hall is made fascinating by its demonstration of the garden's delicate balance with nature. The tree roots form a pattern in the garden that reminds one of the power and tenacity of trees, for example.

that have changed the least, or that represent this time in our history before the Revolution. However, the steadiest indicators and the most reliable icons are perhaps the illustrations of plants found in the literature of the time as well as the plants themselves.

Throughout the South, it was necessary to provide sufficient shade to protect the house and spaces where people were likely to congregate to escape from the intense heat of the summer sun. Many trees were brought in from the wilderness, propagated, and grown in nurseries, and then planted. Some were dug from the forest as saplings and planted directly. The beauty and usefulness of many of our native American trees not only interested the farmers and plantation owners, but made the trees desirable in England, Scotland, and Ireland, thereby constantly encouraging trade in seeds, cones, twigs, and young plants.

The tree that evoked greatest admiration and became of enormous visual importance throughout the south was *Magnolia grandiflora,* which was at that time known as the laurel tree of Carolina and is now commonly known as the southern magnolia. It was used with great skill in the landscape; in the north, where it is not hardy, there is nothing comparable. The great *Magnolia acuminata,* known as the cucumber tree, was another major tree of great ornamental value. The deciduous tree most commonly used, undoubtedly for its beautiful flowers, was *Liriodendron tulipifera* or the Tulip Poplar. It was prized as a landscape subject for its fresh, green foliage that turns a clear, light yellow in autumn and for its multitude of candelabra-like seed pods that persist after the leaves fall. By 1770 the seed was imported annually to England in large quantities.

Other deciduous trees that formed part of the shade-giving complex were *Catalpa bignoniodes,* or southern catalpa, the seeds of which were brought from the piedmont by Mark Catesby. *Ulmus americana,* the american elm, was equally popular in the North and the South and is unequaled for its light shade and beautiful, vase-shaped habit. *Quercus virginiana* (live oak) and the *Liquidambar Styraciflua* (sweet gum) were also of importance not only in the colonial landscapes but in England as well.

It was common practice to grow certain larger ornamental shrubs and smaller flowering trees in beds with flowers and ground covers. Since this was more common in the South than in the North, it may have been done to provide some shade for the flower beds. The laburnum (*Laburnum Vossii*), one of these small trees, was brought from England and was offered by Prince's Nursery in 1790. Another familiar English favorite grown in the colonies was *Koelreuteria paniculata,* the golden rain tree, which was also known in the eighteenth century as "pride of India." Both

laburnum and koelreuteria grew well and were excellent middle-sized trees for the garden, their beautiful yellow flowers being particularly outstanding against the generally monochromatic background of green.

Two small ornamental trees were brought from the wild into gardens and eventually became synonymous with early southern gardens: *Cornus florida,* the flowering dogwood, and *Cercis canadensis,* the redbud. These two trees were often found in the large parterres, where they were appreciated for their beauty of flower in spring and their general character throughout the year.

In addition to the small trees were several large shrubs whose ornamental character made them highly sought after. *Chionanthus virginicus,* the fringe tree, and *Hydrangea arborescens* both have sparkling white flowers and cool, elegant foliage. The hydrangea also combines particularly well with herbaceous plants and ground covers. Numerous other plants were brought in from the wood and were important as new garden ornamentals, many of which are equally popular today, such as *Hamamelis virginiana,* or witch-hazel, which was considered quite remarkable for being in bloom late in the fall. The ornamental small tree *Lindera Benzoin* is the first to put forth its small, pale yellow flowers, which float as a cloud above the bulbs of early spring, and is followed by the *Amelanchier canadensis,* with its pale white flowers.

English boxwood (*Buxus sempervirens 'Suffruticosa'*), now synonymous with southern gardens, was first referred to by John Custis in 1737. The *Camellia japonica* was introduced to southern gardens near the end of the eighteenth century and three of the four original plants still can be found at Middleton Place.

The American wildflower *Lobelia cardinalis,* cardinal flower, was brought in from the wild and became an important garden flower because of its brilliant red color. It was sent to England where it became an extremely popular border flower. On the other hand, dianthus, iberis, and wallflowers were all brought to the colonies from England and flourished in these colonial plantation gardens.

When considering the beautiful Italian villas that became visually important in the seventeenth-century countryside, especially around Florence, Rome, and

Naples, it is immediately apparent that their builders were mindful of the ideal of prospect, of a fine, far-reaching view. In addition to this, the location on the heights provided cooling breezes during the hot summer season and became a distinctive feature in the landscape as old fortified towers were in the hill towns. When Thomas Jefferson came to lay out the house and grounds for Monticello (see illustration on page 83), he chose the site on his mountaintop in keeping with the idea of prospect, of an overlook to the distant landscape being of primary importance. The name Monticello is Italian for "little mountain."

At Mount Vernon, George Washington did not start afresh, as had Jefferson, for there was already an early structure, now included within the fabric of the present house, when he came into possession of the property in 1754. Washington recognized the importance of prospect and designed a vista to be viewed from the spacious verandah that is the hallmark of the house today; he organized the ground plan of the garden to focus on the house, with broad, sweeping views down to the Potomac and over the great lawn to the landscape of the hills beyond.

Most of the larger houses, as well as many of the smaller ones, that commanded a prospect of river view or harbor were consciously designed to clearly establish a powerful visual relationship between the two, which was often reinforced by the planting of trees on either side of the entry to frame the view and to draw the distant prospect into closer proximity. This element of prospect and its necessity in the development of the landscape plans as a whole was well expressed by Washington and Jefferson and is also generally found in much of the work done for more modest houses during this period. Such design underscores the vital connection in the colonies to the artistic ideals of Renaissance Italy.

These ideas of art, as well as of agronomy, horticulture, and animal husbandry were the result of an arduous process of self-education. Since Washington did not travel abroad, it was through the study of the books that formed his library and other titles available to him that he developed his vision for his country estate. He read widely in his garden books, mastered the subject as laid out in them for English

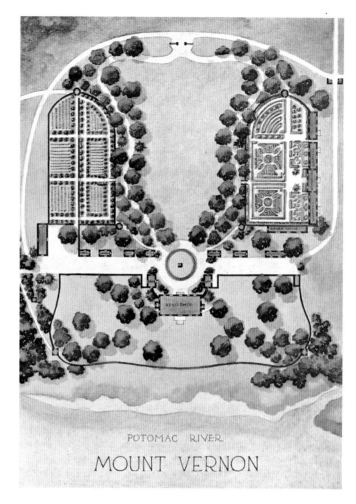

POTOMAC RIVER

MOUNT VERNON

This unusual view of Mount Vernon makes clear the dignity of the structure and the simplicity and breadth of the landscape above the Potomac. Washington had a profound understanding of land form and its relationship to architecture.

and French landholders of means and resources, and proceeded to lay out his own garden of exactly the appropriate size and style for his manor house. Nowhere did he overstep, overdo, overdesign, or overbuild.[6]

Jefferson's library is famous. At Monticello his books and his drafting table can be seen; books were the foundation of his knowledge and of many of the ideas for his gardens. During his years as American minister to France, he went often to Versailles and saw many of the more important châteaux. In 1786, following descriptions in his copy of Whateley's *Observations,* he visited English country places, including

The vegetable garden at Mount Vernon, enclosed within brick walls, is a site renowned for its beauty as well as its usefulness. The patterns employed are similar to those found in French and English garden books of the eighteenth century.

Hampton Court, Stowe, Leasowes, and Blenheim, and commented on them in his *Garden Book*.

Two important English books of the period, Philip Miller's *Gardener's Dictionary* (1731) and Batty Langley's *New Principles of Gardening* (1728) were known by Washington and Jefferson as was the *Works* of William Shenstone (1764). These books reflected the eighteenth-century interest in the juxtaposition of the formal and informal styles of gardening. There was also a keen interest in English works on the ideal of the ornamental farm, which was an attempt to unite utility and art. Both Washington and Jefferson found their way to this vision of an ornamental farm through the influence of English books and engravings and through the essays of Joseph Addison, who

in the early eighteenth century had rhetorically inquired, "Why may not a whole estate be thrown into a kind of garden?"[7]

Washington's design, although symmetrical on the plan, appears to be much more informal on the ground. His vision was that of an idealized landscape, a greensward with trees. The windows of the mansion house overlooked broad vistas of green, on the river side with clumps of trees, on the other, edged by woods. This was the eighteenth-century English landscape ideal and all other necessary parts of the plan had to be accommodated in another way, out of the central line of vision. Washington brilliantly made these vital appendages a graceful part of the design. Fruit, vegetable, and flower gardens were needed, and they are provided, in as handsome a manner as possible without being the central attraction. The vegetables and flowers are within matching gardens surrounded by brick walls, crowned with a picket fence of the most beautiful curvature.

Thomas Jefferson's ideal vision of landscape is perhaps better expressed and more elegantly refined in the plan that he did for the University of Virginia toward the end of his life, than in the much earlier one he made for Monticello. Jefferson's vision of Monticello was a dynamic design, which changed when he had the opportunity to travel abroad and to see examples of landscape design in France and Italy as well as in England. [8]

During the latter half of the eighteenth century, there was considerable interest in the development of horticulture in America, which paralleled and was directly related to interest in the landscape garden and its expression of naturalism. Jefferson was fascinated by exotic botany and was well acquainted with plant collectors such as William Hamilton of Philadelphia and nurserymen such as Bernard M'Mahon. He was a disciple of Linnaeus and adopted his system of plant classification for use with native plants, which he listed in his *Notes on the State of Virginia* (1801). He was especially interested in the journey of André Michaux, the French botanist, who, with his son, toured the Carolinas, the Bahamas, and Canada. Although Jefferson had a deep appreciation for the native trees and shrubs of Virginia and especially admired the holly, the rhododendron, and the magnolia, all of which he included in his shrubberies at Monticello, he especially admired certain exotic plants that he tried unsuccessfully to keep under glass. Of special interest were mimosa, lime, sour orange, and fig, plants from warmer Mediterranean climates that provided a constant visual reminder of his interest in the classical world of antiquity.

Whereas Jefferson was interested in many representatives of the plant world—trees, shrubs, flowers, and bulbs—Washington had a decided preference for trees. He brought in many native saplings from the wild, which he planted closely for immediate effect as well as along the entry drive in a thickly set informal "wildernesse," which created interest and variety in the approach. In gardens of this period, the entry drive usually was not related to a wood but was separate from it. At Mount Vernon the concept of the drive curving through the trees, looking out to the lawn or bowling green, is a brilliant design

accomplishment. Characteristically, straight rows of beautiful trees forming long avenues and shaded walls were considered to be of importance in designed properties of the eighteenth century. Even in relatively small-scale designs order, control, and regularity were expressed by the uniformity of the planting. [9]

The interest in horticulture shared by Washington and Jefferson was fundamental to eighteenth-century ideas of naturalism, which were expressed differently by gardeners in America and abroad. Jefferson was interested in horticulture at an early age and recorded the flowers of garden and woodland. Wood and garden were parallel interests throughout his life. This duality of interest in wood and garden is expressed in the arrangement of plants at Monticello and is one of the reasons why gardens are representative of eighteenth-century attitudes toward the specifically American landscape.

When plants were brought back from the Lewis and Clark Expedition in 1806, Jefferson appointed two people to grow this valuable material. One was the well-known Philadelphia nurseryman, Bernard M'Mahon, who had, just a year previously, published *The American Gardener's Calendar,* the first book devoted to gardening in an American setting. M'Mahon had originally written to Jefferson asking for a small portion of every kind of seed brought back from the expedition. Jefferson, who continued his correspondence with M'Mahon, complied with this request and recommended to Captain Lewis that he commit principal shares of the botanical spoils to M'Mahon and to William Hamilton, also of Philadelphia, the design of whose estate was influential in Jefferson's plans for Monticello. Hamilton was known as a man of taste and was highly regarded as a botanist. He was also an amateur landscape gardener and surrounded his house with extensive gardens and greenhouses containing the most unusual collection of native and exotic plants then known in America.

"Taste," in the latter half of the eighteenth century in America, was expressed in gardens that were in many ways similar to English gardens of the previous half-century. In both countries it meant a presentation that relied primarily on naturalistic rather than formal qualities, with a great deal of open space, particularly around the house, making the house seem to sit on a stage with an apron in front, its ribbons fluttering on either side. The ribbons translated into groves or grovettes near the ends of buildings, such as Jefferson created at Poplar Forest, which gave animation and variety to an otherwise open scheme. [10] These were landscapes of serenity and release where wild nature became domesticated and the strange wood became the familiar grove. All the wild elements were there, but they were subdued, tamed for the enjoyment of the master and his guests.

The horticultural emphasis in these gardens of taste was not on herbaceous plants of vivid color—that was to come later—but on rarity and unusual form of fruit or flower. Of course, the garden was for pleasure and a part of this delight in the eighteenth century came from the joint pleasures of collection and display.

As with so many American gardens of the seventeenth and eighteenth centuries, Washington and Jefferson emphasized plants, both imported and native. Water, which would have been a major feature in contemporary European gardens, was seen from Mount Vernon at a distance, in the Potomac, while at Monticello, Jefferson relied on glimpses of broad lagoons from a river too far away to be important. Fountains, statuary, and objects of the stonecarver's art were not significant in these gardens because the craftsmen who could create such ornament were not available. Even architectural ornament was essentially modest and relatively crude compared to European examples.

Both Washington and Jefferson influenced American garden design because they were public figures held in high esteem. They approached the subject of gardens as men who knew the land as farmers and who, at the same time, possessed original vision and educated taste. The essential modesty of the design of Mount Vernon and the individuality of art and craftsmanship at Monticello today speak of ideals derived from a democratic stance. These men were improvers; on their own lands they carried out projects that emphasized their agrarian interests and that domesticated wilderness and brought the lovely aspects of nature within the boundaries of human domain.

THE ROMANTICISM of historic decay in old Europe, with its collage of ruins and vines, broken pillars and peeling paint, was not seen as an aesthetic worthy of imitation in antebellum America. The deep forest gloom and picturesque, romantic ideals of the English landscape theorists did not impress these Americans. There had always been a naturalism in the relationship of American gardens to landscape, and, from the beginning, the beautiful plants of the wilderness found their way into gardens as well as being sent abroad. The American dogwood and the mountain laurel, the American holly and native azaleas and rhododendrons were allowed to flourish in arrangements that are most accurately called naturalistic. Their organization in the garden, particularly in the old plantations along the James River, was reminiscent of the woodland itself rather than of the artificiality of a semiformal garden design. The splendid magnolias, the yellowwoods and tulip poplars, the Douglas fir, and the amazing sequoia-dendrons, as well as wildflowers like the Jack-in-the-pulpit, bunchberry, and California poppy, all found significant places in gardens as America expanded to the west.

American gardens were practical landscapes for domestic enjoyment, with collections of shrubs, flowers, and trees, both native and exotic. Trees were kept for shade, but also for beauty. The summerhouse was intended to catch the breezes, not to recall Apollo. The formal pattern of the flower garden became a definite design afloat upon a lawn or field, but clearly a fancy to be enjoyed on the way to orchard and vegetable garden, field and pasture. [11]

In the half century before the Civil War, the plantation gardens throughout the South reflected changes in garden design in England during the latter part of the eighteenth century. These new designs were eagerly adopted by plantation owners, as well as by northerners with more modest properties, since the new designs allowed for greater flexibility and more creativity in gardening and provided opportunities for display of new plant varieties.

The connections with Europe, and especially with England, were kept very strong in the South by travel and education. Boys in particular received their ad-

Having made the grand tour, Martha Turnbull made her garden at Rosedown an imitation of gardens she had seen in Europe. She planted trees and shrubs that, today, have achieved impressive size. The clear color of the azaleas is emphasized by their evergreen backgrounds.

vanced education there. Travel meant diplomatic sojourns, visiting relatives "back home," and, at times, the grand tour, with its attendant opportunities to visit palaces and gardens and to view firsthand the crumbling ruins and broken statuary of old Europe, to walk in gardens of ancient origin, and to imbibe inspiration directly from the source.

The design of the beautifully preserved gardens that we see today at Rosedown, in Feliciana parish, Louisiana, is the result of one such grand tour, the honeymoon in 1835 of Martha and Daniel Turnbull.

Martha began to make plans for her garden at Rosedown after she visited Versailles and the gardens of Italy. She saw avenues of trees, statuary, formal parterres, and garden ornaments in the seventeenth-century French style, all on a much larger scale than anything she had previously seen in Louisiana. Although at this time many plantation gardens were being changed from the old formal style to the new naturalistic style, some, such as Rosedown, were being newly laid in a formal design.

The plan of Rosedown is very grand indeed since

Martha Turnbull was a superior gardener. The gardens were extremely well cared for, at least until the war, and they are well cared for now since their restoration. In her garden diary she delineates the activities of each day she directed work in the gardens, and often at the end of a day's work she completed her entry with: "My gardens are in perfect order."

In contrast to earlier gardens, the Turnbulls not only expanded formal areas but they imported marble statuary, pools, fountains, and other ornaments that immediately gave an impressive look to the formal parts. They also imported a great number of exotic trees and shrubs, along with azaleas, camellias, and other plants that were ordered from Prince Nurseries in New York and R. Bruist in Philadelphia as early as 1836. The allée of live oaks is assumed to be about 200 years old and there are many trees and shrubs that are probably more than a century old. Chamaecyparis and Cryptomeria are found in a very large size, as are azaleas, camellias, sweet olives, deutzia, English boxwood, crape myrtle and mock orange, which were to become the signature plants of the average garden in America as the nineteenth century progressed. The gardens extend to parallel the allée of live oaks, with winding paths that are similar to those recommended by A. J. Downing.

In America, this type of garden, with its very high standards of maintenance, was possible only in the South, the only part of the country with adequate labor to make its maintenance possible. Yet, as the nineteenth century progressed, many gardens in America were made in an extravagant manner; they began to be built for show and to display the wealth of their owners. To a significant degree, early American gardens were simpler and were designed with other ideas in mind, especially that of the welfare of the family—whether it was to provide vegetables, fruit, flowers, or shade from the summer sun, or to pique the curiosity of the mind with botanical collections and the growing of exotics. It is no wonder that the desire to return to this simplicity and live in the countryside of the pastoral ideal animates the hearts of so many Americans. The magic shines more brightly the farther it seems to recede in reality. ❧

NOTES

1. About this idea, John R. Stilgoe writes in *Common Landscape of America: 1580 to 1845:* "The frittering away of common land is of great significance because it marked the rise of self-sufficient husbandmen at the expense of the community-supported colonists who first cleared and planted the soil" (p. 55).

2. "Research into inventories, letters, wills, cures for the measles, recipes for cooking eels and jams, travellers' accounts, and especially John Winthrop, Jr.'s 1633 seed bill from a London 'grocer,' identified plants upon which the settlers depended." (Geoffrey Jellicoe, et al., *The Oxford Companion to Gardens,* Oxford: Oxford University Press, 1986, p. 602). This research was undertaken by Ann Leighton (Isadore L. L. Smith) and forms the basis of her book, *Early American Gardens: "For Meate or Medicine."*

3. Leighton, *Early American Gardens.*

4. Stilgoe, p. 317. Tree cutting also precipitated ecological disaster, and "by 1750 agriculturists in several colonies learned that dreaded wildernesses tormented people long after their trees were felled and sawed. Soil erosion troubled husbandmen planting land cleared by loggers, and it angered other colonists who depended, like several Indian tribes, on seasonal migrations of herring and other fish."

5. Most Southern plantations as well as seacoast towns of northern New England and Nova Scotia were intended to be visited and viewed from their ocean and river fronts. Today, arriving by automobile, we approach with an entirely different frame of mind because we have come swiftly by land rather than slowly by water and, in effect, enter by the "back door." In addition to approaching these plantations from the wrong direction, we also have the severe problem created by the encroaching commercial strip and housing complexes that impose a different presence in uncomfortably close proximity.

6. Leighton, *Early American Gardens.*

7. Addison, Joseph. *Essay on Taste.*

8. Jefferson, in his vision of Monticello, wished to do a great number of things and he could accomplish only some of them. Most fascinating are the many drawings and plans (in the collections of the Massachusetts Historical Society) that he prepared for this landscape, which indicate the far-reaching extent of his enthusiasms.

9. Sarudy, *Eighteenth-Century Gardens,* p. 125.

10. Brown, "Poplar Forest," pp. 126–127.

11. Leighton, *American Gardens in the Eighteenth Century,* p. 362.

BIBLIOGRAPHY

Adams, William Howard, ed. *The Eye of Thomas Jefferson.* Washington, D.C.: National Gallery of Art, 1976.

Addison, Joseph, *Essay on Taste. The Spectator,* no. 409.

————. *Essay on Nature and Art in the Pleasures of the Imagination. The Spectator,* no. 414.

Bartram, William. *Travels.* Edited by Francis Harper. New Haven: Yale University Press, 1958.

Beatty, Richmond Croom. *William Byrd of Westover.* Boston: Houghton Mifflin, 1932.

Beverly, Robert. *The History and Present State of Virginia.* Edited by Louis B. Wright. Chapel Hill: University of North Carolina Press, 1947.

Bigelow, Jacob. *American Medical Botany.* Boston: n.p., 1817.

Blunt, Wilfred. *The Art of Botanical Illustration.* London: Collins, 1950.

Brown, C. Allan. "Poplar Forest: The Mathematics of an Ideal Villa." *Journal of Garden History* 10, no. 2 (1990), pp. 117–139.

Burke, Edmund. *A Philosophical Enquiry into the Origin of Our Ideas of the Sublime and Beautiful.* London: 1759. Reprint. Scholar Press, 1970.

Chandler, Alfred. *Illustrations and Descriptions of the Plants Which Compose the Natural Order Camellieae.* (London: John and Arthur Arch, 1831.

Downing, A. J. *The Fruits and Fruit Trees of America.* New York: n.p., 1846.

Emmons, Ebenezer. *Agriculture of New York.* Albany: C. Benthuysen, 1851.

Gilpin, William. *Practical Hints upon Landscape Gardening.* 2d ed. Edinburgh, n.p., 1835.

Hedrick, U. P. *A History of Horticulture in America to 1860.* New York: Oxford University Press, 1950.

Historic Gardens of Virginia. Edited by: Edith Tunis Sale, the James River Garden Club. Richmond: William Byrd Press, 1923.

Hoffy's North American Pomologist. Edited by: William D. Brinkle. Philadelphia: n.p., 1860.

Hogarth, William. *An Analysis of Beauty.* London: n.p., 1753.

Jefferson, Thomas. *Notes on the State of Virginia.* New York: Harper Torchbooks, 1964.

————. *Thomas Jefferson's Garden Book, 1766–1824.* Edited by Edwin Morris Betts. Philadelphia: American Philosophical Society, 1944.

Langley, Batty. *New Principles of Gardening.* London: n.p., 1728.

Le Blond, Alexandre [A. J. Dézallier D'Argenville]. *Theory and Practice of Gardening.* Translated by John James. London: n.p., 1728.

Leighton, Ann. *American Gardens in the Eighteenth Century: "For Use or For Delight."* Boston: Houghton Mifflin, 1976.

————. *Early American Gardens: "For Meate or Medicine."* Boston: Houghton Mifflin, 1970.

Lockwood, Alice G. B. *Gardens of Colony and State.* New York: Scribners, 1931.

Marshall, Humphry. *Arbustrum Americanum: The American Grove.* Philadelphia: Joseph Cruikshank, 1785. Reprint. New York: Hafner, 1967.

McGuire, Diane Kostial. *Gardens of America.* Charlottesville, Va.: Thomasson-Grant, 1989.

Michaux, F. Andrew [André]. *The North American Sylva.* Translated by Robert B. Smith. Philadelphia: n.p., 1852.

Miller, Philip. *The Gardener's Dictionary.* 8th ed. London: n.p., 1768.

Newton, Norman T. *Design on the Land.* Cambridge, Mass.: Harvard University Press, Belknap Press, 1971.

Parkinson, John. *Paradisus in Sole, Paradisus Terrestris* (1629). London: Methuen, 1904.

Rehder, Alfred. *A Manual of Cultivated Trees and Shrubs.* New York: Macmillan, 1974.

Rutland, Robert Allen. *George Washington, Reluctant Statesman.* Williamsburg: 1961.

Sarudy, Barbara Wells. "Eighteenth-Century Gardens of the Chesapeake." *Journal of Garden History* 9 (July-September 1989).

Stilgoe, John R. *Common Landscape of America: 1580 to 1845.* New Haven: Yale University Press, 1982.

Whately, Thomas. *Observations on Modern Gardening.* London: n.p., 1770.

C.A.Flat

Garden and Forest

Nineteenth-Century Developments in Landscape Architecture

❧❧

Keith N. Morgan

❧ *The nineteenth century was a period of enormous change and vitality for horticulture and the landscape. Scientific, cultural, economic, and political factors entered into the disposition of and opinions about the landscape as never before. This chapter locates these issues in terms of garden and forest, a duality that might be seen as order and chaos, man and nature, civilization and wilderness. The fundamental issue was the human relation to the environment. What was our proper role in the natural world?*

The nineteenth century saw both the opening of the West and the declaration that the frontier was "closed." Wilderness preserves, national parks, and open-space organizations were established; the first professional landscape association and numerous formal educational institutions for the study of the landscape were founded. Town planning, the great botanical gardens, and the conservation movement are all products of that century. The full extent of expression of defining the environment was laid out for Americans during this period.

The extremes of the debate were reverence and exploitation, which suggests the range of responses to the environment and the enormous impact that it embodied. The same questions need to be asked in our own time—with one major difference: we now know the inevitable consequences of neglecting the environment and are in a much better position to choose wisely and well. ❧

AT THE END of the nineteenth century, a newly professional landscape and horticulture establishment launched the first magazine to address successfully a wide range of American attitudes toward the land. *Garden and Forest* remained in publication for only one decade (1888–1897), but the active debate that raged in its pages is perhaps the most useful source for understanding the interaction of nineteenth-century Americans with their environment. Topics discussed included horticulture, gardening, professional landscape architecture, cemeteries, town planning, conservation, forest management, and landscape history. The title, while it attempted to be all-embracing, actually reveals the shifting dichotomy that characterized the American idea of the land throughout most of the last century. The closing of the frontier, as announced in 1893 by the historian Frederick Jackson Turner in Chicago, forced Americans to confront their exploitive attitude toward their continent. Was the purpose of civilization to bring the garden to America, or was the forest really the American garden? A look backward over the century will reveal how these ideas emerged and were modified and resolved by its end.

The Garden of the Dead

THE STARTING BELL for the debate was rung by those wishing to find new places Americans could bury their dead. Until the end of the eighteenth century, Europeans and Americans almost universally buried their dead in church graveyards.[1] The overcrowding of these sites and the attendant problems for urban hygiene raised a cry for a better solution. The Parisians launched a new landscape model in their designs for Père Lachaise (1804), the first of a series of extramural graveyards that would ring the capital. The British and Americans quickly followed suit with new "rural cemeteries," landscaped burial grounds around London, Liverpool, and Boston. The American responses were unique in form and purpose.

Boston was one of the earliest centers to enter this debate. In 1825 Jacob Bigelow, a physician, called together a group of his influential friends to consider the creation of a rural cemetery in the Boston area following the Parisian example.[2] Economic instability and the lack of an appropriate site delayed the establishment of their cemetery, named Mount Auburn, until 1831, by which time an important new element had entered the situation. In 1829, the Massachusetts Horticultural Society was founded to allow gentlemen of taste and intellect an opportunity to share and expand their knowledge of horticulture and scientific agriculture and to encourage the creation of

An 1869 exhibition of the Massachusetts Horticultural Society in their building on Tremont Street.

nurseries.[3] Since many of the same individuals were interested in the rural cemetery and the horticultural society, a joint effort soon became a logical objective. Sweet Auburn, a hilly woodland on the border of Cambridge and Watertown, four miles west of Boston, fully satisfied all needs as a site that was well drained, enjoyed panoramic views of the area, and contained a mature collection of trees and plants. The property was developed to accommodate the needs of the cemetery and those of the horticultural society, which planted a garden of specimen trees and shrubs there. Although the cemetery very quickly overwhelmed the space allocated to the horticultural society, Mount Auburn established the ideal of a garden for the dead, which became an important landscape type in nineteenth-century America.

Following closely on the Mount Auburn example was a series of landscaped cemeteries for urban centers throughout the eastern seaboard and the Midwest.[4] Significant among these was the second, Philadelphia's Laurel Hill, laid out in 1836 by John Notman,

View from Consecration Dell, Mount Auburn Cemetery, Cambridge, Massachusetts, with the tower monument to George Washington at the top of the hill.

in Richmond, Virginia; and Spring Grove (1848), designed by Robert Daniels, in Cincinnati, Ohio. Spring Grove represented a further advance from the concept of the graveyard to that of the garden or park—the elimination of monuments and the creation of a lawn cemetery, where the contemplation of nature, rather than of the stoneworker's art, was intended to create the desired mood.

The Private Garden

THE COMMUNAL ENTHUSIASM that the creation of rural cemeteries inspired was rapidly focused on the improvement of rural and suburban residences, especially on the periphery of major urban centers. Indeed, it was a direct step into the garden of the living from the garden of the dead. The obvious link was provided by a nurseryman and writer who became the most influential tastemaker for the landscape in the 1840s.

Andrew Jackson Downing (1815–1852) was born in Newburgh, New York, overlooking the Hudson River Valley, where many of his efforts would be focused. [6] As the editor of *The Horticulturist* from 1846 until his death, Downing was able to campaign for changes in American practices in landscape design and management, including the promotion of the rural-cemetery ideal, as well as to advance the American popular knowledge of issues in horticulture, botany, and his particular specialty, pomology. Downing was the consummate snob, seeing "taste" as the test of a true gentleman and the device by which he could advance his own status in life. He also absorbed and used as his own the words and ideas of others. His most influential publication for landscape design was his 1841 *Treatise on the Theory and Practice of Landscape Gardening Adapted to North America*. Here he promoted the new taste for picturesque suburban villas that had been introduced by his occasional collaborator Alexander Jackson Davis in his 1837 publication *Rural Residences,* and by Humphry Repton's and John Claudius Loudon's earlier publications in England. Downing was not an architect and only advised on the laying out of country seats, such as Springside, the Matthew Vassar estate near Poughkeepsie, New York.

a Scottish immigrant architect who would remain an important force in American landscape gardening for two decades. [5] While Mount Auburn had been the work of horticulturists and landscape enthusiasts, Laurel Hill was the product of an architect, adding a significant new component for the emerging landscape community.

Rural cemeteries soon proliferated. Most noteworthy were Green-Wood (1838) in Brooklyn, New York; Holly-Wood (1848), also a design by Notman,

Idealized view of the suburban streetscape, from Frank J. Scott's *Beautification of Suburban Home Grounds.*

Yet his publications established a new type of American architectural book, the house-pattern book, one aimed at the client rather than the builder and one in which the landscape became an important topic for discussion. Despite Downing's snobbery, the middle and even the working class were here encouraged to move to the country and to develop a villa or cottage, with appropriate attention to the grounds.

Downing's books continued to be published well past his death in 1852 and his influence was felt in American writings on architecture and landscape for several decades. Among the most interesting and in-

fluential of these later authors were Calvert Vaux (*Villas and Cottages,* 1857), an English architect whom Downing had brought to America to serve as his partner, and Frank J. Scott, whose book *The Art of Beautifying Suburban Home Grounds of Small Extent* (1870) still perpetuated the Downingesque formula nearly two decades after the master's death. Of course, most American private landscapes at midcentury remained utilitarian schemes unaffected by Downing's picturesque plans or exotic plant choices, but landscape historians have yet to record or analyze these vernacular gardens.

The Public Garden

DOWNING WAS ALSO INSTRUMENTAL in advancing his landscape ideals for the needs of those who would not or could not escape the city. Like others before him, Downing understood that the rural cemeteries had quickly become favored retreats for the city dweller seeking the solace of green shade and light. Therefore, he used the pages of *The Horticulturist* to argue for the creation of urban parks, focusing on the need of New York City in particular. In 1850, he was invited by President Millard Fillmore to lay out the grounds of the Mall in Washington as a national arboretum and picturesque pleasure grounds. Downing's work in Washington, and similar projects such as John Notman's earlier designs for Capitol Square Park (1848), in Richmond, inaugurated the great age of American park making. Sadly, Downing's death (ironically in a steamboat accident on his beloved Hudson River) removed a major lobbyist from this campaign, but his contemporaries and colleagues soon filled the void.

In 1852 the first Park Act was passed by the New York State legislature to create a central park on the island of Manhattan. After five years of political and real estate negotiating, a competition for the design of the central park was held in 1857. Downing would have been pleased that Calvert Vaux and Frederick Law Olmsted, a young journalist and experimental agriculturalist, carried the day. Olmsted quickly became even more important as the superintendent for construction of the park, which was pursued earnestly

Maurice Prendergast, *Central Park, 1900*, showing the separation of carriage and pedestrian traffic and the mixing of various levels of society.

until the Civil War decreased funding and diverted Olmsted's energies to the cause of the Civil Service Commission.[7]

Nevertheless, the Olmsted and Vaux proposal for Central Park immediately brought America into the mainstream of international activities in park design. Indeed, Olmsted and Vaux, through travel or by birth, were aware of English and continental activities such as the park at Birkenhead, near Liverpool, England, laid out by Joseph Paxton in the early 1840s. Olmsted and Vaux improved on European models, however, in several significant ways. First, they conceived of the park as the ultimate democratic urban institution, a place where all classes of society would come together to experience the restorative forces of nature. Second, the park had a didactic purpose; in-stitutions of culture were to be located in or near the park and the landscape itself was intended as a museum of nature. Ingeniously, their proposal allowed for the park to be an area segregated from the city while not an impediment to transportation or commerce. They accomplished this feat by limiting the number of roads through the park and by suppressing below grade those that were built. Similarly, all transportation routes—for pedestrians, horsemen, carriage drivers, and commercial vehicles—were separated through the use of overpasses and tunnels. The success of Central Park established the reputations and careers of both Olmsted and Vaux, who continued to dominate the new profession of landscape architecture through the end of the century. Olmsted, alone or in partnership with Vaux, was responsible for major parks or park systems that included Prospect Park in Brooklyn (1868), the Buffalo park system (1872), the South Parks, Chicago (1883), and the Boston municipal park system (from 1878 onward).[8]

Plan of Bushnell Park,
Hartford, Connecticut,
designed and executed by
Jacob Weidenmann.

Although Olmsted clearly overshadowed all of his contemporaries in the volume and quality of his work, there were a small number of other designers who were responsible for major public work. After he and Olmsted amicably dissolved their partnership in 1872, Clavert Vaux continued to execute landscape schemes, including his plans for Downing Park, in Newburgh, New York. Olmsted's other early partner was Jacob Weidenmann, author of *Beautifying Country Homes: A Handbook of Landscape Gardening* (1870), who was responsible for Bushnell Park and Cedar Hill Cemetery, in Hartford, Connecticut, and who collaborated with Olmsted on a wide range of landscape problems after 1874.[9]

The only individual who even remotely rivaled Olmsted in achievement was Horace William Shaler Cleveland, the superintendent of the expansive Minneapolis park system from 1883 until his death. Cleveland was a New Englander and briefly maintained a Boston partnership with Robert Morris Copeland in the 1850s. The two men were entrants in the Central Park competition; Cleveland had probably been the author of *A Few Words on the Central Park*

(1856), which argued for comprehensive landscape planning. More influential was his 1873 publication *Landscape Architecture as Applied to the Wants of the West,* written after a brief if volatile tenure with the South Park Commission in Chicago. Little is known about his work in the Midwest except for his role as landscape architect for the Minneapolis Park Commission after 1883, where he could exercise a vision for master planning equal to that of his contemporary, Olmsted.

Town As Garden

AN IMPORTANT American landscape contribution in the middle decades of the nineteenth century lay in the field of town planning and suburbanization. From the opening year of the century, the religious camp meeting had been a uniquely American phenomenon for temporary communing with God in nature. As the settings for these religious revivals were institutionalized, they became a proving ground for new suburban forms. Representative of these experiments was the 1867 design for Oak Bluffs, the

Methodist camp meeting on Martha's Vineyard in Massachusetts, designed by Robert Morris Copeland.[10] Along meandering lanes, small wooden Gothic cottages presented a fairyland appearance of what the modern village could become.

On a secular and more lavish level, the same spirit had been pursued in 1857 by Llewellyn S. Haskell, a real estate developer assisted by the architect Alexander Jackson Davis and the landscape gardener Eugene Baumann in the creation of Llewellyn Park (1857), an idealized, picturesque suburb in West Orange, New Jersey, twelve miles west of New York City.[11] Following Downing's dictates, the suburb was organized along meandering roads that respected the varied topography, with ample space given over to public parks. Olmsted also provided an important model in his 1869 scheme for the new town of Riverside, Illinois, on the railroad line west from Chicago, where landscaped parkways and public open

space became the framework for domestic expansion. Planned communities that incorporated landscaped public space remained relatively infrequent until the end of the century, when the rapid growth of improved mass transportation and the emergence of a professional community of city planners produced a generation of innovative American suburbs.

Forest As Garden

ATTENTION TO THE NEED for preservation and protection of natural areas brought about an international campaign in which the United States held a leadership position. Olmsted, again, was among the earliest to enter this battle. In 1864, while serving as the superintendent of the Mariposa mining community in California, he was appointed chairman of the commission to recommend a policy to the state for the preservation of Yosemite and of the giant

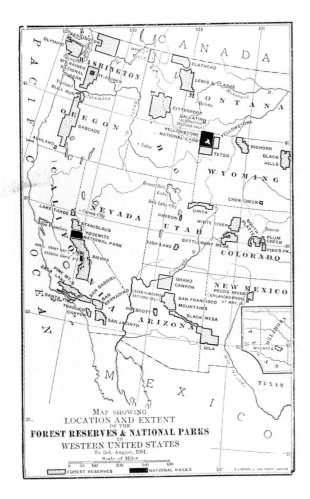

Map of forest reserves and national parks in the western United States to 1901.

natural resources, especially those of the developing West, to the consciousness of the entire country was reinforced by exceptional writers like John Muir. Muir's writings, especially his book *Our National Parks* (1901), were central to the popular understanding of the value of western lands and to the need for preservation and careful access to them.

While the federal example was important, often state and regional efforts led to more creative solutions and the protection of more extraordinary resources. In 1885, the New York State Legislature guaranteed the preservation of the Niagara Falls Reservation, an international effort, and the Adirondack Forest Preserve, safeguarding the watershed for New York City and a mountainous forest district in the East.

Both actions reinforced the determination of Boston landscape architect Charles Eliot to counterattack the destruction of areas of natural, scenic, or historic

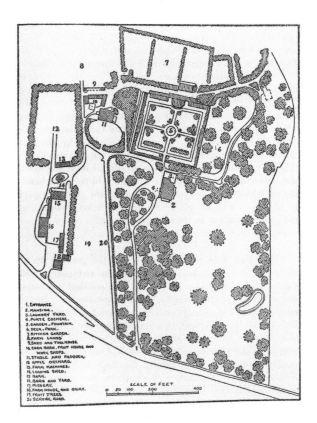

Plan by Charles Eliot for the Cushing-Payson Place, Belmont, Massachusetts; one of six historic estates from Massachusetts and the Hudson River Valley recorded by Eliot and published in *Garden and Forest* in 1889.

redwoods at Mariposa Big Grove.[12] His report established the precedent for public stewardship of areas of natural or scenic significance and inspired a movement that would constantly expand throughout the second half of the century. Equally important was the 1873 legislation that established the first national park, at Yellowstone, with a guarantee that the federal government would acquire and regulate the use of western lands of exceptional beauty or value. The national park movement blossomed in the 1890s with the creation of the Sequoia, Yosemite, and General Grant national parks and through the popularization of America's natural wonders by books such as Charles Fletcher Lummis's *Some Strange Corners of Our Country* (1891). The process of bringing the preservation of

significance in his native Massachusetts. Indeed, Eliot was unique in possessing an historian's appreciation of patterns in the landscape, which he recorded in articles for *Garden and Forest* and in his grand schemes for the Boston region. [13] In 1891, Eliot engineered the passage of a law creating the Trustees of Public Reservations, a private-sector, statewide organization that became the model for the development of the National Trusts in Great Britain, Scotland, and, ultimately, the United States. From the platform of the Trustees' effort, Eliot quickly launched another innovation—the Boston Metropolitan Park Commission—in 1893 to address the open-space needs of the entire Boston basin. This regional plan for the preservation of islands, beaches, tidal estuaries, and forest reservations established a model in Boston that other metropolitan areas and counties soon sought to replicate.

Garden Triumphant

RECOGNITION OF THE NEED to prevent the disappearance of natural areas near urban centers or of larger wilderness districts was partially responsible for a new attitude toward the garden in the closing decades of the century. The dominant practices of either artificial horticultural extravaganzas in carpet bedding and gaudy displays of annuals and exotics or the Olmsted efforts to create a new naturalistic environment for park and homeground were now challenged by the reform initiative of horticulturists who longed for the simpler plants of their grandmothers' yards. This enthusiasm for what became known as the "old-fashioned" garden gathered momentum with the nationalism and interest in colonial roots that the Philadelphia Centennial Exposition of 1876 inspired and grew through the expanding garden literature of the final quarter of the century. [14] One of the most beautiful and influential of these publications was *An Island Garden* (1894), poet Celia Thaxter's description of her old-fashioned garden on the Isles of Shoals off the Maine–New Hampshire coast, illustrated by the watercolors of Childe Hassam.

Another branch of American garden reform oc-

Childe Hassam, *The Garden in its Glory*, showing Celia Thaxter at the doorway to her garden on Appledore Island.

curred with the entrance of more architects, sculptors, and painters into the realm of landscape design. These artists, frequently trained in the academies of Europe, or at least inspired by European travel, preached an art-for-art's-sake philosophy and a belief that a careful study of appropriate historic models would provide for a healthy reform of American garden design. Foremost among these innovators was the landscape painter and etcher Charles A. Platt, who sought inspiration in the villa gardens of Italy for the emerging field of country-house design. [15] In *Italian Gardens* (1894), Platt provided a new formula for a tightly controlled, architectonic garden based upon a knowledge of past forms, just as the architects of his gen-

View toward the central basin of the Court of Honor at the World's Columbian Exposition, the inspiration for the City Beautiful Movement in city planning.

eration looked to European models to improve the quality of American design. In the houses and gardens that Platt designed for himself and fellow members of the art colony at Cornish, New Hampshire, in the 1890s, he established a new schema for domestic architecture and gardens. Soon Philadelphian Wilson Eyre and the New York firms of McKim, Mead and White, and Carrère and Hastings, among others, mounted a winning campaign for formal, geometric, axial landscapes closely integrated with the buildings they embellished.

The same philosophy moved easily into the public domain through the influence of the World's Columbian Exposition in Chicago (1893). Here, Frederick Law Olmsted, at the end of his career, produced a master plan for the Court of Honor, where monumental, monochromatic classical buildings created a fantasy metropolis known as the White City. The

power of this image was transferred to the real realm of city planning in the decades after the fair. [16] Foremost among these imperial visions of American grandeur was the McMillan Commission plan (1901) for the redevelopment of Washington, D.C., which created the uniform look of the governmental public spaces, to designs by Daniel Hudson Burnham, Charles McKim, Augustus Saint-Gaudens, and Frederick Law Olmsted, Jr. Burnham became the most influential link between the fair and the city, especially in his city plans for Chicago, Cleveland, San Francisco, and elsewhere.

These various prejudices in landscape philosophy were increasingly institutionalized in the decades that bracket the emergence of a new century. The American Park and Outdoor Art Association was founded in Louisville, Kentucky, in 1897 with the national mission of creating a constituency for public parks,

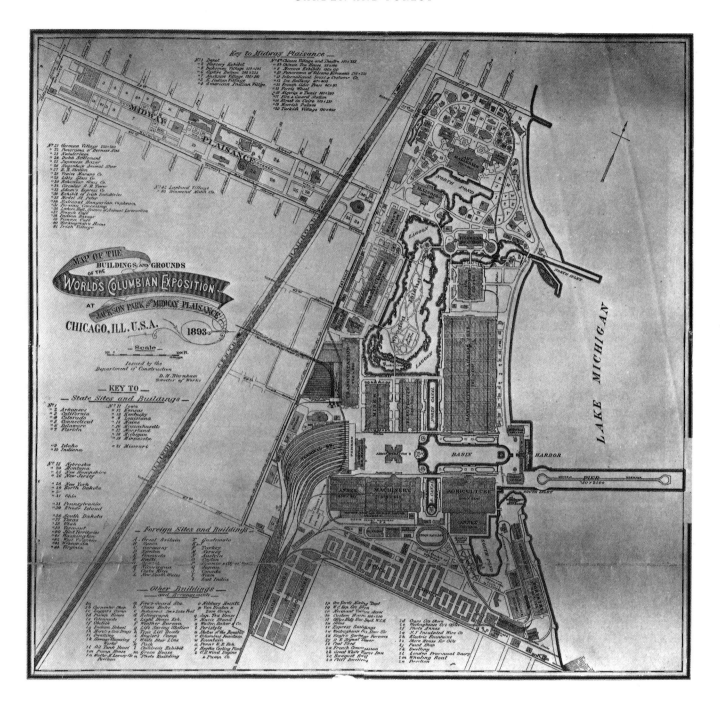

Frederick Law Olmsted, Plan for the World's Columbian
Exposition, Chicago, Illinois, 1893.

41

city planning and beautification, and historic preservation. From this base, discussions concerning the need for a professional organization for landscape architects raged in the later years of the 1890s and finally took a progressive form in the creation of the American Society of Landscape Architects in 1899. American academic training in landscape architecture did not exist until a program was established at Harvard University in 1900 under the direction of John Charles Olmsted and Arthur Shurcliff. The establishment of the American Academy in Rome in 1894 had also certified the legitimacy of landscape architecture within the design community and had underscored the importance of historic precedent for modern form in gardens and cities.

In many ways, in the closing decade of the century, the victory of the garden over the forest could be seen in the work of American landscape architects and in the national mentality. The progressive disappearance of the wilderness signaled the need for the preservation of natural areas and suggested that manmade forms should clearly not attempt to imitate or improve the natural world. ❧

NOTES

1. Richard Etlin, in *The Architecture of Death* provides the most comprehensive overview of the French and English attitudes toward burial and the landscape, focusing on the creation of Père Lachaise, outside Paris.

2. Blanche Linden-Ward has recently published a thorough review of the development of Mount Auburn cemetery and the context from which it emerged, *Silent City on a Hill: Landscapes of Memory and Boston's Mount Auburn Cemetery.* See especially chapter 7.

3. Linden-Ward, 175. The New York Horticultural Society was founded in 1822 and the Pennsylvania Horticultural Society in 1827, following the examples of England, Scotland, and France.

4. The American rural cemetery is discussed in a series of articles in a special issue, edited by David Schuyler, of the *Journal of Garden History* (July–September, 1984), vol. 4.

5. Keith N. Morgan, "The Architecture and Landscapes of John Notman" (master's thesis, University of Delaware, 1973); Constance Greiff, *John Notman, Architect* (Philadelphia: The Athenaeum, 1977).

6. The most recent summary of Downing's accomplishments and influence in architecture and landscape architecture was given at the two-part 1985 conference held at the Athenaeum of Philadelphia and the Center for Studies in Landscape Architecture, Dumbarton Oaks, Washington, D.C. The conference report: George B. Tatum and Elisabeth B. MacDougall, eds., *Prophet with Honor: The Career of Andrew Jackson Downing, 1815–1852.*

7. For the most recent and most thorough analysis of the creation of Central Park, see Charles E. Beveridge and David Schuyler, eds., *The Papers of Frederick Law Olmsted,* vol. 3, *Creating Central Park, 1857–1861.*

8. The best general biographical treatment of Olmsted and overview of his career is still Laura Woods Roper, *F. L. O. A Biography of Frederick Law Olmsted* (Baltimore: Johns Hopkins University Press, 1983). For the Boston park system, the reader should consult Cynthia Zaitzevsky, *Frederick Law Olmsted and the Boston Park System.*

9. *Victorian Landscape Gardening: A Facsimile of Jacob Weidenmann's Beautifying Country Homes,* with a new introduction by David Schuyler (Watkins Glen: American Life Foundation for the Athenaeum Library of Nineteenth Century America, 1978).

10. The best recent study of this phenomenon is by Ellen Weiss, *City in the Woods: The Life and Design of An American Camp Meeting on Martha's Vineyard.*

11. The large literature on American suburbanization is well summarized by David Schuyler in chapter 8 of his book *The New Urban Landscape.* A fuller and more provocative treatment is provided by John R. Stilgoe in *Borderland: Origins of the American Suburb, 1820–1930.*

12. Victoria Post Ranney, ed., *The Papers of Frederick Law Olmsted,* Vol. 5, *The California Frontier, 1863–65,* (Baltimore: Johns Hopkins University Press, 1990) provides the richest account of this important period in Olmsted's career and in the development of an American conservation consciousness.

13. The fullest treatment of Eliot and his accomplishment is still provided in [Charles W. Eliot], *Charles Eliot, Landscape Architect.*

14. Celia Thaxter, *An Island Garden* (Boston: Houghton Mifflin, 1894). Reprint, 1988. See also Virginia Tuttle Clayton, "Reminiscence and Revival: The Old-Fashioned Garden, 1890–1910," *Antiques* (April 1990), 892–905.

15. For Platt's work, see Keith N. Morgan, *Charles A. Platt: The Artist as Architect.*

16. To understand the power and influence of the

Chicago Fair, see Werner Hegemann and Elbert Peets, *The American Vitruvius: An Architects' Handbook of Civic Art* (New York: Architectural Book Publishing Co., 1922).

BIBLIOGRAPHY

Bender, Thomas. *Towards a New Urban Vision.* New York: Columbia University Press, 1975.

Clayton, Virginia Tuttle. "Reminiscence and Revival: The Old-Fashioned Garden, 1890–1910." *Antiques* (April 1990), 892–905.

Cleveland, Horace William Shaler. *Public Grounds in Chicago: How to Give Them Character and Expression.* Chicago: C. D. Lakey, 1869.

Copeland, Robert Morris, and H. W. S. Cleveland. *A Few Words on the Central Park.* Boston, 1856.

Downing, Andrew Jackson. *The Architecture of Country Houses.* New York: Appleton, 1850.

———. *A Treatise on the Theory and Practice of Landscape Gardening Adapted to North America. . . .* New York: Wiley & Putnam, 1841.

[Eliot, Charles W.] *Charles Eliot, Landscape Architect.* Boston: Houghton, Mifflin, 1902.

Etlin, Richard. *The Architecture of Death.* Cambridge: MIT Press, 1978.

Garden and Forest. New York: 1888–1897.

Hewitt, Mark Alan. *The Architect and the American Country House.* New Haven: Yale University Press, 1990.

The Horticulturist. New York: July 1846–December 1875.

Jackson, John Brinkerhoff. *American Space.* Cambridge: Harvard University Press, 1976.

Linden-Ward, Blanche. *Silent City on a Hill: Landscape of Memory and Boston's Mount Auburn Cemetery.* Columbus: Ohio State University Press, 1989.

McLaughlin, Charles, et al. *The Papers of Frederick Law Olmsted.* 5 vols. to date. Baltimore: Johns Hopkins University Press, 1978–.

Morgan, Keith N. *Charles A. Platt. The Artist as Architect.* New York and Cambridge: Architectural History Foundation, Inc., and MIT Press, 1985.

Muir, John. *Our National Parks.* Boston: Houghton, Mifflin, 1901.

Newton, Norman T. *Design on the Land: The Development of Landscape Architecture.* Cambridge: Harvard University Press, 1971.

Platt, Charles. *Italian Gardens.* New York: Harper & Brothers, 1894.

Roper, Laura Woods. *F. L. O. A Biography of Frederick Law Olmsted.* Baltimore: Johns Hopkins University Press, 1983.

Scott, Frank J. *The Art of Beautifying Suburban Home Grounds of Small Extent. . . .* New York: D. Appleton, 1870.

Schuyler, David. *The New Urban Landscape.* New York: Columbia University Press, 1986.

———. ed. Special issue on rural cemeteries in America. *Journal of Garden History* 4 (July–September 1984).

Stilgoe, John. *Metropolitan Corridor.* New Haven: Yale University Press, 1982.

———. *Borderland: Origins of the American Suburb, 1820–1930.* New Haven: Yale University Press, 1988.

Tatum, George B., and Elisabeth B. MacDougall, eds. *Prophet with Honor: The Career of Andrew Jackson Downing, 1815–1852.* Washington, D.C.: Dumbarton Oaks, 1989.

Tishler, William H., ed. *American Landscape Architecture: Designers and Places.* Washington, D.C.: National Trust for Historic Preservation, 1989.

Weidenmann, Jacob. *Beautifying Country Homes: A Handbook of Landscape Gardening.* New York: Orange Judd, 1870.

Ellen Weiss. *Cities in the Woods: The Life and Design of An American Camp Meeting on Martha's Vineyard.* New York: Oxford University Press, 1987.

Zaitzevsky, Cynthia. *Frederick Law Olmsted and the Boston Park System.* Cambridge: Harvard University Press, Belknap Press, 1980.

Regionalism and Modernism

Some Common Roots

∼❧❧∼

Melanie L. Simo

❧ *Modern American gardens have had many regional incarnations, and while they have differed in their expression, they share a similar process of response—to certain local climatic conditions, topographical realities, cultural precedence, or social inclinations. But in each case the regional requirements defined what modernism was. This is not surprising in a country whose very size allows for many interpretations of landscape. The varying climates, geomorphology, historical and social factors, and the ethos of any one region all permit, even make inevitable, a regional approach. Modernism is also defined regionally but always as an expression of that place. It is what traditional garden history calls the genius loci, which warrants "listening" to the needs and aspirations of the place and of those who live in it. In twentieth-century America this has produced some of the most fascinating, beautiful, and respected design ever produced in this country. Sensitivity and care in combining the dictates of place with the aspirations of period have yielded some of the finest approaches to landscape ever offered.* ❧

IF A EUROPEAN VISITOR were to seek out the best modern American landscapes of a truly regional character, he might go straight to Chicago—that is, if he arrived just before the outbreak of World War I. From the early 1900s until about 1914 or 1915, the best work of Chicago-area landscape architects, notably that of Jens Jensen, O. C. Simonds, and Walter Burley Griffin, was distinguished by an appreciation for the natural landscape of the region —expansive prairies, gently rolling meadows and hills, meandering, slow-moving rivers, occasional bluffs, and an unostentatious palette of native grasses, wildflowers, and common deciduous trees such as hawthorns and crab apples—all seen as one calm, harmonious whole, deferring to the horizontal, beneath the vast dome of the midwestern sky.

Jensen and his colleagues in combining these indigenous land forms and native plants in their landscapes, did not mean to dazzle the beholder. Their designs for enhancing the grounds of a home, a park, or a cemetery were adaptations of forms and materials already used by Brown, Repton, and Loudon in England as well as by Downing and Olmsted in eastern North America. Yet contemporary critics recognized differences. Wilhelm Miller, a professor of horticulture at the University of Illinois at the time, saw in

Originally laid out by Jensen beginning in 1918, Columbus Park included this broad swath of former prairie as well as a secluded council ring, a wading pool, and a swimming "hole" or pool. Now a golf course, this area has been well preserved, while other features are in need of restoration.

these designers' work a "new and appropriate type of beauty," an emerging Prairie Style, based on one geographic, climatic, and visually coherent region, and on the practical needs of midwestern people.[1] Frank Waugh, a professor of horticulture and landscape architecture at the State College (now University) of Massachusetts, noticed particularly in Jensen's work something novel, free of formulas, faintly resembling Japanese and modern German gardening, owing something, perhaps, to the Zuni Indians and the flat prairies that Jensen alluded to—but certainly "the most fresh and modern thing in American landscape architecture."[2] Both Miller and Waugh, incidentally, imply a definition of the term "modern" for that particular place and time: something fresh and original, frankly acknowledging local conditions and manners of living, and free of the conventions of any imported style.

This sense of modernism invites one to appreciate

OPENING ILLUSTRATION:
Jens Jensen's design for the Lincoln Memorial Garden in Springfield, Illinois, from the late 1930s, includes a few secluded council rings where people could gather around a campfire and reminisce about the legendary people and events of their common heritage.

landscapes and gardens not as precious jewels but as places to live, work, and breathe deeply. When Miller and Waugh discuss woodlands, the prairie, or wildflowers by the roadside, they evoke the sensibilities of Thoreau, George Perkins Marsh, and others who saw the environment in both the large view and minute details. These two professors also reached out to wide audiences by working within their state landscape extension services. Miller, for example, drew from Jensen's designs for public parks and large private estates some intriguing suggestions for the cottager or weekend gardener. The prairie spirit could be expressed in a small patch of garden with herbaceous plants and shrubs that had flat-topped flowers, such as daisies, elder, and viburnum—flowers that repeated the line of the horizon. The prairie rose—"the symbol of the Illinois way," in Miller's view—could be planted by the front door. Fine old native hawthorns, crab apples, honey locusts, and dogwoods ought to be preserved; and, where a backyard looked out onto cornfields or pastures, a few haws or crabs could frame the view and thus idealize the prairie—as Jensen had done at Douglas Park, in Chicago.[3]

Jensen (who was born on a farm in Denmark and had studied agriculture) and Griffin (who was also a

The calm, expansive horizontal line of the prairie, as seen north of Champaign-Urbana, Illinois, symbolized freedom for Jensen and his contemporaries. Even under cultivation or covered with suburban homes, the primeval lay of the land remained the foundation for the "prairie spirit" in architecture and landscape design.

trained architect and chief designer for Frank Lloyd Wright), worked with some of the most progressive architects of their day—the "Prairie School," or Chicago School. Rejecting imported and period styles, these designers sought a regional—and American—design expression under the generally acknowledged leadership of Louis Sullivan and Wright. Jensen did have some stormy disagreements with Wright while they worked on a house and grounds for Mrs. Abby Longyear Roberts, in Marquette, Michigan, but both men had a profound reverence for the natural form and underlying spirit of the midwestern landscape. They saw the vast prairies as a source of inspiration for design, symbolic of freedom yet stable and sustaining. As Jensen wrote, "All art must grow out of native soil."[4] Native plants, growing profusely, suited to their land, were essential, he believed, whereas the standardization of plants from everywhere would soon make the world commonplace. To enrich the cultural life of the world, then, he made his own gardens and landscapes *regional*. He used local stratified rock and crabapples (with "stratified," or horizontally growing, branches, symbolic of the prairie horizon); goldenrod, asters, and coneflowers in meadows; and stone council rings in forest borders, recalling the campfires of early pioneers.

Echoes of the prairie spirit resound in the novels and poetry of Willa Cather, Carl Sandburg, Edgar Lee Masters, and Vachel Lindsay, whose midwestern subject matter distanced them from writers in the East and Europe. Sandburg's poem "Prairie" is haunting in its defiance of stale precedent:

> I speak of new cities and new people.
> I tell you the past is a bucket of ashes.
> I tell you yesterday is a wind gone down,
>   a sun dropped in the west.
> I tell you there is nothing in the world
>   only an ocean of tomorrows,
>   a sky of tomorrows.

In this poem, Sandburg recalled a song of red hawthorns in autumn, "long as the layer of black loam we go to, the shine of the morning star over the corn belt." Jensen felt the freedom and the "urge to be"

47

Jensen's naturalistic planting of a pool at the side entrance of the Henry Babson house by Louis Sullivan (with George Grant Elmslie, 1907) offered a peaceful retreat within the suburb of Riverside—itself a retreat from bustling Chicago, laid out by Olmsted and Vaux in 1869.

Designed by Frank Lloyd Wright in 1907–8, the Coonley residence, in Riverside, Illinois, still conveys the prairie spirit of openness and simplicity on the grounds of the exterior, said to be laid out by Jensen. Retracing the evolution of his "organic architecture," Wright recalled his childhood days in Wisconsin: "I loved the prairie by instinct as itself a great simplicity; the trees, flowers, and sky were thrilling by contrast. And I saw that a little of height on the prairie was enough to look like much more." (Wright, *The Natural House*, p. 15).

evoked by "red berries" (rose hips) poking up through the snow on a prairie rose bush; and Wright cherished his own home in the Wisconsin countryside (now known as Taliesin East), asserting that "its elevation is the modelling of the hills, the weaving and the fabric that clings to them, the look of it all in tender green or covered with snow. . . . Architecture . . . is no less a weaving and a fabric than the trees are."[5]

This weaving would be difficult to achieve with a collaborator as strong-willed as Jensen. Leonard Eaton, Jensen's biographer, relates that Jensen preferred complete independence from architects and that, consequently, there was little integration between most of Jensen's residential gardens and their houses. And yet a kindred spirit between house and landscape garden emanates from the faded photographs of two places in Riverside, Illinois: the Henry Babson House now destroyed, and the Avery Coonley House.[6] At both places, originally, the long, low, masses of building emphasized the horizontal dimension, while low chimneys, intersecting gables and hip roofs, and changing levels gave some vertical punctuation, in harmony with the tall, round-headed and low, horizontally spreading trees that completed the sweeping landscape compositions. Inside, particularly in the Coonley house, an interior landscape flowed from one living area to another, escaping the confines of traditional, four-walled rooms and corridors. What happened, then, to this architectural and landscape expression of freedom and movement—which, even today, appears modern?

Historians have pointed to shifts in educated taste away from a developing, highly inventive, regional expression toward more cosmopolitan, archaeologically "correct," refined forms. In 1917 the architect Thomas E. Tallmadge reported that the thirtieth annual architectural exhibition in Chicago revealed no evidence that the "Chicago School" as a potent style still existed. "The exhibition would be just as appropriate in the halls of the Boston Museum of Fine Arts, as in our own Art Institute, which stands for art ideals in the Middle West," he regretted.[7] The departures of Wright (to Italy, to Japan, to rural Wisconsin), of Griffin (to Australia), and of Sullivan (into obscurity and sad decline) cannot alone be held

In Wright's scheme for the McCormick house, a natural stream is allowed to flow beneath a wing of the house, on the left, while retaining walls by the water's edge suggest that the entire bluff is a man-made structure integrated with the natural landscape.

responsible for the demise of a once-thriving regional idiom, or style. Jensen remained in the Chicago region through 1935, designing the gardens and grounds of large country places; but the houses that he and Simonds and others typically worked *around* —whether of Georgian or Tudor or any other period style—could never be woven into one fabric expressive of the Prairie Spirit. In fact, another form of regionalism—not geographical, but cultural—must also be recognized.

By the late teens and 1920s, Chicago, like other parts of the United States, was establishing a cultural identity that was drawn less from its geographical location than from its particular economic, social, and cultural development. Its own World's Columbian Exposition of 1893 had already exhibited a dream of buildings and landscapes brought together in a memorable expression of civic order and splendor evocative of imperial Rome (see illustration on pages 40 and 41). Within two decades or so, the refinement of that expression on a domestic level proved irresistible to many well-traveled, cultivated clients in the Chicago area. As early as 1907, the most ambitious residential project of Wright's prairie years (actually a weaving together of gardens and low-rise structures, which might appear, from a distance, as several unpretentious dwellings) was rejected by the client, an heir to the McCormick reaper fortune, Harold McCormick. Apparently Mrs. McCormick, finding Wright's project unsympathetic to her lifestyle, went to New York and contacted the architect/garden designer Charles Platt—who proceeded to design a home faintly reminiscent of the Villa D'Este for the McCormicks' blufftop site, overlooking Lake Michigan.[8] There, on any given weekend, one would not expect to come across a Carl Sandburg or a Willa Cather, but perhaps some relation of Henry James or Edith Wharton.

While the McCormicks' residence, viewed from Lake Michigan, seems almost to have floated there from some secluded lake frontage in northern Italy, views closer to the house are more intimate and somehow more believably "American." Photographs of her-

Designed in 1908–11 by Charles Platt, the McCormicks' terraced gardens recalled the grandeur of the Villa D'Este at Tivoli along the wooded bluffs of Lake Michigan. Within a few years after the gardens' completion, the prairie spirit in midwestern design was clearly declining, while imitations and evocations of period styles from Europe could be found throughout the United States.

baceous borders, with trellises and French doors in the background, make the McCormick place appear pleasantly inviting and quite livable. Thus, the inclusion of such photographs in the May 1912, issue of *The Craftsman* did not in itself confirm the waning of simple, craftsmanlike expression in houses and gardens. *The Craftsman*'s editor, Gustav Stickley, was an outspoken advocate of simplicity, efficiency, integrity of materials, and the interests of working people everywhere. When his magazine featured the McCormick place, it was not the increasingly popular Italianate *style* that was emphasized, but some underlying principles: the close relationship of the house to the grounds, the expression of the owner's way of life, the materials (wood, stucco, and concrete), and the old-fashioned plants (hollyhocks, iris, asters, stock, roses and forget-me-nots).[9] It is true that by 1912 humble, craftsmanlike dwellings were beginning to lose their appeal in the Midwest, as elsewhere in America. (Stickley's magazine ceased publication in 1916 because of this and other cultural and economic changes in America.) Nevertheless, the domains of fashionable and vernacular design in the Midwest were not separated by impenetrable walls.

In 1912, a contemporary writer traced Chicago's cultural development in the design of its gardens: "The first country places were all open, with neither fence, hedge nor shrubbery border about them. Then came the large plantations of shrubbery fostered by Mr. Simonds. But the formal treatment of the grounds immediately about the house is as suitable for a handsome piece of architecture in Illinois as it is in Italy. The whole countryside will become more and more cultivated, more and more civilized. . . . The idea of privacy is gradually growing. A man's garden should be like a room of his house, a place where he can enjoy his thoughts, his books, his friends, his family."[10]

The cultural aspirations outlined here—which know no geographical boundaries—were nourished, for a while, in the kinds of houses and gardens for which Platt, Stanford White, Edith Wharton, Beatrix Farrand, Ellen Shipman, Rose Standish Nichols, and others are now known: homes of a classical manner, more or less Italian in spirit, with regular terraced and walled gardens and planting inspired by Gertrude Jekyll. Jekyll, too, was indebted to Renaissance Italy in her use of water, stone, and perennial verdure to endow relatively new gardens with the impressions of age and venerability.

In the late 1930s, however, drawn in part from the same traditions of Italian villa design, another recognizably modern tradition began to emerge in California in the work of Thomas Church and his followers. In some ways Church did for California gardens what Platt did for gardens of the Northeast: he made appropriate adaptations of European models for the particular geographical and cultural regions he was working in. But, outliving Platt by forty-five

With this sun-dappled view of the Villa Torre Galli, near Florence, Sargent's *Breakfast in the Loggia* (c. 1910) reveals one of the qualities of Italian villas that Platt found particularly appealing: their livability.

years and working in a region and at a time favorable to bold experiment and innovation in the arts, Church went on to become the founder of the modern garden in California.

To be useful, the term "modern" must now be defined for each particular context. As noted earlier, for Jensen, Simonds, and other midwestern designers before World War I, to be modern was to avoid eclecticism of style and exotic plants, to draw inspiration from the region, and to declare cultural independence from the Northeastern American establishment and Europe. For Church and another pioneering California designer, Garrett Eckbo, however, to be modern was to open oneself to a wide spectrum of influences from around the world: to gardens of Renaissance Italy, furniture of contemporary Finland, American jazz, and more. To be modern in California just before and after World War II was also to understand a given region, the culture of which was in flux, rapidly evolving along with its influx of people, ideas, technological innovations, and economic change.

Designing houses and gardens in New England

before World War I, Platt lived in a different, less harried world. Not a modernist, he was nonetheless a pioneer in rural New Hampshire, adapting Italian Renaissance prototypes for the summer homes of a congenial group of artists and writers who were fond of gardening. Platt's genius as a designer in Cornish, New Hampshire, from the 1890s onward, lay in understanding his clients' views of that region and expressing their cultural aspirations in unostentatious built form. [11]

Trained in art schools in New York City and Paris, Platt began to design gardens and houses after he had already made his reputation for fine etching and landscape painting. In 1886 he made his first trip to Italy, where he returned in 1892 accompanied by his younger brother William, then an apprentice to Frederick Law Olmsted in Brookline, Massachusetts. By then, Platt had already built houses for himself and for a client, Annie Lazarus, in Cornish. As Platt's biographer, Keith Morgan, notes, the siting and design of these residences were Platt's (with help from Stanford White on the Lazarus house); planting was usually delegated to someone more

CHARLES A PLATT *Itls Place at* CORNISH

Platt's introduction of features from Italian gardens into the rural landscape of Cornish, New Hampshire, was understated and elegant. When a visitor approached Platt's home from the circular entrance drive, the house and terraced gardens were seen obliquely. The view beyond the lawn toward the mountains is gentle, satisfying.

knowledgeable—to his protegee, Ellen Shipman, for example, or to clients themselves. [12]

The satisfying integration of these houses with their terraced gardens and grounds is still recognizable today, although the gardens and plantings have been much simplified. For that integration Platt was clearly indebted to his Italian journeys. In *Italian Gardens* (1894) Platt revealed the painter/etcher's ap-

preciation for the "evident harmony of arrangement between the house and the surrounding landscape . . . the design as a whole," with its gardens, terraces, groves, and larger environment. Platt also identified a problem that Church and Eckbo would later address: how "to take a piece of land and make it habitable," not only inside but out-of-doors as well. [13] The solution yielded a house-and-garden continuum that was clearly man-made. Though softened by luxuriant planting of perennial borders, vines on trellises, and background trees, the paths, walls, pools, and paving were frank acknowledgments of human use and enjoyment.

Such features were not unknown in New England; simpler structures and less symmetrical layouts could be found in old Colonial gardens. Still, Platt was introducing a greater degree of formality and historical reference. Architectural critics, such as his friend and client, Herbert Croly, were delighted; but some writers regretted the degree of artifice. A reviewer for Charles Sprague Sargent's journal, *Garden and Forest,* was unmoved by Platt's articles, later published as *Italian Gardens.* Acknowledging the sentimental appeal of overgrown, partly ruined Italian gardens, the reviewer stated that the formal garden as a type "expresses no sentiment and carries no inner meaning; it does not address itself to the nobler part of our nature as simple, natural scenery does." One might appreciate the aesthetic beauty of clearly man-made gardens; but only natural scenery could stir "the profoundest feelings of the soul." [14]

Behind this judgment lay Olmsted's contributions in park and residential design; the writings of Emerson, Thoreau, and Ruskin; transcendentalism, with its recognition of divinity in nature; the growth of northeastern metropolitan cities—with the resulting loss of unaltered landscape—among other factors. But underlying the increasing interest in formal gardens were the same social, economic, and cultural factors that would overcome regional pride and cultural independence in the Midwest some twenty years later: increasing personal wealth, travel, residence abroad, and—particularly strong among people of Platt's and Wharton's circle of acquaintances—a delight in imagining oneself in some other part of the world and in designing one's surroundings accordingly.

"In gardening there is a complete freedom from national bonds and the only determining factor is the climate," wrote Helen M. Fox in *Patio Gardens* (1929), her study of Spanish/Moorish traditions. "Whether the land is ruled by a king or a dictator has no influence on the trees and flowers, but rocks and beaches make a difference and so does wind."[15] Variations on this theme of "freedom but for climate" can be found in many writings of the early twentieth century, in which some faraway country is visited and hints for American gardens are brought back.

Landscape architect Charles Downing Lay, who once interviewed Platt, appreciated his "independence of spirit, his refusal to be bound too closely by the natural conditions of the site, but rather to remould them nearer to the heart's desire."[16] The desire of some of Platt's Cornish clients was, frankly, to be in Italy. At times when that was not possible, these clients could at least look out from their slopes of the White Mountains in New Hampshire and *imagine* they were gazing on some hill in Tuscany. Given Platt's restraint and sense of fitness to America and the region, the Cornish clients did not, at any rate,

receive stage sets. In their gardens, "that sacred portion of the globe dedicated to one's self," in Platt's view,[17] they could plant the phlox and larkspur, peonies, daylilies, roses, and irises to suit their own tastes, within a structure of indoor and outdoor spaces that allowed them to dream of Italy.

"Here is our Italy! It is a Mediterranean without marshes and without malaria," wrote New Englander Charles Dudley Warner in 1891. He was referring to southern California. "Now and then some bay with its purple hills running to the blue sea, its surrounding mesas and canyons blooming in semitropical luxuriance, some conjunction of shore and mountain, some golden color, some white light and sharply defined shadows, some refinement of lines, some poetic tints in violet and ashy ranges, some . . . delicate blue in the sky, will remind the traveller of more than one place of beauty in Southern Italy and Sicily."[18] Warner was delighted with the benign climate of southern California. He also appreciated the remnants of the Spanish occupation and thought the old adobe homes, with their light-filled yet enclosed patios were more fitting, and more beautiful, than the prosaic dwellings then being built for wintering and migrating Americans.

Platt's original, richly planted terrace gardens, for his own residence in Cornish, New Hampshire, were evocative of Renaissance Italy, but have since been replaced by a simple lawn. What remains is the impression of a dignified existence in a fairly traditional, rural New England residence, where art and life can freely intermingle.

Noting the need for irrigation and other human intervention in the landscape, Charles Dudley Warner predicted that southern California would become a land of small farms and gardens, picturesque and poetic: "It is the fairest field for the experiment of a contented community, without any poverty and without excessive wealth."

By the time Church was studying landscape architecture at Berkeley in the early 1920s, evidence of Spanish/Moorish, Italian, and other Mediterranean traditions could be found throughout northern and southern California. In the Southland, somewhat drier and sunnier, features of the old Spanish missions and colonial adobe homes were reinterpreted for new communities such as Palos Verdes or Ojai—where Church lived as a boy. Along the northern coast, where fogs swept in from the ocean and kept ancient redwood groves cool and moist during the rainless summers, Spanish and Mexican traditions coexisted, and sometimes merged, with Italian, Anglo-American, and northern European wooden architectural traditions. The San Francisco Bay area, along the northern coast, belonged to a different subregion from that of Los Angeles; yet the two areas shared some common climatic and cultural conditions, including low rainfall (a complete absence of rain for six to eight months a year); subtropical conditions (with rarely a frost); a largely undeveloped landscape, with many hills nearly bare of trees except for the sturdy, contorted-limbed live oak (*Quercus agrifolia*); and a growing population of immigrants from the Midwest, the Northeast, Mexico, and elsewhere, bringing cultural memories and dreams of a better life to a landscape that seemed, to many, a clean slate.

Church was part of that influx. Born in Boston in 1902 and reared from infancy in California, he received a Beaux Arts training in landscape architecture, earning an undergraduate degree at Berkeley and a master's at Harvard. Then, in 1926–27, aware of a lack of coherence in California gardens and houses, Church set off on a Sheldon traveling fellowship in search of ideas that could be adapted for the Mediterranean climate and local conditions of California. The report of his journey contains tiny photographs of overgrown, half-ruined gardens, including the Villa D'Este and the Alhambra, as well as photographs of recently built gardens in California, including El Fureidis, by Bertram Goodhue, home of J. Waldron Gillespie, in Montecito. Sensing poetry and mystery in the beautiful, melancholy gardens of the Mediterranean, Church also saw promise in his own region. "Out of chaos," he wrote, "California is developing a style of its own, suited to its needs and fitting into its hillsides as naturally as the Generalife among its olive groves." [19]

After his travels abroad, Church taught at Ohio State University for two years and returned to the San Francisco Bay area in 1929. He worked for landscape architect Floyd Mick for about two years, then opened his own office during the Depression. Jobs were scarce. Church worked on small residential gardens, making backyards and passageways habitable. For the magazine *California Arts and Architecture,* he edited plant lists compiled by Adele Wharton Vaughan (the landscape architect and wife of Church's friend, Berkeley professor H. L. Vaughan). Church also contributed to that magazine a series of articles on the small California garden, of which he observed, "The small garden is like a small room. It must be neat. . . . Houses have changed. They are down off their stilts. . . . Doors are replacing windows. . . . Dining rooms open to paved courts. . . . I know a bathroom with a garden door; it opens to a court for sun bathing. Everything points to the increasing intimacy of the house and its garden." [20] This, Church pointed out, was not a new idea; the Egyptians, the Greeks, the Romans, and the Renaissance Italians had all integrated their houses and gardens, and *lived* out of doors. Now, as Californians did likewise, function, beauty, adaptability, convenience, and economy of upkeep would become leading principles.

This emphasis on livability and economy of resources, derived as much from rainless summers as from the Depression, was the pragmatic foundation of the modern California garden. The direct influences of modern European art and architecture—the work

Florence Yoch and Lucille Council utilized some features from traditional Spanish gardens in this garden for Casa Santa Cruz, the Santa Barbara residence of Mr. and Mrs. Bernard Hoffman. Church, confident that an appropriate regional style was evolving in California, used a photograph of this pool as the frontispiece for his report on Mediterranean gardens, which was submitted to Harvard University in 1927.

of Miró, Arp, Picasso, Aalto, and Le Corbusier—came later. In 1933 Church departed from his topic of the small garden to write an article on the Villa D'Este. He wrote, "We, today, who stand on the brink of a modern and sensible approach to our garden problems may well revive and restudy the underlying principles which make the Italian Renaissance gardens the greatest achievement of garden building in history." [21]

Just as Stickley studied Platt's McCormick residence, so Church examined the Villa D'Este—for underlying principles of design. Discussing the needs of any garden, great or small, Church's approach remained consistent from the Depression era through the prosperous decades after World War II, when *House Beautiful, House and Garden,* and *Sunset* magazines made him a nationally known designer. Typically, his sentences were short. His mood was cheerful—at times whimsical, at times downright practical—as in discussing where to locate the potting bench and the compost heap. His favorite plants, judging from countless photographs and a few garden tours, included 200-year-old coast live oaks that he typically preserved with great care, designing living spaces around them.

In the 1940s and 1950s, garden editors used to ask designers for lists of their favorite plants for specific situations. Church answered one questionnaire thus: "vine for an arbor: actinidia, wisteria, bignonia; for an architectural planting box: Mugo pine; for fragrance: *Daphne odora;* for a sunny bank: *Nierembergia rivularis;* for a windbreak: six- to eight-foot solid fence; for a window box: 'remove the window box.'"[22] Garrett Eckbo, asked for similar preferences, offered a long list of favorite natives and exotics, including trees that would make any Californian nostalgic: "camphor tree (*Cinnamomum Camphora*), pepper tree (*Schinus species*), California live oak (*Quercus agrifolia*), Pink ironbark (*Eucalyptus sideroxylon rosea*), flannel bush (*Fremontia Mexicana*), California holly (*Photinia arbutifolia*), jacaranda (*Jacaranda mimosaefolia*), coral tree (*Erythrina species*)," and more.[23]

In 1933, Eckbo was an undergraduate at Berkeley, learning about landscape architecture and its history from Vaughan's lectures and Church's occasional visits. Born in Cooperstown, New York, in 1910, and reared from childhood in California, Eckbo was, like Church, also trained in Beaux Arts principles of design. His history and studio courses, however, taught by young professor Vaughan, were imbued with the same pragmatic, open-minded approach to design that Church was beginning to articulate in *California Arts and Architecture.* Eckbo's ponderous, typewritten history notebook, dated May 9, 1934, reveals his efforts to understand gardens of every tradition and era—their uses, influences on their design, and their adaptability to garden design in California.

Bruce Porter laid out this residence, in Woodside, California, for William Bourne in 1915–16. Known today as Filoli, this National Trust property features garden rooms and spatial sequences that delighted young Garrett Eckbo, then a Berkeley undergraduate, in 1934. In the contrast between clipped hedges and other shrubs and trees allowed to grow freely, Eckbo recognized and appreciated the simultaneous expression of formality and informality.

"We are now trying to create a garden of low cost and easy maintenance which will make extra living quarters for the house," Eckbo wrote. While gardens of colonial Virginia and the Alhambra provided models of compact, orderly arrangement, they were not for direct copying. "We can imitate the form," Eckbo observed, "but it will be hollow."[24]

Eckbo's training in landscape architecture at Berkeley was not pointedly "regional," but regional issues were raised as a preparation for practice in California. Among the 2,000 plants that Eckbo and his classmates were required to learn, only about 200 were California natives. Conservation of water, land, and other resources was not emphasized to the degree that it is today. But even during the Depression,

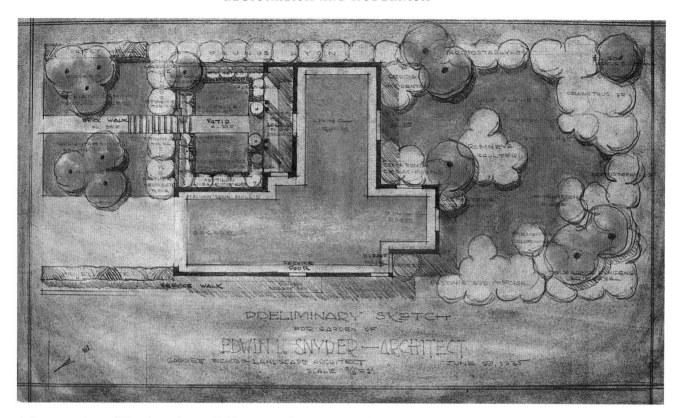

A former student of Vaughan, Garrett Eckbo proposed to terrace the entrance to Edwin Snyder's hillside house, shaping rectilinear spaces with straight paths. The steeply sloping rear of the property is laid out more casually, with many native plants. The style or manner of laying out different parts of the site was determined by the lay of the land.

Eckbo did not ignore the stately country places of the Bay Area; in fact, he learned a great deal about scale, spatial sequences, and relative formality of design during his field trips to gardens such as Filoli, in Woodside, and the Newhall place, in Hillsborough. Examining these European-inspired gardens, he discovered something Church had also recognized in Italy and Spain: that formality and informality were not mutually exclusive qualities. Wherever luxuriant vegetation had been allowed to soften the lines of a path, a wall or a screen, formality and informality need not clash; they could be harmonized, their characters reinforced by contrast.

Church's gardens, published in *California Arts and Architecture* in the mid-1930s, and Eckbo's gardens of 1935-36, designed mostly for clients of Armstrong Nurseries, in Southern California, are not particularly modern. [25] Yet modern traits can be found in their work of that time: spaces tend to be clear, unclut-tered, shaped by walls and clipped hedges; bordering plants are neat, sparse, many in pots; hillsides are terraced and paved in brick—or left wild, shaded by a few live oaks and a tangle of native plants; nowhere is nature imitated. These gardens are creations by and for human beings.

Accustomed to such gardens, Eckbo was shocked when, in 1936, he entered Harvard's graduate program in landscape architecture on a scholarship (which he won in a national competition) and discovered that gardens of a frankly man-made character—formal gardens—were somehow inferior to informal gardens—that is, imitations of someone's *ideal* of nature! Eckbo's Harvard textbook on landscape design, first published in 1917, had been written by Professor Henry Vincent Hubbard (who was on the landscape faculty at Harvard) and Theodora Kimball (the librarian of the Harvard Graduate School of Design and, eventually, Hubbard's wife). [26] Their prin-

This sketch suggests Eckbo's frame of mind as he and a few Harvard classmates began to investigate the new phenomenon of modern architecture and its implications for garden design.

In the view of Henry Vincent Hubbard and Theodora Kimball, landscape design imitative of nature, following nature's own ways, represented a higher art than clearly man-made alterations of nature. This judgment is exemplified by this scene near the entrance to the Arnold Arboretum in Jamaica Plain, Massachusetts.

ciples were impeccable, yet their views were deeply rooted in the moist, temperate, summer-green, naturally picturesque, and gradually self-healing landscapes of New England. Eckbo, accustomed to terracing, irrigating, and otherwise altering the summer-brown hills of California, knew that every act of making *that* land fit for human habitation required undisguisable artifice. He was also accustomed to designing *spaces,* rather than pictures of nature. As the only Californian in his graduate class, he was outnumbered; but, finding like-minded spirits among fellow students Dan Kiley and James Rose, he joined them in rebelling against preconceived notions of design. By 1937-38, when Walter Gropius became head of Harvard's department of architecture, Eckbo was already prepared to investigate some of the ideas of European Modernism then in the air.

In 1937 Church, in San Francisco, and Eckbo, in Cambridge, were independently experimenting with garden designs inspired by European modernists. In February, the San Francisco Museum of Art opened an exhibition, "Contemporary Landscape Architecture and its Sources," featuring models and photographs of houses and gardens by Church, Fletcher Steele, William Wurster, Richard Neutra, Wright, Le Corbusier, Mies van der Rohe, and others. [27] Church's prize-winning model, published in *Landscape Architecture* that April, featured a house and garden on a 25-foot city lot, by Ernest Born and Carl B. Lund. The house, garden, connecting ramp, and spiral staircase owed much to Le Corbusier's houses and projects of the 1920s.

Eckbo was intrigued by Le Corbusier and other Europeans who were trying to express the spirit of their age: an era of quickening pace, urbanization, mechanization, and scarcity of space and time. In September, 1937, Eckbo's own designs for "Small Gardens in the City" were published in *Pencil Points.* The similarity between Eckbo's and Church's designs is remarkable; dynamic in their diagonals and asymmetry, both gardens are extensions of the form and spirit of their modern houses. Today, Eckbo does not recall having been aware of Church's prize-winning design. In 1937 his interests lay not in sources or styles, but in "an open-minded, uninhibited,

Growing up in the San Francisco Bay Area, where terracing, irrigation, and other alterations were necessary to make the land fit for human habitation, Eckbo could not understand why naturalistic design constituted a higher art than clearly man-made design. He brought his beliefs to bear on his design for the Blake garden in Kensington, California.

straightforward solution of a problem on its own conditions." [28]

The individual paths of development followed by Eckbo, Church, Platt, and Jensen cannot be retraced here. The modern Bay Area tradition, or style, for instance, to which Church, Eckbo, Robert Royston, Lawrence Halprin, and others would contribute, working with architects such as William Wurster and Gardner Dailey, was just beginning to emerge in the 1930s. What should be clear, however, considering the regional influences, is that Modernism, however defined for a particular context, whether recognized as part of an international movement or simply noted in isolation, is a development typically arising from a particular time, place, and/or spirit. Regionalism, which is normally determined by geography, can also depend on a form of culture that transcends geographical or topographical boundaries.

Strands of regionalism and Modernism are often woven together; and running through that fabric may be a few threads of tradition—timeless in their use and beauty. As Eckbo, endowed with one of the most penetrating minds that ever discussed Modernism, wrote during the ascendancy of that movement, "The serious and intelligent modern artist does not reject tradition, he only rejects imitation of past segments in the stream. . . . When we understand that the Japanese garden, far from being quaint, picturesque or naturalistic, is the most highly refined, most sensitive, most organized, and therefore *most* formal landscape expression in history, we may be ready to go forward with our own problems on their own terms."[29]

NOTES

1. Wilhelm Miller, *The Prairie Spirit in Landscape Gardening* (Champaign-Urbana: Department of Horticulture, University of Illinois, 1915).

2. Frank Waugh, *The Landscape Beautiful* (New York: Orange Judd, 1910), pp. 198–99.

3. Miller, *The Prairie Spirit in Landscape Gardening,* pp. 1–16.

4. Jens Jensen, "The Naturalistic Treatment in a Metropolitan Park," *American Landscape Architect* 2 (January 1930): 34.

5. See Jens Jensen, *Siftings* (1939; reprint, Baltimore: Johns Hopkins University Press, 1990); Frank Lloyd Wright, *An Autobiography* (New York: Duell, Sloan & Pearce, 1943).

6. Early-twentieth-century photographs of the Babson house and grounds are reproduced in Eaton, *Landscape Artist in America,* pp. 108–15. For contemporary photographs of the Coonley residence (garden courtyards by Wright; peripheral landscape by Jensen), see Grant Manson, *Frank Lloyd Wright to 1910* (New York: Reinhold, 1958), among many other works.

7. Thomas E. Tallmadge, "The Thirtieth Annual Architectural Exhibit in Chicago," *The Western Architect* (April 1917): 27–28 ff.

8. See Manson, *Frank Lloyd Wright to 1910,* for an account of the McCormicks' rejection of Wright's project. Manson believes that had this prominent Chicago couple not rejected Wright's scheme, the prairie spirit might have flourished for many more years.

9. For more *Craftsman* gardening articles, see the issues for April 1910 and April 1912.

10. Anthony Hunt, "Landscape Architecture in and about Chicago," *Architectural Record* 32 (July 1912).

11. Platt later designed houses and gardens in other regions of the United States, but only his early work in New Hampshire is discussed here.

12. For Platt's influence on Shipman, see Leslie Rose Close, "Ellen Biddle Shipman," in William H. Tishler, ed., *American Landscape Architecture, Designers and Places* (Washington, D.C.: National Trust for Historic Preservation and American Society of Landscape Architects, 1989).

13. Charles Platt, *Italian Gardens* (New York: Harper & Brothers, 1894), p. 6. This book was composed of two articles Platt published in *Harper's Magazine,* July and August 1893.

14. *Garden and Forest* 6 (August 2, 1893): 322.

15. Helen M. Fox, *Patio Gardens* (New York: Macmillan, 1929), p. 195.

16. Charles Downing Lay, "An Interview with Charles A. Platt," *Landscape Architecture* 2 (April 1912): 130.

17. Platt, *Italian Gardens.*

18. Charles Dudley Warner, *Our Italy* (New York: Harper & Brothers, 1891), p. 18.

19. Thomas D. Church, "A Study of Mediterranean Gardens and their Adaptability to California Conditions" (report of his Sheldon traveling fellowship, 1926–27), in archives of the Frances Loeb Library, Harvard Graduate School of Design.

20. Church, "The Small California Garden; chapter 1, A New Deal for the Small Lot," *California Arts and Architecture* (May 1933): 16.

21. Church, "The Villa D'Este at Tivoli," *California Arts and Architecture* (October 1933): 15.

22. Church, "To Help You Choose the Right Plant for the Right Place," *Sunset* (April 1949): 30–33.

23. Church, "Choose Plants to Suit Your Climate," *House and Garden* (January 1953): 63. *Fremontia* has since been renamed *Fremontodendron; Photinia arbutifolia* is now known as *Heteromeles arbutifolia;* and *mimosaefolia* is now spelled *mimosifolia.*

24. Garret Eckbo, "A History of Landscape Design," May 9, 1934 (private papers at Eckbo's home in Berkeley, California). Typescript.

25. Church's articles and photographs appeared frequently in this magazine during the middle 1930s; later his work often appeared in *House Beautiful* and *Sunset.* Eckbo's papers, photographs, plans, and drawings are to be preserved in the archives of the University of California at Berkeley, Department of Landscape Architecture.

26. Eckbo's own copy of this textbook, Hubbard and Kimball's *Introduction to the Study of Landscape Design* (New York: Macmillan, 1917) is heavily annotated in the margins, showing precisely where he disagreed with the authors.

27. *Contemporary Landscape Architecture and its Sources* (San Francisco: San Francisco Museum of Art, 1937). Compare Church's model with Eckbo's garden plans and perspectives in his "Small Gardens in the City," *Pencil Points* (September 1937): 573–86.

28. Eckbo, "Small Gardens in the City."

29. Eckbo, "What Do We Mean by Modern Landscape Architecture?" *Journal of the Royal Architectural Institute of Canada* 27 (August 1950): 268–271.

BIBLIOGRAPHY

The Art of Home Landscaping. New York: F. W. Dodge Corp., 1956. Revised as *Home Landscape: The Art of Home Landscaping.* New York: McGraw-Hill, 1978.

Brooks, H. Allen, ed. *Prairie School Architecture: Studies from "The Western Architect."* Toronto: University of Toronto Press, 1975.

Byrd, Warren T., Jr., ed. *The Work of Garrett Eckbo: Landscapes for Living.* Proceedings of the Second Annual Symposium on Landscape Architecture, February 11, 1984, the University of Virginia, Charlottesville, Va.

Church, Thomas D. *Gardens Are for People.* New York: Reinhold, 1955. 2d ed., edited by Michael Laurie and Grace Hall. New York: McGraw-Hill, 1983.

Cutler, Phoebe. *The Public Landscape of the New Deal.* New Haven: Yale University Press, 1985.

Dobyns, Winifred Starr. *California Gardens.* New York: Macmillan, 1931.

Duncan, Frances. "The Gardens of Cornish." *Century Magazine* (May 1906).

Eaton, Leonard K., *Landscape Artist in America: The Life and Work of Jens Jensen.* Chicago: University of Chicago Press, 1964.

Eckbo, Garrett, *Landscape for Living.* New York: F. W. Dodge Corp., 1950.

Gelbloom, Mara. "Ossian Simonds: Prairie Spirit in Landscape Gardening." *Prairie School Review* 12, (1975): 5–18.

An Interview with Garrett Eckbo, edited by Karen Madsen. Watertown, Mass.: The Hubbard Educational Trust, 1990.

Jensen, Jens. "Some Gardens of the Middle West." *The Architectural Review* (Boston) 15, (May, 1908): 10–14.

Laurie, Michael, "The California Influence on Contemporary Landscape Architecture." *Landscape Architecture* (July 1966): 292–98.

Meacham, Barbara Brent. "Garrett Eckbo, A Retrospective." Master's thesis, University of California at Berkeley, 1980.

Messenger, Pam-Anela. "The Art of Thomas Dolliver Church." Master's thesis, University of California at Berkeley, 1976.

Miller, Wilhelm. "How the Middle West Can Come into Its Own." *Country Life in America* 22, (September 15, 1912): 11–14.

Miyakoda, Tooru, ed. *Garrett Eckbo: Philosophy of Landscape, Process Architecture* 90. Tokyo: Process Architecture Publishing, 1990.

Morgan, Keith N. *Charles A. Platt: The Artist as Architect.* Cambridge, Mass.: MIT Press, 1985.

Reiss, Suzanne. *Thomas Church, Landscape Architect.* 2 vols. Bancroft Library series of oral histories. University of California at Berkeley, ca. 1978.

Simo, Melanie Louise. "The Education of a Modern Landscape Designer" (on Garrett Eckbo). *Pacific Horticulture* 49, (Summer 1988): 19–30.

————. "Garrett Eckbo and Dan Kiley: Some Notes on Rebellion and Reconciliation." In Patrick M. Condon and Lance M. Neckar, eds., *The Avant-Garde and the Landscape: Can They Be Reconciled?,* Proceedings from the conference held April 14-16, 1989, at the University of Minnesota, Twin Cities Campus, Minneapolis, Minnesota. Minneapolis: Landworks Press, 1990. Proceedings include Eckbo's article, "Avant-Garde and Status Quo Landscapes, How Do They Relate?" and Diane W. Shirvani's article, "The Works and Thoughts of Thomas Dolliver Church."

Starr, Kevin. *Americans and the California Dream, 1850–1915.* New York: Oxford University Press, 1973.

————. *Material Dreams: Southern California Through the 1920s.* New York: Oxford University Press, 1990.

Streatfield, David. "Evolution of the Southern California Landscape." Parts 1–3. *Landscape Architecture* (January and March, 1976; May 1977).

————. *A Circle of Friends: Art Colonies of Cornish and Dublin.* Catalogue of an exhibition at the Thorne-Sagendorph Art Gallery, Keene State College, Keene, New Hampshire, March 9–April 26, 1985; and the University Art Galleries, University of New Hampshire, Durham, September 9–October 30, 1985. (A cooperative exhibition project of these two galleries). Durham: University of New Hampshire, 1985.

Wright, Frank Lloyd. *The Natural House.* New York: New American Library of World Literature, 1963.

Breaking New Ground:
Twentieth-Century American Gardens

❧

William Howard Adams

❧ *Appropriately enough, many of the issues of landscape and gardening addressed in twentieth-century America have caused more introspection and soul-searching than those of previous decades. Enormous and rapid growth during the century, intense urbanization, often-changing social mores, and new ideas of what a garden is: all of these are of concern to landscape historians. In "Garden and Forest," Keith Morgan lines up the categories for the nineteenth century as does Diane Kostial McGuire for the previous two in "Early Gardens Along the Atlantic Coast." In the twentieth century, however, the problems begin to become more burdensome, more complicated. Multiculturalism, the sprawling of suburbia, technological advances, environmentalism, and the role of landscape architecture are among the issues that affect the way we look at gardens. Change is quicker, more frequent, and more intense, and gardens are not immune from fluctuations in values and opinions of taste. In the twentieth century we have seen models from Europe and from within, preservation and restoration movements, and completely original approaches to gardens and landscape along with overdevelopment and the rise of environmental awareness in landscape architecture. In the midst of these complex issues, gardens remain symbols of the way we view nature, ourselves, and our culture. In the almost one hundred years since the turn of the century, America has changed in myriad ways; the garden has comforted us, reminded us of our past, and expressed our aspirations. While it will continue to evolve in our collective psyche, it will also serve these purposes and, ironically, remain both constant and ever new, whatever it may become in the next millennium.* ❧

The faint spring loveliness reached her some-how, in long washes of pale green, and the blurred mauve of budding vegetation; but her eyes could not linger on any particular beauty without its dissolving into soil, manure, nurs-erymen's catalogues, and bills again—bills. It had all cost a terrible lot of money; but she was proud of that too—to her it was part of the beauty, part of the exquisite order and suit-ability which reigned as much as stimulated the wildness of the rhododendron glen as in the geometrical lines of the Dutch garden.

EDITH WHARTON, *Twilight Sleep* (1927)

IN BOTH HOUSES AND GARDENS, Edith Whar-ton was determined to set a new direction for American taste. Having drawn a blueprint for the reform of the interior life of houses in *The Decoration of Houses*, a book she wrote with Ogden Codman in 1897, she then turned to the garden. In 1904, when *Italian Villas and Their Gardens* was published, money and taste were rarely combined as they would be by Mrs. Wharton's character Pauline Manford, who had yet fully to learn Wharton's garden dicta in the late 1920s, when the novel *Twilight Sleep* came out. "Sev-enty-five thousand bulbs this year! she thought, as the motor swept by the sculpted gateway, just giving and withdrawing a flash of turf sheeted with amber and lilac, in a setting of twisted and scalloped evergreens."[1] For one thing, according to Wharton's well-bred standards, Pauline displayed too much en-thusiasm for flowers. Writing of the Italian garden as a not-so-subtle model, it was difficult "to explain to the modern garden-lover, whose whole conception of the charm of gardens is formed of successive pic-tures of flower-loveliness . . . [the] enchantment . . .

OPENING ILLUSTRATION:
Americans find it difficult to confront the increasingly overwhelming realities of the technological world that surrounds them. These windmills at Altamont, California, provide clean, safe energy, but when stretched across the landscape they do not fit the model romantic image of how nature ought to appear.

produced by anything so dull and monotonous as a mere combination of clipped green and stone-work."[2]

By the end of the nineteenth century, the gar-dens of the well-to-do were as overstuffed with or-namentation and flowers—especially anything that "weeped"—as the parlors were with bric-a-brac and flotsam gathered on the Grand Tour. All sense of design had been lost in the detail of shrubbery and bedded-out annuals. Except for the older parts of the East—around Boston, the Hudson River Valley, and Philadelphia—and sections of the South, newly re-covered from the Civil War, there was little tradition and few models to follow, especially for the rich and ambitious. Wharton's use of the Italian garden to make her case was shrewd strategy. She had employed a similar approach on the overloaded decor of houses of the nouveau riche by using chaste examples of Louis XVI as her tool of criticism.

In the era of Wharton and Theodore Roosevelt, Andrew Jackson Downing's *Treatise on the Theory and Practice of Landscape Gardening*, first published in 1841, still extended its influence over suburban res-idential design and gardening. Edith Wharton's worldly efforts to reform unruly American taste at the beginning of the twentieth century found roots in an old native custom of reforming one's fellow citizens. In a way, Wharton's silk slippers were fol-lowing in Downing's humble footsteps. Dedicated to John Quincy Adams, Downing's book included in a later edition a supplement written by Henry Win-throp Sargent to appeal to the affluent new leaders of the Gilded Age. "Rural pursuits," in the democratic spirit of the Founding Fathers, had been Downing's theme—one that was passing out of fashion in the higher gardening circles. "In the United States, it is highly improbable that we shall ever witness such splendid examples of landscape gardens as those abroad,"[3] he wrote. "Here the rights of man are held to be equal; and if there are no enormous parks, and no class of men whose wealth is hereditary . . . [there is] a large class of independent landholders who are able to assemble around them, not only the useful and convenient, but the agreeable and beautiful, in country life."[4]

Wodenethe, near Fishkill Landing (now Beacon), New York, was the country estate of Henry Winthrop Sargent, a member of the influential Boston banking family. His friend and neighbor Andrew Jackson Downing called it "a bijou full of interest for the lover of rural beauty."

The American ideal of the picturesque for Everyman was never so succinctly spelled out. The words "independent landowner" are still operative at the end of the century and the appeal continues to lure the city dweller to suburban lots where a hint of the "agreeable and beautiful" is attempted in smaller and smaller spaces.* Yet there is hardly a fig leaf to hide the fact that all vestiges of country life have utterly vanished.

A vision of how people thought they wanted to live until well into the second half of the twentieth century, the pastoral ideal was and continues to be Jeffersonian in its optimism. "With us, a feeling, a

---

*A recent Harris poll confirmed the pastoral ideal when the majority of Americans questioned declared that "green grass and trees all around me" was the most important quality of a livable residence.

taste, or an improvement is contagious; and once fairly appreciated and [once] established in one portion of the country, it is disseminated with a celerity that is wonderful, to every other portion," said Downing.[5]

Twenty-three years after Downing's tragic death in a steamboat accident in 1852, his neighbor and friend Henry Winthrop Sargent brought out the expanded seventh edition of Downing's book on landscape architecture. Sargent was himself a sophisticated plantsman and amateur who had established his estate across the Hudson from Downing's nursery and laid out one of the most magnificent gardens on the East Coast. Wodenethe was not large by European standards, as Sargent, who had traveled widely in Europe, was quick to point out. But its formal beds near the house, long allées, temples, greenhouses, and kitchen gardens spread out on rolling hills overlooking the river placed it far beyond the means of the modest citizen whose garden on an acre or two had been envisioned in Downing's idealism. The cataclysm of the Civil War is bracketed between Downing's small but contagious "improvements" and Sargent's luxu-

Another member of the Sargent family, Charles Sprague Sargent, lived with his family at Holm Lea, their Brookline, Massachusetts, estate, a horticultural showplace assembled in the mid-nineteenth century.

Although under control, nature appeared to be left to its own inclinations at Holm Lea by the aloof, patrician Sargent, who became the first director of Boston's Arnold Arboretum in 1873.

rious Wodenethe. The war would permanently alter the cultural and political landscape of America and would also overwhelm the landscape of the virtuous husbandmen whom Downing had set as his ideal citizen-gardeners.

In 1892, Henry Sargent's cousin, Charles Sprague Sargent, author of the *Manual of the Trees of America*, was professor in charge of the Arnold Arboretum near Boston. The Boston Sargent knew Edith Wharton and her niece Beatrix Jones, a woman who, later, as Beatrix Farrand, would become one of the outstanding landscape architects of her generation. It is im-

portant to emphasize the ties of this sophisticated, small but influential, circle of Americans, symbolizing a kind of genealogy of landscape design early in this century. Their interests were wide-ranging and embraced science, horticulture, and plant collecting along with a firsthand grasp of garden traditions in Europe, where all of them had traveled and studied. Any one among them could have written a creditable book on the subject.

Beatrix had expressed an interest in becoming a professional landscape and garden designer, a field that still had little definition or focus, so Sargent encouraged her to study a year with him before traveling abroad as part of her education. Beatrix lived with the Sargents at Holm Lea, their estate outside Boston, itself one of the best American interpretations of the English school of the Picturesque to be seen in this country.

Taking Sargent's advice, Farrand traveled to Europe in 1895. There she first saw the work of Gertrude Jekyll at Penshurst and took the opportunity to call on the famous English gardener, who was to have a substantial influence on Farrand's designs for both public and private commissions. (Not surprisingly, the recent revival of American interest in Jekyll has also stimulated a similar resurgence for Farrand.) Returning late that same year, Farrand opened her own office on the top floor of her mother's New York brownstone.

The final decade of the nineteenth century was marked by a growing professional self-awareness culminating in the founding in 1899 of the American Society of Landscape Architects, of which Beatrix Farrand was a founding member. Her serious preparation of study and travel, her impeccable social connections, and the encouragement of her aunt, all advanced her career at an early stage. During her fifty years of practice, she designed major private gardens, her most famous being Dumbarton Oaks in Washington, D.C. By the turn of the century, numerous American universities had launched major building programs adopting the Romantic Gothic motif drawn from Ruskin and the English Arts and Crafts movement. It was a style that called for architecture to be set in ideal nature, and Farrand was asked to create the settings for the new campuses at Yale, Princeton, Oberlin, and later at the University of Chicago.

Beatrix Farrand's quadrangles and gardens at Yale, Princeton, and other universities were attempts to create an ideal country setting for what were essentially urban institutions. Seen here is Farrand's plan for the President's Garden at Yale.

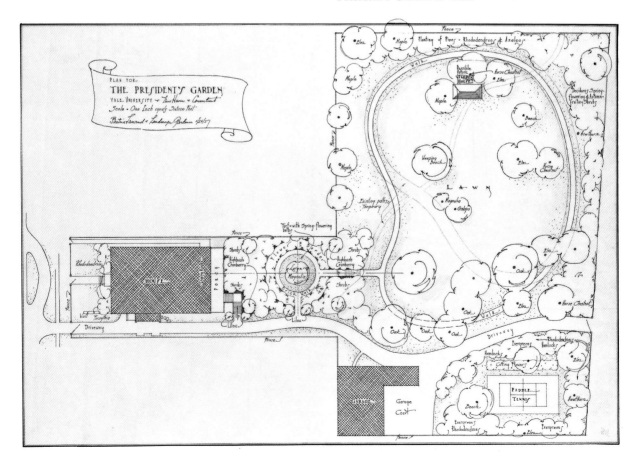

IN 1900, HARVARD UNIVERSITY began formal instruction in landscape architecture. The field of architecture as a profession and as an academic discipline had itself gone through a similar awakening and had only recently established a professional body and new academic programs at Harvard and other universities. There is no doubt that this self-conscious emergence of the architects had stimulated the landscape field to clarify and establish its own standards of accreditation. But historically, such strict professional divisions of labor did not exist and certainly not in the Renaissance, when the architect considered the design of the garden an extension of that of the building. The question remains whether this separation has perpetuated the subordinate and collaborative role of American landscape architects in this century, a role that has reduced them to something less than a full partnership in the design process as a price for professional comfort in a secondary position.

With previously unimagined wealth pouring into the centers of American capitalism at the beginning of the century, the extravagant possibilities for house and garden seemed limitless, especially if they were orchestrated by architecture firms like McKim, Mead and White, Carrère and Hastings, or Delano and Aldrich. These high-powered offices continued to control the design of entire estates, delivering polo fields, Italian terraces, greenhouses, and stables along with the house and its gardens and parks. Not only the popular Italian models but French, English, and, as Pauline Manford noted, Dutch traditions, were rifled for ideas to fill the void of enthusiasm for a cultivated mise-en-scène. Magazines began to reproduce photographs of seventeenth- and eighteenth-century English, French, and especially Italian gardens, as did books of the period, providing numerous sources of inspiration for parvenu connoisseurs. The journal of the then new Society of Landscape Architects regularly ran articles on these historical styles.

In its most inventive form, the American estate garden in the first quarter of the twentieth century could be distinctively original. The style did not always copy a European prototype, especially where the open American approach to spatial organization and the use of materials, both in buildings and in

plants, had no European precedent. Loggias and terrace balustrades were often copied in wood from Tuscan stone originals, then painted a glistening white. Native evergreens replaced Italy's cypresses.

The absence of the inevitable patina deposited over the centuries in Europe was immediately apparent in Newport, Brookline, and Long Island. Wharton, Henry James, and other trans-Atlantic visitors complained about this cultural and aesthetic shortcoming. But telltale marks of palpable history could not be easily bought or imported. The other quality that distinguished these American estates, as Malcolm Cairns has pointed out, is the bold way in which "the spatial hierarchies in [the] architecture were transferred directly to the garden and landscape. Porches and loggias opened to outdoor formal terraces. Central foyers and halls extended to outdoor vistas through formal lawns, parterres or water cascades."[6]

In this there was something of the Arts and Crafts aesthetic of Edwin Lutyens and his partner Gertrude

Created between 1891 and
1895 for George W.
Vanderbilt, the gardens
and grounds for Biltmore,
in Asheville, North
Carolina, were laid out by
Frederick Law Olmsted in
the style of "High
Eclectia" then favored by
the rich.

The gardens of Old
Westbury, the best
preserved of all the great
Long Island gardens, were
laid out in 1906 for John
S. Phipps the steel
magnate. His garden
designer was George
Crawley, an English
interior designer cum
landscape designer and
architect.

Working with her client Mildred Bliss, Beatrix Farrand designed Dumbarton Oaks, in Washington, D.C., which remains the quintessential country house estate in an urban setting. It now belongs to Harvard University.

Jekyll, although the usual new estate in Chicago or Los Angeles lacked those old, vernacular features of fences, farm buildings, and ancient orchards that the Lutyens-Jekyll partnership so brilliantly exploited in their work before World War I. The eighteenth-century house and grounds in the center of the Dumbarton Oaks estate in Georgetown, which confronted Farrand when she began her new design, comes closest to the kind of thing that inspired Lutyens and Jekyll.

During the first decades of the new century, post–Civil War towns suddenly emerged as booming cities. New boulevards, parks, esplanades, and subdivisions were planned wherever railroads had set off civic energy to "bring order out of chaos," in the words of Daniel Burnham and Edward H. Bennett, two of the architects responsible for the World's Columbian Ex-

position in Chicago. They were singing the battle hymn of the evangelical—not to say "Protestant"—City Beautiful movement, demanding a new standard of grandeur in the country's architecture, parks, and city planning. The City Beautiful movement had received its big boost from the Columbian Exposition, which had opened on the shores of Lake Michigan in 1893. The firm of Frederick Law Olmsted, headed by the country's leading landscape architect, carried out the plans of the exposition. Olmsted's son John Charles, who had also been involved in the great Beaux Arts extravaganza, declared in an address to the American Institute of Architects in 1900 that America's architecture and its landscaped settings must conform to the new classicism. They must be "strongly formal whether they are perfectly symmetrical or not, and this formal quality ought to be recognized in the plan of their surroundings if the total effect is to be consistent."[7]

The long shadows cast by the imperial facades glistening in the hard light of Illinois did not take long to reach the nation's capital. Daniel Burnham was named head of the newly created McMillan Commission in Washington to redesign the Mall in 1901, a date almost as important to classical America as that of the Columbian Exposition itself. The mystique of the McMillan plan still holds Washington's Fine Arts commission in thrall. A number of impresario planners emulated Burnham's role in the exposition and later in Washington, leading to the interdisciplinary, amorphous profession of city planning. It was a career that would also be recognized by the new landscape programs in universities. By 1915, fourteen landscape architects had taken the lead to establish the American City Planning Institute. This organized approach to produce a totally planned urban landscape was to be a dominant force in all aspects of design throughout much of the remainder of the century.

Garden design as a vital art form, reflecting the experimental and unpredictable vitality of the modern movement in architecture, painting, and sculpture, held little appeal for new generations of landscape architects who had become civic engineers with a moral cause in the name of Order and Beauty.

The Beaux Arts influences that had shaped the

thinking of the generation of architects and planners leading to the Columbian Exposition, had, of course, already quickly extended to the houses and gardens of the well-to-do who also upheld order and beauty. Clients had traveled in Europe and felt that even an American interpretation would be an accepted garden status symbol required by the Georgian or Italian villas they were commissioning. To make the settings more authentic, boatloads of urns, columns, pergolas, and balustrades were imported from Europe just as were the furniture and often the paneling for the interior. An outstanding example is Villa Vizcaya, a Florida palace on Biscayne Bay in Miami. Begun in 1913 by James Deering, heir to a Chicago farm-implement fortune, it was a remarkable pastiche of foreign garden themes translated into an original American creation complete with a stone barge apparently inspired by one built by the last empress of China in front of the Summer Palace in Peking.

Inventing the past in America had taken on a special vitality with complex and obscure motives intertwined with fundamental aspects of American life and the modern world. Both in classicism and the parallel phenomenon called the Colonial Revival, we are constantly surprised, as Alan Axelrod has written, "by the fertility of the imagination in creating meanings from the unsuspecting past."[8] The invention and reinterpretation of what was vaguely identified as the country's "colonial" legacy, although the cut-off date extended well into the nineteenth century, affected not only architecture but the decorative arts and garden design as well. These changes in style reflected new myths and values associated with American history. And as Axelrod has pointed out, patriotism was central to the national interest in preservation and restoration.

Without doubt, the restoration and re-creation of Williamsburg, Virginia, begun in the late 1920s by John D. Rockefeller, Jr., had a major influence on architectural and landscape design, as well as on city planning and commercial developments. Williamsburg's small residential gardens with their box and ornamental shrubs were enormously appealing to the average visitor who came to admire them, extending the influence of the Colonial Revival via the amateur

The most ideal American gardens (sans dogs and children), the vernacular museum gardens of Colonial Williamsburg were first created in the 1930s and 1940s. They became a kind of model for small suburban gardens throughout the country, but with dogs and children added.

gardener across the country.* But, as in most things, the origins of the forces that rebuilt Williamsburg as we know it today cannot be pinpointed to a single event such as turning the first spade of archaeological dirt or removing a modern porch on an eighteenth-century building to reveal the "true" colonial capital of Virginia.

*Recently, the international couturier Hubert Givenchy actually created a garden near Paris that has its historical roots in Virginia gardens designed earlier in this century.

Some time after the close of World War I, the members of the James River Garden Club began to assemble the history of gardens throughout their state dating from the "colonial and early Republican" period. Nearly eighty gardens were surveyed and briefly documented by the club in a book called *Historic Gardens of Virginia*. All the contributors were amateur gardeners. This is only one example of the contributions made by the energetic network of amateurs throughout the country who continue to sustain a remarkable tradition of gardening and garden research. This book was and remains an important contribution to regional garden history because the period and the region has the most coherent and longest tradition of gardening in the United States. While Mount Vernon and its gardens had been a national shrine for over seventy-five years, that other patriotic shrine, Thomas Jefferson's estate at Monticello, was just then passing into a public foundation and its gardens would not be restored until the beginning of World War II with funds from the Garden Club of Virginia.

This impulse to rediscover the outline of Virginia's garden tradition by James River gardeners anticipated the work that would later go on in Williamsburg, even though the more sophisticated techniques of modern garden history had yet to be invented. In fact, the dedicated garden club amateurs collecting documents, memoirs, and old photographs may have come closer to an accurate picture of colonial garden art than the elegant, over-maintained gardens that would soon appear along Duke of Gloucester Street in Williamsburg. The restoration and more often re-creation of the gardens of Colonial Williamsburg was directed by the noted Boston landscape architect Arthur A. Shurcliff as a part of the architectural team organized by the Boston architectural firm Perry, Shaw and Hepburn. The entire enterprise was run by the architects, and while restoration experts and planners debated the correctness of Shurcliff's versions of gardens past, the landscape architect usually won the argument to perpetuate a blissfully harmonious version of what life ought to have been during the colonial period. The results are examples of twentieth-century garden design of enormous influence.

WRITING ON "The American Country House" in 1919, the art historian, critic, and some-time restoration expert Fiske Kimball observed that "the striving for a style which shall be specifically modern and American has had to face heavy odds since the overwhelming popular victory of the classical in Chicago in 1893."[9] But, he pointed out, the "conscious revival or perpetuation of local traditions of style, materials and workmanship . . . is one of the dominating forces in the whole architectural world today."[10]

One of the outstanding architects who was inventing his own version of Virginia architecture and gardens, whom Kimball might have had in mind, was William Lawrence Bottomley of New York. Bottomley had been trained in the classical Beaux Arts school dominated by McKim, Mead and White, but by the 1920s he was successfully exploring and adapting earlier American, rather than European, styles for both urban houses and modern country villas. "Free handling of style, instead of imitating some old example and often copying it badly is a sign of life,"[11] he wrote. His strong ideas about the landscape and garden setting followed the same principles.

By the early part of the decade following World War I, Bottomley had begun to leave his mark in a series of stately town houses along Monument Avenue in Richmond, Virginia. While there was not much room for the development of extensive gardens on these town lots, the settings did carry the classy Bottomley stamp. By the eve of the Depression, he had moved west along the James River to the new suburban subdivision Winsor Farm, "a development with an ideal," according to its publicity. It is here, working closely with the landscape architect Charles F. Gillette, that Bottomley would demonstrate his sure and influential interpretation of a regional garden style, reflecting a sense of balance and proportion while freely translating his romantic readings of what he saw as a comfortable and congenial American past. Although Bottomley's landscape designs—which he claimed as the traditional domain of the architect—were not directly linked to nearby Williamsburg, his neo-Georgian villas and their Colonial Revival grounds seemed to merge in photographs and books

The suburban district of Windsor Farms, just beyond the city boundary of Richmond, Virginia, contains a superb collection of small estates designed by William Lawrence Bottomley. One of them, Milburn, was begun in 1934 and traces its design to the colonial past of the commonwealth but its landscape setting is an idealized version of Virginia vernacular with a pronounced English accent.

illustrating the work at Mr. Rockefeller's new town and publications documenting the new "ideals" of the contemporary Winsor Farm in Richmond, in which is found Milburn, a fine and representative example of Bottomley and Gillette's collaboration.

Not every aspiring garden designer of Bottomley's generation concentrated on the grand manors of the establishment, orchestrating "good taste" and fitness for an admiring clientele. Light years away from this fashionable, conservative style were the avant-garde gardens exhibited in 1923 at the Paris Exposition des Arts Décoratifs. The International Style had yet to be identified by New York's Museum of Modern Art, but a fresh, creative energy in architecture and design had already moved out from the centers of Vienna and Paris, where it was first felt, and had reached a few quarters in the United States. Fletcher Steele, only two years younger than Bottomley, was decidedly more adventuresome, turning up to admire the "concrete trees" of Robert Mallet-Stevens at the Paris exposition. After ten years of successful practice as a landscape designer, creating settings of "charm and beauty," in the words of his biographer, he was restless to find new directions. The year before, in his small, down-to-earth book called *Design in the Small Garden*, he made no sweeping, theoretical claims for the direction of garden design. Rather he addressed the concerns of the average, middle-class amateur who wanted to improve the unpretentious yard of his tract development. Steele recognized the realities of the dynamic American society fueled by a mass-production economy, and while he continued to design bespoken gardens for the rich in the Berkshires, he also knew there was a whole world beyond those rarified precincts.

In 1936 a young landscape architecture student from California met Steele at Harvard, where Steele was lecturing. Garrett Eckbo was impressed with the older man's openness to new ideas and his critical attitude toward the mystique of the profession, something his book had also reflected. Later Eckbo was joined by James Rose and Dan Kiley, who together wrote a three-part argument for *Architectural Record* in 1939–1940. None of the changes that Steele had seen in Europe had touched the preeminent architecture department at Cambridge even though the dean, Joseph Hudnut, had brought Walter Gropius from England to help bring the department, which included landscape architecture, into the twentieth century. When Gropius arrived, Eckbo recalled how the landscape faculty believed that since they were not manufacturers, the profession did not need to bother with unsettling new ideas spawned by technological revolution that was in fact changing forever the direction of all the arts. There were those who rarely thought of garden design as an art form on a par with painting, dance, and architecture.

There is no question that surging charges, if not changes, were in the air throughout the thirties, a decade in the history of landscape design that has not yet been fully explored. At the beginning of the decade, the old guard was defensive. The editor of *Architectural Record* had written that the designs of "the modernist school are deplorably lacking in those qualities which make for liveableness, charm, satisfaction and . . . hospitality," [12] qualities in fact that young students at Harvard and particularly in California would also agree were important. In his introduction to the San Francisco Museum of Art catalogue

Contemporary Landscape Architecture (1937), Henry-Russell Hitchcock thought liveableness in the form of outdoor living rooms and terraces was geared for the California climate and "in keeping with the character of modern architecture," [13] a quality that was in tune with the new direction of small domestic gardens. As for a theory of modern gardening, he pronounced, the general rule and guide must be "the preservation of all possible values in existence in the landscape setting." [14] Man-made intervention must be held to a minimum. Nature's sacred benevolence must be protected and embraced in a Virgilian reunion. The dictum that less is more would now extend beyond the "machine for living" into a "leave-it-alone" environment.

What disturbed the younger landscape architects about such a theory was its implicit limitation of the possibilities of creative garden making for the individual house. Hitchcock's answer was that it would free the designer from the concerns of the *retardataire* private garden and allow him to press his aesthetic attentions on the "fields of regional and even national planning," thereby restoring the profession to the historic calling it had enjoyed in the Baroque and Romantic ages.

Christopher Tunnard, a landscape architect in England who had recently come to America to join the Harvard faculty, also had misgivings about the future of the private garden. His landmark *Gardens in the Modern Landscape* wrestled with the issue of "whither" the garden, recognizing that "the modern garden architect has as much to discard as has the painter, sculptor and architect of a decade or two ago." [15] Published in 1938 and revised in 1957, Tunnard's book was a valiant attempt to provoke critical discussion on the subject. He was not successful nor have succeeding decades seen much improvement in criticism of landscape design in the United States. Tunnard seemed to endorse Hitchcock with a notable failure of prescience when he wrote, "The garden of tomorrow will not be a hedged, personal, half acre of today, but a unit of green landscape itself, controlled for the benefit of all." [16] It was a misty theme that seemed to envelop critical writing of the period.

The exhibition in San Francisco did manage to

spark some attention in the press and in a few journals, and the small exhibition garden of Thomas Church, then a promising young professional, was favorably noted. Church had already designed a number of small city and suburban gardens around San Francisco. Even though he usually worked within severe restraints of space, he never seemed to lose his conviction that a garden was a work of art regardless of scale. Later, his influential book *Gardens Are for People*, published in 1955, documented his belief that the garden of the second half of the century must address the pragmatic realities of American mobility, outdoor family living (by no means limited to California), irregular plots, and the overriding need for low maintenance. His raised planting beds, wooden-screen walls, stone or concrete paving, and timber decks introduced a new vocabulary of domestic garden design that still exercises an influence in schools and in practice.

Even though Eckbo and Church had grown up in California in the decades between the wars, there had been no atmosphere for radical change in the arts or conscious efforts by organized artists and architects to "go modern" any more than there had been in Chicago, Boston, or Richmond. In Los Angeles, A. E. Hanson, a high school dropout who had worked in a nursery, discovered his true talent by creating extravagant Hollywood-set gardens for movie stars of the 1920s and 1930s. His most elaborate period piece was the estate of Harold Lloyd in Benedict Canyon. It was literally an instant success, since it was completed in a remarkably short few months. Such work had no appeal for Eckbo or Church any more than the reactionary philosophy of Norman T. Newton of Harvard, who preached "changeless principles" in landscape design, declaring that the question of "modern" or "not modern" was irrelevant. His followers of a later generation still swear by "Newton's Law."

Like Church, Eckbo concentrated on small domestic gardens but later moved into a wider practice, entering the domain in which city planners had staked out their territory. Taking up Tunnard's argument, he also lobbied for a more responsible use of land development. Eckbo believed strongly that there was

With an implicit snub to nature, Los Angeles, like most human settlement in California, was built in a hostile environment. The eleven acres in Beverly Hills that A. E. Hanson transformed into a garden for movie star Harold Lloyd had previously been a piece of god-forsaken real estate. Helped by irrigation and bulldozers, the result became one of pure illusion, Hollywood style.

a fundamental contradiction between community values and policy that allowed greed to determine land use that undermined those values. It was an idealism to which later members of the profession would continue to give lip service with little evidence of any change in the land-use/developer equation.

More than one critic of the period had raised the possibility that the aesthetics of Japan, with its underlying philosophy regarding the importance of nature as a creative force, offered an alternative direction for Western art in the twentieth century. The example of Japanese art and Japanese religion enabled its admirers to move beyond the economic, pragmatic arguments offered by Eckbo and his followers. It seemed that for centuries, as Tunnard had pointed out in his book, Western civilization had carried on a war with nature; a war that had separated people from nature's constructive, healing powers. The unity of Japanese architecture with its environment, the use of native materials, and the subtle manipulation of space both inside and out had an undeniable appeal to the modern sensibility.

Tunnard did not mention Frank Lloyd Wright in *Gardens in the Modern Landscape*, or for that matter, Richard Neutra, an architect who, like Wright, intended his interventions to fit into nature and to be at one with it and its immutable laws. Wright's autobiographical writings are filled with lyrical passages in homage to nature, as if he had tapped some mysterious source of its creative power. His earliest Prairie houses are organically wedded to their natural surroundings. Opening out with their terraces, balconies, and cantilevered roofs, they acknowledge their debt to Japanese inspiration. Wright understood the unity between nature and form in Japanese art when he translated the Japanese interpenetration of indoor and outdoor space into his revolutionary American houses. Beginning with his own house, Taliesin, in Wisconsin, and including Fallingwater, one arrives at two major examples of Wright's lifelong affair with nature and the landscape, representing the artist's spiritual commitment to nature's high calling.

Richard Neutra, who had grown up in the heady atmosphere of Josef Hoffman's Vienna at the turn of the century, intuitively shared Wright's sensitivity to the natural landscape. The young Austrian had also had some training in landscape design and worked as one of Wright's California assistants after he arrived in the United States in 1923. After finishing his revolutionary Health House (1927) in Los Angeles, Neutra lost no time in making plans for his first trip to Japan. His response to the natural simplicity of Japanese design was immediate. This was an aesthetic kinship that Wright before him had also shared.

Neutra never wrote much about garden design, but his *Mysteries and Realities of the Site* and his mem-

oirs, *Life and Shape*, in which a number of early landscape drawings are reproduced, provide a useful background to the intelligent and responsive settings he created for his houses in the 1930s and 1940s. His ideals are summed up in what he called his "search for elemental environment factors . . . to which a human organism already has an adaptation of long standing, and to fit them into our design, applying in all this the insight of the biologist."[17]

The Kaufmann House, in Palm Springs, Neutra's masterpiece completed in 1947, captures the essence of Neutra's twenty years of experimentation in California. By removing the walls of the living area, he was able to articulate the connection between the architecture and the landscape as he had tested earlier in the Health House, drawing on what the dynamic natural scene had been for a hundred millennia, making it a human habitat once more. The living space

OPPOSITE:
The unity of architecture with its natural setting at Frank Lloyd Wright's Fallingwater is seamless. Few works of the twentieth century have been orchestrated into such a duet of admiration between human works and nature.

Richard Neutra's most celebrated postwar house was built at Palm Springs in 1946 for Edgar Kaufmann, who had earlier been a patron of Wright. Sited with spectacular views of the mountains and desert, the Kaufmann house, as Thomas Hines has observed, is a man-made artifact designed to observe the scenery, yet it is sympathetic to its natural setting. Like the building materials, the shrubs and plants are unapologetic imports.

and pool are projected into the bare, rocky desert, framed by the distant hills, scaled for human intimacy through its elegant appropriation by the architecture.

SELF-DOUBT HAS REPEATEDLY assailed landscape architects and garden designers throughout much of the twentieth century. In spite of an impressive list of accomplishments, the record seems uneven and lacks the dynamic thread of coherent evolution or focus that informs the narrative account of architecture and other arts subject to the same atmospheric influences. Any reasoned idea for the focus of the field seems repeatedly to elude those who have diligently questioned and searched for answers. One is haunted by the recent admission by members of this profession to what appears to be a lack of self-esteem when, in the introduction to a book on "how landscape architects had shaped America," they cheer-

fully admitted that they have always been "comfortable in a collaborative role." [18] The generalities and abstractions that have afflicted garden journalism have failed to move the debate forward in any meaningful way.

In his 1954 book *Modern Gardens*, the English designer Peter Shepheard intended to identify some masterworks of contemporary landscape architecture but confessed that examples were hard to find. To his dismay, he concluded that he could find no modern examples that would qualify. All tradition of design was dead and the time-honored system of apprenticeship had disappeared. More recently, the landscape architect and critic Steven Krog also searched for examples and admits that "the body of works indicating that the contemporary landscape is equal to the highest challenges" [19] (of the artist) is minuscule. The enemies of promise have been myriad, and it is difficult to assess their true influence or to overcome their demoralizing power. The failure to produce a modern movement in landscape design may well stem from the absence of professional opportunity, as it is claimed, as well as the basic conflict between the traditional techniques of garden making and the revolutionary technological forces that have revolutionized architecture.

Ian McHarg's *Design with Nature* has provided recent generations of designers and city planners with stirring moral dicta on the environment, but the author has been unable to indicate just what form the landscape of his purified environment should take. Grasping at labels such as "postmodern" had encouraged a liberal use of contrived historical references in self-conscious garden designs as a kind of mask or decoration with hope of journalistic appeal but with little relevance in the world of the last decade of the twentieth century. These visual narratives invoked by obvious references to the past or to misunderstood myths do have a certain attraction for garden writers, but the resultant writing seldom approaches criticism. There seems to be little grasp of historical developments of landscape design in this country on which to build a body of critical appraisal of the past or of contemporary achievements. Nor does there appear to be an awareness that a critical evaluation is a missing ingredient in the recurring crisis of sorting out future directions, in the same way that such discussion advances other fields of the arts.

The decades of the seventies and eighties have produced a large body of landscape design, some of the most arresting of which has been created for corporate headquarters, industrial parks, and shopping malls. Yet it is difficult to sort out a significant direction, a coherent vocabulary, or a consistency in quality on which the future might build with confidence. Many of these projects have a sterile, hermetic, ephemeral quality that is inspired by the architecture. In few cases do these vast and expensive schemes relate to the stark realities of the larger setting of thruways, overpasses, high rises or, as I often note on approaching lower Manhattan, the elegant rows of oil-storage tanks near the Statue of Liberty, which we are supposed to ignore.

J. B. Jackson has spoken of some of these issues from his perspective as a geographer, and he views the landscape in the broadest terms of the study of the earth and its life. He suggests that despair is premature and that it is perhaps too early to attempt any full understanding of those man-made details that have been the subject of this brief essay (including those of the most recent decades, which have been left out). At best, Jackson advises, we should rely most intently not on the technicians and planners but rather on the artists, philosophers, and, of course, geographers: "They are the most trustworthy custodians of human traditions, for they seek to discover order out of randomness, beauty within chaos, and the enduring aspirations of mankind behind blunders and failures."[20]

Geographers have not often been looked to as "custodians of human traditions" but it is a provocative thought. Critics like Jackson have been willing to look without prejudice at the American landscape strewn with parking lots, elevated highways, electrical substations, and television aerials and have seen that this everyday landscape may well hold instruction that would demoralize most garden designers.

"The visible influence of technology is ubiquitous and nearly inescapable," Robert Thayer, Jr., has written, yet "we are often uncomfortable in its presence."[21] The short sketch I have attempted indicates an all but total denial of this central, overwhelming reality throughout the century. Edith Wharton's Pauline Manford may seem a figure out of a distant, irrelevant past. Yet her fervent efforts to avoid the reality of her time by ordering each year twenty-five thousand more tulips than she had the year before may not be all that remote from the waning pastoral dreams that some garden designers still seem to harbor. The issue of technology versus the designed or the quotidian landscape is profound, and it raises fundamental questions about our image of the garden and its future in the century that arrives day after tomorrow. ✍

NOTES

Epigraph: Edith Wharton, *Twilight Sleep* (New York: Scribner, 1927), p. 233.

1. Ibid., p. 253.
2. Wharton, *Italian Villas and Their Gardens*, p. 5–6.
3. Downing, *Treatise on the Theory and Practice of Landscape Gardening*, p. 23.
4. Ibid., p. 23.
5. Ibid., p. 24.
6. Malcolm Cairns, "Country Estates," in *American Landscape Architecture: Designers and Places,* William H. Tishler, ed. Washington, D.C.: Preservation Press, 1989, p. 133.
7. Quoted in Wilson, p. 84.
8. Axelrod, *The Colonial Revival in America*, p. 5.
9. Quoted in O'Neal and Weeks, p. 8.
10. Ibid., p. 3.
11. O'Neal and Weeks, p. 6.
12. [editor] *Architectural Record*, 1940.
13. Henry-Russell Hitchcock, introduction to *Contemporary Landscape Architecture*, p. 15.
14. Ibid., p. 19.
15. Tunnard, *Gardens in the Modern Landscape*, p. 69.
16. Ibid., p. 138.
17. Neutra, *Life and Shape*, p. 10.
18. *American Landscape Architecture,* op. cit., p. 14.
19. Krog, "Whither the Garden," p. 103.
20. Jackson, The Necessity for Ruins, p. 75.
21. Thayer, p. 1.

BIBLIOGRAPHY

Axelrod, Alan. *The Colonial Revival in America: A Winterthur Book*. New York: Norton, 1986.

Byrd, Warren T., Jr., and Rainey, Reuben, eds., *The Work of Dan Kiley*. Charlottesville: University of Virginia Press, 1983.

Cleveland, H. W. S. *Landscape Architecture as Applied to the Wants of the West*. Pittsburgh: University of Pittsburgh Press, 1975.

Contemporary Landscape Architecture. San Francisco: San Francisco Museum of Art, 1937.

Creese, Walter S. *The Crowning of the American Landscape*. Princeton: Princeton University Press, 1985.

Eckbo, Garrett. *The Art of Home Landscaping*. New York: F. W. Dodge Corp., 1950.

———. *Landscape for Living*. New York: F. W. Dodge Corp., 1950.

Hanson, A. E. *An Arcadian Landscape*. Los Angeles: Hennessy and Ingles, 1985.

Harwood, Kathryn Chapman. *The Lives of Vizcaya*. Miami: Banyan Books, 1985.

Hines, Thomas S. *Richard Neutra and the Search for Modern Architecture*. New York: Oxford University Press, 1982.

Jackson, John Brinckerhoff. *American Space*. New York: W. W. Norton, 1972.

———. *The Necessity for Ruins*. Amherst: University of Massachusetts Press, 1980.

Jensen, Jens. *Siftings*. Chicago: Ralph Fletcher Seymour, 1930.

Kassler, Elizabeth B. *Modern Gardens in the Landscape*. New York: Museum of Modern Art, 1964.

Kimball, Fiske. [WLB].

Krog, Steven. "Whither the Garden." In *Denatured Vision*, edited by W. H. Adams and Stuart Wrede. New York: Museum of Modern Art, 1991.

McHarg, Ian. *Design with Nature*. New York: Doubleday, 1969.

Meining, D. W., ed. *The Interpretation of Ordinary Landscapes*. New York: Oxford University Press, 1979.

Neutra, Richard. *Life and Shape*. New York: Appleton Century-Crofts, 1962.

Newton, Norman. *Design on the Land*. Cambridge: Harvard University Press, Belknap Press, 1971.

Noguchi, Isamu. *The Isamu Noguchi Garden Museum*. New York: Harry N. Abrams, 1987.

O'Neal, William B., and Weeks, Christopher. *The Work of William Lawrence Bottomley*. Charlottesville: University of Virginia Press, 1985.

"Landscape Design: Works of Dan Kiley." *Progress Architecture* 33 (October 1982).

Ray, Mary Helen, and Nicolls, Robert P., eds. *The Travellers's Guide to American Gardens*. Chapel Hill: University of North Carolina Press, 1988.

Shepheard, Peter. *Modern Gardens: Masterworks of International Garden Architecture*. New York: Praeger, 1954.

Steele, Fletcher. *Design in the Small Garden*. Boston: Atlantic Monthly Press, 1924.

———. *Gardens and People*. Boston: Houghton Mifflin, 1964.

Thayer, Robert, Jr. "Pragmatism in Paradise," *Landscape*, vol. 30, no. 3, 1990, pp. 1–11.

Tunnard, Christopher. *Gardens in the Modern Landscape*. New York: Scribner, 1938.

Van Valkenburgh, Michael. *Built Landscapes: Gardens in the Northeast*. Brattleboro, Vt.: Brattleboro Museum and Art Center, 1984.

———. *Transforming the American Garden*. Cambridge: Harvard University Press, 1986.

Wilson, Richard Guy, ed. *The American Renaissance, 1876–1917*. New York: Brooklyn Museum, 1979.

Graces and Modest Majesties

Landscape and Garden Traditions of the American South

Catherine M. Howett

While all regions of the country have traditionally seen land as a sign of wealth and even power, and certainly as a necessity for agriculture, none has perceived it as so integral to its identity as the South. Tamara Plakins Thornton, in "Horticulture and American Character," examines how certain segments of the populace have looked upon land ownership as showing divine approbation and as a sign of being among the elect. In the South the importance given to land, especially its cultivation and beautification, goes beyond economics and theology to the realm of myth. The dual role played by the land for the South's landed gentry underlay their assumptions of grandeur, which referred in American fashion to the aristocracy of Europe. The large estates in Virginia, the Carolinas, and Georgia bespoke a way of life much older and grander than the nation itself. The other role played by the land was expressed in the magnificent care taken of such properties. The concern for the beauty of the natural world also betokened a certain refinement and gentility that was not common or, indeed, indigenous to this country but rather an attitude that sprang from a way of life common to the haute culture of many periods of western civilization.

The land also was a way of defining the South itself. It held together various cultures in one larger culture that was united by its sense of place, of belonging to the land. In this spirit the care taken to preserve, record, and protect such expressions of glorifying the land as the plantations and gardens of the South brought about garden history organizations (as discussed by Walter Punch in "The Garden Organized") and the important role the South has assumed in the conservation of its old and cherished places and landscapes.

THE INHERITANCE of shared history and shared societal values that defines the American South as a region—however much it may constitute a complex, ambiguous, and even contradictory cultural mythos—has historically attached symbolic importance to the land itself. The idea of the land as a source of meaning and value for Southerners derives, certainly, from the dominance of an agricultural economy over more than three centuries. Almost from the beginning, regional voices of conscience were periodically raised against those who exploited land as mere commodity. Late in the nineteenth century, for example, the poet Sidney Lanier chastized farmers who committed all of their resources to cotton production, "scorning the slow reward of patient grain," and moving on to new territories when their fields were exhausted. Lanier celebrated instead the beauty of corn, "steadfast dweller on the selfsame spot/ Where thou wast born . . . Type of the home-fond heart," and token of those "graces and modest majesties" that inhere in places where generations of men and women have wisely cultivated and cherished their land.[1] Ties to a settled and traditional rural life, whether they are actual or simply nostalgic, have had a persistent hold on the imaginations of Southerners, even as the physical character of their world has undergone accelerating change late in the twentieth century. Southern fiction and poetry, no less than the lyrics of country music, amply testify to the tenacity of this ideal.

That sense of the land as a carrier of mythic communal values constitutes, moreover, the substrate and source of another, related passion: the love of gardening. The propaganda literature that in the seventeenth and eighteenth centuries was aimed at luring European settlers to the southern coast of North America compared the bounties to be discovered there to those of the biblical Garden of Eden—a land of spontaneous fruitfulness holding the promise of easy

OPENING ILLUSTRATION:
The gradual acceptance of the wooded park, espoused by seventeenth-century English garden design, is documented in this watercolor (dated 1800) by Charles Fraser of the seat of Julius Pringle, Esq., on the Ashley River, near Charleston.

sustenance, wealth, health, and leisure. Yet while an atmosphere of luxurious fecundity may indeed have surrounded them on every side, Southern colonists soon discovered that they inhabited the Garden after the Fall, where troubles of every sort, risk, and considerable toil attended the adventure of building farms and towns in the wilderness. The metaphor of the South as primal garden—exotic, and in some measure unknowable—lingered in the national psyche, however, accommodating as it did the notion of a dark original sin that ultimately brought about the South's own fall—its historic surrender to the seduction of chattel slavery.

The distinctiveness of the Southern gardening experience is grounded, then, not just in such easily measured physiographic factors as climate, soils, and native vegetation, but in more elusive historical and cultural factors as well. Many other regions of the nation shared the legacy of an agricultural economy; only in the South was that legacy associated with the failed dream of a plantation empire, closer in its imagined form to the tropic empires of the Caribbean and Latin America than to the republic of yeoman farmers envisioned by Thomas Jefferson. Rich infusions from French, Spanish, and Indian cultures on the Gulf coast, and Spanish and Indian culture in Florida, tempered the dominance of northern European, mostly Anglo-Saxon and Celtic (Scottish and Scotch-Irish), traditions. No less important, although scarcely acknowledged until recent times, was the impress of African food and folkways upon Southern gardening practice. The regional tradition of the "swept yard," for example—a ground surface of sand or packed dirt kept free of grass and other vegetation by frequent brooming or raking, sometimes in decorative patterns—may have at least one possible source in the practice of many West African tribal villages.

The association of Southern landscape and gardening traditions with the history of plantation agriculture based on staple-crop monocultures—tobacco, rice, indigo, and cotton—nourished the myth of a society presided over by a class of wealthy and well-educated planters able to build mansions, gardens, and landscaped parks on the scale of the princely

During Jefferson's lifetime, this view over Monticello's vegetable garden from the west lawn would have been screened by the garden fence and the buildings along Mulberry Row.

palaces of Europe's aristocracy. The reality, in terms of both the relatively small percentage of the South's planters who worked very large holdings and owned many slaves, and in terms of the actual physical layout of most working plantations, was very different from this popular conception of a vanished Golden Age of plantation culture.

Yet Thomas Jefferson was himself a curious representative of the myth, arguing as he did for a nation of self-sufficient husbandmen even as he operated plantations of almost ten thousand acres with several hundred slaves. Moreover Jefferson was indeed driven by a dream of what the landscape of his cherished plantation home at Monticello should become—a *ferme ornée,* or ornamental farm, on the model celebrated by early theorists of the eighteenth-century English landscape-gardening school. He had been from early manhood an eager student of the literature of this school, and in 1786 visited, with John Adams as his companion, some of the famous estates described by Thomas Whately in *Observations on Modern Gardening* (Jefferson owned a copy of the 1770 second

edition). [2] He formed ambitious plans over many years for various architectural and landscape features to embellish the grounds of Monticello, laying out its drives, walks, and flower beds—as well as its functional fields, orchards, vegetable garden, and dependencies—in ways that he hoped would contribute to an effect of harmonious, evocative, and picturesque scenic composition.

As the English themselves discovered, however, the integration of a thriving agricultural enterprise with the refinements of the new "natural" landscape-gardening style was difficult to achieve. Whately had warned his readers that "an apparent attention to produce . . . obliterates the idea of a garden." [3] Jefferson intended, for example, that the paling fence and all of the buildings along Mulberry Row—slave cabins and service buildings at the edge of Monticello's west lawn, overlooking the vegetable garden terrace—should eventually be removed. He proposed to substitute a ha-ha for the ten-foot-high fence, thus creating a pleasing open vista over the planted terrace and slope from the level of the upper lawn, without

OPPOSITE:
The slave quarters at
Mulberry Plantation, near
Charleston, present a vivid
contrast to the master's
residence (at back) in this
painting from about 1800.

The avenue of twenty-
eight oaks at Oak Alley on
the Mississippi River,
north of New Orleans, was
planted in the early
eighteenth century, while
the present mansion dates
from 1839.

sacrificing the security from predatory animals that
the fence had provided for his garden. These plans,
and similar ones inspired by his enthusiasm for the
English landscape gardening style, remained largely
unrealized owing to economic and other practical considerations.

It is not simply, then, the predictable conservatism of a colonial society that predisposed most Southerners to favor the older, more formal and geometric
traditions based on European Renaissance and Baroque classicism in laying out their gardens. Formal
styles, with their conventions of axiality, symmetry,
and enclosure, were more easily adapted to the layout
and functioning of a plantation—or, for that matter,
to those of much smaller residential properties in
cities and towns, the shape of which was usually
determined by a grid pattern of streets and lots. At
the same time, it is hard to resist the suggestion that
formal styles may have appealed to Southerners at
some unconscious level because of their association
with the aristocratic culture of traditional and hier-
archical Old World societies.

This ambivalence toward the fashionable "naturalism" of the English school, and a hint of how the
problem was frequently resolved, may be seen in a
charming portrait of the Tannatt family of Charleston
and Savannah, painted by Henry Benbridge in the
years just before the American Revolution, when family loyalties were divided and several Tannatts chose
to return to England. The foreground of the painting
shows family members within a determinedly picturesque woodland setting of ancient mossy trees, at the
edge of a lake or pond in which the two gentleman
at the right have been fishing. The background, however, shows us a handsome country house with col-
umned entrance portico, cupola, Palladian window,
and a wide piazza at the side; in front of the house,
a formal garden of parterres and clipped evergreen
shrubs is depicted. Whether or not this house and
garden reflect some actual Tannatt plantation residence, their style is clearly meant to convey an
impression of the family's wealth, good taste, and
refinement by associating them with the residential-
design traditions of Europe's aristocracy. This tradi-

tion had its sources in the great age of Italian villa design that began about the middle of the fifteenth century and culminated two centuries later in the French style epitomized by André Le Nôtre's transformation of Versailles for Louis XIV. At the same time, the Tannatt family's being pictured at leisure within a wooded grove is probably meant to suggest their cultivation of that sensibility toward the beauty of the natural world that had been a motive force of the English reaction against French formalism early in the eighteenth century.

In an analogous way, many Southerners sought to join these two values—and the styles that represented them—in the design of their properties. An arrival drive lined with a formal planting of trees was one convention of antebellum landscape design, but so was the preservation or planting of groves of randomly positioned large trees in areas close enough to the house to provide shade or fine views—an invocation of the wooded park that was a central feature of the landscape-gardening style of English country houses. Writing in the 1850s, Mrs. Mary Jones, of Liberty County, Georgia, described the house of her plantation, Montevideo, as "fronting a lawn of twenty or thirty acres covered with live oak, magnolias, cedars, pines, and many other forest trees arranged in groves or stretching out in lines or avenues or dotting the lawn here and there."[4]

The design of the gardens at plantations like Montevideo would, by contrast, have been quite formal in character—both the kitchen gardens that provided a ready supply of vegetables, salad greens, herbs, and perhaps fruits for the table (Mrs. Jones's coastal garden included "sweet and sour oranges and the myrtle orange, pomegranates, figs, the bearing olive, and grapes"[5]) and the pleasure garden that ornamented some area close to the house. Such gardens were usually enclosed within sturdy fencing as a necessary protection against the depredations of animals, both domestic and wild. The compartments thus formed constituted units within a much larger landscape of work, divided into zones demarcated by an assortment of fencing types—paling, post-and-rail, log or "worm" fences around fields—or by hedging chosen

OPPOSITE:
The plan of the parterre
for the garden of Mrs.
Joseph Manigault, Argyle
Island, Georgia.

The parterre garden of the
Battersby-Hartridge House
in Savannah, Georgia.

for its impenetrability. Watercolors from the sketch-book of the Charleston, South Carolina, artist Charles Fraser document the appearance of a number of the "rural seats" of well-to-do planters settled along the Cooper and Ashley rivers in the opening years of the nineteenth century; several of these illustrate typical uses of fencing to enclose garden areas.

In the kitchen garden, planting in rows might organize the space very simply, or else a grid of planting beds and borders might be established, hardly changed in its form from the gardening practice of medieval Europe. In the domestic landscapes of Southerners of modest means, and therefore more limited gardening ambitions, the area set aside for the kitchen garden might include some flowering plants, especially in the perimeter beds. Similarly, flowers, bulbs, and ornamental shrubs might be set within a few simple geometrically shaped beds in the front yard—small islands of color, texture, and fra-grance in a clean-swept dirt yard in which plants garnered and exchanged among family and friends were lovingly tended, usually by the women of the house. The traditional form of such vernacular gardens, set within the landscape of work that dominated most rural and small-town properties, is continuous —however different in scale, complexity, and in the range and quality of materials—with the pleasure gardens that were so important a feature of high-style Southern landscape tradition.

To create and maintain the handsome ornamental pleasure gardens to which many wealthy Southerners aspired, some part of the work force of slave labor usually had to be committed to the labor-intensive tasks demanded by the fastidious order and clipped geometry of the formal gardening tradition. Indeed, the intricate geometric play of the planted beds served an important aesthetic function in such gardens. Often, in fact, the linear pattern of the clipped box-

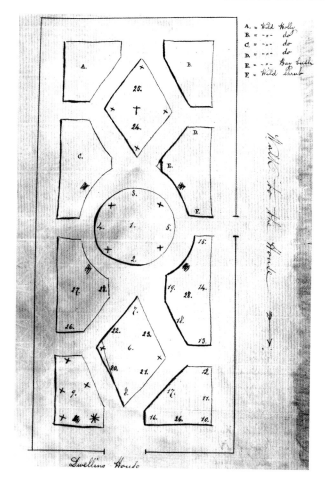

wood or other evergreen edging was the primary ornamental feature, and topiary figures or mottoes or intricate mazes—however despised by theorists of the English school—were popular in antebellum Southern parterre gardens. Miss Almira Coffin of Buxton, Maine, had never seen a "labyrinth of hedges" until her visit to Chancellor Charles Dunkin's Midway plantation near Charleston in the spring of 1851. In her letter to a friend back home, she described her pleasure in this landscape feature:

> You enter it, near the house, & the path will lead you about in a zigzag direction, in the center is a circle with a summer house covered with flowering vines &c, then you go on & on, round & round, first coming to a hedge of wild orange then again to Arbor-vitae, then to Casina, & between them are plots in a variety of shapes, filled with flowers.

Some of the hedges are so high & broad that you can just peep over them & so thick that a chicken couldn't get through, & trimmed beautifully, looking like one mass of deep green leaves, these looked best from the chamber window & gave one a better idea of a labyrinth to look down into it. . . . Many times a day we girls would take a run through it.[6]

More commonly, of course, the shrubs used to form the parterres would be trimmed low, so that their pattern was easily read from eye level. Occasionally the spaces within the hedging were left bare or covered with sand, pebbles, or similar material, in the classic manner of that French garden tradition within which the concept of the *parterre de broderie* had been developed. (Le Nôtre preferred to use inert materials such as brick dust, iron filings, or colored earths, rather than flowers, to provide vivid contrast to the scrolled tracery of the evergreen hedging.) The French school's canon also accommodated, however, the type of the *parterre fleuriste,* or flower garden. The designer Alexandre Le Blond, disciple of Le Nôtre, had defined as one of four possible types of the parterre the "Parterre of Cut-work," in which flowers were planted within boxwood-edged planting beds arranged in a pattern. In this form, sanded walks delimiting the planted beds allowed visitors to walk within the parterre.[7] It is this version of the parterre garden that was most favored by Southern gardeners until about the last quarter of the nineteenth century.

Surviving documentation of the actual plan and plantings for such gardens is quite rare; most often, gardens were simply laid out and planted without being recorded in a drawing. For this reason, the plan and accompanying plant list in the Louis Manigault family papers provide useful evidence of an antebellum plantation garden. The plan records the design of Mrs. Manigault's garden at the family's rice plantation on Argyle Island, Georgia, with numbered locations keyed to a separate plant list of trees and shrubs ordered from nurseries in Charleston and Savannah, and their prices. A note on the list provides an approximate date for this garden project, since a group of shrubs from the order was "set out" on December 23, 1859. The large number of specific rose varieties itemized suggests that roses were a major feature of the planting scheme; weeping cypress, American and Chinese arborvitae, variegated pittosporum, spirea, and "Cape Jasmine"—our gardenia—were included among the trees and shrubs.

As was suggested earlier, gardens of this type were well suited to city and town lots, particularly as a feature of the entrance forecourt, since rear yards usually had to accommodate a myriad of service functions. A visitor to New Orleans in 1801 observed that gardens were "disposed in the old still formal style—the border and circles kept up with strips of board."[8] The design of the garden of the Battersby-Hartridge House on Lafayette Square in Savannah is believed to be the oldest surviving parterre garden in that city based on an original design. A Cherokee rose and white Lady Banks rose of venerable age— "both a full three stories high"—may date from the garden's earliest beginnings.[9]

These examples make clear that the widespread popularity among Southerners of the parterre garden that also functioned as a flower garden provided them with an incentive to indulge the same enthusiasm for horticulture that engaged a large segment of upper- and middle-class society in England and other parts of America during most of the nineteenth century. Following the period toward the end of the eighteenth century in which the so-called Picturesque wars had divided English theorists on the question of the merits of pastoral versus picturesque scenery in the landscape garden, the English designer Humphry Repton ratified the suitability of more formal and architectural gardens and terraces in the immediate vicinity of the house. His younger contemporary, the prolific writer, editor, and landscape gardener John Claudius Loudon, moved English taste still further toward a return to formal design elements, although he believed that these should be integrated within a larger plan based on the irregular, informal compositional principles of the "natural" style. Both of these men called for a reinstatement of flower gardens, greenhouses, and conservatories at a time when the discovery and importation of exotic plants from Asia and an expanded

supply from North and South America made English gardeners anxious to create or enlarge domestic gardens. Loudon apparently coined the term "Gardenesque" to describe a style that aimed, in his words, "to add, to the acknowledged claims of the Repton School, all those which the sciences of gardening and botany, in their present advanced state, are capable of producing."[10] Jefferson's interest in establishing "shrubberies" within his woodlands, and the assymmetrical arrangement of nongeometric flower beds along his west-lawn walk, show the influence of this transitional phase in English landscape-gardening theory on his design ideas.

The renewed interest, among English property owners and gardeners in the 1830s and 1840s, not just in floriculture but in old-fashioned formal and geometric gardens, made Loudon fear that he had unleashed a dangerous movement of reaction against the higher goal of scenic composition that had been the hallmark of the landscape-gardening style. He warned his readers against the use of angular and figural shapes for their planting beds and lamented "the introduction of these angular beds, in the most romantic or otherwise strongly marked scenes, that no man of taste would dare to touch."[11] Melanie Simo has pointed out that Sir Walter Scott had helped to foster the national nostalgia for the older, formal styles by inveighing against the substitution of bare grounds around the house for the flower parterres, straight walks, brick walls, and high hedges of earlier Tudor and Stuart gardens and those of the period of Queen Anne.[12]

Southerners were among the most avid readers of Scott's novels; romantic tales of chivalry and of the age of the cavalier nourished their view of their own culture as feudal and of themselves as the latter-day embodiment of courtly and aristocratic traditions that had their roots in the European Middle Ages and the Renaissance. Most Southerners had never committed themselves to the "modern" style of landscape gardening in the way that Jefferson and some few others had done; a New Orleans horticulturist writing under the pen name Sylvanus said in 1851, "Notwithstanding all the praise bestowed upon the sunny south, in this part of it, at least, Landscape Gardening is half a century behind the age."[13] Yet the English travel writer Harriet Martineau had remarked that she saw more roses in New Orleans gardens during a morning's walk in 1837 than she had seen in the whole course of her life up to that time.[14]

Thus if Southerners seemed *retardataire* in their lack of enthusiasm for the English landscape gardening style in its purer forms, their persistent preference for formal gardens and their avid horticultural pursuits allowed them to participate in the newly fashionable return to traditional garden forms and escalation of garden enterprises that Repton and Loudon had, almost inadvertently, set in motion. In his *History of Horticulture in America to 1860,* U. P. Hedrick averred that in rapidly growing Southern cities like Nashville and Memphis in the first quarter of the nineteenth century, "gardening was recognized as the chief recreation of wealthy men."[15] Joseph and Adelicia Acklen's Nashville estate, Belmont, for example, had 180 acres of "ornamental grounds" and three greenhouses, each three hundred feet long, housing plant collections that included a large camellia collection and plants of the red water-lily *Victoria regia* that were reputed to have been the first of this species to bloom in the United States.

The Northern horticulturist, editor, and author Andrew Jackson Downing, preeminent spokesman for the theory and practice of English landscape gardening "adapted to North America" in the years before the Civil War, acknowledged a considerable debt to J. C. Loudon in the preface of his *Treatise on the Theory and Practice of Landscape Gardening,* published in 1841. The opening chapter of this work, "Historical Sketches," describes country seats that Downing considered outstanding examples of architecture and "modern landscape gardening." But he concludes this inventory, which had no Southern examples, with the observation that "at the south are many extensive country residences remarkable for trees of unusual grandeur and beauty . . . but they are, in general, wanting in that high keeping and care, which is so essential to the charm of a landscape garden."[16]

In spite of this bias against a part of the country and a landscape tradition of which he had little knowledge at the time, Downing had sufficiently

TOP: An early photograph of Belmont and its grounds, near Nashville. BOTTOM: An early photograph of the greenhouses and water tower at Belmont.

absorbed Loudon's Gardenesque theory to advocate "architectural" terraces and walks and flower gardens close to the house. He argued that these were essential

The greenhouses and this formal seasonal display occupy only a small part of the sixty-five acres of gardens created by Mr. and Mrs. Walter Bellingrath at their Theodore, Alabama, home, south of Mobile.

"embellishments" that gracefully united the architecture of the house with the surrounding grounds, whose lawns and massed tree groups were meant to form a scene—either Beautiful or Picturesque in character, depending upon the style of the house and the natural character of the landscape. Downing's descriptions of suitable flower gardens and shrubberies evoke images of a long tradition of Southern gardens. When he describes the advantage of being able to "descend from the terrace by a few steps" into a flower garden, [17] the passage recalls an account of a visit in 1828 to a South Carolina plantation by Captain Basil Hall of Edinburgh, who admired the way one moved easily "from the drawing-room . . . into a verandah or piazza, from which, by a flight of steps, we found our way into a flower garden and shrubbery, rich with orange trees, laurels, myrtles, and weeping willows, and here and there a great spreading aloe." [18]

The difference between the two kinds of residential properties being described is significant for our understanding of Southern gardening tradition. Downing insisted that beyond the boundaries of the flower garden, a parklike "landscape garden," free of all traces of formal geometry, should extend from the house and frame it in a scenic composition. What Basil Hall saw over the hedge that enclosed the South Carolina garden were the rice fields, stretching "over the plain for miles, their boundary line being the black edge of the untouched forest." [19] Southerners of means, in the years before the Civil War, might develop wooded groves and lakes or ponds to ornament their grounds in the English manner; they might hire English gardeners to build rustic bridges, seats, and summerhouses to add a note of picturesque scenery; but these added features seldom replaced a formal structuring of their properties and a primary commitment to classical design traditions, especially that of the ornamental pleasure garden. They steadfastly resisted, for the most part, the view of the English school in its late phase and of its American interpreters like Downing that the primary goal of landscape design was to frame a scenic view of the house within its landscaped setting.

One Southern editor, in fact—the Alabaman Charles Peabody, horticultural editor of *Soil of the South*—proposed an alternative "Southern system of landscape gardening" to counteract the influence of Downing's notion that the landscape about a house should be composed with the view from the road in mind—a goal of ostentatious display, according to Peabody, that ought to offend the refined good taste of Southerners. Peabody advocated instead a landscape composition that centered the house within a clearing that protected it from damp shade while allowing views outward toward massed groupings of trees and shrubs, screening the house from view and creating privacy. Flower beds, of course, would adorn the open area near the house. The Southern historian James C.

Bonner also credited Peabody with successfully promoting regional pride in the South's indigenous vegetation, since he campaigned for the use of native trees and shrubs—the magnolia and live oak, cedars and pines, mountain laurel and wild azaleas—rather than such popular exotics as the crape myrtle, gardenia, and camellia. [20]

In spite of such criticism, Downing did find a receptive audience among some Southern readers of the agricultural journals, especially those interested in scientific farming and in horticulture, and a smaller group open to his prescriptions for architecture as well. Whatever they may have thought of his advocacy of Gothic Revival architectural styles and Picturesque landscape scenery, many Southerners used his writings as an authoritative source of information on desirable plants and their horticultural requirements, and on other technical matters related to house, garden, and grounds. Godfrey Barnsley, a cotton factor from Savannah who built an Italianate country house in a remote corner of north Georgia in the 1850s, used a plan adapted from one in *Villas and Cottages* (1857), by Calvert Vaux, Downing's partner for a brief time before the latter's untimely death in 1852 (and later a partner of Frederick Law Olmsted for the design of Central Park in New York City). Barnsley clearly studied Downing for information on the technology of a hydraulic ram to raise water from a low-lying pond to supply a marble fountain, and for such design features as the "rockwork" mounds, illustrated in Downing, which Barnsley built to frame the circular parterre garden at the entrance to his villa—what Downing would have classified as an "architectural flower-garden."

The breadth of Godfrey Barnsley's gardening interests was typical of that group within the pre–Civil War Southern population interested in new developments in horticulture—and, very frequently, in enlightened alternatives to an agricultural system so heavily invested in staple-crop monoculture that a stable economy and stewardship of land resources was impossible. The collapse of the Southern economy in the aftermath of war ironically did not significantly increase the ranks of those interested in scientific farming and agricultural reform, but the period of

Reconstruction did produce some erosion of strong regional traditions in landscape design and a new openness to northern models. A Hancock County, Georgia, planter newly returned from the war observed that his wife "consults 'Downing' with renewed pertinacity and, with busy thought, plans future improvements." [21] Especially in urban areas, and in the suburbs that began to develop around major cities late in the century, the styles that have come to be associated with "Victorian" garden design replaced the familiar geometry of the boxwood parterre and flower garden.

The importance of the flower garden within this late-nineteenth-century design aesthetic represents nothing less than the final full flowering of seeds planted in Downing's writings—seeds imported from England through the agency of his mentor Loudon. Downing had described in the first edition of the *Treatise* the current fashion in England for a type of garden that restricted the plant palette within individual beds to a limited number of brightly colored massed species:

> The beds are either in symmetrical forms and figures, or they are characterized by symmetrical *curved* outlines. The peculiarity of these gardens . . . is, that each separate bed is planted with a single variety, or at most two varieties of flowers. Only the most striking and showy varieties are generally chosen, and the effect . . . is highly brilliant. [22]

Commenting on this new English style, Downing introduced to Americans the English practice of maintaining a "reserve garden," the function of which was to provide potted replacements for the massed flowers in the beds: "As soon as a vacuum is made in the flower-garden by the fading of any flowers, the same are immediately removed and their places supplied by fresh plants just ready to bloom, from the pots in the *reserve garden*." [23]

Enter Victorian "bedding out" and the beginnings of what shortly became a national fashion in garden design. When Perez Dickinson, a transplanted New Englander who became one of the wealthiest businessmen in Knoxville, Tennessee, built gardens to

OPPOSITE:
Villa Vizcaya, James
Deering's palatial Italianate
estate on Biscayne Bay in
Miami, is now a city park
and museum. Diego Suarez
designed ten acres of
formal gardens to
complement the palazzo
designed by F. Burrall
Hoffman, Jr., completed
in 1916.

Island Home, the Perez
Dickinson residence in
Knoxville, Tennessee.

grace his Italianate mansion Island Home, the planting beds incised in the lawn provided a dazzling
display of crisply edged color, accented by plants of
exotic texture and form. Although this garden style
ultimately came under heavy criticism as too
artificial—the English garden writer William Robinson led a revolution against it, inspiring Gertrude
Jekyll's experiments with softer and more complex
massing of herbaceous plants and shrubs—one may
still encounter examples of the style in many public
gardens.

The changes in garden design and gardening prac-
tice that were occasioned by the ascendancy of Beaux
Arts classicism at the end of the century and beyond
were largely a national, not a regional, phenomenon.
The South had remarkable examples of the revival of
Renaissance and Baroque landscape design traditions
—best represented, perhaps, by Frederick Law
Olmsted's formal esplanade and "Italian" gardens at
Biltmore, George Vanderbilt's estate outside Ashe-
ville, North Carolina, begun in 1888, or by Villa

Vizcaya, near Miami, Florida, designed by F. Burrall
Hoffman for James Deering in 1914.

But more significant, perhaps, for the purposes
of this narrative, is the degree to which the historic
gardens of the American South became the focus of
national interest in the opening decades of the twentieth century. Included in Guy Lowell's landmark
survey *American Gardens,* published in 1902, were
photographs of the gardens and grounds of such
Southern plantations as Mount Vernon, Wye, Brandon, and Shirley in Virginia; the Carroll garden in
Annapolis, Maryland; and Drayton Hall and Middleton Place in South Carolina. The second edition of
Louise Shelton's *Beautiful Gardens in America,* published in 1924, included twelve Southern gardens,
half of them having some continuity with eighteenth-
and nineteenth-century gardens on the same site.
Classical garden traditions that were part of our own
country's historic past acquired new importance for
Americans, and that tradition was better represented
in the South than anywhere else in the nation.

For their part, Southerners celebrated the rediscovery of regional tradition, finding themselves before long in the vanguard of an historic-preservation movement that traced its beginnings back to Ann Pamela Cunningham's organization of the Mount Vernon Ladies' Association in 1858. The architectural historian Kenneth Severens has suggested that "preservation may be the South's major contribution in the twentieth century."[24] Interest in the preservation and interpretation of historic landscapes—and by extension, the adaptation of historic regional traditions to contemporary garden design—has been an important outgrowth of preservation activities initially addressed to individual buildings or to neighborhoods. The Southern Garden History Society, formed in 1982,

was the first such organization in the country dedicated to the promotion of the study of regional landscape and garden history and the collection and conservation of relevant documentary resources.

Southerners pouring through archives and traveling back-country roads to visit the sites of old gardens are not pursuing the vestiges of a vanished Golden Age of great houses and landscapes in order to reclaim its aura for the present. Rather, they are seeking an authentic understanding of the past history of some part of the world they have come to care a great deal about, in the hope that they might then design, plant, and care for gardens that are carriers of memory, binding individuals and communities to nature, to place, and to one another over time. ❧

NOTES

1. Sidney Lanier, "Corn," first published in the February 1875 number of *Lippincott's Magazine*.

2. Frederick Doveton Nichols and Ralph E. Griswold, *Thomas Jefferson, Landscape Architect* (Charlottesville: University Press of Virginia, 1978), p. 81.

3. Thomas Whately, *Observations on Modern Gardening* (London, 1770), quoted in William A. Brogden, "The *Ferme Ornée* and Changing Attitudes to Agricultural Improvement," *Eighteenth Century Life* 8, n.s., no. 2 (January 1983), 43.

4. From an undated note in the collection of Tulane University, quoted in Robert Manson Myers, ed., *The Children of Pride: A True Story of Georgia and the Civil War* (New Haven: Yale University Press, 1972; repr., New York: Popular Library, 1972), vol. 1 Prologue, n.p.

5. Ibid.

6. Almira Coffin to Mrs. J. G. Osgood, quoted in Katherine M. Jones, *The Plantation South* (Indianapolis: Bobbs-Merrill, 1957), 187–88.

7. Julia S. Berrall, *The Garden: An Illustrated History* (New York: Viking Press, 1966), 186, 197. Although Berrall cites Le Blond as the author of *La Théorie et la Pratique du Jardinage*, Kenneth Woodbridge has noted that the first publication of Dezallier d'Argenville's work of this title in 1709 "owed much to the plates of Jean-Baptiste Alexandre Le Blond, engraver and architect, who had produced designs for parterres published by Pierre Mariette. Although Mariette gave Le Blond as the author of the book in some later editions, the text was undoubtedly by Dezallier. . . ." Woodbridge, *Princely Gardens: The Origins and Development of the French Formal Style* (New York: Rizzoli, 1986), note 4, 267, 299. William Howard Adams states that Dezallier d'Argenville was "assisted by Alexandre Le Blond . . . in the third [1747] edition." Adams, *The French Garden, 1500–1800* (New York: Braziller, 1979), 105.

8. Quoted in David Lee Sterling, ed., "New Orleans, 1801: An Account by John Pintard," *Louisiana Historical Quarterly* 34 (July 1951): 228.

9. William Mitchell, *Gardens of Georgia* (Atlanta: Peachtree Publishers for the Garden Club of Georgia, 1989), 14.

10. J. C. Loudon, ed., *The Landscape Gardening and Landscape Architecture of the Late Humphry Repton, Esq. . . .* (London: Whitehead, published for the Author, 1840), ix.

11. Loudon, *Gardener's Magazine* 5 (October 1829), quoted in Melanie Louise Simo, *Loudon and the Landscape: From Country Seat to Metropolis, 1733–1843* (New Haven: Yale University Press, 1988), 175.

12. Simo, 173–75.

13. "Sylvanus," *The Horticulturist* 6, quoted in U. P. Hedrick, *A History of Horticulture in America to 1860* (New York: Oxford University Press, 1950), 356.

14. Harriet Martineau, *Western Travel*, vol. 1, quoted in Hedrick, 353.

15. Hedrick, 338.

16. A[ndrew] J[ackson] Downing, *A Treatise on the Theory and Practice of Landscape Gardening, Adapted to North America . . .* (New York: Wiley and Putnam, 1844) 45.

17. Downing, *Treatise*, 349.

18. Captain Basil Hall, *Travels in North America, in the Years 1827 and 1828*, vol. 3 (Edinburgh, 1830), quoted in Katherine M. Jones, 98.

19. Ibid.

20. James C. Bonner, "House and Landscape Design in the Antebellum South," *Landscape* 21, no. 3 (Spring-Summer 1977), 4–5.

21. Letter of Edgeworth Bird to his daughter Sallie, 2 September 1866, quoted in John Rozier, ed., *The Granite Farm Letters: The Civil War Correspondence of Edgeworth & Sally Bird* (Athens: University of Georgia Press, 1988), 258.

22. Downing, *Treatise,* 1841 ed., 358.

23. Ibid., note, 364.

24. Kenneth Severens, *Southern Architecture: 350 Years of Distinctive American Buildings* (New York: E. P. Dutton, 1981), 186.

BIBLIOGRAPHY

Brandau, Roberta Seawell, ed. *History of the Homes and Gardens of Tennessee.* Nashville: Parthenon Press for the Garden Study Club of Nashville, 1964.

Briggs, Loutrel W. *Charleston Gardens.* Columbia: University of South Carolina Press, 1951.

Bonner, James C. "House and Landscape Design in the Antebellum South." *Landscape* 21, (Spring-Summer 1977): 2–8.

Christian, Frances Archer and Susanne Williams Massie. *Houses and Gardens in Old Virginia.* Richmond: Garrett & Massie, 1929.

Cooney, Lorraine M., comp. and Hattie C. Rainwater, ed. *Garden History of Georgia, 1733–1933.* Atlanta: Peachtree Garden Club, 1933.

Davis, Ben. *The Southern Garden: From the Potomac to the Rio Grande.* Philadelphia: J. B. Lippincott, 1971.

Davis, Evangeline. *Charleston: Houses and Gardens.* Charleston: Preservation Society of Charleston, 1975.

Dillon, Julia Lester. *The Blossom Circle of the Year in Southern Gardens.* New York: A. T. De La Mare, 1922.

Draper, Earle Sumner. "Southern Plantations." *Landscape Architecture* 23 (Oct. 1932): 1–14.

———. "Southern Plantations: Notes on the Carolinas." *Landscape Architecture* 23 (Jan. 1933): 117–38.

Forman, Henry Chandlee. *Tidewater Maryland Architecture and Gardens.* New York: Architectural Book Publishing, 1956.

Fraser, Charles. *A Charleston Sketchbook, 1796–1806.* Rutland, Vermont: Charles E. Tuttle for the Carolina Art Association, 1959.

Gardens of the South. New York: Simon and Schuster for Southern Accents Press, 1985.

Gray, Lewis Cecil. *A History of Agriculture in the Southern United States to 1860.* Introd. by Henry Charles Taylor. 2 vols. Washington, D.C.: Waverly Press for the Carnegie Institution of Washington, 1933.

Hartzog, Mattie Abney. *Garden Time in the South.* Harrisburg, Pa.: J. Horace McFarland, 1951.

Hudson, Charles J., Jr. *Hudson's Southern Gardening.* Atlanta: Tupper and Love, 1950.

Hume, H. Harold. *Gardening in the Lower South.* Rev. ed. New York: Macmillan, 1954.

Hunt, William Lanier. *Southern Gardens, Southern Gardening.* Durham: Duke University Press, 1982.

Krochmal, Arnold, and Connie Krochmal. *Gardening in the Carolinas.* New York: Doubleday, 1975.

Lawrence, Elizabeth. *Gardening for Love: The Market Bulletins.* Durham: Duke University Press, 1987.

———. *A Southern Garden: A Handbook for the Middle South.* Chapel Hill: University of North Carolina Press, 1967.

———. *Through the Garden Gate.* Edited by Bill Neal. Chapel Hill: University of North Carolina Press, 1990.

Leblanc, Joyce Y. *Pelican Guide to the Gardens of Louisiana.* Gretna, La.: Pelican Publishing, 1974.

Lockwood, Alice G. B., comp. and ed. *Gardens of Colony and State.* 2 vols. New York: Charles Scribner's Sons for the Garden Club of America, 1934.

Maccubin, Robert P., and Peter Martin, eds. *British and American Gardens in the Eighteenth Century.* Charlottesville: University Press of Virginia for the Colonial Williamsburg Foundation, 1984.

Mason, Hamilton. *Your Garden in the South.* Princeton: Van Nostrand Reinhold, 1961.

Mitchell, William. *Gardens of Georgia.* Photography by Richard Moore. Atlanta: Peachtree Publishers for the Garden Club of Georgia, 1989.

Nichols, Frederick Doveton, and Ralph E. Griswold. *Thomas Jefferson, Landscape Architect.* Charlottesville: University Press of Virginia, 1978.

Rion, Mary C. *Ladies' Southern Florist.* Columbia, S. C.: Peter B. Glass, 1860.

Shaffer, E. T. H. *Carolina Gardens.* Foreword by DuBose Heyward. Chapel Hill: University of North Carolina Press, 1939.

Squibb, Robert. *The Gardener's Calendar, for South Carolina, Georgia, and North Carolina.* Charleston: Samuel Wright & Co. for R. Squibb, 1787. Reprint, Athens: University of Georgia Press, 1980.

Wedda, John. *Gardens of the American South.* New York: Galahad Books, 1971.

Welch, William C. *Perennial Garden Color.* Foreword by Neil Sperry. Dallas, Tex.: Taylor Publishing, 1989.

White, William N. *Gardening for the South.* New York: C. M. Saxton, 1856.

Williams, Dorothy Hunt. *Historic Virginia Gardens.* Charlottesville: University Press of Virginia, 1975.

Western Expansion

❧❧

David C. Streatfield

❧ *In 1803 the Louisiana Purchase opened up the West and doubled the land area of the United States. It also offered botanists and gardeners many new and "exotic" plants. Additionally it presented new landscapes to consider, consult, and respond to. Early settlers of these regions found remnants of other cultures, notably French and Spanish, and also brought with them their own ways, styles, and uses of gardens and gardening.*

In time the new lands inspired new ways, and the pioneers, now citizens of the new states, relinquished old ones, especially in the West and Southwest. The results of experimentation, along with topographical and climatic demands not previously experienced, led to some marvelous and very creative gardens. The influence of novel surroundings is not measurable, but surely unfamiliar landscapes and the lack of tradition encouraged a great deal of trial and error as well as reflection on the meaning, purpose, and design of gardens.

The gardens of the American West, especially those in California and the southwestern states, have been influential far beyond their regions, and even beyond our national boundaries, for their guiding principles of environmental appropriateness, "livability," and boldness in imaginative design are not limited to any one region. Indeed, such characteristics have always been the hallmark of great gardens. ❧

WHEN SETTLERS moved westward across the North American continent in the nineteenth century, they encountered landscapes of great diversity. These physical landscapes ranged from the huge midwestern plain between the Appalachian and Rocky mountains to the desert states of the Southwest, and the states on the Pacific Coast. Embracing the rolling and fertile parts of the eastern Midwest, the flat expanses of the prairies, the arid parts of the Southwest, which range in elevation from below sea level to over thirteen thousand feet, these regions include mountains, canyons, mesas, plateaus, and the dramatic coastal landscapes of the Pacific States. The latter include the temperate, glacially scoured valleys of the Puget Sound lowlands, the dry Willamette Valley, the redwood forests of northern California, the varying microclimates of the San Francisco Bay region, the hot and dry Sacramento-San Joaquin Valley, the semidesert of the Los Angeles basin, and the more arid mesas of the San Diego uplands. The climate to the east of the Rocky Mountains is one characterized in the northern parts by severe winters and hot and humid summers, while the Pacific Northwest region is characterized by a much more temperate climate with far less humidity. The Southwest, by contrast, is characterized by intense light and extreme aridity.

Before the settlement of this huge area by people from the Northeast and the Atlantic coastal states and by European settlers in the nineteenth century, it had been settled in distinctive ways by a number of earlier immigrant groups. The French ruled much of the central part of the Midwest from 1534 to 1759, establishing forts and farms in a pattern of settlement identical to that of French Canada. Similarly, the southwestern states of Arizona and New Mexico were settled in the sixteenth century by the Spanish, moving northward from Mexico: it was not until 1769 that they moved into Alta California. All of these early forms of settlement are classic examples of "cultural Colonialism," in which familiar patterns of land distribution, cultivation of plants in gardens, the layout of towns, and, in the Spanish colonies, the distribution of water, followed traditional patterns that had been established in the centers of these colonial empires many centuries before.

The nineteenth-century settlement of this vast region did not immediately produce new garden forms. Gardens of this period were, in fact, completely consistent with the norms of taste that were accepted in the Eastern states and in Europe. However, inherent American inventiveness and love for experimentation eventually produced gardens that were distinctive expressions of some of these regions —most notably on the West Coast and more recently in the Southwest—with regard to ecological limitations and opportunities for growing plants or for living harmoniously with the environment. The gardens of the late nineteenth century and the modernist gardens of the immediate post–World War II era possessed a regional character that, in the latter pe-

OPENING ILLUSTRATION:
Marcus Bollinger designed this desert-plant garden in the 1980s for a home in the Pinnacle Peaks area of Scottsdale, Arizona.

riod, was of national if not international, significance. Gardens created recently in the Southwest and in California may prove to be of equal significance by establishing new standards of ecological appropriateness for arid and semiarid regions.

Initial Settlement

EARLY PERCEPTIONS of the horticultural potential of newly opened areas differed considerably. As late as 1847, Horace Greeley visited northern Illinois and informed the readers of the *New York Tribune* that a deficiency of water was a great drawback to farming, a deficiency, furthermore, that he did not believe would ever be remedied. Similarly, the region between the Wisconsin River and St. Paul was regarded as a wilderness "uninhabited and uninhabitable." As late as 1846, Thomas Allan of St. Louis, Missouri, could find little to praise in the gardens of the Mississippi Basin. In an article in *The Horticulturist,* he describes gardening in the West as "tending a truck patch." The principal object of having such a garden, he said, was "the daily plentiful supply of 'garden truck' in the kitchen pot." By contrast, the rich soils and benign climate of such areas as the Willamette Valley in western Oregon and the coastal and inland regions of California were looked upon jealously by Yankee and European traders and visitors before this Mexican region was ceded to the United States. Initial settlement on the Pacific Coast occurred in the Willamette Valley. The discovery of gold in California turned this tide of settlers towards that state, where a small number had already penetrated. A number of the Yankee traders had married the heiresses of large Mexican ranchos and had, to some extent, adopted the lifestyle of their parents-in-law. The gardens they created were a fusion of the Spanish tradition of the courtyard garden and the gardens they had known in New England. These gardens were synthetic and were not a direct translation of the traditions of the Iberian Peninsula to California. Indeed, they should more properly be regarded as representations of the New England traditions of simple, formal gardens containing old-fashioned flowers. The myth of the "elegant half-seigneurial life" of the Mex-

The courtyard garden at Rancho Camulos in Piru,
California (c. 1852), united the simple form of Spanish
courtyard gardens and the formal gardens of eighteenth-
century New England.

icans portrayed so beautifully by Helen Hunt Jackson
in her famous novel *Ramona* is a romantic fiction.
Mexican California was in reality a world without
elegance that could be emulated by the eastern settlers. The ranchos were exceptionally crude domestic
establishments, frequently lacking any kind of garden. In distinct contrast, the remains of the Spanish
occupation in the Southwest recalled, at times, some
of the elegance of the Iberian Peninsula precedents.

National Taste on the Far West Frontier

APREREQUISITE for the creation of fine gardens
is a reliable supply of good plants. One of the
most remarkable aspects of western expansion was the
relatively early appearance of plants from other regions. In the earliest settlement of the Midwest, seeds
were brought from Canada into Illinois, which continued for some time to be a testing ground for the
development of new and appropriate plants. A nursery

was established at Paris, Illinois, in 1810 and another
one at Waukegan in 1844. However, it was Henderson Lewelling who transferred this early cultivation
of plants to the far West, when he moved from Salem,
Iowa, to found a nursery outside Portland, Oregon.
Several decades later, he moved to California, giving
him the unique distinction of having worked as a
nurseryman in Indiana, Iowa, Oregon, and California.

The lack of a cross-continental railroad, the long
overland route from the East Coast to the West, and
the long sea voyage around the Horn apparently were
not barriers to the rapid establishment of nurseries in
the Pacific states. In the early 1850s, they were set
up in Sacramento and in the San Francisco Bay region
at San Francisco, Oakland, and San Jose. What is
especially remarkable about these California nurseries
is the initiative and imagination shown by their owners in selling an extraordinarily wide range of temperate and subtropical plants. Plants came from nurseries on the East Coast, Europe, and Australia, the
latter providing acacias and eucalyptus. Despite the
breadth of range of available plants, especially those
available in West Coast nurseries, the gardens of the
Midwest and the Far West, until the early 1870s,

were remarkable for their conservative reliance upon the prevailing design conventions in the Eastern states and Europe. The books of John Claudius Loudon and Andrew Jackson Downing were consulted. [1] However, many garden creators simply replicated the gardens they had known previously. The use of established norms of taste enabled them to feel "rooted" in an unfamiliar landscape and also remain part of the civilized culture of the nation, despite their geographical separation. A number of gardens recalled specific places rather than relying upon contemporary theoretical precepts. Places as diverse as a farm in Kentucky, a New England garden, or an old-fashioned English flower garden were emulated.

By contrast, in the 1860s and 1870s elaborate gardens were created on the San Francisco peninsula that bore more resemblance to European manorial estates. Usually at least five hundred acres in size, they belonged to totally self-sufficient establishments that included mansion, pleasure grounds, at least one farm, and, frequently, sporting facilities such as race tracks. Such establishments continued the earlier cultural preferences. An Italian count built an Italian villa overlooking a series of formal terraces. Antoine Borel, a Swiss banker, built a summer home surrounded by extensive lawns decorated with mosaiculture, a birch grove, and an extensive rock garden with a meandering stream; it attempted to imitate the dramatic landscapes of the Swiss Alps. The garden of Faxon Dean Atherton combined the simple formality of New England gardens with the tropical lushness of Chile, uniting his boyhood origins and a place of later residence. Despite stylistic differences, these gardens on the San Francisco peninsula were all highly introverted, seeming to express a marked antipathy toward the local landscape. Indeed, these highly ordered and "green" gardens made a compelling statement of the conquest of the Western frontier by Eastern culture.

By contrast, gardens created in midwestern states were more conventional. A typical example was Terrace Hill, the Benjamin Franklin Allen estate in Des Moines, Iowa, designed by Job T. Elletson, an Englishman who had immigrated to Rochester, New York. It was later modified by Jacob Weidenmann of New York, whose book *Beautifying Country Homes*, published in 1870, became an important source for design practice, in addition to the work of Downing and his disciple Frank Scott.

A New Californian Identity (1870–1900): The "Tropical"

IN CALIFORNIA from the 1870s until the end of the century, an increasing degree of elaboration was evident, especially in the larger gardens. This development reflected the expanding economy and the growing importance of southern California, known from this period onward as the "Southland." It also reflected a conscious attempt to celebrate the remarkable, if not unique, opportunities for gardening that California offered. It included "natural" and formal gardens and culminated at the end of the century in "tropical" gardens.

"Natural" gardens were advocated by John McLaren. [2] However, his diaries recommended plant associations of an extraordinarily diverse range drawn from the subtropical and temperate regions. McLaren's naturalism was clearly not ecological. It was derived from the Gardenesque and Picturesque of Loudon and William Sawyer Gilpin, to whom he frequently refers in his diaries. McLaren sought, by using a wide range of plants, to create natural places that he had visited in Scotland and California.

Lavish formal gardens also appeared on the San Francisco peninsula early in the 1870s. Rudolf Ulrich's Linden Towers was an extravagant and flamboyant example, with a large cast-iron fountain and carpet bedding, beyond which were extensive groves of oak trees lavishly underplanted with ornamental trees and plants, flowers and beds of mosaiculture, and flanked by lawns containing exotic specimen trees. Ulrich was one of the first designers in California to use color in a consciously organized way. Linden Towers was designed around the theme of cream and gold, and the garden at Château Fresno centered on pink and white.

Associated with these formal designs were "Arizona" gardens, collections from deserts of Arizona. While these could be seen as a form of regionalism,

TOP: For Linden Towers, in Menlo Park (1878), Rudolf Ulrich incorporated an elaborate cast-lead fountain made by Ducel et Cie of Paris into his formal design. It was surrounded by shrubberies with cream and gold flowers.

BOTTOM: A decorative collection of plants brought from the deserts of Arizona was used by Ulrich in his c. 1880 design for Stanford Ranch, in Palo Alto.

Huntington Gardens's Palm Garden in San Marino, California, was created about 1895 by William Hertrich. The grand scheme contains a series of outdoor spans that evoke different garden modes. This collection of palms shows the continuity of the mania for plant collecting.

their use appears to reflect a desire for flamboyant exoticism.

The first systematic attempt to address the needs of California gardeners was Charles Shinn's *Pacific Rural Handbook* (1878). Much of Shinn's advice was a synthesis of earlier work, but his advice reflects the bias of a northern Californian. He advocated a very carefully controlled use of conifers, since they provided too much shade. Gardeners in the Southland, however, felt the loss of such trees in their landscape. A garden in Riverside created in the 1880s reveals the desperate means used in this region to shut out views of the surrounding desert.

Shinn's magazine, the *Pacific Rural Press,* contains the first reference to the suitability of the tropical for California.[3] Tropical plants began to appear in the 1870s. Japanese plants arrived in the San Francisco Bay region, and several nurseries specialized in tropical plants in the Southland. The apogee of tropical taste was achieved at such gardens as Canon Crest Park in Redlands and Henry Huntington's estate at San Marino. These were eclectic gardens, but the eclecticism was an expression of moods rather than a choice of styles or associations.

The taste for the tropical in garden design occurred throughout the West Coast region and its appearance emphasized two central differences between the various subregions. In the Pacific Northwest, gardens were created as spaces "carved out" of the primeval coniferous forest. In northern California, existing oak trees were invariably incorporated into garden designs and used as visual anchoring devices. By contrast, in southern California, where little vegetation had previously existed, the long growing season enabled the creation of a landscape of instant maturity of a remarkably florid and lush character in a physical setting treated as a tabula rasa.

The principal negative aspect of this tropical lavishness was the prodigal use of water, which appears to have been unremarked by most Californians. A lone voice, remarkably perceptive in 1913, was that of the English visitor Arthur T. Johnson. He pointed out that the splendor of Californian gardens depended on "the liberal use of the hose-pipe and garden sprinkler which are turned on with lavish generosity in the gardens and parks which has been the main factor in making the wilderness bloom as the rose."[4]

The Golden Age: 1900–1929

THE FIRST THREE DECADES of the twentieth century were a golden age of garden design in several American regions. A plentiful supply of creative and highly skilled landscape designers served the needs of a large number of rich and well-traveled clients who commissioned elaborate gardens and had the means to maintain them properly. It was also a time when the differences between the various regions of the Midwest and the Pacific Coast states became more apparent. Chicago became the center of what Wilhelm Miller dubbed "the Prairie School of Landscape Architecture," practiced by such designers as its originator, Ossian Simonds, and Jens Jensen. This style combined a rigorous use of native plants with an aesthetic that was derived from the Picturesque naturalism associated with Humphry Repton. At its best, it produced lyrical designs that, while not exactly replicating the forms of the landscape of the prairie, sought to celebrate its essential spirit.

By contrast, Californian designers sought to address critical regional issues in different ways. The population of the region expanded dramatically during this period. In the Pacific Northwest, the rivalry for dominance in the region between Seattle and Portland was decisively won by Seattle, which served as the staging ground for the Alaskan gold rush. San Francisco remained the leading city in California until the beginning of the twenties, when it was supplanted by Los Angeles, the most rapidly growing region in the country. The expansion of existing industries and the development of new ones, such as moving pictures, produced great wealth that was frequently reflected in the creation of fine gardens.

During this period, gardens were designed by a variety of individuals who displayed a greater professionalism than the gardeners and nurserymen of the previous century. There had been few professional garden designers in any of the subregions until the twenties and many gardens in the Pacific Northwest were designed by outside design firms such as Olmsted Brothers. Nurseries provided design services and many architects designed gardens.[5] The great passion for plant collecting that had been such a distinguishing aspect of the second half of the nineteenth century continued but was now practiced on a much more scientific basis, as in the work of the Southern California Acclimatizing Association.

The presence of an ever-expanding number of plants from the various regions of the world ensured the continuity of the tropical and natural garden modes. However, the first two decades of the century

saw a turn toward a greater sense of order in garden design throughout the U.S. Bruce Porter called for a new kind of garden that spoke of care under great difficulties.[6] The architectural critic Herbert Croly proposed a landscape architecture that expressed a mixture of "daring and discretion." The Italian villa garden was the perfect vehicle for such expression.[7] The Berkeley poet Charles Keeler despised the lavish tropical garden and advocated a garden that could be used for play and work and would uplift the souls of the users by references to both Spanish and Oriental traditions.[8]

In fact, garden design in the first two decades of the twentieth century was distinguished not by the single-minded adoption of any of these new ideas but by a plurality of design modes. The Mediterranean and Oriental idioms were pursued individually as well as in synthesis with the former passion for tropical gardens and naturalism. The entire West Coast region also witnessed and embraced the Arts and Crafts movement. In the Pacific Northwest, the Olmsted Brothers developed a modified version of the Olmstedian Picturesque which was probably the first truly regional approach adopted there.

Mediterranean gardens created on the West Coast during the first two decades of the century represented a remarkably broad spectrum of approaches. El Fureidis, in Montecito, is a poetic and highly abstract version of the great terraced water gardens of Persia.[9] Italian villa gardens and Spanish gardens were evoked in ways that continued the Victorian tropical tradition, while the Italian gardens in the San Francisco Bay region have a graver and more sober quality reminiscent of the villas around Rome.

The dark and somewhat gloomy native conifer forest of the Pacific Northwest did not lend itself particularly well to the formality and crisply detailed architectural ornament of the Italian gardens, and it was not particularly popular in this region.

Another formal style adopted to confer order and civility was the French Baroque. However, the exquisite visual subtleties of André Le Nôtre's designs were never attempted. Formal allées were carved through groves of eucalyptus whose shaggy foliage did not accord well with this idiom.

OPPOSITE:
The David Gamble garden
in Pasadena was a 1900
project by Charles and
Henry Greene. This fluid
landscape is a poetic
interpretation of a Japanese
garden by designers whose
only acquaintance with
Japan was through
photographs.

The Japanese Garden on
the Andrew Welch estate
in Hillsborough (c. 1910)
is a literal copy of a
traditional Japanese
garden.

Oriental gardens were quite popular on the West Coast after 1894. But despite the area's large Asian populations, this was not a regional celebration, but a decorative fascination with the visually exotic and fantastic with little or no appreciation for the spiritual and intellectual dimensions that informed the authentic style.

The Arts and Crafts movement, an approach rather than a design style, was taken up on the West Coast with great intensity. Derived from English practice, the goals of this movement were regionalism, appropriateness, fine craftsmanship, and the use of local materials. As in England, the actual achievement of such goals was often highly ironic in character. The sheer cost of creating well-crafted gardens usually put them well beyond the means of ordinary people. Nevertheless, the work of professional designers had a considerable effect through books that popularized some of their design features. There was no single style advocated by the Arts and Crafts theoreticians, and one can detect the influence of Japanese

and English, as well as Mediterranean, traditions in the work of a number of Arts and Crafts designers. Almost all of them conformed to a spatial arrangement that continued through the twenties. Houses were invariably surrounded by paved terraces and pergolas, from which it was possible to look out over rolling lawns or a focal point such as an irregular pond. The principal movement through the garden took the form of a perimeter path that provided views of the garden and the house as well as linking detached terraces, pergolas, and other places where the owners and their friends could sit in the partial shade and read or converse. The rhetoric of Arts and Crafts proposed an outdoor living room and encouraged the idea of informal living. However, despite this rhetoric, the actual use of the garden as an outdoor room was limited to partially covered sitting areas. Some features of the style were the finely crafted garden walls, terracotta flower pots, glazed ceramic tiles, and art that provided bright or subtle points of color although, for the most part, colors were rather muted.

A new approach to garden design was created by Olmsted Brothers throughout the Pacific Northwest. In these gardens, nineteenth-century Olmstedian Picturesque principles were carefully used to screen out undesirable views such as local industry. John Charles Olmsted's marked antipathy to the native fir and cedar trees produced a new and distinctive garden character through use of facer plantings of smaller and more ornamental trees and shrubs in front of them and setting off the latter with a carefully sculptured ground plane. The gardens were centered around large, irregularly shaped lawn areas, carefully designed to provide long, diagonal sight lines that would create a greater sense of space. Immediately adjacent to the house the designers placed formal features such as terraces and pergolas to extend the geometry of the architecture out into the landscape.

The twenties saw the creation of an exceptionally large number of gardens in southern California. Here, the economy boomed, owing to the expansion of the moving-picture industry, the discovery of oil at Long Beach, carefully orchestrated property development, and tourism. By contrast, growth in the San Francisco Bay region and in the Pacific Northwest was relatively sluggish, although this by no means prohibited the development of fine gardens. The social diversity of the era naturally produced numerous expectations. For some clients, the garden was simply a background for entertainment; for others it recalled specific places they had visited abroad. Some clients permitted their designers considerable freedom, so that the garden was as much an expression of the designer as it was of the personality of the client. In Los Angeles, a significant number of talented landscape designers came to the fore, in contrast to the smaller group of landscape architects practicing in the San Francisco Bay region and the Pacific Northwest.[10]

Furthermore, fine craftsmen, well-stocked nurseries, and gardeners who had been trained in England, France, Belgium, and Italy were all readily available. Mature trees were moved on a scale that reminds one of the movement of Birnam Wood, demonstrating

Ralph Stevens's Spanish garden for George Steadman (Montecito, 1926) was created with the assistance of two experts on Spain. Yet this bench with its Spanish and Art Deco tilework exhibits visual eclecticism.

that there were no barriers to the creation of any effect desired by the designer or by the client.[11]

A decisive shift in taste occurred in this decade. In the Southland, the Mediterranean traditions became far more popular than before. Attempts to re-create Italian gardens were now matched by an equal passion for Spanish gardens, referring to what was incorrectly believed to have been the elegant seigneurial tradition of the Spanish and Mexican periods. Various forms of English influence could still be found, the earlier formal traditions as well as the more spacious English Picturesque park as at Paul Thiene's design for Greystone, Beverly Hills, and Florence Yoch's design for Mrs. Frank Emory's garden in Pasadena. The Norman-French style, as in other parts of the country, also made an appearance.[12] The

regionalism of the Arts and Crafts period was no longer popular, although Charles Greene created two fine gardens in this mode: the D. L. James garden at Carmel and Green Gables at Woodside.

In the case of these national styles, it was the use of beautifully detailed architectural features, especially walls, and other elements such as gazebos, vases, fountains, and benches, that marked a particular style. Gardens displayed a wide range of regard for specific periods ranging from actual copying to, in extreme instances, a kind of stripped-down abstraction. A few designers went beyond mere stylistic exercises to experiment with simple, abstract solutions using only plants.

The spatial conception of the gardens of this decade was essentially no different from that of the Arts and Crafts gardens: a series of formal terraces, sometimes incorporating the partial shade of pergolas, were wrapped around a house and led to a system of axial or irregular walks, depending upon the style, which led the visitor through the garden around its perimeter. Terraces continued to be used as outdoor sitting places and were invariably sited facing east or south so that the occupants would be sitting in the shade during the extreme heat of the afternoon. While the character of the house invariably determined the character of the immediate gardens, farther from the house one might encounter gardens in other styles, including English park-like lawns, Spanish or Japanese gardens, or desert gardens.

Formal styles permitted modern features such as tennis courts and swimming pools to be incorporated into an historicist framework using devices like formal enclosures with overlooks or belvederes derived from historical precedents. The addition of a fountain to a swimming pool could convert what might otherwise have been a utilitarian feature into a decorative and ornamental pool.

While many attempts were made to create Spanish gardens in this decade, few manifested the true qualities of the simple but elegant geometry of the originals with their brick-paved paths, tiled fountains, boxwood parterres, pergolas, and tile-lined benches. Even a garden created with the advice of Mildred and Arthur Byne, the leading American experts on Spanish gardens, mixes Andalusian and Moroccan tiles.

Smaller gardens were often conceived with romantic and eclectic subtlety. Features such as fountains and benches established reference to a historic period. Flower beds invariably recalled the loose rumpus of color of English cottage gardens. Scattered trees often implied the passage of time, an idea that had fascinated designers since the rediscovery of classical Italy in the eighteenth century.

References to England were most commonly made in the detailed planting of flower beds, to which great attention was paid by many designers who provided meticulous instruction on their seasonal replanting. In the intense heat of southern California, such planting was largely restricted to the winter months.

Interest in native plants for their own sake was infrequent. [13] In some ways Lockwood de Forest's experimentation with native and native-like plants is far more significant. [14] His own garden was remarkably prophetic of the kind of garden created in the postwar period. The lawn was planted with Kikuyu grass, which was never irrigated, and thus turned a golden yellow in the summer months. His children played simple ball games here. The deep bed beyond held native shrubs and a California live oak tree. The simple, formal geometry, colors, and textures were intended to create a strong visual link with the bold mountain landscape beyond.

De Forest made such visual connections with the surrounding regional landscape in an even more abstract way in his design for a garden at Hope Ranch. The theme of this garden was silver. In the late afternoon narrow flecks of light defined the edges of a grove of oak trees, and the silver theme was contained in a planting of proteas from South Africa and a spectacular allée of leucodendron trees underplanted with bird-of-paradise. These silver plants echoed the silver of the distant ocean and the mountains. The garden became part of the regional landscape in an extraordinary and subtle way.

Native plants were used in other regions to create a new regional character or identity. In the Pacific Northwest, the practice of such designers as F. C. Cole and Otto Holmdahl resulted in gardens that

Lockwood de Forest's own small garden was designed in 1926 as a place to be experienced as a visual foreground to the mountains.

superficially resembled the earlier work of the Olmsted Brothers. However, the combination of using extremely subtle grading and calling attention to the Northwest evergreen forests, by bringing forward to the edge native small trees and shrubs, such as the native dogwood, rather than screening it with exotic

A range of plants carefully selected for their textural qualities, combined with a sensitive use of concave and convex curves, makes the space of the Edmund Hayes garden in Portland, Oregon—designed in 1941 by John and Carol Grant—seem larger.

ornamental trees and shrubs, produced a distinctive aesthetic comparable to the spiritual expressiveness of the Prairie School of landscape architecture.

In the Southwest, designs for the Jokake Inn and the Tangere Verde Inn, both at Phoenix, and Stephen Child's design for the subdivision Colonia, Solana, at Tucson, also used native vegetation as an expression of regional character and a way to live in harmony with a stressed environment.

Toward a New Regional Identity: 1930–1940

THE DEPRESSION brought permanent changes to garden design throughout the region. Although the Southland's economy remained relatively buoyant because of the moving-picture industry, enabling its leading figures to commission fine gardens, there was a concomitant, marked reduction in size and elaboration. Gardens were made to appear larger through the subtle use of optical illusions. Most gardens were committed to sport and entertainment, albeit on a reduced scale.

New gardens had to confront vastly changed social circumstances. Low maintenance now became a critical design factor, achieved by the use of hard surfaces, narrow slabs of paving to eliminate trimming the edges of grass lawns, ground covers, and a greatly reduced palette of plants. Gardens, therefore, took on a much more architectonic character. In addition, consciously reductionist and simplified historicism culminated at the end of this decade in a totally new design idiom.

In the Pacific Northwest, these new challenges were addressed in a different way that spoke of considerable confidence in the possibility of a regional expression. The Aubrey Watzek house and garden in Portland was a seminal design that influenced both architecture and the treatment of landscape throughout the region. Perched on a level hilltop and commanding panoramic views toward Mount Hood, the design centered around a single-story house derived from the barns of the Willamette Valley. [15] A courtyard with carefully controlled and coordinated flower colors constituted a simplified and reordered interpretation of the Roman courtyard garden. Outside the house, its designer, John Yeon, rigorously eschewed using anything but native plants, since he believed that evolution had produced a range of colors and textures harmoniously adapted to the climate and physical character of the landscape.

An equally important and more influential regional design style was established by John and Carol Grant. The Grants expanded their vocabulary of plants to include nonnative species that had similar physical and horticultural characteristics to native ones. By the carefully coordinated use of concave and convex curves, they sought to create visual illusions to make small spaces seem larger. Their style represented an emphasis on plant textures, rather than color, that was reminiscent of the principles underlying Japanese gardens, although their work is largely derived from the work of Gertrude Jekyll. Their scalar range was perverse, however, since they frequently used fine textures in the foreground and coarse textures in the distance. This contradicted that inherent understanding of textural qualities related to human perception first introduced and recognized by Picturesque theory at the end of the eighteenth century. The Grants' books were highly influential, since they were the first written principally for the Pacific Northwest that showed any real understanding of the region's unique opportunities.

An equally distinguished but unfortunately short-lived practice was that of Elizabeth Lord and Edith Schryver, who had worked for Ellen Biddle Shipman. They brought to the Northwest an exemplary plantsmanship and visual sensitivity that represented the very best of East Coast eclecticism. Their gardens were distinguished by beautifully designed structures, and carefully selected pieces of garden furniture placed in formal settings. In their own garden, perimeter planting was used to establish a high level of privacy and sense of enclosure. The more detailed planting beds were filled with delicate washes of color that changed with the seasons.

The decade also witnessed the architectural Pueblo Revival in the Southwest, which was centered in the work of John Gaw Meem. His Los Poblamos ranch was an attempt to re-create the character of

Elizabeth Lord and Edith Schryver gave Lord's elaborate formal garden of boxwood hedges in Salem, Oregon (1930), an asymmetrical quality through the use of delicate, irregular washes of color.

simple haciendas created by the Spanish in the area around Santa Fe, New Mexico. This ranch was surrounded by a walled garden designed by the eastern landscape architects Rose Greeley and Cecil Pragnell that re-created the enclosed-paradise nature of true Spanish gardens. At the same time Bud Hollied, designer of Roosevelt Park in Albuquerque, and Cecil Pragnell established what has been termed the "Rio Grande style," characterized by a mixture of enclosed courtyards, the use of masonry paving, naturalistic English planting, and traditional adobe walls.

OPPOSITE:
The open, pavilionlike character of this house, designed in 1950 by Richard Neutra for James Moore, in Ojai, California, is visually integrated with the lush oasislike character of the water garden so that house and garden—also by Neutra—are a seamless unity.

In 1948, Thomas Church designed this abstract swimming pool for the Dewey Donnell Ranch in Sonoma, California. The line of the pool's edge "implodes" and "explodes" simultaneously, like a piece of Cubist sculpture, establishing relationships to the sculpture and the forms of the outer landscape.

Modernism on the West Coast: 1939–1965

SOME OF THE EARLIEST manifestations of modernism in the American garden occurred on the West Coast. Modernism was diverse and embraced at one end the understated "commonplace" and at the other conscious abstraction. Thomas Church and Garrett Eckbo, whose work was published in the fifties in articles and books, were enormously influential. The influence of exhibitions held by the Museum of Modern Art in San Francisco, the model houses built by residential developers, and the Case Study House Program initiated by *Arts and Architecture* magazine also brought modernism to a much broader audience. While much of the publicized work was produced by Californian designers, the movement was by no means confined to that state. Indeed, *Sunset Magazine* was

quite justified in talking about "western" gardens since most Pacific Northwest designers embraced the fundamental principles underlying the work of their Californian counterparts.

By the late thirties a recognizable modern style had appeared. It respected, and indeed derived much of its character from, the architecture of the house, seeking to establish functional and visual relationships between exterior and interior spaces so that house and garden formed an indivisible unity. This achievement was made possible by site planning, a process of equal collaboration between the client, the architect, and the landscape architect that divided the garden into four distinct zones: the entry zone, which provided parking and established relationships to the street and local neighborhood; the service zone, which accommodated lathhouses, greenhouses, vegetable plots,

and garbage storage; the social zone, which was used for entertaining and dining; and the recreation zone, which was used for swimming, sunbathing, tennis, and children's play.

The aesthetic realization of these ideas varied considerably. Church sought an abstract "visual endlessness" that would not weary the eye. His most famous design was conceived like a piece of Cubist art, with the ground plane as a series of overlapping surfaces creating visual dissonance and focusing the eye upon the swimming pool, which "implodes" and "explodes" simultaneously. Visual relationships occur inward to the sculpture and outward to the sensuous forms of the outer landscape.

The design is paradigmatic. The abstract treatment of the horizontal ground plane, the treatment of trees as pieces of living sculpture, the expansion of space by the use of fluid lines, and the principle of borrowed scenery were all adopted at a variety of scales. Even very small and modest gardens could use all of these principles successfully.

The principles of modernism were sometimes handled in ways that eschewed the use of fluid, abstract forms. Edward Huntsman-Trout's garden in West Los Angeles was "modern" in that it respected the spatial characteristics of the various zones. Stylistically, however, it was a reinterpretation of earlier sensibilities, looking back to the simple forms of the Spanish-Mexican garden and recalling Arts and Crafts tenets in its use of local materials. It also reflected its designer's desire to create a garden that appears not to have been designed at all but is entirely appropriate to its setting.

The most advanced houses and gardens developed in this period in the Southland treated the house as a pavilion sitting in the garden. This spatial integration of interior and exterior spaces, which was one of modernism's goals, was achieved more successfully here than anywhere else in the world, using strong geometric cadences and a loose treatment of the landscape.[16] Richard Neutra, for example, believed that modern architecture was universal in nature and that it was the landscape that established the sense of place. Many of his houses seemed to disappear into the garden, an illusion achieved by their siting and by the apparent interpenetration of water features inside the house.

A bolder conjunction of hard and natural materials occurred in the work of the more avant-garde designers. Garrett Eckbo's approach to design was consciously sculptural. Trees and shrubs were used as pieces of sculpture, panels of ground cover were used in a highly architectonic fashion and plants were placed against walls, on screens, and pergolas to create extremely rich, textured environments in which a counterpoint is established between structure and nature. These designs were experimental and were intended to contain the germ of solutions to any landscape design problem.

The use of structures and abstract forms was frequently employed to create visual illusions, drawing the eye of the viewer out into the natural landscape along diagonal sight lines, thereby extending the sense of space. Such designs used abstract elements to reflect and refract forms of the landscape. [17]

Clear and distinct differences are discernible within the different subregions in the West. San Francisco's pattern of small and narrow back gardens produced designs that were to be both used and gazed down upon from the living rooms, which were often one floor above.

As in previous decades, the inherent character of the regional landscape affected the design character of gardens. Those in the San Francisco Bay region were invariably centered around existing trees, whereas the gardens of the Southland were essentially created de novo. In the Pacific Northwest, gardens still appeared to have been carved out of the primeval forest. Decks and screens were used to provide usable areas and to extend the geometry of the house out into the landscape. The design for the Russell house in Medina reflected careful siting in relation to existing trees. An architectonic approach was sometimes adopted in which abstract structure revealed the "true" nature of the landscape by contrast.

By the 1960s, a more restrained and less strident approach had been adopted by many designers. Gar-

dens frequently relied less upon built structure than upon a carefully arranged sequence of many shrubs and decorative trees. Unlike the Grants' approach, these gardens explored a rich vocabulary of color, form, and texture but shared their concern for creating garden spaces principally through the use of plants. [18]

A more imaginative attempt to create a new garden mode was made in a garden in Kirkland that manipulated plants in ways derived from England. This is a synthesis of elements from different formal gardens, such as pyramidal yews, a riot of form and color so characteristic of traditional or cottage gardens, and a medieval "flowery mede" attained by using plants that would support light walking, in place of grass.

Other designers continued to find inspiration in the English Picturesque tradition. In a large garden in Pasadena, Ruth Shellhorn complemented a grove of existing trees with a collection of new conifers and shrubs designed to create a beautifully restrained garden of light and dark with exquisitely graded textures, a superb restatement of the principles of the Picturesque. Miss Shellhorn always sought to create gardens that were essentially a series of "pictures."

The Seventies and Beyond: Contemporary Trends

BY THE 1970S, new gardens were frequently exceedingly small. California's commitment to an outdoor life centered around exercise frequently ensured that a pool, even a modest lap pool, was an essential element of a garden. The Leland Burns garden in Santa Monica contains a room in which the pool occupies the center of the space, defined in this case by walls rendered in subtle variations of peach, with a small number of plants. Other imperatives come to the fore, such as a concern for development on steep hillsides, limitations of water and energy, new levels of self-sufficiency, and broader concern for environmental than for aesthetic issues. A garden in Berkeley is a brilliant and unusual solution for a garden space in the middle of an extremely steep slope. Its "weeping" wall of slump stone suggests a giant Mayan ruin.

This Pasadena garden, designed by Ruth Shellhorn during the twenty-year period between 1965 and 1985, demonstrates an exquisite and subtle use of the pictorial principles of composition, color, and light associated with the English Picturesque movement.

Isabelle Greene's sculptural design for a Montecito garden uses succulent plants in a way that recalls the forms of the water paddies of Indonesia.

113

An acknowledgment of the needs and limitations of a given site has led to the creation of remarkable gardens in areas of the West once thought to be hostile to landscape efforts. Steve Martino created this garden of native plants for the Cliff Douglas home in Mesa, Arizona.

In Mediterranean California, the issue of water has begun to take on a new significance. Santa Barbara County has been the leader in initiating water rationing. Designers have responded to this challenge by using drought-tolerant plants and a variety of other devices to lessen reliance upon imported water. A garden in Montecito, developed on a steep hillside site, presents a poetic solution by recalling the water paddies of Indonesia with a series of concrete walls of different heights enclosing beds of succulents tilted up to avoid a sense of vertigo that would make the garden appear to tip downward. The water-saving

potential of gardens was taken up in the seventies, most notably in a garden created in Berkeley for the Farallones Institute. This garden coupled the use of gray, or slightly dirty, water, a wind-controlled fish tank, and different ways of capturing solar energy to enable a family of four to survive without reliance upon water, sewage, and energy utility systems. Most of the garden was given over to the cultivation of fruits and vegetables, and to hutches for small animals. The lawn disappeared completely. It remains to be seen whether such ideas will become popular. Much will depend upon the willingness of municipalities to change current restrictions so that such innovative approaches could be used on a widespread scale.

Many designers in the southwestern region began to address similar issues of water conservation and of regional appropriateness by looking back to Spanish precedents, and to the work of earlier designers, including those associated with the Rio Grande style, and the Pueblo Revival, and to Frank Lloyd Wright at Taliesin West (1938). In New Mexico designers and plant growers such as Judith Phillips and H. Baker Morrow have extended the work of the Rio Grande school. Morrow's designs are a balance of formal and informal elements, using stonework, trickling water, and such native plants as oaks and Mexican elders. Small green areas are set around the houses, while the outer parts of the gardens are xeriscapes of native plants.

In Arizona, the landscape designer Steve Martino inspired by earlier precedents—such as Frank Lloyd Wright's Taliesin West, the Jokake Inn, and Tangere Verde Inn—developed a design mode of shaded and colorful gardens using native plants. His subtle use of simple, bold, geometric shapes and the beautiful forms and colors of Sonoran desert plants are a splendid celebration of that landscape, into which the garden appears to be completely integrated visually.

The West Coast region has developed from a frontier whose gardens were classic examples of cultural colonialism to a region whose gardens express a distinct and appropriate lifestyle quite different from that in other regions of the United States. Its modern gardens, especially those of California, have influenced designers in other regions, marking the passage from a regional appanage influenced by national norms to a self-confident place of influence. Whether this influence can be sustained in the future is uncertain. The cohesiveness of the West Coast garden designers that existed from the forties to the midsixties has been replaced by a plurality of approaches that range from ecological sensitivity at one extreme to self-indulgent triviality at the other. It is to be hoped that, in the future, issues such as the conservation of water and energy, greater self-reliance, and regional appropriateness will be addressed by designers with the same degree of energy, boldness, and imagination displayed in the best eras of this region's rich heritage of gardens. ✒

NOTES

1. For the influence of Loudon and Downing in California, see David Streatfield, "The Evolution of the Southern Landscape I: Settling into Arcadia," *Landscape Architecture* 66 (1976): 45–46, 79. For their influence in the Pacific Northwest, especially Oregon, see Wallace Kay Huntington, "Victorian Architecture," in *Space, Style, and Structure: Building in Northwest America,* ed. Thomas Vaughan and Virginia Guest Ferriday (Portland: Oregon Historical Society, 1974), 1, pp. 261–301.

2. References to John McLaren's gardening activities at El Cerrito, Hillsborough, are contained in his daybooks and diaries in the John McLaren Collection in the San Francisco Room, San Francisco Public Library.

3. *The Pacific Rural Press* 7 (1874), May 30.

4. Arthur T. Johnson, *California: An Englishman's Impressions of the Golden State* (London: Stanley Paul, 1913), p. 27.

5. In the Pacific Northwest, E. O. Schwagerl (Seattle) and L. M. Theilan (Portland) were trained as landscape architects. In San Francisco in the midteens, Horace Cotton, Willa Cloys Carmack, and Howard Gilkey all practiced as residential landscape architects. In addition, the McLaren Nursery provided design services. The artist-landscape designer Bruce Porter designed several gardens on the San Francisco Peninsula. The architects Willis Polk and Lewis Hobart also designed a number of significant gardens. In Los Angeles, Wilber D. Cook, Jr., and George Hall were the only landscape designers who had been trained as landscape architects. The Beverly Hills Nursery, the Armstrong Nursery, and Howards Nursery provided design services. In addition, David Farquhar, Myron Hunt, Elmer Grey, and Irving Gill designed numerous gardens.

6. Bruce Porter, Introduction to Porter Garnett, *Stately Homes of California* (Boston: Little, Brown, 1915), pp. ix–xv. Bruce Porter's most significant garden design was Filoli, San Mateo. See Diane Kostial McGuire, *Gardens of America: Three Centuries of Design* (Charlottesville: Thomasson-Grant, 1989), pp. 118–123.

7. Herbert D. Croly, "The California Country House," pp. 24–29.

8. Keeler, *The Simple Home,* p. 16.

9. J. Waldron Gillespie took his architect, Bertram

Grosvenor Goodhue, on a year-long trip throughout the Mediterranean Basin to search out possible models for El Fureidis. They were especially impressed by the terraced water gardens of Persia. Gillespie had planted extensive groves of palm trees and pine trees before construction of the house began. *House and Garden* 3 (September 1903): 53–62.

10. In Los Angeles and Pasadena: Charles Gibb Adams, Ralph Cornell, Katherine Bashford, Lucile Council, A. E. Hanson, Edward Huntsman-Trout, Paul Thiene, and Florence Yoch; Santa Barbara: Ralph Stevens, Lockwood de Forest, Jr., and Francis Underhill; San Francisco Bay region: Horace Cotton, Willa Cloys Carmack, Howard Gilkey, and Floyd Herbert Mick; Portland: L. M. Theilan; Seattle: F. C. Cole, F. Fabi, and Otto Holmdahl.

11. The moving of semimature and mature trees has a long history going back to the beginning of civilization. It was introduced to the West Coast early in the twentieth century by William Hertrich, curator of the Huntington Botanical Gardens from 1905 to 1949.

12. The finest example of a Norman-French garden was the elegant service road of the Harvey Mudd estate in Beverly Hills.

13. Charles Gibbs Adams created two large montane wildflower reserves for George Owen Knapp and C. K. G. Billings. Theodore Payne developed an extensive collection of native plants, including a large natural flower meadow for Mrs. Laura K. Knight on her estate in Montecito.

14. Lockwood de Forest was one of the most creative landscape designers practicing in California from the twenties to the early forties. A definitive study of his work has yet to be prepared. See William Frederick Peters, "Lockwood de Forest, Landscape Architect: Santa Barbara, California, 1896–1949," master's thesis, University of California, Berkeley, 1980.

15. A famous photograph of the entrance court with a shadow line on the eaves of the living-room gable echoing the profile of Mount Hood in the distance was, according to John Yeon, a happy accident rather than a deliberate design decision.

16. In particular, see Thornton Ladd's design for Hilltop, Pasadena. Herbert Weisskamp, *Beautiful Homes and Gardens in California,* pp. 154–159.

17. The work of Garrett Eckbo and Robert Royston especially contain these qualities.

18. The qualities are especially evident in the work of Robert Chittock in Seattle and the surrounding area. See also the work of Barbara Fealy.

BIBLIOGRAPHY

Angier, Belle Sumner. *The Garden Book of California.* San Francisco: Paul Elder and Company, 1906.

Beatty, Russell. "Greening of the Brown Sward." *Pacific Horticulture* 49 (1988): 30–39.

Boesiger, W., ed. *Richard Neutra: 1950–60. Buildings and Projects.* New York: Frederick A. Praeger, 1959.

Braunton, Ernest. *The Garden Beautiful in California: A Practical Manual for All Who Garden.* Los Angeles: Cultivators Publishing Co., 1915.

Brown, Thomas. "California Mission Gardens." *Pacific Horticulture* 49 (1988): 3–11.

Butterfield, Harry M. "The Introduction of Eucalyptus to California." *Madroño* 3 (1935): 149–154.

———. "The Introduction of Acacias into California." *Madroño* 4 (1938): 177–182.

———. "History of Ornamental Horticulture in California." *California Horticultural Society Journal* 26 (1965): 47–50.

———. "European Sources of Ornamental Plants in California." *California Horticultural Society Journal* 26 (1965): 109–112.

———. "Some Pioneer Nurseries in California." *California Horticultural Society Journal* 27 (1966) I: 70–77; II: 101–108; 28 (1967) III: 132–138.

———. "Some Old Homes and Estates in California." *California Horticulture Journal* 30 (1969): 90–94.

Byne, Mildred Stapley, and Arthur Byne. *Spanish Gardens and Patios.* Philadelphia: Lippincott, 1922.

Chase, J. John. "Artist and Earthscape: The Native Plant Palette Artfully Applied." *Landscape Architecture* 79 (1989): 64–68.

Church, Thomas D., Grace Hall, and Michael Laurie. *Gardens Are for People.* 2d rev. ed. New York: McGraw-Hill, 1983.

Church, Thomas. *Your Private World: A Study of Intimate Gardens.* San Francisco: Chronicle Books, 1969.

Croly, Herbert D. "The California Country House." *Architect and Engineer* 7 (1906): 24–29.

DeForest, Elizabeth. "Old Santa Barbara Gardens." *Pacific Horticulture* 38 (1977–78): 31–36.

Dobyns, Winifred Starr. *California Gardens.* New York: Macmillan, 1931.

Eckbo, Garrett. *Landscape for Living.* New York: Architectural Record with Duell, Sloan, and Pearce, 1950.

Farallones Institute. *The Integral Urban House: Self-Reliant Living in the City.* San Francisco: Sierra Club Books, 1979.

Garnett, Porter. *Stately Homes of California.* Boston: Little, Brown, 1915.

Grant, John, and Carol L. Grant. *Trees and Shrubs for Pacific*

Northwest Gardens. Seattle: S. McCaffrey, 1943.

———. *Garden Design Illustrated.* Seattle: University of Washington Press, 1954.

Gross, Susan Jane. "The Gardens of Edward Huntsman-Trout." Master's thesis, California State Polytechnic University, Pomona, California, 1976.

Hanson, A. E. *An Arcadian Landscape: The California Gardens of A. E. Hanson, 1920–1932,* ed. David Gebhard and Sheila Lynds. Los Angeles: Hennessey and Ingalls, 1985.

Harvey, Robert R. "Documenting a Victorian Landscape in the Midwest." *Bulletin of the Association for Preservation Technology* 9 (1977) 73–99.

Hedrick, U. P. *A History of Horticulture in America to 1860.* New York: Oxford University Press, 1950.

Helphand, Kenneth I., and Nancy D. Rottle. "Cultivating charm, in the Northwest's first female landscape architecture firm, created a lasting legacy at Deepwood Gardens." *Garden Design* 7 (1988): 26–38, 88.

Hertrich, William. *The Huntington Botanical Gardens: 1905–1949. Personal Recollections of William Hertrich, Curator Emeritus.* San Marino: The Huntington Library, 1949.

Keeler, Charles E. *The Simple Home.* San Francisco: Paul Elder, 1904.

Lockwood, Alice G. B. *Gardens of Colony and State: Gardens and Gardeners of the American Colonies and of the Republic before 1840.* Vols. 1 & 2. New York: Charles Scribner's Sons, 1931.

Lutsko, Ron. "Designing the Dry Garden: Perennials for Sun." *Pacific Horticulture* 50 (1989): 30–38.

Makinson, Randall L. *Greene and Greene: Architecture as Fine Art.* Salt Lake City: Peregine Smith, 1977.

McLaren, John. *Gardening in California: Landscape and Flower.* 3d ed. San Francisco: A. M. Robertson, 1924.

Messenger, Pam-Anela. "Thomas Church: His Role in American Landscape Architecture." *Landscape Architecture* 67 (1977): 128–139, 170.

———. "El Novillero Revisited." *Pacific Horticulture* 43 (1982): 23–29.

Montgomery, William. "Studies in Southern California: Landscape History Applied to the Development of the Rancho Los Cerritos." Master's thesis, California State Polytechnic University, Pomona, 1975.

Murmann, Eugene C. *California Gardens.* Los Angeles: Eugene C. Murmann, 1915.

Padilla, Victoria. *Southern California Gardens: An Illustrated History.* Berkley: University of California Press, 1961.

Panich, Paula, and Nora Burba Trusson. *Desert Southwest Gardens.* New York: Bantam, 1990.

Shinn, Charles. *Pacific Rural Handbook, containing brief and practical essays and endnotes on the cultivation of trees, vegetables, and flowers adapted to the Pacific Coast. Also hints on home and farm improvements.* San Francisco: Dewey and Co., 1878.

Streatfield, David C. "The Evolution of the Southern California Landscape I: Settling into Arcadia." *Landscape Architecture* 66 (1976): 39–46, 78.

———. "The Evolution of the California Landscape II: Arcadia Compromised." *Landscape Architecture* 66 (1976): 117–126, 170.

———. "The Evolution of the California Landscape III: The Great Promotions." *Landscape Architecture* 67 (1977): 229–239, 272.

———. "The Evolution of the California Landscape IV: Suburbia at the Zenith." *Landscape Architecture* 67 (1977): 417–424.

———. "Thomas Church and the California Garden, 1929–1950." *Festschrift: A Collection of Essays on Architectural History.* Salem: Northern Pacific Coast Society of Architectural Historians, 1978, 68–75.

———. "Landscape Design in Washington." In *A Guide to Architecture in Washington State: An Environmental Perspective,* edited by Sally B. Woodbridge, Roger Montgomery, and David Streatfield. Seattle: University of Washington Press, 1980.

———. "Echoes of England and Italy: 'On the Edge of the World': Green Gables and Charles Greene." *Journal of Garden History* (1982): 377–398.

———. "'Paradise' on the Frontier: Victorian Gardens on the San Francisco Peninsula." *Garden History* 12 (1984): 58–80.

———. "The Garden at Casa del Herrero." *Antiques* 130 (1986): 286–293.

Vaughan, Thomas, and R. Virginia Guest Ferriday (eds.). *Space, Style and Structure. Buildings in Northwest America.* Vols. 1 & 2. Portland, Oregon, Historical Society, 1974.

Weisskamp, Herbert. *Beautiful Homes and Gardens in California.* New York: Harry N. Abrams, 1964.

Wickson, E. J. *California Nurserymen and the Plant Industry, 1850–1910.* Los Angeles: The California Association of Nurserymen, 1910.

Yoch, James J. *Landscaping the American Dream: The Gardens and Film Sets of Florence Yoch, 1890–1972.* New York: Harry M. Abrams/Sagapress, 1989.

R. & J. FARQUHAR
& Co.
6 AND 7 SOUTH MARKET ST.
—BOSTON—

FARQUHAR'S
PAEONY FLOWERED
DAHLIAS
$2.00 per Dozen
$12.00 per 100

Plants of American Gardens

❧❧

Peggy Cornett Newcomb

❧ *It is easy to overlook the obvious. In writing of American garden history many social, artistic, and cultural issues are considered and analyzed. Plants, the most essential factor in a garden, have their history, too.*

In the early years of ornamental gardening, settlers and colonists often relied on Europe for plants and style, perhaps finding some comfort in old ways and familiar sights and scents. This tendency continued into the early nineteenth century, when exploration of the new lands of America as well as foreign realms yielded new and exciting—even exotic— plants. Economic conditions allowed for trade in plants, and nurseries began increasingly to appear. New technology developed, as Keith Crotz explains in "Science and Technology in American Gardens," which made the transport and "improvement" of plants easier, cheaper, and more common. Also, as Elisabeth Woodburn shows, in "American Horticultural Books," a literature developed that both promoted ornamental gardening and offered instruction in it. Various organizations were established to bring together people interested in gardening and horticulture. These, in turn, sponsored shows that themselves promoted new plant introductions and experimentation.

Flower gardens, and their plants, have undergone many transformations over the last century and on into this one, all the while demonstrating a way of gauging the tone and temperament of the time. Whether formal beddings in the strict geometrical fashion of the staid Victorians or a more relaxed, naturalistic garden in more recent times, the flower garden has been not only a place of retreat, recreation, and enjoyment but has reflected varying degrees of sophistication and knowledge of plants. In addition, our flower gardens have chronicled a delightful and ancient way of finding for ourselves a place in the "wilderness." ❧

THE FLOWERS found in early American gardens have unique histories capable of filling volumes. In the traditional gardens of the eighteenth and early nineteenth centuries, Americans of European origin generally looked back across the Atlantic for their plant sources. They studied Old World techniques and patterned their gardens after early, rather formal styles. But flower gardening, like everything else during the early 1800s, would change dramatically with the influx of new discoveries and ideas that entered the scene from all parts of the world. Explorations of the Orient, pan-tropical regions, and North America's Pacific Northwest brought new and unusual plants into the trade. Fashions came and went, often dictating the types of plants most desired.

A number of distinct gardening styles determined the types of flowers chosen, from the florists' highly refined cultivated varieties, or cultivars, to the wildflowers of the surrounding countryside. This look at a selection of both native and cultivated plants popular from the late eighteenth through the twentieth century incorporates many of the most evident trends or patterns in the development of flower gardening in America.

A Parade of Florists' Flowers

ALTHOUGH SCIENTIFIC plant breeding on a commercial scale did not evolve until the latter half of the nineteenth century, numerous plants were highly developed and refined by the time they reached American shores in the eighteenth century. Books, periodicals, and advertisements from abroad fostered these images of floral ideals, molded expectations, and inspired the horticulturally inclined despite the inherent difficulties of obtaining viable seeds, bulbs, and plants by means of lengthy and damp transatlantic passage. Even the earliest broadsheets and lists

OPENING ILLUSTRATION:
Richly colored lithographs found in late-nineteenth-century catalogues and periodicals enticed American gardeners with such flowers as the double dahlia, the standard by which many double forms of flowers were measured.

offered by seed merchants in America promised many of the latest and most coveted forms available in Europe.

Centuries of cultivation, combined with the careful selection of choice sports by keen growers or "florists," resulted in waves of plant crazes. Tulipomania, perhaps history's best-known plant madness, could not have had the same impact in America as it did in Europe, where it originated and became a passion among collectors during the mid-seventeenth century. Yet the ripple of this phenomenon persisted in American literature through the nineteenth century. Though criteria for a fine garden tulip (*Tulipa gesneriana*) changes through time, generally the variegated or striped forms caused the greatest excitement. The manner in which the richly colored petals were streaked, feathered, or penciled defined their quality and determined their rarity. Appropriately called "Bizarres," these variegated sorts arose by chance through intensive cultivation of solid-colored sorts, or "breeders," often grown from sets or seed. This process, which actually constituted a weakening of the bulb by growing it in poor soils, could take from one to twenty years. Parrot tulips, which have not only variegated but also heavily fringed petals, grew in popularity during the early 1800s and were favorites of such tulip fanciers as Thomas Jefferson.

But dabbling with tulips was not merely a pastime of the well-to-do. As diary accounts reveal, even humble craftsmen, such as Chesapeake clockmaker and silversmith William Faris, grew tulips with a passion, developing and naming their own varieties. The availability of "all sorts of tulip seed," as listed in a 1786 Maryland journal, suggests a general interest in and market for growing "breeder" tulips for the purpose of achieving a distinctly unique form.[1]

This tulip obsession in America was encouraged by massive public displays such as a planting of over six hundred cultivars in the Linnaean Botanic Garden, on Long Island, in 1845. The finer tulips were still considered quite costly by the mid-1800s, although lists of "cheap" tulips appeared in the century's latter half.

Few of these prized tulips exist in commerce today. Many garden historians consider the mixed Rem-

striped with two colors; Bizarres or bizards, flowers irregularly striped with three or more different colors; picotees (from the French *piquettes*), flowers spotted with scarlet, red, purple, and so on, or bordered with a dark, narrow margin on a pale ground; and finally painted-ladies, with petals red or purple on the upper side and white underneath.

The popularity of these forms shifted through the decades. In 1754 Philip Miller noted in *The Gardener's Dictionary* that although picotees were considered foremost in the past, "at present" the flakes were most favored by florists.[3] By 1806 Bernard M'Mahon observed in *The American Gardener's Calendar* that the bizards seemed preferred to the flakes. Picotees resumed supremacy in the 1840s, by which time their

The variegated and deeply fringed petals of parrot tulips captivated eighteenth- and nineteenth-century American gardeners.

brandt sorts currently available to be poor approximations of the once vast array of "Bizarres." A twentieth-century shift toward the solid pastels partially explains this situation: the virally induced striping can actually spread disease to solid-colored forms, making it unwise to grow both types in close proximity. Holland bulb growers are therefore reluctant to risk the infection of whole crops.[2]

Dianthus, another group of plants refined by the hands of the florists, likewise intrigued an American audience. Many popular garden species exist in this genus, including *Dianthus chinensis* (China pink), *D. barbatus* (sweet William), *D. plumarius* (cottage pink), and *D. Caryophyllus* (clove gilliflower or carnation). Grown since medieval times, this last species, the fragrant garden carnation, evolved, much like the tulip, into several distinct forms. Florists eventually distinguished four classes: flakes, flowers boldly

Like tulips, striped forms of *Dianthus* were considered choice both here and abroad. This one was among the type known as "Bizarres."

121

thin band of color was more refined along the smooth petal edge.

Although many border carnations were lost in the flurry of Victorian bedding plants, the tender sorts, first improved in France, evolved into the cut-flower carnation grown under glass today. This became a major American industry beginning in the 1880s and the first American Carnation Society gathered in Philadelphia in 1891.

The nineteenth century witnessed the entrance of the chrysanthemum, *Chrysanthemum sinensis* X *indicum,* into the realm of the florists. Originally from China, where they had been cultivated for centuries, three types of chrysanthemum were imported into Europe in 1789: a purple, a white, and a violet. Of the three, only the purple survived and hence became known as 'Old Purple.' By 1820 fifteen cultivars had been imported from China. According to Charles M. Hovey, of Boston, Massachusetts, the first chrysanthemum arrived in the United States around 1805 or 1806, although others put the introduction of 'Old Purple' at 1798.

The center of chrysanthemum seed production and plant breeding had moved to the island of Jersey by the 1830s, and the first National Chrysanthemum Society in Britain was formed in 1846. That same year Robert Fortune brought the Chus'an daisy back from his travels in China. This would become the parent of the pompom cultivars so popular in France during the mid-nineteenth century. The in-curved, quilled, and feathered types from China were superseded by the shaggy, reflexed Japanese cultivars brought back from Fortune's fourth journey to the Orient, in 1861.

Initially, the problem with chrysanthemum culture in America resulted from the plant's habit of late flowering, rendering their blossoms extremely vulnerable to the season's first freezes, especially in the northern states. Many early-nineteenth-century instructions on chrysanthemum cultivation specified leaving the plants in open ground until frost, then lifting and potting for the "sitting room" while flowering, and finally returning the roots to the ground or the cellar over winter.

Hardier, outdoor strains were developed in France by the 1880s. With the advent of early-blooming forms, chrysanthemums gained popularity in America. Soon their development in the United States would outpace that in Europe. By 1888, Peter Henderson would exclaim, "Next to the rose, no plant is now so popular. . . ."[4] A National Chrysanthemum Society was formed in America the following year by a group of commercial growers.

At the beginning of the twentieth century, the chrysanthemum developed in several directions—as a cut-flower, potted plant, and garden flower. September-blooming cultivars entered the market by 1914, widening the appeal of the "Queen of Autumn."

Many annual flowers also became the object of the florists' attentions. China aster, *Callistephus chinensis,* was introduced into England and France in the 1780s by a Jesuit missionary who discovered the single, purple-flowered plants growing in a field near Peking. Germany became the western center of China aster seed production and breeding during the early 1800s and these plants, which were introduced into America during this period, were commonly called German asters.

By the 1860s asters were considered indispensable in parterres and carpet beds as well as mixed borders. Their late season of bloom made them particularly desirable. In 1865 James Vick commented on their wide popularity:

> No class of flowers has been so much improved within the past twenty years as this splendid genus, and none has advanced so rapidly in popular favor. They are now as double as the Chrysanthemum or the Dahlia, and almost as large and showy as the Peony, and constitute the principal adornment of our gardens during the autumn months.[5]

Distinct forms from this period included reflexed types ('Truffaut's Peonia-flowered Perfection'), double imbricated types ('New Rose'), and dwarf forms ('Dwarf Chrysanthemum' and 'Dwarf Pyramidal Bouquet'). It was not uncommon to find the chrysanthemum, rose, peony, and dahlia used as descriptive images for many sorts of flowers throughout the nine-

N.° 327

Pub by W. Curtis S.ᵗ Geo: Crefcent Feb. 1. 1796

By the turn of the nineteenth century, chrysanthemums had begun to arrive from China in European and American gardens. *Chrysanthemum indicum* was one of the first of these flowers to be imported.

teenth century. Indeed in many illustrations it is often difficult to discern which kind of flower is actually depicted.

Changes in gardening styles and tastes led to a preference for the looser-growing, branching types of China aster developed in the late 1800s. Improved forms introduced at this time included Semple and Vick's branching asters developed by American breeders.

Decline in the popularity of China asters occurred not as a result of the caprices of taste, but from the onset of two devastating diseases during the early twentieth century: wilt (caused by soil- and seed-borne fungus of the genus *Fusarium*); and yellows (a virus spread by a species of leaf hopper). These diseases plagued the seed industry until resistant strains were developed by breeders in the 1920s and 1930s. Although China asters still exist in gardens today, they have never regained their former status.

"The single is pretty, but the double is splendid . . . ,"
ROLAND GREEN, *Treatise . . . ,* 1828

T HE NOTION that double flowers were the choicest, which was certainly a preoccupation with the florists, seems to have been an obsession that developed quite early. The seventeenth- and eighteenth-century herbals and gardening dictionaries of John Parkinson, John Gerard, and Philip Miller all made special note of double forms, many of which have vanished today. The fact that many could be maintained only through asexual means such as cuttings or root divisions made their occurrence rare and their perpetuation difficult, since seeds could be stored, exchanged, transported, and passed down more easily. So if interest in certain double forms waned, their demise from cultivation was almost surely imminent.

The obvious appeal of the doubles was their showier, more dramatic appearance. In many instances, the additional petals also created a more intense fragrance. Furthermore, because these forms were also sterile, and thus not in the business of producing seed, they bloomed more prolifically over longer periods of time.

Among the many double forms of bulbs and corms that were favored over their single counterparts, into the twentieth century, was the Persian ranunculus.

References to double forms exist throughout the literature of the eighteenth and nineteenth centuries. Lists of double ranunculus, anemones, hyacinths, poppies, pinks, balsams, and later, dahlias, were endless. Even double tulips were considered choice by some and offered "in sorts" by M'Mahon in the early nineteenth century, though he deemed them monstrosities.

The rare occurrence of many double flowers enhanced their desirability. Joseph Breck described the double dame's rocket, *Hesperis matronalis,* as uncommonly fragrant and beautiful, though seldom seen because of the difficulty of preserving it. The prized double-flowered snapdragons (*Antirrhinum majus*), developed in the 1880s, seem to exist now only in the imagination, as today the infertile strains are unlikely to be maintained by cuttings.

Likewise, double scarlet lychnis or Maltese cross is quite scarce today and a double-white form has likely vanished from cultivation. Though illustrations of double lychnis are rare, the earliest rendering can be found in Parkinson. Also known as nonesuch, flower of Constantinople, and Jerusalem cross, this flower has been cultivated since the Crusades. Philip Miller noted that the *"Lychnis chalcedonica, flore pleno miniato . . . is only propagated by parting the Roots, or planting the Cuttings of its Flower stem. . . ."*[6] Joseph Breck repeated Miller's advice one hundred years later and added that it was "one of the most splendid decorations of the border."[7] The double-white and double-scarlet lychnis, both equally admired, were considered superior to the singles because they continued blooming into autumn. Although Bailey's *Standard Cyclopedia of Horticulture* would list double-white lychnis into the 1940s, it appears to have generally disappeared by the 1920s.

Double hollyhocks (*Althaea rosea*) date to the late seventeenth century in America and were quite popular during the 1700s. They could be propagated from seed, and thus their continuation was less precarious, though Miller suggested exchanging seed every three to four years "with some Person of Integrity who lives at a considerable Distance, and is exact to save Seeds from none but double Flowers."[8] Hollyhocks would be taken up by the florists of the mid-nineteenth century, during which time they would be refined even further.

"Old fashioned flowers not to be Discarded"
JOSEPH BRECK, *The Flower Garden,* 1851

WHEN CONSIDERING PLANTS cultivated in American gardens over broad periods of time, the concept of "old-fashioned" becomes a relative term. During the colonial period, ancient Old World

plants—the pinks and sweet William, campanulas and foxglove, rose campion and gallica roses—were regarded as old-fashioned. As flower gardening moved into the 1800s, many of the unimproved flowers became the old standards—globe amaranths, Joseph's coat, love-lies-bleeding, and Marvel of Peru (four o'clocks), for example. By mid-nineteenth century, as the American industrial revolution led to unprecedented "progress" and an overall acceleration in the pace of life, a desire ensued to somehow preserve the old. Flowers that evoked this nostalgia gained greater significance.

By that century's end, old-fashioned flowers gained favor as a reaction against the controlled, bedding-out style of the Victorian era. This longing for the "good old days" when life seemed simpler can best be exemplified in a late-nineteenth-century shift in attitude toward the resilient hollyhock:

> This grand landscape flower will never cease to be a favourite with the artists and the whole of that happy race who love the country, though the florists may solemnly assure us that it has fallen from its high estate.[9]

Joseph Breck viewed this desertion of old favorites by florists and gardeners as folly:

> Of all inconstant lovers, gardeners must surely be the most inconstant. To-day they are at the feet of a Dahlia; to-morrow there is no beauty like a Pansy. . . . We remember when Cape plants were the rage . . . these were thrown aside, and New Holland beauties supplanted them; to be succeeded by the flaunting, or shy and delicate, natives of South America. . . .[10]

Garden writers helped revive interest in many ornamentals through such essays.

Climbing nasturtium (*Tropaeolum majus*), in cultivation since the late sixteenth century and grown in America by the turn of the nineteenth, assumed numerous identities in the comings and goings of garden fashion. Its edible qualities were recognized early and often nasturtium seed was found listed with the vegetables. As the common orange-scarlet forms

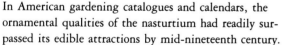

In American gardening catalogues and calendars, the ornamental qualities of the nasturtium had readily surpassed its edible attractions by mid-nineteenth century.

The primitive "medicine hat" form of the wild zinnia (*Zinnia elegans*) hampered the desirability of this flower before mid-nineteenth century double forms evolved.

gave way to the more brilliantly colored Tom Thumb cultivars in the 1850s, these new dwarf, bushy plants became "modern" as carpet-bedding candidates. Forms with variegated foliage drew interest in the 1880s. Eventually a bizarre combination of mottled flowers and variegated leaves was introduced as 'Queen of Tom Thumb Chameleon.' But as old-fashioned gardens returned in popularity, the trailing, informal habit of nasturtiums was once again its main feature. Likewise, its edible qualities returned to the forefront, as the following notice in David Landreth's 1914 catalogue mentions:

We call the attention of table epicures to Nasturtium sandwiches, the effect being most novel, and to the palate most delicious, both greens and flowers being used. [11]

Although introduced as late as 1796, zinnias (*Zinnia elegans*) seem always to have carried the reputation of "old maid of the garden." [12] During the first half of the nineteenth century, this coarse flower with plain scarlet and crimson blossoms persisted reluctantly in the trade. With the advent of double types in the late 1850s, enthusiasm for its possibilities increased. Charles Hovey observed in 1864 that, although still improving "under the hands of skilled cultivators . . . there is no reason to suppose it will not in time give us as great a variety as the dahlia."[13] Dwarf, double forms did arise to enter the ranks of bedding-out plants, but their ungainly or unattractive habit and unreliable colors from seed rendered their value questionable in highly controlled situations. Giant or mammoth strains entered the trade by the late 1880s, allowing the zinnia's ungainly character full expression. This branching, freely growing flower delighted the creators of the "old-fashioned border" during the early twentieth century. But as late as 1929 we are reminded of the zinnia's earlier reputation. As Hume observed, "Today it has grown forth into the prize and pride of many a garden . . . gorgeous and self-assured, new formed, new faced, new named, its despised position of former years entirely forgotten."[14]

The culture and development of sweet peas, *Lathyrus odorata,* exemplifies this tension between the old and the new coming full circle. The earliest form introduced into England—in 1699 from Sicily—was weedy and small-blossomed, distinguished primarily by its sweet fragrance. The flowers remained small until the mid-nineteenth century; distinct forms selected in white, purple, black-purple, striped, and a reddish-pink bicolor known as 'Painted Lady.' The appearance of 'Blue Hybrid' and 'Scarlet Invincible' in the 1860s drew the interest of American seedsmen, such as James Vick and Peter Henderson, who kept abreast of all the latest developments from England. By the turn of the twentieth century, the sweet pea had assumed cult status, more vigorous and substantial forms appearing yearly. The first dwarf form entered the market in 1893 through the Burpee Seed Company in California, and was named 'Burpee's Cupid.' But by this time, reviews of dwarf forms were mixed. During the age of post-Victorian revivals, Louise Beebe Wilder, William Robinson, Gertrude Jekyll, and others longed for the old hedge of sweet peas, which, unlike their offspring, could still fill the air with a sweet, nostalgic fragrance.

Climbers, Twiners, and Scramblers

VINES WERE CONSIDERED an adjunct to every garden throughout the eighteenth and nineteenth centuries and into the twentieth. They were grown to cover arbors and pergolas, to provide shade and to screen unsightly objects and areas. The Victorians considered vines especially useful to frame windows, climb sides of houses, and cover architectural features deemed harsh or unpleasing. Both native and imported vines were cultivated. M'Mahon's 1806 *Calendar* suggested collecting the native *Wisteria frutescens* from the wild and introducing it into gardens. This woody perennial climber, formerly called *Glycine frutescens,* was commonly known as "cluster-flowering glycine" and called "Carolina kidney bean tree" by Lady Skipwith, who grew it in her

By the beginning of the twentieth century, sweet peas had attained cult status in the flower-gardening world.

Plate II

Clematis

128

OPPOSITE:
Both native and exotic vines were admired for their beauty, fragrance, and architectural usefulness beyond the Victorian period. The clematis, shown here, is still extremely popular as the twentieth century nears its close.

The heady fragrance and luxuriant growth of this early-nineteenth-century introduction from Asia drew attention away from many less invasive native species of wisteria.

southern Virginia garden during the late eighteenth century.

Other prized, indigenous perennial vines included coral honeysuckle (*Lonicera sempervirens*), Carolina jasmine (*Gelsemium sempervirens*), perennial pea (*Lathyrus latifolius*), and virgin's bower (*Clematis virginiana*). The trumpet creeper, *Campsis radicans* (previously *Bignonia radicans*), with its magnificent trumpet-shaped orange-scarlet flowers, was regarded as extremely ornamental. Even poison ivy, *Rhus toxicodendron*, admired by early botanists and plant hunters, was given high praise by Joseph Breck who, in 1851, wrote that it "would be desirable for covering walls, trees, etc., were it not for its poisonous qualities."[15]

In addition to the nasturtiums and sweet peas mentioned earlier, other annual vines found in gardens since the late eighteenth century include various types of flowering beans such as scarlet runner (*Phaseolus coccineus*) and hyacinth bean or "black-seeded dolichos" (*Dolichos Lablab*). Morning glories such as cypress vine (*Ipomoea quamoclit*) and curious vines such as the balsam apple (*Momordica Balsamina*), with their strange, succulent, bright-orange seed pods, attracted many admirers.

Fragrance, always a sought-after quality in flowers

grown in early American gardens, was part of the attraction of many invasive Asian vines imported during the 1800s. *Lonicera japonica,* the Japanese honeysuckle, was freely recommended in gardening magazines and books. The introduction of Chinese and Japanese wisteria, with their heavily perfumed, luxuriant, purple flower clusters, caused quite a sensation during the early nineteenth century. A white-flowering form, brought to England by Robert Fortune, had found its way into American gardens by the 1860s. The vine's rampant growth habit seemed to enhance the fascination further, as evident in Breck's description of his own planting of Chinese wisteria:

> They are planted against a bank wall, on the south side, and run in and out of it at pleasure, sending out long branches in every direction, making free with all the trees in the neighborhood, and running at random in a strange manner.[16]

The steady march of these foreign vines from the neighborhoods out across the countryside attests to their wide popularity in the past century.

Cultivating Natives—Naturalizing the Tamed

Is it because they are indigenous, that we should reject them? . . . What can be more beautiful than our Lobelias, Orchis', Asclepias', and Asters . . . Solidagos and Hibiscus' . . . Violas, Rudbeckias and Liatris'; with our charming Limadorum, fragrant Arethusa and a thousand other lovely plants, which if introduced, would grace our plantations, and delight our senses?[17]

WHEN BERNARD M'MAHON made these observations at the turn of the nineteenth century, he was making a case for a naturalistic movement in this country to parallel that in England. But here the land was too new and the concept too radical. Americans wanted their "foreign trifles" from abroad as reminders of Old World civility and refinement. In England, with its countryside tamed for centuries, the notion of creating wild places seemed appealing. So, while Americans grew hollyhocks in their cultivated spaces, Philip Miller suggested intermixing them in "large Wilderness-borders or Avenues, [where they might] afford an agreeable Prospect during their season of flowering."[18]

As a result of the great expeditions into the western regions of America by plant hunters such as Lewis and Clark and David Douglas, many new and unusual plants began arriving in American gardens by the early nineteenth century. Often these natives took a circuitous route through Europe and Britain before returning to their country of origin. Such was the case with many of the perennial mainstays of the garden, such as purple coneflower, *Echinacea purpurea,* as well as the "California annuals," including clarkia (*Clarkia pulchella*), gilia (*Gilia sp.*), and California poppy (*Eschscholzia californica*). In 1835, Charles M. Hovey wrote that the native plants of the northwestern coast discovered by David Douglas on the Columbia River "will probably in a few years take the place of many of the old varieties, which scarcely deserve to be cultivated."[19] This prediction never proved to be as sweeping as Hovey thought at the time because of the eventual discovery that these western natives often performed better in the moist, English climate

PETER HENDERSON & CO.'S CATALOGUE OF SEEDS. 25

Phlox Drummondii.
A beautiful assortment.
Page 32.

Many flowers native to America found their way into American gardens through a circuitous route via the botanical gardens of Europe and Britain during the early nineteenth century. *Phlox Drummondii* is an example of such a well-traveled plant.

than in the eastern regions of North America. But nevertheless, catalogues of the nineteenth century attest to a strong interest in these new flowers.

Drummond's phlox (*Phlox Drummondii*), discovered in Texas by Thomas Drummond in the 1830s, intrigued both British and American gardeners soon after its introduction. *Curtis' Botanical Magazine* carried a lengthy description of this flower and its ill-fated discoverer (who died during his last expedition) by Sir William J. Hooker, the recipient of Drummond's last shipment of seeds in 1835. This annual

"NATURALIZING" HARDY BULBS
FOR PERMANENT EFFECTS IN
LAWNS AND GARDENS.

Beautiful and permanent effects may be obtained by planting hardy bulbs in groups and masses on the lawn, in shady nooks, where they find a congenial and permanent home, flowering abundantly in their season, and requiring little or no care after being planted. This mode of planting is termed "naturalizing," and is now generally followed in Europe. It adds a charm to tangled and half-wild places, heightens the natural effects of light and shade, and imparts a natural grace and beauty to the scene. The following are admirably adapted for this purpose:

Anemones, Apennina, Blanda and Hepatica. *Partial shade.*

Allium Moly. *Open and sunny position.*

Bulbocodium. *Partial shade.*

Camassia. *Shady woods.*

Chionodoxa. *Open or shady banks.*

Colchicum. *Open and sunny position.*

Crocus. *Open and sunny places.*

Eranthis (Winter Aconite). *Partial shade, under trees, etc.*

Erythronium. *Partial shade.*

Grape and Feather Hyacinths. *Partial.*

Hemerocallis. *Open, sunny, moist.*

Hyacinth. *Sheltered but open.*

Iris Germanica. *Moist rich banks.*

Iris Kæmpferi. *Banks of streams, etc.*

Jonquils. *Open and sunny.*

Liliums. *Various sorts. Open and sunny position.*

Lily of the Valley. *Shady woods.*

Narcissus (Daffodil). *Open or shady.*

Pæonias. *Open and sunny.*

Puschkinia. *Partial shade.*

Scillas. *Shady banks and woods.*

Snowdrops. *Partial shade, under trees.*

Snowflakes. *Open or partial.*

Sternbergias. *Open and sunny.*

Triteleia. *Open and sunny.*

Trillium. *Shady woods.*

Tulips. *Open and sunny.*

Zephyranthes. *Open and sunny.*

"Wild" and "natural" styles of gardening emerged during the early twentieth century, reflecting in part a movement away from Victorian artifice.

phlox was one of the few that found its way into the Victorian carpet beds. This was especially true for many of the dwarf forms developed by the late 1800s. But it was treated best in the mixed borders and open gardens of the early twentieth century.

It was during this period that a "country life" movement, as embodied in the *Country Life in America* magazine, exploded into the American consciousness. This was an idea rooted in the English naturalistic movement of the eighteenth century and redefined by the William Robinson style of gardening at the turn of the twentieth. In 1909, Mrs. Stephen Batson would write in *The Summer Garden of Pleasure*: "Of the many delightful ideas which the closing years of the nineteenth century have restored to the earnest gardener [the most delightful is] the art of making the grass meadow, the wood, and the orchard a part of the garden scheme. . . ."[20] The English wild gardens planted at Wisley and Kew, with their broad sweeps of naturalized narcissus, powerfully inspired a Western audience as periodicals and books of this period overwhelmingly confirm. Lists of bulbs suitable for naturalizing included many vigorous, long-lived daffodils: *Narcissus obvallaris, N. poeticus, N. pallida praecox, N. moschatus,* and the like. The florists' cultivars of hyacinths and tulips were considered out of place, but the grape hyacinth (*Muscari botryoides*) and the spreading Florentine or yellow wood tulip (*Tulipa sylvestris*) were planted in great masses. Other minor bulbs such as wood hyacinths, including English (*Endymion non-scriptus*) and Spanish (*E. hispanicus*) bluebells, and winter aconite (*Eranthis hyemalis*) were recommended for woodlands and under conifers. Plants allowed to naturalize included the greater celandine (*Chelidonium majus*) and even the biennial sweet William (*Dianthus barbatus*).

It might be argued that the advent of the automobile played a role in the appeal of this style of planting, especially on large country estates. Early twentieth-century periodicals even described automobile tours through New England, the Hudson Valley, Long Island, and Morristown, New Jersey, where "ravishing pictures" planted on the countryside could be viewed at a distance from fast-moving vehicles. [21]

But while a vast population busily set about introducing and naturalizing many foreign species, there were others who saw the unadulterated American landscape itself as a garden—one that, sadly, was rapidly disappearing. A century after Bernard M'Mahon appealed to gardeners to look to the meadows and woods around them as a source for their horticultural palettes, Liberty Hyde Bailey would share a similar perspective:

> To most persons the wild flowers are less known than many exotics which have smaller merit, and the extension of cultivation is constantly tending to annihilate them. Here, then, in the informal flower-border, is an opportunity to rescue them . . . a border half full of weeds is handsomer than the average well-kept geranium-bed, because the weeds enjoy growing and the geraniums do not. [22]

The use of native plants as well as introduced plants suitable for wild and informal gardens continues to the present day. The current ecological movement in the face of burgeoning development adds a sense of urgency to the efforts of wildflower societies and conservation groups. But an interest in preserving the native flora can be traced back in our history at least two hundred years.

Likewise, the popularity of refined florists' plants continues to ebb and flow with trends and tastes. The development of countless cultivars of tulips and sweet peas gives way to a vast array of roses, irises, and even rhododendrons. This intense focus, almost to the point of overrefinement of certain plants, has at times distanced them from the average gardener, placing these plants instead among the collections of connoisseurs.

A look back through the centuries at the types of plants grown and admired in American gardens reveals a rich complexity of interests, needs, and tastes. An even closer look at the development of plants reveals ever-improving methods of hybridization, distribution, and marketing—techniques originating during the mid-nineteenth-century Industrial Revolution in America. The push and pull of fashion continues to propel gardeners of all sorts toward the latest novelties depicted in the glossy photographs of slick catalogues mailed to millions of American customers. But at the same time, our "looking back" has grown more refined and sophisticated in the "modern" realm of historic garden restoration. It can only be through careful examination of early documentation—revealed in seed lists, diaries, letters, and botanical illustrations—that we may accurately determine the character of plants from precise periods of American gardening. ❧

NOTES

1. Sarudy, "Eighteenth-Century Gardens of the Chesapeake," p. 154.
2. 'Shirley,' a modern cultivar, is a type whose striping is not virally induced.
3. Miller, *Gardener's Dictionary*, pp. 263–264.
4. Henderson, *Gardening for Pleasure*, p. 147.
5. Vick, *Catalogue*.
6. Miller, *Gardener's Dictionary*, p. 814.
7. Breck, *Flower Garden*, p. 134.
8. Miller, *Gardener's Dictionary*, p. 835.
9. Hibberd, *Amateur's Flower Garden*, p. 134.
10. Breck, *Flower Garden*, p. 28.
11. David Landreth Seed Co., *Landreth's Seeds*, p. 89.
12. Hume, *Gardening in the Lower South*, p. 301.
13. Hovey, "Floricultural Notes," p. 10.
14. Hume, *Gardening in the Lower South*, p. 302.
15. Breck, *Flower Garden*, p. 204.
16. Ibid., p. 307.
17. M'Mahon, *Calendar*, p. 78.
18. Miller, *Gardener's Dictionary*, p. 835.
19. Hovey, *American Gardener's Magazine and Register*, p. 102.
20. Batson, *The Summer Garden of Pleasure*, p. 5.
21. "Growing Tulips like Wildflowers," *Country Life in America* 24 (Sept. 1908): 450–452.
22. Bailey, L. H. "Use of Wildflowers in Cultivation," *The House Beautiful* (June 1902): 51.

BIBLIOGRAPHY

Bailey, Liberty Hyde. *The Garden of Pinks.* New York: Macmillan, 1938.

———. *Standard Cyclopedia of Horticulture.* New York: Macmillan, 1939.

Batson, Mrs. Stephen. *The Summer Garden of Pleasure.* Chicago: A. C. McClury, 1909.

Breck, Joseph. *The Flower Garden; or Breck's Book of Flowers.* Boston: John P. Jewett, 1851. Reprint. Guilford, Conn.: Opus Publications, 1988.

Bridgeman, Thomas. *The Florist's Guide.* 3rd ed. New York: C. M. Saxton, 1840.

———. *The Young Gardener's Assistant.* New York: published by the author, 1863.

Buist, Robert. *The American Flower Garden Directory.* New York: C. M. Saxton, 1862.

Coats, Alice M. *Flowers and Their Histories.* London: Adam & Charles Black, 1968.

David Landreth Seed Company. *Landreth's Seeds.* 1914.

Downing, Andrew Jackson, ed. *The Horticulturist.* Vol. 1 (June 1846—June 1847). Albany, NY: Luther Tucker, 1847.

Emsweller, S. L., et al. "The Improvement of Flowers by Breeding." In *Yearbook of Agriculture 1937.* Washington, D.C.: Government Printing Office, 1937.

Fessenden, Thomas G. *The New American Gardener.* 7th ed. Boston: Otis, Broaders. Philadelphia: Thomas, Cowperthwaite, 1845.

Green, Roland. *Treatise on the Cultivation of Ornamental Flowers.* Boston: J. B. Russell, 1828.

Henderson, Peter. *Gardening for Pleasure.* New York: Orange Judd, 1888.

Hibberd, Shirley. *The Amateur's Flower Garden.* London: Groombridge & Sons, 1871. Reprint. Portland, Oreg.: Timber Press, 1986.

Hogg, Thomas. *A Practical Treatise on the Culture of the Carnation.* London: Whittaker & Co., 1839.

Hovey, Charles M. *American Gardener's Magazine and Register of Useful Discoveries* 1. Boston: Hovey, 1835.

———. "Floricultural Notes." *Magazine of Horticulture, Botany, and All Useful Discoveries and Improvements in Rural Affairs,* January 1864.

Hume, H. Harold. *Gardening in the Lower South.* New York: Macmillan Co., 1929.

Leighton, Ann. *American Gardens of the Nineteenth Century: "For Comfort and Affluence."* Amherst, Mass.: University of Massachusetts Press, 1987.

Leighton, Ann. *American Gardens in the Eighteenth Century: "For Use and Delight."* Amherst, Mass.: University of Massachusetts Press, 1976.

M'Mahon, Bernard. *The American Gardener's Calendar,* 1806.

Miller, Philip. *The Gardener's Dictionary.* Reprint of 1754 abridged edition. New York: Wheldon & Wesley, Ltd., 1969.

———. *The Gardener's Dictionary.* 8th ed. London: "printed for the author," 1768.

Morton, James. *Southern Floriculture.* Clarksville, Tenn.: Titus Publishing, 1890.

Rand, Edward Sprague, Jr. *Garden Flowers: How to Cultivate Them.* Boston: Tilton, 1866.

Sarudy, Barbara Wells. "Eighteenth-Century Gardens of the Chesapeake." *Journal of Garden History* 9, no. 3 (1989): 103–159.

Strong, A. B., MD. *The American Flora*; or, *History of Plants and Wild Flowers.* Vols. 1, 2. New York: Green & Spencer, 1848.

Stuart, David, and James Sutherland. *Plants from the Past.* New York: Viking Penguin, 1987.

Vick, James. *Illustrated Catalogue.* 1865.

Science and Technology in American Gardens

❧❧

D. Keith Crotz

❧ *Upon first glance a garden may seem to be the most natural, the most unscientific thing in the world, all plants, soil, and elements. The fact, of course, is that American gardens—and gardeners—are the recipients of almost two centuries of concerted effort to alter, assist, refine, improve, and control nature. The results are both simple and complex, from improved hand tools (which are extensions of the hand) to genetic manipulation. Some of these efforts have resulted in great benefit to both people and nature, as is the case with hoses and sprinklers, bringing water where and when it is needed. Other attempts have had tragic consequences: chemical pesticides and herbicides, huge fire-spitting trimmers, and some aspects of hybridization have proven to be directly or potentially dangerous, as in the case of monospecific staple crops with exact gene pool resources, therefore capable of being eliminated altogether.*

All of the scientific and technological advances (and retreats) have in one way or another spoken of our attitude toward nature and shown what, over the centuries, we have believed a garden is and should be. In more recent times there are trends suggesting that listening to nature and not shouting at it may be the better way to proceed. Contemporary signs imply that science, technology, and nature can have a positve and fruitful working relationship and that it is not only beneficial but preferable to cooperate with natural and biological procedures rather than to impose human schemes on natural processes.

The history of science and technology as applied to the garden in America reflects both the abuses and the great benefit that can be derived from these activities when they are seen as another tool to be used properly and appropriately by the right hands. ❧

SCIENCE AS I SEE IT is mankind's search for the hows and whys of nature. The application of the secrets wrested from the natural world constitutes the realm of technology. Gardeners often take for granted the influence and assistance we receive from both, but much of what we grow and many of the implements that we wield are technologically improved, direct descendants from earlier days.

The first gardens were products of hoes, hands, and strong backs. Between 1600 and 1800, American yards and gardens were touched by little change or technological innovation that resulted from scientific discovery. Certainly the number of new plants available for use in gardens increased as a result of scientific explorations, but methods for garden preparation, maintenance, and harvesting did not change.

Perhaps the first major technological advance to have significant impact on gardening was in the realm of printing. Changes in methods of gardening were very difficult to disseminate to practitioners in colonial America. The laborious setting of type by hand and printing of books a few pages at a time limited access to books to all but the well-to-do. But in the 1830s, stereotyping—the ability to reproduce entire pages of type through a molding process—immediately increased the accessibility of garden books and periodicals. The development of steam-powered printing presses once again increased the production capacity for publications.

Increased printing capabilities were congruent with the greater number of leisure hours. Life was still arduous on the burgeoning continent, but ornamental plants were gaining ground in America and demand for books dealing exclusively with their culture was increasing as was the ease with which they could be obtained. And, while work-simplification

OPENING ILLUSTRATION:
The ease with which the new models of lawnmowers could be operated was often advertised by showing their use by a woman or child (or both!), as in this trade catalogue. Clean, smooth, and close-cut lawns took on an almost moral character in the mid- and late nineteenth century, when they were a sign of domestic bliss and civic pride.

and productivity-enhancing methods were sought by many, printing became a wonderful tool by which manufacturers could create a perceived need for their products through intensive marketing.

The first colonial settlers were amazed by the productive capacity of American soils. Perpetuation of soil productivity by the application of animal manures was of considerable interest to early gardeners. The role and source of nitrogen and its role in plant growth was a very important field of study for scientists in the 1840s. Justus Liebig, a German chemist, published *Organic Chemistry in Its Applications to Agriculture and Physiology* (1840), which was received with great enthusiasm since it combined science with application for an audience that was very aware of problems arising from possible land exhaustion. [1]

Interest in agricultural chemistry had begun to be addressed in the pages of agricultural and horticultural periodicals during the 1830s. Liebig's book appeared at just the right time, as it helped explain processes occurring in the soil. Since 99 percent of living plant tissue is composed of a mere eleven elements, a limiting factor in plant growth and vigor is often the lack or imbalance (or both) of one or more of these elements. Plants also require trace elements, or micronutrients, to remain healthy and productive. Before Liebig's publication, it was not widely known how plants used air, light, and water to grow and produce seeds and fruit. An understanding of soil formation, its chemical constituents, and fertility proved a great boon to gardeners.

During the 1840s, mineral fertilizers such as gypsum, lime, and crushed bone earned acceptance as additives that enhanced soils' value. Superphosphates and artificial manures became available in the 1850s, but they were not commonly used in gardens until the 1880s. [2] While the study of plant nutrition was enhanced, it was not until the twentieth century that soil microbiologists discovered the role of microorganisms in ammoniafication and nitrification.

The study of micronutrients, soil science, and plant biochemistry is still very much at the forefront of research. Work is continuing in an effort to learn why compost promotes plant growth better than a three-part artificial manure. Soil scientists are search-

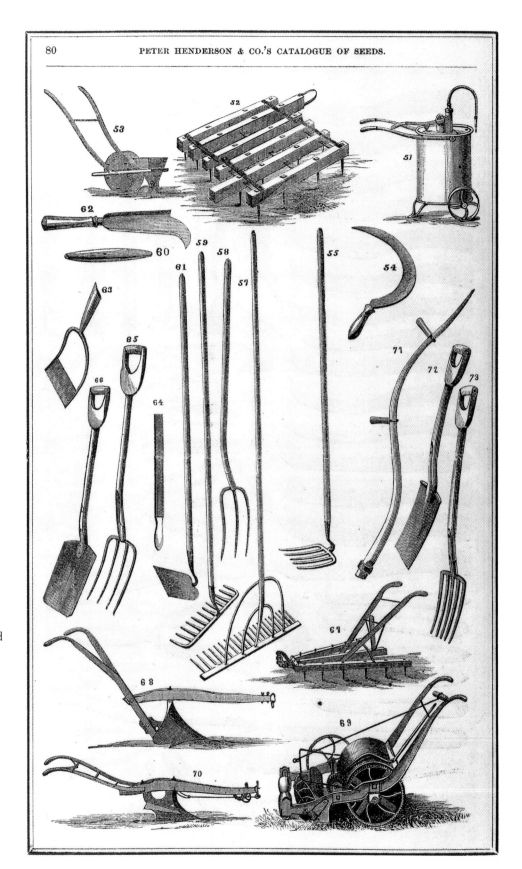

In the nineteenth century, the wide range of tools and machines used for gardening and horticulture provided easier working conditions and focused application for specific tasks. Perhaps in democratic fashion, America did not have regional tools for local conditions, as were prevalent in England, where many counties had their own variations of numerous types of tools.

ing for optimum nutrient combinations for plant growth and development. Researchers want to understand what effect ratios of nitrogen, phosphorous, and potassium have on plants, and what differing nutrient ratios do to the plants' ability to utilize the micronutrients in the soil.

Hand tools in American gardens have changed little from those brought ashore by the Pilgrim fathers in 1620. They were simple and to the point, hoe, rake, spade, fork, shears, knife, and wheelbarrow having been listed as essential by the early horticultural writers. The basic tools entered an era of greater proliferation at the close of the Civil War, after which industrialization made it possible to create specialized articles for the toolshed.

Smaller gardens were most often prepared by turning the ground with a fork or spade, which was time-consuming but ensured the gardener an intimacy with the soil. For larger gardens, horse-drawn equipment—literally hundreds of different plowing and cultivating machines—was available. Even after the invention of the steel plowshare, many plows and cultivators were products for a decidedly regional market, owing to the difficulties of transporting them. Only with the expansion of steam power to rail and water transportation did markets for larger gardening devices gain national attention. Many gardeners obtained their equipment from relatives and friends, ensuring continued employment for the village blacksmith. Little change was seen in the larger tillage devices until after the First World War as the horse was quickly replaced by the internal combustion–powered tractor.

One need only look at the pages of advertisements in the more than two hundred garden periodicals of post–Civil War America to see the expansion of the use of hand tools. The advertising carried all the hype of modern-day products—"scientifically improved," "new and improved," "redesigned and improved"— aimed at securing customers from the ranks of the emerging suburban gardener.

In the 1880's, a new introduction to garden maintenance coincided with suburban development and municipal water systems. Hoses, hose reels, and sprinklers were innovations that no true gardener could be without and were featured prominently in seed catalogs and horticultural periodicals. Sprinklers have evolved from simple wrought-iron devices designed to spin and cover an area with water to seemingly intelligent machines of space-age polymers that can send water in elaborate patterns at the whim of the owner.

One of the greatest technological changes to have an impact on the garden has been the internal combustion engine. No other invention has brought about such profound change on the human race. The first internal combustion engines were produced in the 1830s and gained ground slowly. It was not until 1886 that Gottlieb Daimler invented the "petrol motor," which was lighter and more powerful than those of the previous generation of internal combustion engines and found its way into use for garden implements.

The lawn mower offers a prime example. Before 1830, any expanse known as a lawn was kept cut by wandering sheep or herds of gardeners armed with hand scythes. Lawns were never neat, well-groomed places for taking a leisurely stroll, but rather served as foreground for estates. Edwin Budding, an Englishman employed as a textile-mill engineer, offered the first machines for cutting lawns in 1830. Budding's early advertising announced: "Country gentlemen may find in using my machine themselves, an amusing, useful and healthy exercise."[3]

It took twenty-five years for Budding's mower to become available in America. Henry Winthrop Sargent, of New York, imported the first of them. The smallest of these machines was 12 inches wide, weighed 150 pounds, and was hand and leg powered; the largest available was 42 inches wide, requiring a

OPPOSITE:
The lawn—the suburb's response to the meadow—had become so much a part of domestic life by the turn of the century that implements used for its care were made in whimsical, if not artistic, fashion. The lawn generated its own industry over the years, as this page of watering devices from a 1902 Henderson's catalogue shows.

HENDERSON'S "Siamese" Lawn Sprinkler Attachment

"SIAMESE" ATTACHMENT.

By Using These Several Sprinklers can be operated at one time,

Providing the pressure and volume of water are sufficient. A three-quarter inch hose and thirty to forty pounds pressure will operate three sprinklers; a forty to fifty pound pressure, four sprinklers; with one inch hose and a good pressure, six sprinklers can be operated satisfactorily. This method of watering is valuable for thoroughly saturating large areas of lawn or garden, distributing the water more evenly and thoroughly than can possibly be done with a hose nozzle.

We found the "Water Witch" Lawn Sprinkler (*with spur to stick in the ground*) the best sprinkler for the purpose. One of these sprinklers and the "Siamese" was applied at the end of every twenty-five foot length of hose. PRICE, "Siamese" Attachment for ¾ inch hose, 60c., by mail, 70c.; for 1 inch hose, 75c., by mail, 85c.

For prices of Water Witch Sprinklers see opposite page.

Lawn Sprinkler Carriage.

Can be used with any sprinkler, having a spur to stick in the ground—the carriage enables the sprinkler to be moved without shutting off the water. PRICE, 75c. each.

Brass Hose Nozzle.

Brass with stop cock in the large end, spray rose and straight stem. PRICES, for ½ and ¾ in. hose, 75c.; for 1 in., 90c. Postage, 10c. each extra.

The "Graduating" Spray Nozzle.

Will throw a coarse or a fine spray, a large or a small solid stream. The spray can be closely contracted or made to cover a large area. These results are obtained by revolving it part way round. PRICE, ¾ in., 50c.; 1 in., 60c. Postage, 5c. each extra.

Hudson's Hose Menders.

Practical, simple, perfect. PRICE, per box of 6 tubes, 20 bands and 1 pair pliers, 75c.; or by mail $1.00. (*Give size of hose.*) TUBES, ½ in. 2c.; ¾ in. 3c.; 1 in. 4c. each. BANDS, 20c. per dozen. PLIERS, 30c.; by mail, 35c.

Paragon Hose Nozzle.

It throws either a stream or a flat, fan-shaped sheet spray as desired; splendid for watering lawns and flower beds. For ¾ in. hose, 60c.; postage 5c. each extra.

The "Frog" Lawn Sprinkler.

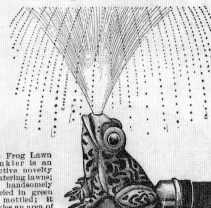

The Frog Lawn Sprinkler is an attractive novelty for watering lawns; it is handsomely enameled in green and mottled; it sprinkles an area of 30 to 40 feet in diam.; fits on ¾ inch garden hose. PRICE, 50c. each, or delivered in U. S., 75c.

Gem Nozzle Holder.

For watering lawns and flower beds. The hose is held firmly and can be adjusted to any elevation in an instant. 25c. each, by mail 30c.

The "Cooper" Brass Hose Mender.

PAT'D SEPT. 22. 96.

Made of thin brass tubing; will not rust or wear out; scarcely decreases the flow of water. Easily applied by any one; simply cut out your bad piece of hose and force the ends of the good hose over the mender until they meet in the centre. No other fastening is required; the barbs will hold it firm, and no matter what strain is put on the hose it will be as good as new at the point mended, and will not leak. PRICE, for hose with ½ in. bore, 7c. each, 75c. doz.; for hose with ¾ in. bore, 7c. each, 75c. doz.; for hose with 1 in. bore, 8c. each, 85c. doz. If wanted by mail, add 5c. per doz., at the single price postage free.

Hydrant Swivel Connection.

Turns in any position, prevents hose from kinking. For ¾ in. hose, 90c., by mail, $1.00. **Hose Reducer.** 1 in. to ¾ (*mailed free*), 35c.

Lightning Hose Coupler.

NO. 2 · NO. 1

Instantly attached or disconnected, no twisting of the hose, no bruising fingers, water-tight. (*State if wanted to replace old couplings, or to be attached to them.*) PRICE, post-paid, per set two pieces, ¾ in., 35c.; faucet attachment extra, 15c.

Florists' and Gardeners' Hose Sprinkler.

A wide face nozzle. The holes are made small and are numerous, so that a copious yet gentle shower is given without washing or packing the soil. PRICE, for ¾ in. hose, 3 in. face, 60c.; 4 in. face, 85c. Postage, 10c. each extra.

Caldwell's Hose Strap.

The best device for attaching hose couplings. Pliers, 35c., by mail, 50c. pair; hose straps for ½ in. hose, 50c. doz.; ¾ in. hose, 60c. doz.; 1 in. hose, 80c. doz.

Lawn and Stable Barrow.

Extra Large
and
Extra Strong.

Our Lawn and Stable Barrow is designed for extra heavy work and has a large capacity, adapting it for manure, lawn litter, etc.; box 25 inches wide by 32 inches long by 18 inches deep.

Price, $5.00.

THE Regulation

Garden Wheelbarrow.

A superior barrow, handsomely painted and striped; iron leg braces, bolted, not screwed on, run under the legs, forming a shoe to slide on, avoiding racking the barrow; iron bands shrunk on hubs. No pine used in these barrows.

Number.	Size.	Length Box.	WIDTH OF BOX.		Box Depth.	Diam. Wheel.	Tread.	Price.
			Wheel End.	Handle End.				
No. 2.	Boy's.	21 in.	15½ in.	18 in.	9 in.	16 in.	1¼ in.	$2.75
No. 4.	Medium.	26½ "	18½ "	23 "	12 "	20 "	1½ "	3.50
No. 5.	Large.	28 "	20 "	24 "	12 "	22 "	1½ "	4.00

Tubular Steel Frame, Steel Tray Barrows.

The trays are made of one piece of steel the edges of which are turned over a ⁵⁄₁₆ inch steel rod, which prevents breaking at the edge. These barrows are made to dump forward, and are so constructed that at the dumping point they will not run back on the operator. The trays are about the same size as ordinary wooden canal barrows. These barrows will last a lifetime. Weight, about 70 pounds.

Price, $6.00.

Steel Garden and Farm Barrow with Tubular Steel Frame.

This style is especially adapted to wheeling dirt, manure, etc., having a deep steel tray, made in one piece, with the edges turned over a ⁵⁄₁₆ inch steel rod; the frame, of tubular steel, is so constructed that in dumping forward the barrow does not run back. Size of tray, 27x33 inches; weight of barrow, about 70 pounds.

Price, $6.50.

The "Henderson" Barrow.

This barrow is light, strong and durable, has a steel wheel and axle and oil-tempered springs, and we do not hesitate to say that it is the best barrow on the market and as well painted, striped and varnished as a buggy. While its carrying capacity is from 300 to 500 pounds, its weight is less than 40 pounds; fully warranted to stand the roughest usage.

The tire being wide makes it more desirable for lawn and garden use and a stronger wheel for the pavements. The shoe brace, running from the rear of the body to the foot of leg, is a great protection to the leg against breakage, and prevents it from sinking into soft ground. The barrow is made of selected material, and will outlast several of the cheaper, heavy, clumsy barrows. Weight, 39 pounds; body, 26 inches by 22½ inches by 12 inches deep; diameter of wheel, 20 inches; width of tire, 1¾ inches.

Price, $5.00.

Steel Tray, Wood Frame, Steel Wheel Canal Barrow.

Frame of selected hard wood; iron braces form a shoe so the barrow slides when set down, without racking it. Heavy steel wheels 17 inches in diameter; tread 1⅜ inch. Trays of one piece of sheet steel, about the size of an ordinary wood canal barrow, 28 inches long by 31 inches wide; the edges are turned over a ⁵⁄₁₆ inch steel rod, passing entirely around the tray; painted one coat of heavy paint.

Price, $4.00.

Bolted Wooden Canal Barrow with Steel Wheel.

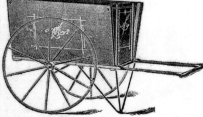

One of the strongest canal barrows made. The front of tray is supported by a wooden cleat, bolted as well as by the heavy iron braces; handles and legs of hard wood. Tray full size with edges shaved; steel wheel that will not fall to pieces like the common wooden wheel.

Price, with steel wheel, $2.25; with wooden wheel, $1.85.

Henderson's "All-about" Hand Carts.

Strong and durable, adapted for a great variety of uses. They are handy about the orchard, garden, farm, lawn and stable for carrying tools, vegetables, fruits, etc. All finely painted, striped and varnished.

☞ The undermentioned prices are for Carts without springs; if springs are wanted, add $1.50 per cart extra. Any of above carts can be furnished with a third wheel in front, in place of the iron rest, for $1.50 extra.

No. 1, 36 in. wheels, Box 40x23 in., 10 in. deep, 1 in. tire, $8.50; 3 in. tire, $10.00
No. 2, 30 " " 32x20 " 9 " " 1 " " 7.50, 3 " " 9.00

Henderson's Lawn AND Leaf Hand Cart.

Especially adapted for carrying large quantities of light material, such as cut grass, leaves and litter; the box is deep and flaring—measures at the bottom 28 inches wide by 48 inches long. 10 inches wider at the top; it is 24 inches deep; nicely painted green and vermilion, striped and varnished; 30 inch wheels.

Price, $15.00

horse to pull it, but the mower allowed suburban landscapes the luxury of a finely clipped expanse of grass. [4]

The first application of an internal combustion engine to a lawn mower occurred in 1902, when Edwin George, a Detroit industrialist and real estate developer, attached the gasoline engine from a washing machine. Thus the revolution of the gas-propelled mower began. [5] The reel-type mower was the dominant feature of lawn mowing until the Second World War, before which very few rotary mowers were produced. After the war, however, the number of rotary mowers skyrocketed.

The gasoline engine has recently been applied to a shear-action cutting bar originally designed and built in 1826. This new generation of sickle-bar mower allows the landowner to cut medium-size wild and overgrown areas with ease and greater safety.

The gasoline engine was made available in the 1940s for tilling small gardens. The Rototiller has been one of the most important mechanical devices for the home gardener, and the variety of tillers is endless. Today, tillers are categorized by engine size: two- to three-horsepower tillers are considered minitillers, suitable for the small garden; mid-size tillers are suitable for all but the most ambitious gardens; and heavy-duty tillers—those with rear-mounted tines—are designed for very large gardens, where they are used for more than just soil preparation.

Rototillers provide an ease in soil preparation available with no other machine. They offer a one-pass method of preparing the seed bed with less work and time. (Turning the ground over by hand produces clods of earth that require manual pulverization.) The modern tiller is a descendant of the six-hundred-pound walk-behind tractor of the 1930s.

OPPOSITE:
The multiplicity of carts and barrows in different dimensions and sizes (including one for boys) indicates the intensity of the work done on gardens in the nineteenth and early twentieth centuries. Steel, a technological improvement, was featured prominently in the construction of these vehicles. Although the steel wheels were heavy, they lasted much longer than their wooden counterparts and could be refitted onto other cart bodies.

The chainsaw is another technological innovation made possible by the gasoline engine. As carburetors and engine materials have been improved, the weight of the saws has been drastically reduced, making the machines ideal for clean-up work in the larger garden.

With the reduction in engine size, gasoline-powered trimmers have surpassed nearly every other piece of power equipment on the market. First introduced in 1972 to trim around trees and fenceposts, these trimmers now sport chain flails, circular saw blades, and numerous other attachments designed to enhance cosmetic clean-up of the home grounds. Electric models are increasingly popular as they require less maintenance and don't spit fumes.

The list of equipment made possible by light, gasoline-powered engines is truly amazing. Yard sweepers, hedge trimmers, and leaf blowers are just a few of the many power devices tempting the gardener of today.

Although generally not motor-driven, another important mechanical garden tool is the one used to move articles around in yard and garden, the general style and design of which has changed dramatically. Wheelbarrows reputedly were invented by the Chinese nearly six thousand years ago. [6] The tried and tested wheelbarrow is slowly being replaced by the garden cart, which is less likely to be mired in the mud or tip over than its single-wheeled cousin.

AMONG THE GREAT scientific discoveries that benefit gardeners today were Gregor Mendel's biological theory of heredity and the related discovery of the chromosome, which was predicted by Mendel. These discoveries led in turn to the science of plant breeding in the 1930s, by which modern hybrids were introduced to gardeners.

In America, during the second half of the nineteenth century and into the early twentieth century, Luther Burbank's work in plant breeding had an immeasurable impact on the varieties of plants available to gardeners. Burbank was deeply influenced by the writings of Darwin and went on to become a pioneer in the field of plant improvement. He and his colleagues carefully selected plants that looked different from others of their species; unique characteristics of these select plants were then exploited for the development of new varieties. Such experimental breeding work has yielded thornless blackberries, ever-bearing strawberries, and larger, sweeter plums and apples, among many other permutations that today are considered to be the norm.

Until the 1930s nearly all of the seed available to the flower and vegetable gardener had been self-fertile. Unless a gardener wanted a new variety of plant, the seed could be saved year to year with little need to return to the seed store or catalogue supplier. A gardener would select the best seeds from each of the vegetables grown and save them for next year. By selecting the largest and healthiest-looking seeds, the gardener ensured that the following year's crop would be successful, weather and insects permitting.

Even when seed purchase was necessitated by the need to expand or by adverse conditions, many of the nineteenth-century seed establishments were regional, so the local seed supplied was ideal for that specific climate. As seed companies merged or went out of business, however, the seed available might no longer reach its full potential because it had been grown far from the area in which it was planted, with its own specific soil conditions and climate.

At the beginning of the twentieth century, the discoveries of chromosomes and the principles of heredity encouraged breeding experiments by seed companies. Efforts were made to create uniformity in the vegetable and flower seeds offered for sale. As hybrids appeared on the market, they heralded a new era in gardening in which the productivity of plants increased, the number of plants a gardener needed to feed the family decreased, and the amount of space required for individual plants was reduced. Greater productivity in a smaller space left room for gardeners to try new and unusual flowers and vegetables. For example, kohlrabi and the Chinese leafy vegetables were unusual specimens in the 1930s, even though both had been available—but not particularly popular—at the turn of the century.

Hybrids removed the necessity for a gardener to sort and retain the best fruits of labor as seed for the next season. All of the produce could now end up on the table or in a pot. In order to grow a hybrid, one need only place an order with the seed company that originated the variety.

In the 1980s, plant breeders developed bush and container varieties of plants that previously required twenty or more square feet to produce a modest amount of food. The new varieties of squash, for example, can grow in a three-square-foot area, climbing up a pole, and produce as many or more squashes as the original vining ancestor.

One of the problems with these marvels of plant breeding is the gardener's inability to save seed and regrow the plant next year. Hybrids are crossed to develop the best characteristics of both parents, and if that offspring's seeds are sown, the result might be a plant even less desirable than either of the two original parents.

An example of how hybridization has affected gardens over the years is the tomato. Before 1870 tomatoes were primarily a curiosity, though Thomas Jefferson is known to have grown several in his garden at Monticello. Plant breeders have worked on increasing the tomato's resistance to disease, insects, and pests, and have tried to establish some cold tolerance in this semitropical taste treat. Thus far, tomatoes are resistant to nematodes, verticillium wilt, and fusarium blight; some are now being grown in Alaska. As more and more research is done in tomato genetics, the day will dawn when yellow and red tomatoes will be just two of the many colors available. Plant breeding offers great hope for the home gardener with little space and fresh-food ambitions.

DURING THE NINETEENTH CENTURY, pest and weed control was attempted through intensive cultivation and crop rotation. When the undesirable elements became unbearable, armies of children were recruited to walk through the garden, picking off the pests and insects and dropping them into kerosene while the weeds were pulled or hacked to death with hoes.

As the life cycle and physiology of the insects were learned, poisons and pesticides were developed to destroy the invaders. Early insecticidal dusts were made of arsenic and copper or of Bordeaux mixtures, a blend of arsenic-copper and copper sulfate with

Luther Burbank, shown here with his assistant Mr. Hasegawa, was responsible for introducing more than six hundred varieties of plants, from plums (113 types), quinces, and grapes to potatoes, peas, and asparagus. By turning his attention to flowers, he also introduced new roses, gladioluses, zinnias, and dahlias, among others.

lime. Although restricted to being a last line of defense against insects, they were poisonous and dangerous to use and they frequently left residues.[7] DDT, a popular insecticide of the 1960s, also turned out to be toxic to the environment and to humans and was banned. Research continues today into the use of general garden sprays and dust. While in many cases these chemicals are effective against the plant predators, their long-term environmental hazards are not as yet clear.

With the discovery of sex-attractant pheromones, scientists expressed great hope of attracting insects into traps. But, in some cases, more traps would need to be employed than is economically feasible. One positive use for these traps might be as indicators, telling the gardener when to spray or to be on the lookout for a specific garden pest.

Organic approaches to weed and insect control are also being researched and developed. Such approaches as companion planting and the use of predator insects were introduced in the late nineteenth century and are enjoying the renewed attention of gardener and scientist alike. In a sense, we are applying the technology of the late twentieth century to methods espoused, then all but abandoned, a hundred years ago.

The science of plant biochemistry has made considerable progress over the years. In the 1830s arguments and research revolved around discovering just

Tissue culture allows whole plants to be generated from small tissue samples or even from a single cell. One notable use of this procedure has been in the commercial growing of orchids, shown here in progress. First, callus cells are grown *in vitro* in appropriate media (TOP LEFT), from which plantlets develop (TOP RIGHT) and grow into full-fledged *Phalaenopsis Daryl Lockart* orchids.

what a plant was made of. Today, with such discoveries as gibberellic acid as an inducer of blooms in camellias, plant chemists are confident that methods of forcing plants to bloom in any growing condition are possible.

Numerous ornamental plants, such as roses and hosta, require several years to mature before they can reproduce, and many of the hybrid roses are exceptionally difficult to propagate. The science of tissue culture has guaranteed ample supplies of these popular plants at reasonable prices. In tissue culture, a small number of actively growing cells is removed, sterilized to remove any contaminants, then grown in germ-free culture until a clump of cells, or callus, develops. From this callus, with the help of nutrient-growth chemicals, a new plant grows. Hundreds or thousands of perfect copies of the original plant are possible with this method.

One way in which tissue culture is having an impact on contemporary gardening is in the practice of shade gardening. As the taste for large expanses of grass grown under trees is slowly being abandoned, a need has arisen for ornamental plants that will grow in the shade, where grass won't grow. Tissue culture opens the door to the creation of an affordable supply of popular plants that are difficult, if not impossible, to grow from seeds.

Tissue culture is a practice that was barely dreamed of a generation ago. Likewise, new technologies that are difficult for the average gardener to envision are already being pursued by today's plant and soil scientists. While some are in the realm of improvement and creation of new plant varieties, perhaps the area of most interest for the next generation of gardeners will be that concerned with the responsible use of existing natural resources and the reclamation and restoration of those dwindling gifts of nature that were so readily squandered by what, not long ago, was considered cutting-edge technology. ✥

NOTES

1. Margaret W. Rossiter, *The Emergence of Agricultural Science: Justus Liebig and the Americans, 1840–1880* (New Haven, Yale University Press, 1975), p. 11.

2. Rossiter, pp. 149–150.

3. White, William, "Follow These Suggestions for Safe Mowing," *Horticulture* (August 1966): 32.

4. Ibid.

5. Ibid.

6. Holtzman, Jay, "The Tool Shed, Wheelbarrows and Garden Carts," *Horticulture* (January 1980) 16.

7. Weed, Clarence, *Insects & Insecticides* (New York: Orange Judd, 1897), pp. 49–52.

BIBLIOGRAPHY

Fowler, Cary and Pat Mooney. *Shattering Food: Politics and the Loss of Genetic Diversity.* Tucson: University of Arizona, 1990.

Gorer, Richard. *Living Tradition in the Garden.* London: David & Charles, 1974.

Howard, H. L. *Luther Burbank's Plant Contributions.* Berkeley: University of California, Bull. 691, 1945.

Kloppenburg, Jack. *First the Seed: The Political Economy of Plant Biotechnology.* Cambridge: Cambridge University Press, 1988.

Kraft, Ken. *Garden to Order.* Garden City, N.Y.: Doubleday, 1963.

White, Katherine. *Onward and Upward in the Garden.* New York: Farrar, Straus, & Giroux, 1979.

The City and the Garden

❧❧❧

Phyllis Andersen

❧ *Over the last three hundred years, since the inception of the city in America, gardeners and planners have adopted various attitudes toward urban gardens. From William Penn's plan for Philadelphia to the current concern about green spaces as necessary for a full human life, gardens and landscape in the urban environment have evolved into their own forms and functions.*

Early American towns were laid out with great green spaces in mind. By the eighteenth century a true urban culture had developed, and the distinction between town and country had become quite pronounced. City gardens—both public and private—reflected a growing cultural sophistication and European influences.

In the rapidly expanding nation of the nineteenth century, the city and images of it changed drastically. As the cities grew they became hubs of industrial activity and, in time, burgeoning sources of goods made available by the railways. The century also saw unprecedented poverty and urban blight. These and related factors gave rise to a plethora of parks for physical, emotional, and moral wholeness for those who remained in the city as well as the birth of suburbs for those seeking to live in more peaceful and idyllic surroundings.

The form and content of urban gardens have continued to change. Victory gardens brought new vigor to gardening in the city. Urban renewal resulted in more space for community gardens, making them a cohesive and unifying factor of urban life. Other twentieth-century expressions in urban landscape, including shared gardening and roof gardens, are unique inventions that allow for both socialization and solitude.

In their various forms, city gardens have been agents in the organization of city living and occasions of civilized life, bringing the need for nature and the amenities of city life together in a pleasant unity. ❧

THERE ARE TWO prevailing views of the garden in the city. One, clearly a utopian view, holds that the city should, in fact, *be* a garden with all the harmony of experience and sense of refuge and nourishment offered by a life close to nature. The garden is advanced as the ultimate salvation of cities— a form that transcends political, moral, and religious differences while bestowing a righteous order on a form of human settlement rank with temptation and bad deeds. A differing view defines the city as the highest form of human endeavor: a dynamic, evolving organism that accommodates the garden only as an extension of man-made geometry and relegates nature to its appropriate place, the country. These sharply contrasting attitudes join a debate that goes back to that faintly patronizing country mouse of Aesop's fable who returns to his home in a hollow tree smugly secure in the belief that his misguided city cousin is condemned to a life of terror.

The early settlers of the American colonies came determined to create the ideal pastoral city, a marriage of the culture of the European capitals and the freedom of the countryside. Unlike European cities, which were laid down layer upon layer over centuries to celebrate royal power, the victories of war, or the glories of the church, American cities were carved directly out of the wilderness in a relatively short period of time to provide ever-expanding opportunities for human enterprise.

Americans are uniquely committed to the continuous transformation of their cities—wilderness into town, swamp into park, parking lot into garden— in a nostalgic search for an idealized verdant past that continues to be elusive. Today, when three quarters of our population lives in urban centers, we continue to raise the banner of a rural utopia where nature rules.[1] That banner has been dropped many times,

then dusted off and picked up again by new generations. The literature of urbanism is mined with garden metaphors to describe the success or failure of our utopian ideals—"garden cities," "city wilderness," "granite gardens." We still exhibit a curious uneasiness in the presence of the man-made landscape. We still need rural images to sustain our pursuit of the perfect way of life.

Rus in Urbe: *Town Plans and Green Space*

THE EARLY TOWN-PLANNING efforts of the colonists were extremely important in establishing prototypes for the relationship between buildings and landscape. Looking to the great cities of Europe, the colonists recognized that regulating growth and providing public and private green space was a civic responsibility of the highest order; they identified the green square, the tree-lined avenue, and the town common as civilizing influences useful to convert a raw settlement into a sophisticated town.

The topographic advantages of the regional capitals—the great natural harbors, access to river systems, the natural prospects—favored their expansion from small trading centers into thriving market towns. But before they could develop the degree of civic pride needed to sustain growth the people who lived in such regional centers as Philadelphia, Boston, New York, and Charleston still needed the amenities that residents of European cities took for granted.

The early town planners employed simple ideas of symmetry and repetition of elements to impose order on sprawling settlements. The most beguiling attempt to use landscape to attract new residents was William Penn's well-publicized plan for Philadelphia. Raised in London, Penn greatly admired Christopher Wren's plan for that city conceived after the great fire of 1666. Penn's scheme, drawn by the surveyor Thomas Holme in 1683, was the first and most fully conceived proposal for a new town in the colonies. Organizing his plan around five green squares set in a traditional rectangular grid, Penn borrowed the simplest ideas from Wren—the grid street layout, the residential lots fronting on a green square. Penn's plan was first published in a promotional pamphlet

OPENING ILLUSTRATION:
Central Park, indisputably one of the greatest urban parks in the world, was the collaborative work of Frederick Law Olmsted and Calvert Vaux. It was opened to the public in 1859 and continues to be the premier open space of New York City.

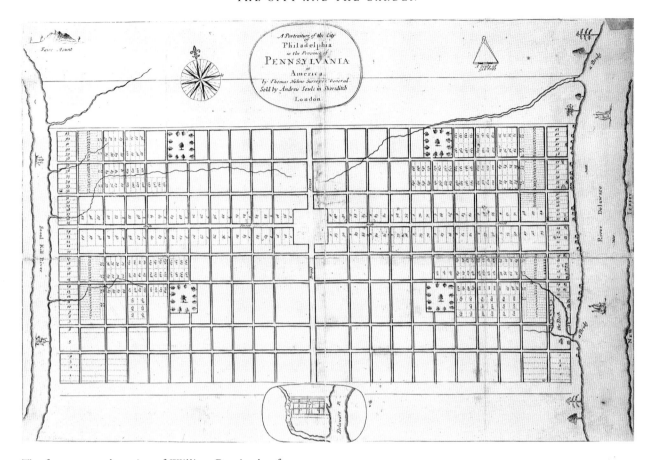

The first engraved version of William Penn's plan for Philadelphia was drawn by Surveyor General Thomas Holme in 1683 and shows the central square and four district squares.

written to lure an English audience to settle on his gracious site on the banks of the Schuylkill River. It read in part:

> Let every house be placed, if the person pleases, on the middle of the plat, as to the breadth way of it, that so there may be ground on each side for gardens or orchards, or fields, that it may be a free country town, which will never be burnt and always be wholesome. [2]

While not precisely implemented, the town did remain faithful to the principles of Penn's plan, and the five green squares inspired a system of parks and gardens that contributed greatly to the prominent position Philadelphia came to play in the history of American horticulture. Penn's emphasis on a planted city attracted new residents sympathetic to his vision. In 1700 Philadelphia passed a law requiring each citizen to plant one or more trees to produce shade and a healthy atmosphere—one of the first civic statements to equate tree planting with public health. Penn's "country town" plan provided deep lots for substantial homes and surrounding gardens. It suggested the possibility of achieving that ideal of town planning, a seamless merging of public green space and private garden.

New York, by contrast, initially grew without an official plan. The early colony of New Amsterdam reflected the Dutch origins of its first settlers. A small, tightly knit community at the tip of the island, New Amsterdam, like all the other colonies, demanded a common green space, and its first public park, the Bowling Green, was established at the lower end of what is now Broadway. In 1811 city engineers prepared Manhattan's famous grid street plan. The

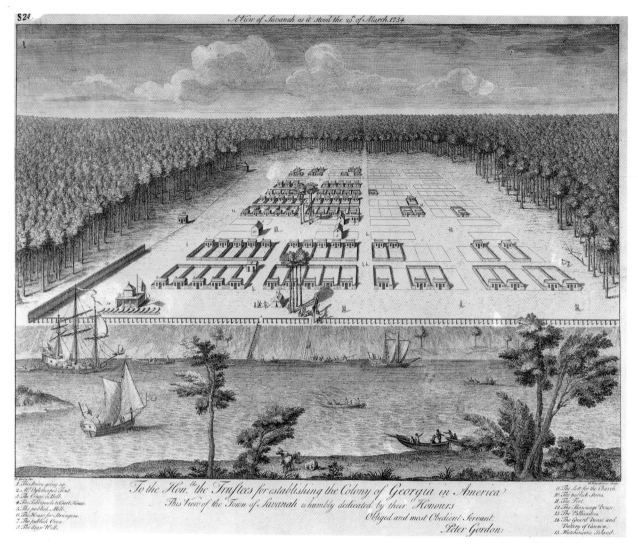

S24.

A View of Savanah as it stood the 29.th of March. 1734.

To the Hon.ble the Trustees for establishing the Colony of Georgia in America
This View of the Town of Savanah is humbly dedicated by their Honours
Obliged and most Obedient Servant.
Peter Gordon.

1. The Stairs going up.
2. M.r Oglethorpe's Tent.
3. The Crane & Bell.
4. The Tabernacle & Court House.
5. The publick Mill.
6. The House for Strangers.
7. The publick Oven.
8. The draw Well.

9. The Lott for the Church.
10. The publick Stores.
11. The Fort.
12. The Parsonage House.
13. The Pallisadoes.
14. The Guard House and Battery of Cannon.
15. Hutchensons Island.

Early engraving depicting Savannah in 1734 prepared after the plan of General Oglethorpe, who founded the colony of Georgia. It shows the distinctive squares creating permanent open space in the gridiron plan.

layout, which has great clarity and strength, imposed substantial limits on an intimate relationship between public green space and residential areas. The engineering commission defended their solution by stating, "Straight and right angled houses are the most cheap to build and the most convenient to live in."[3]

New York's plan, which encouraged development and put intense pressure on sites reserved for green space, nonetheless included park spaces as adjuncts to residential and commercial development. Battery Park and City Hall Park, both remnants of the colonial period, have gone through several resurrections as civic spaces. Gramercy Park, New York's homage to the English square, was developed as a private enclave of trees and turf open only to abutters who owned shares of the space. Ironically, the restrictions of the grid created an icon of modern park design: Paley Park in midtown Manhattan. Reclaimed from an empty building site in the middle of a dense block, the park is one of the most elegant statements of restrained design in the country and virtually defined the term "pocket park."

Boston arrived at systematic planning even later than New York. The early settlement of the Shawmut Peninsula mimicked an English town with small, regular streets accommodating the hilly topography. The city's first major planning effort was the mid-

150

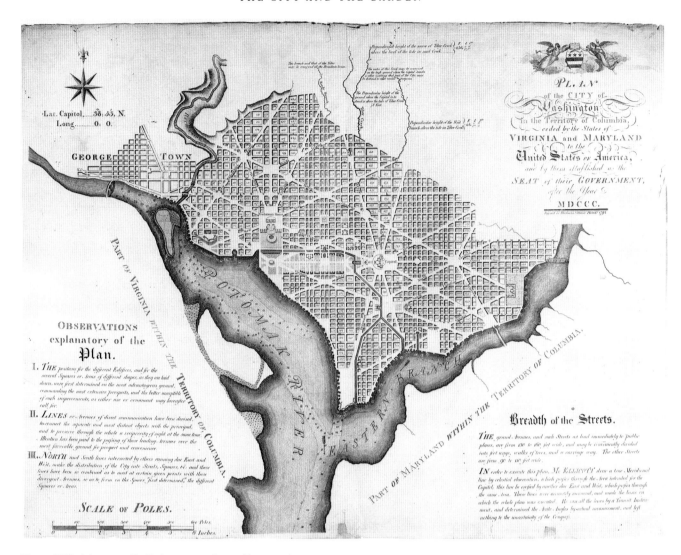

Plan of Washington, D.C. in 1792, the earliest version. It depicts Pierre L'Enfant's design and was taken from the official survey by Andrew Ellicott.

nineteenth-century layout of the Back Bay with its Parisian-inspired mall and the South End with its English-style squares. Boston's distinction in the landscape history of America was the 1640 designation of the Boston Common as a commonly held green space. Reserved first as pasturage for the town's cows and later as a drill area for the militia, the legal stipulation created America's first public park.

America's southern colonies, based on a strong agricultural economy and blessed by a benevolent climate, reveled in the creation of garden cities. Charleston's town plan took form during the late seventeenth century and, like Philadelphia, used a generous grid layout. James Oglethorpe's plan for Savannah relied on classical geometry and an elegant system of green squares. He proposed an ordered grid that organized residential streets around the squares while allowing for broad avenues that by-passed the square system to facilitate passage through the city. Both Charleston and Savannah were well known throughout the eighteenth century for their beautiful and horticulturally varied private gardens and for their shaded streets and squares. Savannah, still admired for its gardens, proves the point that faithfully implemented planning efforts can sustain a civic reputation for many generations.

When the time came to build a national capital, the need to combine the best values of both city and country life was made very clear to its designer, Pierre L'Enfant. L'Enfant was a French military engineer, trained in a number of skills, including landscape painting. George Washington himself selected the general site for the capital on land along the Potomac River. L'Enfant refined the site selection to allow grand prospects equal to that of any European city. He noted that the numerous springs and creeks would provide water for fountains and reflecting pools. L'Enfant brought to his design all of his admiration for French garden layout. His plan overlaid a traditional grid of streets with a series of radiating avenues, their intersections punctuated by monuments. Residential lots were generous to allow for stately homes surrounded by gardens. L'Enfant was dismissed after completing his plan because of his unwillingness to compromise with government administrators who tried to restrain a scheme they considered too grandiose for the young democracy. Thomas Jefferson, who had been so involved with L'Enfant in the planning process, wrote the letter of dismissal. But L'Enfant's ideas prevailed, and succeeding attempts to refine the city's plan—namely Frederick Law Olmsted's work in the 1850s, and that of the McMillan Commission in 1901—remained highly respectful of L'Enfant's original concept.

Colonial Town Gardens

THE EARLY COLONISTS used their town gardens to grow fruit trees, vegetables, and herbs for the family table. But garden space had to be shared with wood storage, stables, and privies and the town gardener was continually fighting dust, deeply rutted streets, lack of proper garbage disposal and free-roaming dogs and livestock. Ornamental gardening took a backseat to such infrastructure improvements as street paving, rudimentary lighting, or bollards set up to protect pedestrians from horses and carriages. By the early eighteenth century, however, the colonies were beginning to develop a genuine urban culture, and the acquisition of things supplanted issues of survival. Economic growth brought increased trade with Europe, imported books on architecture and garden arts became popular, and seed houses were established to cater to both agricultural and horticultural interests. Small nurseries and market gardens sprang up on the periphery of towns, offering a limited selection of ornamental plants for town gardens.

The survival of horticulture in any age depends on healthy competition in the guise of communication, plant exchange, and some form of exhibition. By the mid-eighteenth century ornamental gardens had become fashionable and hence objects of emulation. As the century progressed, many town dwellers accumulated the means to create private gardens of distinction as displays of position and affluence, but, more important, as a form of activity remote from the physical and spiritual constraints of commerce.

The eighteenth-century gardens of Boston were impressive, horticulturally varied, and the object of much commentary. European visitors, who had been expecting rude huts and wild animals in the streets, were amazed at the level of sophistication of the residents and their homes. One of the most visible gardens was "The Green," owned by Governor Winthrop, who used it extensively to entertain visitors from abroad. In the same area Gardiner Greene constructed a terraced back garden on the slope of Pemberton Hill, one of the peninsula's three original hills, only one of which—Beacon Hill—still stands. Greene grew the black Hamburg grape and an impressive array of fruits: peaches, apricots, nectarines, plums, and pears. Although he maintained one of the first greenhouses in the colonies, he is reputed to have grown the tender fruits out-of-doors.

In Philadelphia, where Penn's vision of generous house lots and large gardens was fading owing to a real estate boom, the pursuit of horticulture was nonetheless advanced by the extraordinary circle of plantsmen who settled there. John Bartram, the great botanist and naturalist, created a botanical garden just outside the city. Two pioneer plantsmen opened seed houses in town: David Landreth in 1784 and Bernard M'Mahon by 1802. Philadelphians planted their colonial gardens elaborately, with fine shade trees and flowering shrubs. Having made an early commitment to a green town, eighteenth-century Philadelphia boasted public and private garden spaces of handsome maturity.

Watercolor of Boston Common, 1768, by Christian Remick, showing the house of Thomas Hancock in the upper right corner along with the row of elms he planted. Some of Hancock's elms continued to grow at the edge of the Common until the 1970s.

The interest in new plant introductions that swept Europe in the eighteenth century also reached the colonies; botanical collections promised the excitement of scientific contributions along with an aura of exoticism and adventure. André Michaux, a French botanist and plant collector, established a private botanical garden near Charleston in 1787 to act as a holding area for native American plants eventually to be shipped to France for use as ornamentals. Michaux's "French garden" introduced new azaleas and other native flowering shrubs to an already notable garden scene.

A further mark of civilization was Charleston's waterfront promenade, the Battery, one of the earliest park spaces in the colonies. Meanwhile Savannah's earlier town-planning efforts yielded streets lined with deep front gardens surrounded by elaborate wrought-iron fences. Residents of both of these southern towns began to build back gardens made uniquely private by the construction of high walls upon which were displayed rock plants and vines.

The Nineteenth Century: When Towns Became Cities and Cities Became the Wilderness

UNFETTERED ECONOMIC GROWTH, western expansion, and a population with a voracious appetite for goods and culture produced the true urbanization of the American colonies. This precipitated a process of landscape differentiation that would change the face of the country forever. The only valid subdivisions of the eighteenth-century American landscape were wilderness, country, and town. Nature was to be explored, transformed, or civilly accommodated. In the nineteenth century, industrial expansion and economic opportunity transformed the colonial regional centers into full-fledged cities—a new category of American landscape. That energetic century also saw the invention of the last vital division, the suburb. Disaffected with life in cities, Americans began to drift to urban edges to pursue a more ordered life within a garden setting. Those who remained in cities either by choice or necessity needed a more expansive existence, with opportunities for privacy and recreational pursuits. The city garden and

Union Park (now Union Square) was one of the earliest open spaces integrated into Manhattan's early-nineteenth-century grid plan. This mid-century view shows the extensive tree planting both within the square and on the street side.

The St. Charles Street residence and expansive gardens of Colonel Augustus May were typical of the substantial Italianate homes built around Lee Circle, in New Orleans, in the mid-nineteenth century.

the public park, in all of their diverse forms, offered asylum from the intensity of urban life.

The burst of horticultural activity in the nineteenth century could not have occurred without the propellant of urbanization. The postrevolutionary city became the stage that launched plant explorers to the American West and to the far corners of the world. Wealthy city dwellers funded many of these expeditions, perhaps identifying vicariously with the mystique of daring and adventure. The seed houses and nurseries, which in the eighteenth century had provided a cozy environment for the exchange of horticultural information, became inadequate for the quantities of information flowing back into cities from American plant collectors and European publications. There followed an inevitable institutionalization of horticulture, epitomized by the founding of the great American horticultural societies. The urban-based societies sponsored exhibitions both for their members and for the general public. They built libraries and offered lectures and courses. New journals were launched to satisfy the insatiable demands for information about plants.

By the early nineteenth century the town garden had been transformed by urbanization and by the pronounced social and economic distinctions created by intense growth. Gardens took on new meaning as people were less tied to the production of food crops. Market gardens sprang up on the edges of cities. Over time, such land became too valuable for crop production. Railroads then served to bring fresh produce to city markets. City dwellers throughout the nineteenth century thus had access to a far greater variety of fresh fruits and vegetables than most rural residents.

The relationship between house and garden was slowly formalized by social conventions, and only the most eccentric gardener would deviate from accepted landscape models. The front garden space, usually too small for a lawn, was minimally planted with small trees or a few shrubs while the back garden, customarily fenced off from neighbors, became a truly personal space planted with favorite flowering plants. The implicit control of garden space by proper standards of conduct was even more evident in suburban gardens, where the cultivation of green lawns, un-

fenced and unimpeded, was a requirement of good manners.

AFFLUENT AMERICANS have never had to narrow their options to a choice between life in the city or life in the country. By the late eighteenth century men of substance had established country retreats where they could assume the role of gentleman farmer and amateur horticulturist while maintaining homes in the cities where they conducted business and kept a hand in civic affairs. The nineteenth-century expansion of these country estates outside the original colonial towns was responsible for creating a distinctive American gardening style. But the gentlemen's gardening urge did not extend to their city properties, where, throughout the century, they limited their horticultural interests to potted plants and conservatory displays.

While the southern cities did not escape the pressures of urbanization, their reliance on a predominantly agricultural economy, their emphasis on the elaboration of domestic space over civic monuments, their passion for horticulture over landscape design, generated cities with a gentler pace of life and a romantic atmosphere of domestic embellishment. The horticultural variety and steamy texture of New Orleans were particularly noted by European travelers, who were seduced by streets filled with live oaks, magnolias, and sour orange. Roses bloomed everywhere. Visitors also admired the gallery gardens. Wrought-iron-framed, glass-enclosed galleries, covered on the exterior by vines and filled with house plants were typical features of New Orleans houses. The cultural influences on New Orleans were French rather than English, and domestic life was conducted in a more private, Mediterranean manner. Accordingly, privacy, shade, and abundance were valued over a more public and institutionalized garden art.

Cincinnati, a center for horticulture between 1820 and the Civil War, was the final destination of the legendary English traveler, Frances Trollope, whose *Domestic Manners of the Americans,* an acerbic chronicle of America, was widely read if not always appreciated. While not enamored of the city, she

Until recently, municipal park departments produced thousands of plants and seedlings for the embellishment of public spaces around their cities. Municipal greenhouses and conservatories, such as the Lincoln Park Conservatory of Chicago (pictured here in 1910), were once an important part of the urban landscape.

nonetheless commented favorably on its public gardens, remarking upon their profuse flower displays. Cincinnati's planners had used Philadelphia as a model but laid their grid on an irregular topography that includes a flat basin on the Ohio River whose banks rise rather abruptly into a series of hills. Despite the awkwardness of access created by this plan, Cincinnati was known for beautiful homes with gardens that commanded magnificent views over the Ohio Valley. The city also earned much praise for Spring Grove Cemetery, founded in 1845 and modeled on the first garden cemetery in the United States, Mount Auburn, in Cambridge, Massachusetts. Spring Grove exemplified the rural tastes of the mercantile society that controlled the growth of the self-described "Queen City" on the Ohio River.

Chicago originated as a small settlement along Lake Michigan, and by the late nineteenth century its importance as a railroad hub and as a center for banking and commerce made it a formidable rival for any city of the East Coast. Chicagoans made a strong commitment to parks and plantings, and tree-lined streets were an early mark of the growing sophistication of the town. It took as its motto *Urbs in Horto,* soon to be translated into "The Garden City," a designation later used by numerous chambers of commerce and town booster clubs across the Midwest.

Midcentury Chicago was a lively and sociable city. It perfected the very popular institution of the garden restaurant, ranging from elegant winter garden conservatories where one might drink and dine amidst tropical flora to the humble beer garden where plants provided privacy and atmosphere. Frederick Law Olmsted and Calvert Vaux were commissioned to develop a park system for the city in 1870. Their preliminary proposals were taken over by the landscape architect Horace Cleveland, a transplanted New Englander and colleague of Olmsted. Cleveland carried the park system work forward, working on proposals for the city's two major park sites, South Park and Jackson Park. Cleveland also made an intriguing proposal to line Chicago's Lake Shore Drive with a ten-mile-long planting of native trees—a linear arboretum for the enjoyment of the public.

The booming midwestern cities—often in fierce competition with one another for new residents—constantly looked eastward for planning advice and cultural inspiration. Horace Cleveland developed park and parkway systems for Minneapolis and St. Paul, allowing those cities to protect prime open space before development removed it forever from public enjoyment. St. Louis, "Gateway to the West," was the fourth largest city in the United States after the Civil War. A bustling town, laid out with Philadelphia as a model, its great love of horticulture and plant collecting resulted in the founding of the Missouri Botanical Garden in 1859. Ralph Waldo Emerson, on an extended lecture tour in the Midwest, commented favorably on the city's spacious squares.

The rectangular plots and divisions of the midwestern landscape were a direct result of a federal land ordinance of 1785 that mandated a grid of townships to settle the new territory. This gridded survey, which completely ignored topography and natural features, could have resulted in banal, undistinguished cities. Fortunately, the transformation of special natural features into park spaces and the supporting squares and gardens gave a distinctive character to these midwestern cities even as they grappled with the problems of extraordinary growth.

If the life of any city in the country is tied inextricably to its topography, it is San Francisco. The grid overlaid on the city's hills created dramatically steep streets and memorable vistas. European influences on the city are immediately apparent. The English-square model was adopted by the mid-nineteenth century, and the three squares established then—Union Square, Washington Square, and Portsmouth Square—still serve as meeting places and focal points for their neighborhoods. South Park was, in fact, laid out by an Englishman, George Gordon, and was a copy of Berkeley Square, in London. The most famous of San Francisco's nineteenth-century park attractions had more to do with the pleasures of amusement and display than with any profound ideas about landscape. Woodward's Gardens was a privately owned establishment open to the public. It contained a zoo, a botanical garden, a Museum of Curiosities, and a roller-skating rink. The garden of Adolph Sutro, just outside the city, was a bonanza of Victorian garden features; conservatories, carpet beds, statues, and exotic plants from around the world. The garden was opened to the public in 1885 and was at its height when Sutro was mayor in the 1890s.

The climate of San Francisco, sufficiently cool to allow plants from the East Coast to thrive, was also mild enough to encourage the introduction of many plants from the Far East, from Australia, and even South America. Waves of immigrants have added a special character to the private gardens of San Francisco. The nineteenth-century settlers brought English and French garden ideas to the city, and the strong Italian community brought a formal Italianate sensibility to many of the small gardens. The Chinese and Japanese communities have added their own special knowledge of garden techniques.

A Day in the Country

THE AMERICAN CITY nurtured horticultural institutions, promoted the cultural value of gardens and plants, and created the great fortunes that sponsored estate-garden design and botanical exploration. The variety of public and private green spaces of the colonial towns were admired by European travelers and served their citizens well. But the pressures of growth after the Revolutionary War rendered these spaces inadequate. The spread of factories, warehouses, and transportation facilities reduced private garden space and isolated public parks from the part of the population that most urgently needed them. By the middle of the nineteenth century it was clear that all citizens of many cities were not equally well served by public amenities. The socially prominent supported by family fortunes could escape to country estates, and the affluent middle and professional classes could build town gardens as private retreats. But the economically underprivileged of the cities were remote from these pleasures. The Golden Age concept of the founding fathers—that desire to meld

The Long Meadow of
Prospect Park, Brooklyn,
with its seventy-five acres
of rolling turf and trees, is
the centerpiece of this
superbly designed park,
built from the 1866 plan
by Olmsted and Vaux.

agrarian values and urban culture—was obscured by
the excesses of urban growth and the housing built
to hold the rapidly expanding populations. Substandard housing, offering little natural light, poor heating systems, outdoor privies, and no space for children to play in the open air, forced a great number
of city families into lives of deprivation and poor
health.

Civic leaders and social reformers might disagree
on how to solve poor housing and sanitary conditions,
but both groups turned with enthusiasm to the city's
antithesis—nature—to provide a new image of civic
pride. In no other period of American history has the
intellectual tension between urban values and the
moral superiority of nature been more hotly debated.
The park solution, termed "Parkomania" by Andrew
Jackson Downing, coalesced around Frederick Law
Olmsted and his "Greensward" plan for Central Park,
in New York City. Olmsted believed in the redemptive power of landscape. He deplored the inflexibility
of the grid plan and the decorative use of plants that
embellished the traditional park, feeling that subtropical plants and long lines of iron-work fencing

had turned the simple beauty of English parks into
"hospital wards for convalescents." Olmsted conceived
of his urban parks as a narrative of landscape pictures:
bucolic scenes of modified nature, meadow and grove
alternating with water features and simulated wilderness. He recreated the pastoral landscape of England
within the confines of the American city. Discouraging active recreation and encouraging a passive engagement with the landscape, Olmsted revealed the
beauty of native plant communities, the power of
rolling turf, and quiet ponds.

One of Olmsted's greatest contributions to the
American city was the development of park systems,
a series of park segments distinguished by unique
topography and landscape features connected by
broad, tree-lined parkways limited to the traffic of
pleasure vehicles only. The park systems he developed
for Boston, Louisville, Baltimore, and Buffalo transformed those cities, but, of course, Central Park
remains the crown jewel of Olmsted's career. The
widespread publicity the park received upon its completion was unprecedented. From popular magazines
to town newspapers the glories of the park were pre-

sented to a public eager for ideas on how to improve their own cities and towns suffering from crowded housing conditions and limited green space. Central Park, with its expansive scenery and its accommodation of all segments of society, transcended the familiar urban park spaces derived from European models: the square, the promenade, the plaza. Olmsted went on to create other jewels—Prospect Park in Brooklyn, Belle Isle in Detroit, Mount Royal in Montreal. He worked on parks in Seattle, prepared a proposal for Golden Gate Park in San Francisco, and designed hundreds of small parks across the United States. Finally, he took his ideas on how people should live and applied them to the design of Riverside, Illinois, the first residential community designed as a park. Olmsted has become the pivotal figure in the renaissance of urban park-making in the nineteenth century. He inspired and taught others who carried his ideas into the twentieth century: his stepson, John Charles Olmsted, his son, Frederick Law Olmsted, Jr., Horace Cleveland, Warren Manning. Olmsted rejected the old order of the American city, which was predicated on a simple geometry and

a controlled access to green space. He imposed a new order based on the composition of pictures of nature and proved that the two could be successfully fused.

From the Victory Garden to the Green Guerrillas: Community Gardens in America

NO OTHER FORM of gardening has done more to enliven American cities than the cultivation of vacant city lots for food production. In the space of less than a hundred years the community gardening movement has evolved from an activity of charity to one of aggressive self-help. Allotment gardens, the earlier term for community gardens, are not unique to the United States. They have a long history dating back to the English land-enclosure acts of the late eighteenth century, which gave small gardening patches at the edge of towns to tenant farmers who had lost their right to cultivate the property of large landholders. Similar small garden plots soon became part of many European cities, combining an opportunity for city dwellers to retain a connection to the land with the charitable activity of providing food to poverty-stricken families. It was this last function that first popularized allotment gardening in the United States.

The first formal programs to convert vacant city land to food-producing gardens occurred during the economic depression of the 1890s when banking and factory failures produced widespread unemployment in the nation's cities. In Detroit, Mayor Hazen Pingree persuaded owners of vacant land to lease it to the city for use as allotment gardens where unemployed men could grow food for their families. Four hundred thirty acres were secured and over nine hundred families participated in the program. Critical to Mayor Pingree's plan was limiting gardeners to a single crop that had good nutritional value and could be easily grown and stored. He chose the potato. Forever immortalized as "Pingree's Potato Patches," Detroit's allotment gardens touched a responsive chord across the country, and by 1895 twenty other cities had initiated similar programs with more varied crops. Chicago, Kansas City, Philadelphia, Providence, all developed allotment gardens as a charitable gesture to alleviate poverty in their cities. Not surprisingly, it was quickly observed that gardeners provided themselves and their neighbors with produce far superior to anything available in local stores. Chicago's Bureau of Associated Charities leased forty acres for a garden program. Here, for the first time, the gardeners made an attempt to organize themselves and created "People Friendly Clubs" to exchange growing information and promote sociability among the gardening families. This small attempt to detach the gardening program from the paternalism of local charities was so successful that the Chicago program was sustained for ten years.

These early allotment programs, well-meaning and responsive to real social problems, were nonetheless vulnerable to fashions in charitable giving. Land was leased rather than owned and could be removed from the program by landowners seeking a more profitable use.

World War I reenergized the allotment-garden movement and turned food production in cities into a patriotic duty. Gardening was not an occupation for the unemployed but a spare-time activity for all

citizens to produce food locally and thereby ease the strain on the nation's food production system. The World War I garden program was formalized into the National War Garden Commission and headed by Charles Lathrop Pack, a wealthy Cleveland lumberman. Pack's organizational and promotional skills were formidable. He convinced the nation that gardening was a true test of patriotism. Demonstration gardens were set up on the Boston Common as well as in Bryant Park and Union Square in New York. Across the country local park agencies allowed park land to be converted to garden plots. Newspapers printed daily gardening hints.

Pack is credited with coining the term "Victory Garden" at the end of World War I, encouraging people to continue their gardening efforts so that the United States could still make significant food contributions to Europe. When the allotment gardening movement was resurrected during World War II, the name Victory Garden was a resonant tie to an earlier war and an earlier success. During 1944 twenty million gardeners produced 44 percent of the vegetables on America's tables. [4]

The Victory Garden movement was truly a family and community effort. The gardens went well beyond food production and included seating and children's play areas, barbecue pits and small summer houses. Skilled gardeners were admired and encouraged to share with their neighbors techniques for high-yield growing. The public was deluged with slogans, pamphlets, and demonstrations.

The World War II gardening effort not only produced prodigious amounts of food at the local level but made a lasting connection between residents and local governments. Gardeners learned planning and organizational skills in cooperation with city agencies. By the end of the war city residents had not only become good gardeners; they had also removed the stigma of charity from the community garden movement by taking an active role in its implementation.

Victory Gardens dwindled at the end of World War II as the need for food production diminished. By the end of the 1940s popular gardening interest had shifted to creating the perfect suburban lawn. But the community garden spirit never completely

World War II saw an explosion of victory gardens in American cities. Nurseries, such as Peter Henderson & Co., supported the movement and supplied special Victory Garden seed collections for small home gardens.

died and the complex urban problems of the 1960s inspired a revived interest in the food garden in the city. The government policy of urban renewal left whole blocks of city land vacant. Informal community groups began to clear rubble, improve soil, and create small gardens both for food production and neighborhood improvement. To the delight of many, ethnic diversity created gardens of unique character, and gardening techniques from all corners of the globe were discussed and displayed.

The community garden movement gathered momentum throughout the 1970s, with informal groups coalescing into citywide initiatives. Boston Urban Gardeners (B.U.G.), Philadelphia Green, and New York City's Green Guerrillas were pioneers in organizing support for community gardens and other beautification projects. The history of the community garden movement in the United States is a record of changes in attitude toward land use in cities and of the shift of a small charitable program to an urban gardening activity of great vitality.

OPPOSITE:
The garden treated as an outdoor room is a typical solution to small city-garden spaces. This Boston garden turns the restrictions of shade and dampness into a virtue by using woodland species to form a green oasis behind a typical Beacon Hill townhouse.

Communal gardens—private back gardens opened up and shared by a number of owners—were popular in the early part of this century. The recently restored Jones Wood Garden, originally completed in 1919, is a hidden treasure just off New York City's Third Avenue.

The Comfort of a Small Garden

THE MODERN GARDEN in the city is a talisman against the sensory overload of daily life. The modern city gardener resists the lure of suburban calm (as his nineteenth-century equivalent resisted the rustic country life) and instead chooses to create a private oasis in an atmosphere of constant change. From the small delights of the window box to the miniature Taj Mahal on the rooftop, the city garden continues to give its owner a retreat from the relentless intrusions of the city and a direct connection with soil, seeds, and plants. The modern city gardener has developed unique techniques to cope with diminishing space and dense population. Behind the formal facades of row housing one finds not only private garden "rooms," but a sense of communal sharing unique to American cities.

By the 1920s town house owners in New York had combined backyards into shared gardens of flowering trees and shrubs, fountains, turf, and garden sculpture. The Jones Wood Garden, completed in 1919, was one of the first attempts to combine small backyards to form a garden space of great elegance for use by all the residents. Back fences were removed and a garden shaded by great elms and planted with flowering trees and shrubs was constructed. Fountains, garden sculpture, and seating were part of the overall design. The Neighbors Garden, just off Riverside Drive, allowed each of the abutters a small private garden opening onto a communal space with winding brick paths, fruit trees, roses, an oriental teahouse, and a view of the Hudson River.

The hidden gardens of Boston's Beacon Hill also included a series of connecting gardens tucked away behind the traditional red brick walls of Louisburg

OPPOSITE:
Charleston's nineteenth-
century preference for
private garden spaces
hidden behind gates and
walls continues to this day.
This garden exhibits the
fine wrought-iron work
and lush azalea planting so
characteristic of the
Charleston town garden.

Dense evergreen plants in
terra-cotta pots, herbs, and
annuals create a private
outdoor dining space on a
balcony in the middle of
San Francisco.

Square. The notion of shared space and shared ideas is characteristic of city gardening, where the logistics of planting a garden are often overwhelming.

Creating a small private garden space in the city challenges owners to seek nontraditional solutions. Fire escapes, balconies, light wells, the edges of parking areas, have all been extravagantly planted and patiently nurtured by generations of city residents. Perhaps the most significant contribution to city garden history in the twentieth century has been the growing popularity of the roof garden. Even as early as the 1920s roof gardening was seen as an efficient way to use dead space. Extravagant plans were proposed to build playgrounds and athletic facilities on New York roofs just before World War II. Lifting garden spaces off the street, a recommendation made

by generations of modern architects starting with Le Corbusier, not only offers a gardening opportunity for residents without rights to ground-level space, but creates a rich texture of layered planting reaching out in all corners of the city.

City gardeners have pressured the nursery industry to provide plants that thrive in a stressed environment with limited water and reduced planting areas. After many years when it was a struggle to find experts who could advise gardeners on planting in city conditions, a number of specialty firms were created in the 1960s to provide plants and advice on this unique gardening situation. City garden clubs from New York to San Francisco provided sustaining support and educational activities for urban gardeners. The Society of Little Gardens in Philadelphia was

American cities have achieved some semblance of that utopian goal. The garden district of New Orleans, San Antonio's Riverwalk, San Francisco's Golden Gate Park, Boston's Emerald Necklace, the great public spaces of Washington, D.C., have become emblems of their cities—Central Park may well supplant the Empire State Building as the symbol of New York City. American cities demonstrate that public parks and gardens stimulate private garden endeavors. The private gardens of Savannah, Charleston, and San Francisco demonstrate that gardening can become a municipal value. The American city still evokes a complicated set of emotions: fear, ambivalence, irony, awe. Our gardens can expand those feelings, adding pride in the masterworks of our designed parks and public gardens and delight in the unexpected pleasure of the tiny private garden behind a city wall. ✍

NOTES

1. Wright, John W., ed., *The Universal Almanac* (Kansas City, Mo.: Andrews and McMeel, 1991), p. 181.

2. Quoted in John Reps, "William Penn and the Planning of Philadelphia," *Town Planning Review* 27 (April 1956): 29.

3. Quoted in Richard Sennett, *The Conscience of the Eye: The Design and Social Life of Cities* (New York: Knopf, 1990), p. 53.

4. Warner, *To Dwell Is to Garden*, p. 19.

BIBLIOGRAPHY

Boyer, M. Christine. *Dreaming the Rational City: The Myth of American City Planning.* Cambridge, Mass.: MIT Press, 1983.

Bridenbaugh, Carl. *Cities in Revolt: Urban Life in America, 1743–1776.* New York: Knopf, 1955.

———. *Cities in the Wilderness: The First Century of Urban Life in America, 1625–1742.* New York: Ronald Press, 1938.

Hedrick, U. P. *A History of Horticulture in America to 1860.* New York: Oxford University Press, 1950.

Warner, Sam Bass, Jr. *To Dwell Is to Garden: A History of Boston's Community Gardens.* Boston: Northeastern University Press, 1987.

founded in 1914 and did important work with settlement houses and civic projects. The City Garden Club of New York (1918) set itself to work with neighborhoods to create communal back gardens. The San Francisco Garden Club (1926) worked closely with school garden clubs, offered study courses and educational exhibits, and was significantly involved in many civic planting projects.

The history of the urban garden in America is less a story of horticultural triumphs than a documentation of how people really live. A commitment to planned green space both as an organizing principle of city design and as an essential component of a civilized life has given many American cities a distinctive character. The term "garden city" is not an oxymoron or an empty slogan of town boosters. Many

American Artists, American Gardens

❧❧❦

Mac Griswold

❧ *The garden, in all its perceptions and manifestations, has long been a subject for artists, and not less so in America. Whether as place or idea, the garden is depicted variously in American art as imposition of "civilization" upon the wilderness, expression of wealth and power (in much the same way that Catherine Howett, in "Graces and Modest Majesties," describes the impulses behind plantation gardens in the South), imaginative embellishment, realistic duplication, or metaphor for the intricacies of human consciousness.*

All of these approaches bespeak a view of the natural world and our relationship to it—as celebrant, interpreter, creator, caretaker, and admirer. The recording of gardens and "the garden" in American art display the myriad feelings and attitudes toward the land formed by changing social, cultural, and technological factors. The application of these factors forms an engaging dialogue between art and gardens, enriching both. The mutual influence has become a part of the American cultural consciousness in many instances, such as the work of Currier and Ives. In other instances, such as the paintings of Thomas Cole or Georgia O'Keeffe, for example, one finds great personal meaning and discovery.

The enormous variety of knowledge and delight derived from the interplay of art and garden can suggest new ways of looking at our land, our art, and ourselves in a manner that places mankind within the natural order and counteracts a modern alienation from the natural world. This harmony can but be good for people and nature. ❧

WILDERNESS, EUROPE, and the power of print—these were the three great forces that shaped Americans' images of their gardens over the course of five centuries. From the beginning of the seventeenth century, when settlement began in earnest, feelings about the wilderness were complex and ambivalent, a struggle barely reflected in the rare surviving examples of the art of the day that depicts gardens. The conflict is more apparent in literature, where initial descriptions (often intended to attract new settlement) celebrate America's fertility, describing the entire continent as the Garden of Eden. At the same time accounts in journals and letters record struggles with forest, swamp, fever, the land's original inhabitants, and the unknown in tones of fear, awe, and exhaustion.[1] The two notes—celebratory and fearful—have resounded ever since.

In Western art, the idealization of nature as a garden quite separate from its wild surroundings dates back to the Persian *paradeisos*, the fenced park. But in early American imagery it had particular resonance because the wilderness was so extraordinarily *present*, defying the colonists who wished to transform it into field and plot. Nature began to be idealized as wilderness only in the nineteenth century, when the dangers the actual wilderness presented were perceived to be distant. Then, all too quickly, such idealization became elegiac—a reminder of something precious that had vanished. (The process of "taming the land," as it is often called, took barely five hundred years in America, compared to Europe's thousand-year-long forest-clearing effort.)

Whatever the political conditions, and whatever nationalist noises were made, Europe, especially England, was the inspiration for American garden design, and in the first centuries, garden plants and seeds were imported as well. Beautiful and useful American plants were admitted to the garden on a one-by-one basis, but the framework was European. A similar situation existed in American art until the twentieth century: when American artists depicted their native surroundings, including gardens, and even if they endeavored to express a distinct American character, their artistic theories and models were European, and their struggle was to match European artistic achieve-

OPENING ILLUSTRATION:
"I have made much of green rectangles in my drawings and landscapes," says painter and architect Barbara Stauffacher Solomon. "They are paragon, paradigm, panacea and paradise. . . . Here the rectangles are lavender. Order is in the furrows of the fields. . . . Order is orientation and cultivation; enclosure makes a landscape into a paradise; magic is where illusion is reality and opposites merge. A greenhouse is a garden. A cypress wall is architecture. A roofless room is a garden. Within a wisteria arcade there is architecture." *Solomon's Drawing No. 1*, one of a set of five paintings entitled *2 Fields + 3 Houses = A Landscape*, takes its forms from the simplest of farm patterns: the field.

ment. How was it possible otherwise, since their cultural perspective was European?

The power of print in terms of illustrative material was not widely felt until the nineteenth century, but it has more than made up for this short time span in its pervasive influence on gardens since, with the rapid circulation of ideal garden images continuing today in many forms. Photographs in shelter magazines, earthworks by artists like Mary Miss, and even the Jolly Green Giant tell us what to expect from a garden and how it should look.

Images of the garden, whether we consider them works of art or merely iconographic signs, imply the imposition of order on the part of the artist; choice and elimination are part of creation. Gardens themselves were already part of the massive ordering of the wild landscape, an ordering perceived by European arrivals to the "new continent" to be a gigantic struggle between the agriculture they brought with them and what they called the wilderness, where Native Americans had long lived and gardened before the arrival of white men and women.

Works of art that show just the colonial garden, as opposed to the entire farmscape so arduously shaped by ox, ax, and plow, are nonexistent among the handful of depictions that predate 1750. Rather one finds near-cartographic images of place, like the drawing-room overmantel painting at Holly Hill in Anne Arundel County, Maryland, painted between 1717 and 1733. Early images of gardens, quite separate from the flowers of forest, swamp, and meadow magnificently limned by artists like John White or Mark Catesby, almost always *were* parts of maps: the embroideries of (perhaps imaginary) planting beds that European cartographers used to fill the empty spaces on urban plans, for example.[2]

Colonists during the first century of European settlement were hopeful but homesick; they grew familiar European plants, and garden archeology reveals traces of European land forms and planting patterns.[3] Garden symbolism and imagery used in sermons, letters, diaries, and descriptions, and seen in the floral motifs used in the decorative arts, was largely biblical in inspiration and had to do with fruitfulness, safety, and beauty.

An unknown painter aboard Sir Francis Drake's pirate vessel recorded the lively richness of American aboriginal life in about 1573. One section of this extraordinary manuscript, which is entitled *Histoire Naturelle des Indes*, is a courtship narrative. In an illustration entitled "The Manner and Style of Gardening and Planting of the Indians," the eager suitor "sows several kinds of grain for his food . . . to please his fiancée and sufficient to feed his wife and children [to be]; the soil being so fertile as to bear fruit all the time."

Colonel George Boyd's stoutly fenced, south-facing pleasure garden had a "broad Ally" lined up with the front entrance of his house, set close to his shipyard at the mouth of Islington Creek, in Portsmouth, New Hampshire. In this canvas of 1774, the anonymous painter included such details as the turned posts at the garden gate, the elegant weathervane that crowned a smokehouse or garden house, and neat rows of blooming plants along the walks. By choosing a stance atop a nearby hill, the painter was able to create a near-bird's-eye view of Boyd's civilized and prosperous domestic universe.

After 1750, American colonists on the eastern seaboard began to feel safe and confident in a land that had become theirs by settlement, if not by political right. Like their European counterparts, the landholding elite began to want pictures of what they had wrought, which by now included ornamental gardens. During the eighteenth century one could find "American gardens" filled with American plants in England, and French and German "wildernesses" that celebrated the life of the noble savage, but Americans' ornamental gardens, with few exceptions, were formal, fenced, symmetrical, and simplified versions of late-seventeenth-century European gardens. The 1774 painting of Colonel Boyd's garden in New Hampshire is an icon that means "country seat" after the English model.[4] Simplification of the garden experience empowered the folk artist who created this work. What mattered to him (or, most doubtfully, her) were the outlines of the garden and its place in the landscape; for the garden-making owner, perhaps

the greatest value of the work of art was its confirmation of his stability, wealth, and culture and its summary of his "improvements." For us, the finest pleasures are the anecdotal details of a vanished country life, such as Colonel Boyd's fancy pond, or "basin," in the middle of his radially laid out garden, or the line of hitching posts outside his picket fence. As is usually the case in topographic views of gardens, what Boyd actually grew remains tantalizingly conjectural, since there is no supporting documentary confirmation. Travelers' accounts do tell us that places like this New Hampshire "country seat" were perhaps not as neat and green as the artist imagined, but the wish to idealize is as old as the artist's brush, and certainly a truly American impulse as well.

In general, painters of gardens, unlike flower painters, seldom dwell on details of species or cultivar. Artists are more concerned with creating a total impression, one hazards. Perhaps such vagueness, such generalization, has to do with the changing nature of gardens thanks to the plants in them. After all, light and distance are what transform architecture, while artists, along with gardeners, surely perceive that other forces—growth and decay—are at work in the garden. It is only possible to say that, over time, the stance generally adopted by artists, both American and European, changes from that of a distant bird's eye (perhaps an implicit statement about a mastery of the land not yet achieved, or the dominant place of man in nature) to the close-up that seems to merge the artist's experience with that of his subject.

After 1785, when they found themselves to be Americans, and no longer colonists, garden makers still longed for the European. Classical imagery, and the paraphernalia of eighteenth-century European gardens—temples, chinoiserie bridges, busts, obelisks, and the like—were associated with culture, and culture with power. A garden like William Paca's, in Annapolis, with a temple for a cold bath, and a bridge as "Chinese" as a Chippendale chair, was as sure an assertion of status as his beautiful blue coat or his diaper-patterned (and bulging) white silk waistcoat. It would be quite wrong, however, to imagine that status was Paca's only concern; he must also have loved the art and craft of gardening, for he made a flowery pleasance at every house he owned.[5]

European aesthetic baggage included the classifications of the Sublime, the Picturesque, and the Beautiful, which had been circulated first by Joseph Addison in the *Spectator* at the beginning of the eighteenth century. Certainly as early as the 1730s, visitors to America and educated Americans alike used the language of "landskip" to describe natural scenery *and* gardens, and garden makers began to include views of the countryside beyond the garden in their calculations, but it would not be until close to the end of the century that "country-house paintings" such as the series of Francis Guy's chairback views of Baltimore estates (in the Baltimore Museum of Art), or actual paintings of Picturesque garden landscapes would appear. John Penn, Jr., a grandson of the founder of Philadelphia, was raised in England and brought to the landscaping of his country seat on the banks of the Schuylkill River (now the site of the

From the tiny detail of the temple and bridge seen in the background of Annapolis nabob William Paca's portrait by Charles Willson Peale, and from painstaking on-site research, an accurate restoration has been created of Paca's 1783 garden—just one of the documentary uses of garden works of art.

Philadelphia Zoo) a complete understanding of the Picturesque. He named his place The Solitude, an appropriately romantic name, and John Nancarrow's handsome sketch plan of 1784 shows the flower garden set far away from the house in a plantation of trees. A vista was cut through to the river at an angle to the house, and a Brownian clump of trees set close to the shore is an artful interruption of the view.[6]

But the Picturesque in gardens and garden images did not endure; what lasted seventy-five years in Eng-

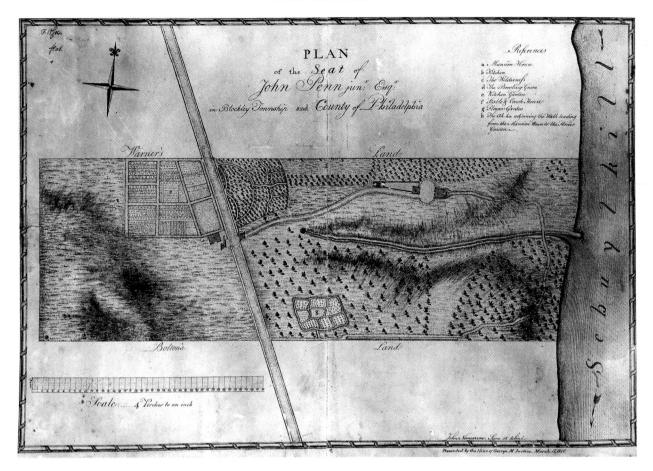

Fine plans can often convey the characteristics of place and garden style better than any sketch or painting, as does this 1784 ink rendering by artist John Nancarrow of John Penn's country seat, Solitude. Note the flower garden at bottom, far from the house, which sits among lawns and woods.

land was telescoped into about thirty in the United States. And even as a limited vogue for the Picturesque style flourished in sophisticated gardens and garden art, formal gardens were recorded by other artists working in vernacular traditions, such as the anonymous painter of *The Plantation*. In 1825 he recorded an inescapable fact of American garden reality: the wilderness was still there, still able to reclaim whatever had been so briefly cultivated. This untamed nature in its wilder aspects was celebrated by the transcendentalist writers and found visual expression in the paintings of the Hudson River school. Additionally, in these paintings the grandeur and beauty of the American wild landscape became identified with the power and nationalistic aspirations of the new republic. However, most gardeners in the

1840s happily turned to tamer stuff than the cliffs and cascades of Cole and Bierstadt for their backyards, specifically to Downing's rendition of John Loudon's theories of garden design, *A Treatise on the Theory and Practice of Landscape Gardening* (1841), the first book for Americans by an American-born landscape gardener. Along with the Picturesque and the Beautiful, Downing included Loudon's new style, "the Gardenesque," which advised planting as many exotics as possible, both to enrich what had been a quite limited palette of trees in the home landscape and to make clear the distinction between garden and unimproved nature. A wide range of newly introduced summer-flowering tropical annuals meant that flower beds for the first time could be resplendently in bloom from May to frost. The American flower garden, long cor-

Wild fox grapes stretch out their tendrils and forest trees their shadows over the cultivated land in this powerful painting of a plantation by an anonymous artist in 1825. The archetypal "big house" of the Southern experience is set off from the slave quarters and other plantation outbuildings by a garland of a garden, fenced and terraced. Below, a sailing ship takes the tobacco to market. Three generations of tobacco exhausted the soil forever.

seted by protective fences and kept close to the house, now burst out in curving beds over the grounds of the home place.

Early-nineteenth-century garden symbolism and imagery also took a different twist: in the seventeenth century, a well-tended and bounteous garden had been a sign of God's favor toward man; during the Enlightenment it came to be seen as a sign that the clockwork of the cosmos was in good working order. By the nineteenth century, however, a fine garden had become a mark of personal character and moral rectitude. Many a household, according to the books of the day at least, rose or fell in public opinion according to the state of its garden.[7]

In art, the single most important factor in the depiction of gardens throughout the nineteenth cen-

tury was the democracy of print. Its low cost and wide dissemination meant that new garden ideas and images spread rapidly to a growing middle class. Downing's *Treatise* went through nine editions between 1841 and 1875, for example, and the century saw the publication of more than a hundred horticultural periodicals. New uses for garden images, such as seed packet illustrations and catalogue covers, were born as the technology of reproduction, color as well as black and white, advanced. By the mid-nineteenth century women had been given charge of the garden and the moral atmosphere of the home, and illustrations in women's periodicals such as *Godey's Lady's Book* and *Peterson's Magazine* promoted the garden setting as ideal for family pursuits. Prints by Currier and Ives, among many others, and books such

When General Nathan Whitfield wrote, "We have had very few roses as yet, the hyacinths, the crocuses, and some few other blooms are out and the rose bushes are full of buds," in 1848, he was probably referring to the parterres seen in the distance at his magnificent Greek Revival house, Gaineswood, in Demopolis, Alabama. Whitfield was said to be his own architect (probably with a master builder) and his own garden designer as well. The house—seen here in an 1860 engraving by John Sartain—survives today; the fifteen-acre landscape garden does not.

Only nine years after the Civil War, nostalgia had set in for antebellum days—and perhaps also for a flowering wilderness that Americans were just beginning to notice was disappearing. Harry Fenn's wood engraving of Magnolia, near Charleston, appeared in poet William Cullen Bryant's two-volume compendium, *Picturesque America*, in 1874. Bryant was also one of the earliest to speak out for a public park in New York City.

FORMER RESIDENCE OF **J.F.D.LANIER** ESQ. AT MADISON IND. NOW OCCUPIED BY **A.C.LANIER**

Civil War financier J. F. D. Lanier laid out this garden in Madison, Indiana, on terraces below his Greek Revival house designed by architect Francis Costigan in the 1840s. Lanier's son, A. C., elaborated the garden and kept it going for many years afterward. The parterres, the dogs, at right, and the magnificent conservatory at back right were all recorded for posterity in the Jefferson County atlas of 1876. Such atlases, and the compendiums of country houses published locally in many regions, are invaluable sources of garden information.

as William Cullen Bryant's *Picturesque America* (1874), with its superb engravings by such artists as Harry Fenn, fostered the association of history, nostalgia, and reverie with the garden. These associations were by no means new, but they *were* new to such a large popular audience.[8]

By the 1880s, in the world of high art, as opposed to folk art, popular art, and book illustration, a generation of European plein air painting had altered the traditional salon formulas for the landscape with fig-ures. Plein air painting fostered a new enthusiasm for the direct experience of nature; perhaps the finest expressions of this movement were the works of American Impressionists living or visiting Connecticut, who included Childe Hassam and Julian Alden Weir. Hassam's best garden paintings were those of the garden of his friend Celia Thaxter, on the island of Appledore, off the Maine-New Hampshire coast (see illustration on page 35).

As the ripples of consciousness spread from the

RIGHT:
Scientific interest in the interaction of plants with their environments, spurred by the publication of Darwin's *On the Origin of Species* (1859), led to the creation of works of art depicting plants in their natural settings. This watercolor by Fidelia Bridges, painted in 1876, is a fine example.

FAR RIGHT:
Intimacy, informality, and privacy are some of the hallmarks of late-nineteenth-century garden painting, qualities shared by James Wells Champney's small gouache. But the hollyhocks and poppies of the charming, straggly "old-fashioned" border in *Garden in Old Deerfield* (c. 1900) are emblematic of something else. Revivalists like Champney looked back to a lost American innocence: the hopeful strength of colonial days, when the nation's spiritual, economic, and social dilemmas lay in the future. Even flowers, they seemed to say, were simple —single and self-sowing!

LEFT:
An image of a rare African-American garden is *The Cabbage Patch*, a painting by Kentucky-born artist Thomas P. Anshutz, who was a student of Thomas Eakins. Though perhaps somewhat sentimental, this 1879 portrait of a vernacular garden and its gardeners does not seem idealized.

impact of Darwin's theory of natural selection, the commitment on the part of painters like John Trost Richards, Fidelia Bridges, and Maria Oakey Dewing to represent new scientific insights into the organic rhythms of the plant world gained momentum.[9] Often a microcosm (a single clump of plants, sometimes in the wild, sometimes in the garden) stood for the natural universe, a visual counterpart to Darwin's "entangled bank."[10] The English Arts and Crafts movement, and its American echo, the Aesthetic movement, also had an effect on the depiction of gardens[11] as artists looked to the conventions of woodcut and nonperspective art for a simplification and strengthening of form. In garden design, the Arts and Crafts movement, with its nostalgic look back at a holistic preindustrial world and its emphasis on regional materials and styles led to the examination of America's own preindustrial past, and thence to the "old-fashioned garden," recorded by painters such as James Wells Champney, and to the Colonial Revival.[12]

Around the turn of the nineteenth century a perfectible world, and man's place in the hierarchy of creation, no longer seemed assured. Paradoxically, a great spate of garden paintings, part of the heightened garden consciousness of the late Victorian and the Edwardian world, seemed to proclaim the garden as the last, best refuge from the combat of nature, or at least the combat of human nature. Though artists like Maurice Prendergast continued to depict a harmonious society at play in the parks and on the beaches of America (see illustration on page 35), the counterimage was the dreamer with eyes averted, sealed in a separate contemplative envelope even in the presence of others, as are Charles Curran's lotus lilies.

Which are the flowers Charles Curran is referring to in his title, *Lotus Lilies* (1888): the sheltered, dreaming women in the boat or the pale, fragile blossoms also afloat on the sunny pond? The women's sunshade, whose shape echoes that of the giant lotus pads, strengthens the frequently made implicit parallel. The rower of this boat is the painter or the viewer; the women are passengers, seemingly as powerless to move themselves as are the rooted lilies.

In 1916 an unknown photographer took over a hundred pictures of millionaire Morton F. Plant's "Branford House," in Groton, on the Connecticut coast. Hand-tinted and presented to Mr. and Mrs. Plant in an immense album, they tell us all we know about this colossal, classical vanished garden. Its sunken pink marble pools, fountains, and flights of stairs designed by Boston landscape architect Guy Lowell stretched out below the Gothic Revival house. Stairposts and niches were adorned with platoons of fashionable hothouse plants, such as this immense agave in the foreground.

Gardens themselves, while still indicators of status, increasingly symbolized safety and privacy rather than culture. A similar shift occurred in garden design in the late twenties and thirties, where what could be called the late nineteenth century's "postcard mentality" of wholesale, eclectic importation of European garden effects and architecture slowly gave way to a more considered use of space, and stone architecture gave way to the architecture of plant forms.

The high-art cataloguing of the wonders of nature, including those seen in the garden, stopped in the twentieth century. Reasons were many and various. For example, the advent of photography as an art form shifted the balance of artist-as-observer. Art became personal expression, while photography, as it was at first quite untruthfully perceived, was heralded as a way to reproduce actual, unmediated experience. In the early years of the twentieth century, print sequences by photographers such as Mattie Edwards Hewitt[13] interpreted the American garden experience in a narrative way just as seventeenth-century artists such as Israël Silvestre had done in their suites of

Garden photographs of the twenties, like Mattie Edwards Hewitt's portrait of the border at "Breaknolle"—car-manufacturer George Studebaker's "cottage" at the resort colony of Little Boar's Head, New Hampshire—captured the soft fullness of a short New England summer.

Hewitt, who specialized in landscape architectural photography, took her pictures with an 8 × 10 or an 11 × 14 view camera mounted on a heavy wooden tripod. Many of her prints were bromide silver, as was this beauty.

prints of palace gardens. [14] (Videos, such as Mary Lucier's multiscreen experiences, have continued still farther down this narrative path.) Even more than stance, or distance, framing defines the representation of a garden: to experience a garden in actuality is to move through space along paths or across lawns, but for an artist, garden depiction has traditionally most often meant choosing a single fragment of that experience and holding it as a "still." One can argue that twentieth-century multiple images such as Hewitt's have another meaning besides quantification of the garden experience, however; they can also be understood in an almost cubist way as simultaneous perceptions of the same reality.

With the advent of Modernism and the influence of psychology, artists began a direct investigation of their own perceptions; they attempted to find within themselves, and within their art, an order that would represent the new order of nature, an order at once cosmic and cellular. [15] Art became self-referential, and images of the garden became symbols of artists' interior landscapes.

During the twentieth century artists have abstracted images of the garden to serve subjective aims. From the farm fields of Virginia that Armenian immigrant painter Arshile Gorky visited in the forties came inspiration for *One Year the Milkweed*. Gorky, a close observer of nature, repeats a skeletal structural form derived from the milkweed pod, inventing a pictorial language that is both expressive and mysterious.

Alfred Caldwell, Jens Jensen's assistant in the twenties, understood even then that we must begin to look at the nature of things, instead of imposing ourselves on nature. His delicate and fanciful drawing, *Sun House*, indicates one way to begin. The curved house at upper right (which is not a solar house but takes advantage of the high and low seasonal arcs of the sun) finds circular echoes in the landscape. Besides a circular pool and garage, Caldwell more subtly uses a rose arbor to extend the curve of the house at top center. At lower left is a marvelous (though probably wildly impractical) circular vegetable garden.

OPPOSITE:
Climbers make lacy screens
of leaves and flowers in a
garden; artist Patsy
Norvell's *Climber* (1982) is
a screen too. Sandblasted
patterns echo the shape of
the see-through glass
screen—or do the climbers
set the pattern for the
shape of the screen? In a
garden and in art, synergy
is often the best answer.

Georgia O'Keeffe, *Jack-in-
the Pulpit No. 5*, 1930.

Images that directly present the natural world, such as Patricia Norvell's sinuous, sandblasted glass screen, *Climber,* abstract and isolate plant movement and habit until the work of art becomes a strange simulacrum of experience. A valid and moving pictorial garden image is Arshile Gorky's great *One Year the Milkweed,* where the artist structures his abstract, subjective work with fragments of botanical description taken from the dissection of milkweed flowers. [16]

Landscape architects' drawings of the seventies and eighties present a less subjective, though perhaps more visionary, version of what part gardens and garden imagery can play in the world of today. Process, rather than permanence, becomes the order of salvation. Drawings like Alfred Caldwell's *Sun House* and Barbara Stauffacher Solomon's *2 Fields + 3 Houses = A Landscape* express a longing to reforge links with the old patterns of agriculture and with those of the earth itself. They also celebrate the continuity of the seasons, the beauty of the solar system, the preciousness of water.

As with portraiture or still life, a close look at garden and landscape art as a genre reveals as much about our history, thought, and social organization as it does about the subject itself. Early American artists probably drew as much comfort from the aesthetic order they projected on the landscape as they did from the beauty of the farms they saw and captured on wood or canvas; Thomas Cole and other Hudson River School painters found self-definition as Americans; late-nineteenth-century garden and nature painters used their art as a stage where religion and science struggled against each other. The garden in art has provided room for Hassam's experiments with color, as well as for the kinds of exploration of sexuality and self-liberation that Georgia O'Keeffe made in her gigantic close-ups of flowers. Alfred Caldwell found hope in the planned landscape for a future that projects harmony with nature, not dominance over it. The garden has indeed been fertile ground for American artists. ✒

NOTES

1. See Stilgoe, *Common Landscape,* for a detailed description of the wilderness and its longstanding associations with the powers of darkness.

2. See Leighton, *Early American Gardens,* p. 168, for plate of a late-seventeenth-century French drawing of New York City, presently in the Bibliothèque Nationale in Paris.

3. See Nicholas Luccketti, "Archaeological Evidence at Bacon's Castle, Surry County, Virginia," in Kelso and Most, *Earth Patterns,* pp. 23–43.

4. For a description see Abbott Lowell Cummings, "Eighteenth-Century New England Garden Design: The Pictorial Evidence," in Maccubbin and Martin, *British and American Gardens,* pp. 130–135.

5. Paca maintained an estate on the Eastern Shore, Wye Hall, and between 1834 and 1852 also had a garden at Mount Pleasant, in Harford County, Md. See Historical Society of Talbot County, *Art of Gardening,* p. 30.

6. For a discussion of gardens and garden styles around Philadelphia, see Elizabeth McLean, "Town and Country Gardens in Eighteenth-Century Philadelphia," in Maccubbin and Martin, pp. 136–147.

7. Scott, *The Art of Beautifying Suburban Home Grounds,* is an example of how entwined gardening became with the concepts of virtue and morality.

8. See Tice, *Gardening in America,* for the impact of the popular garden image on the American public.

9. See Ella Foshay's treatment of the place of nineteenth-century scientific development in artistic theory and practice in *Reflections of Nature,* pp. 51–93.

10. Darwin, *Origin of Species.* In the last paragraph of the book, Darwin uses the image of "an entangled bank, clothed with many plants of many kinds, with birds singing on the bushes, with various insects flitting about, and with worms crawling through the damp earth" as the model of the universe created by natural selection.

11. See Gerdts, *Down Garden Paths,* for a discussion of the Aesthetic movement's effect on the depiction of gardens.

12. For a succinct treatment of the "old-fashioned garden," see Clayton, *Gardens on Paper,* pp. 158–159. For the characteristics of the colonial revival in the garden, see William Butler, "Another City upon a Hill: Litchfield, Connecticut, and the Colonial Revival"; Charles B. Hosmer, Jr., "The Colonial Revival in the Public Eye: Williamsburg and Early Garden Restoration"; and Edward Teitelman and Betsy Fahlman, "Wilson Eyre and the Colonial Revival in Philadelphia," all in Axelrod, *Colonial Revival in America.* For visual documentation of "old-fashioned" and colonial revival gardens, see the glass lantern slides and black-and-white 35 mm. slides of the Archive of American Gardens at the Office of Horticulture, Smithsonian Institution.

13. Garden photography as a separate genre was a field in which many women found career opportunities, as they did in landscape architecture. A new discipline, its structure was not yet rigid enough to exclude women. See Close, *Portrait of an Era in Landscape Architecture,* for a discussion of Mattie Edwards Hewitt, one of the most prominent women garden photographers of the teens and twenties.

14. French artist Israël Silvestre (1621–1691) documented the gardens of more than fifty châteaux and palaces, including Fontainebleau, Vaux-le-Vicomte, and Versailles.

15. See Foshay, *Reflections of Nature,* pp. 149–179.

16. For Gorky's familiarity with botanical dissections see Foshay, *Reflections of Nature,* pp. 89–90, and nn. pp. 130–134.

BIBLIOGRAPHY

Archive of American Gardens, Office of Horticulture, Smithsonian Institution, Washington, D.C.

Axelrod, Alan, ed. *The Colonial Revival in America.* New York: Norton, for the Henry Francis du Pont Winterthur Museum, 1985.

Blazer, Werner. *Architecture and Nature, The Work of Alfred Caldwell.* Boston: Birkhauser, 1984.

Clayton, Virginia T. *Gardens on Paper: Prints and Drawings, 1200–1900.* Washington, D.C.: National Gallery of Art, 1990.

Close, Leslie Rose. *Portrait of an Era in Landscape Architecture: The Photographs of Mattie Edwards Hewitt.* Bronx, N.Y.: Wave Hill, 1983.

Darwin, Charles. *On the Origin of Species.* London: J. Murray, 1859. Reprint. New York: Avenel Books, 1979.

Foshay, Ella M. *Reflections of Nature; Flowers in American Art.* New York: Knopf, 1984. Reprint. New York: Weathervane Books, 1990.

Griswold, Mac. *Pleasures of the Garden: Images in the Metropolitan Museum of Art.* New York: Metropolitan Museum of Art and Harry N. Abrams, 1987.

Gerdts, William H. *Down Garden Paths: The Floral Environment in American Art.* Cranbury, N.J.: Associated University Presses, 1983.

Hedrick, U. P. *A History of Horticulture in America to 1860.* New York: Oxford University Press, 1950. Reprint, *with an Addendum of Books Published from 1861–1920,* by Elisabeth Woodburn. Portland, Oreg.: Timber Press, 1988.

Jellicoe, Sir Geoffrey, and Susan Jellicoe, consultant eds, with Patrick Goode and Michael Lancaster, executive eds. *Oxford Companion to Gardens.* New York: Oxford University Press, 1986.

Kelso, William M., and Rachel Most, eds. *Earth Patterns: Essays in Landscape Archeology.* Charlottesville: University Press of Virginia, 1990.

Leighton, Ann. *Early American Gardens: "For Meate or Medicine."* Boston: Houghton, Mifflin, 1970.

Lockwood, Alice G. B., ed. and comp. *Gardens of Colony and State: Gardens and Gardeners of the American Colonies and of the Republic before 1840.* 2 vols. New York: Charles Scribner's Sons for The Garden Club of America, 1931–34.

Maccubbin, Robert P., and Peter Martin, eds. *British and American Gardens in the Eighteenth Century: Eighteen Illustrated Essays on Garden History.* Williamsburg, Va.: Colonial Williamsburg Foundation, 1984.

Pisano, Ronald G. *Long Island Landscape Painting 1820–1920.* vol. I. Boston: Little, Brown, New York Graphic Society, 1985.

Sarudy, Barbara Wells. "Eighteenth-Century Gardens of the Chesapeake." *Journal of Garden History* 9 (July–September 1989).

Scott, Frank J. *Victorian Gardens, Part I: Suburban Home Grounds by Frank J. Scott.* Originally published as *The Art of Beautifying Suburban Home Grounds of Small Extent.* New York: D. Appleton, 1870. Reprint. Watkins Glen, N.Y.: American Life Foundation and Study Institute, 1977.

Stilgoe, John. *Common Landscape of America: 1580 to 1845.* New Haven: Yale University Press, 1982.

Stritikus, George R., ed. *Alabama: Her People, Houses, and Gardens.* Catalog for a traveling exhibit for the Alabama Cooperative Extension Service, in Cooperation with the Alabama Historical Commission, 1986. n.p.

Tice, Patricia M. *Gardening in America, 1830–1910.* Rochester, N.Y.: The Strong Museum, 1984.

Van Valkenbergh, Michael R. *Transforming the American Garden: 12 New Landscape Designs.* Cambridge, Mass.: Harvard University Graduate School of Design, 1986.

The Ladies' Floral Cabinet

AND PICTORIAL HOME COMPANION

Entered according to Act of Congress, by HENRY T. WILLIAMS, in the year 1871, in the Office of the Librarian of Congress, Washington, D. C.

BY HENRY T. WILLIAMS.   VOL I.   NEW YORK, DECEMBER, 1871.   INITIAL No.   PRICE 10 CENTS.

Home Comforts and Pleasures.

Horticulture and American Character

❧❧❧

Tamara Plakins Thornton

❧ *What does gardening have to do with moral stature? Is a rose salvific? Can planting an orchard improve the quality of one's interior life? In the context of the nineteenth century, these questions assume a serious tone. At first, involvement with horticulture was seen as an antidote or as curative to the greed then rampant in this country. The more money one had, therefore, the more one could benefit from horticultural and rural pursuits. Because horticulture was not seen as a product or commodity (it was too natural, too pure) it was a way of associating oneself with something at once useful and noncommercial. Further, men who had gardens did not move about and would consequently have a greater interest in the affairs of their community, and in bringing about a more stable society.*

Having used horticulture for their own moral improvement, the upper classes then turned their attention to the plight of the poor, especially the urban poor and the great numbers of newly arrived "foreigners." Horticulture, it was thought, would instill virtue and rid people of many vices associated with poverty and the "laboring classes." Children were especially targeted, which led to the school garden movement. To be sure these projects did much good but their motivation was a belief that horticulture taught republican virtues: hard work, thrift, and the sacrosanct worth of private property.

All of these perceptions of horticulture can still be felt today, not because they are simply held over but because there is some truth in them. We are now in the midst of a "back-to-the-earth movement," a concern with the greening of our cities to enhance the quality of life for all, especially those who are unable to have a garden. Gardening is also considered psychologically restful. An awareness of the role plants play in our lives is essential to the good stewardship of our planet, making it all the more important for children. And, in the end, being in the garden gives us a chance to start over, to be in Eden once again and be confronted with the original choice. ❧

COLONIAL AMERICANS gardened for show or for necessity, but for the most part, they did not garden for pleasure. Although wealthy merchants and planters laid out their estates in the style of English aristocrats, and ordinary people cultivated kitchen gardens for food and medicine, it was not until well into the nineteenth century that it occurred to many of our countrymen that horticulture might be undertaken as a form of recreation. Then, around 1820, the place of horticulture in America underwent a tremendous change, to the point that gardening assumed a significance for our national culture well beyond what it holds even today. Horticulture entered the mainstream of American life as no mere hobby, but as a movement. As it took shape in horticultural periodicals and societies, the horticultural movement promised far more than relaxing Sundays in the garden; it promised moral benefits to an entire nation. Whatever ailed America a good stiff dose of gardening was sure to cure. Were Americans too boorish? Plant some vines. Were they too materialistic? Cultivate flowers. Were they too restless? Plant some trees. Did they drink too much? Start an orchard. Were the men too greedy and the women too fragile? Get thee to a garden.

The foremost propagandist for this nineteenth-century horticultural movement was a nurseryman from Newburgh, New York, Andrew Jackson Downing. Downing's origins were relatively humble, but his social aspirations were high. He greatly admired, and probably envied, the manor lords of the Hudson River Valley whose elegant estates he provided with plant materials. Downing married into the local aristocracy, but there was a good deal more to his ascent of the social ladder than an astute match. More critical was his campaign to raise the status of his profession

from a manual occupation to a full-blown fine art with great cultural import for America. Downing was successful in his efforts because he fashioned this new role for horticulture in the context of Americans' hopes and fears for their rapidly changing nation.

Downing lived in a time of unprecedented economic and social transformation. To Americans of the pre–Civil War era, the scope and pace of change was dizzying. Within the space of a mere three decades, a once rural and agricultural nation underwent an explosion of trade and manufacturing. Along the settled seaboard, older towns—Boston, New York, Philadelphia—mushroomed into bustling commercial entrepôts. Brand-new cities—Rochester, Cincinnati, Chicago—appeared along the transportation corridors of the nation's ever-expanding interior. This modern world was a paradise of opportunity to be sure, but it also loomed as a nightmare of instability and immorality. Young men flocking to the cities in search of wealth were warned against the fatal temptations of liquor and loose women. Revival preachers castigated Americans for worshipping at the altar of Mammon, while highbrow foreign travelers humiliated them by portraying America as a land of uncouth tobacco spitters and philistine moneygrubbers. Americans, it appeared, were engaged in a fevered scramble for wealth and power, discarding whatever did not advance their personal fortunes as just so much excess baggage. What would become of such an America, so newly born, so quickly doomed? Middle-class reformers came up with many a cure. Some regarded evangelical Christianity as an effective counterweight to modern immorality. Others looked to virtuous wives and pious mothers to impress the husbands and sons of America with the importance of morality and religion. Downing and his fellow horticulturists confronted the same anxieties and proposed a novel cure.

Why is it, Downing asked, that in England even the meanest hovel is ornamented with flowers and vines, while in America there is no such interest in gardening? Because, he answered, we suffered "from that lowest species of idolatry, the love of money." Because, answered a second horticulturist, while "the mind [is] absorbed at the shrine of Mammon, although Eden's beauties are everywhere displayed in

For Downing, a vine-covered cottage (designed here for a workingman) suggested both a refined appreciation of beauty—"because mere utility would never lead any person to plant flowering vines"—and the refining influence of women—"whose very planting of vines is a labor of love offered upon the domestic altar."

rich profusion they will be neglected or despised." Replied a third: "Because we Americans are so particularly *practical,* and so possessed of the demon of trade, that nothing is valuable which cannot be sold."[1]

Horticulture, promised Downing, would counter this American tendency toward materialism. By cultivating the products of nature for their beauty and perfection, we would prove our appreciation of that which had no market value. "Surely," insisted one confident horticulturist, "[he who plants a garden] looks beyond the mere *profit* of his labors and rejects the insinuation, that his every act is an act of cold calculating indemnity for toil and attention."[2] Downing eagerly seized on evidence of a growing interest in gardening as "one of the most striking proofs of the progress of refinement, in the United States," a portent of our final triumph over greed and boorishness.[3]

Just how would horticulture work this moral change? In the contemplation of God's works, the horticulturist would be brought to an appreciation of divine beauty and perfection, thus purifying his soul and refining his sensibilities. "Who," asked one enthusiast rhetorically, "when his attention is directed to the simplest petal in the great floral family, but feels his intellect elevated and enlarged, and withdrawn from the cold calculations of everyday existence?" Horticulture, explained Downing, "has the incalculable advantage of fostering only the purest feelings, and, (unlike many other occupations of business men,) refining, instead of hardening the heart." The "toil, the hurry, the speculation, the sudden reverse," wrote Lydia H. Sigourney, the "restlessness and din of the rail-road principle," the "spirit of accumulation which threatens to corrode every generous sensibility"—these are all "modified by the sweet friendship of the quiet plants." Perhaps only Jacob Lorillard, cigar king and president of the New York Horticultural Society, managed to break free of the literally florid prose when he toasted "Horticulture—free from the perplexities of Wall Street."[4]

Nor were materialism and boorishness the only moral failings to be corrected by the practice of horticulture. Also worrisome to contemporaries was what

Philip S. Van Rensselaer of Clinton Point, New York, was among the Hudson River horticulturists who spared no expense on their great estates. Costly greenhouses sheltering exotic plants represented an aristocratic disdain for thrift and practicality.

Downing identified as the "spirit of unrest" manifest in the penchant to be always on the move—farther west, to the metropolis, up the social scale. "Much as we admire the energy of our people," he wrote, "we value no less the love of order, the obedience to law, the security and repose of society, the love of home, and the partiality to localities endeared by birth or association, of which it is in some degree the antagonist."[5] Communities filled with men on the make constituted a shaky basis for a virtuous and stable republic. But how to make people stay put? Downing's answer was to plant roots—literally. A man who planted a garden would develop an attachment to the very soil and be unlikely to hazard transplanting. Children raised in a home embellished with nature's ornaments would ever think fondly of the family homestead and be unwilling to leave what had assumed the status of sacred ground. Horticulturists counted on decreasing social friction by keeping the humble quite literally in their place. "Absorbed in the cultivation of his favorite flowers, his patch of vegetables, or his orchards of fruit," commented one Boston horticulturist, "the poor man envies not the wealthy, nor is his sane and well-braced mind dis-

turbed by the diseased and empty dreams of the ambitious."[6]

The same dedication to domestic adornment promised to cure America's drinking problem as well. What man on his way home from work would linger at the dram shop when the charms of orchard and garden were calling him? And once at home, the breadwinner could slake his thirst not with "the fiery products of distillation"[7]—for Americans drank enormous amounts of whiskey—but with the relatively benign products of his own apple trees or vineyards.

It was these sorts of moral claims that lay behind what amounted to an explosion of popular interest in horticulture. By the 1820s, periodicals catering largely to gentleman farmers began to carry items of interest to gardening enthusiasts as well. By the 1830s, periodicals specializing in horticulture appeared. Most were published in the cities of the Northeast, but others, such as the Reverend Henry Ward Beecher's *Western Farmer and Gardener,* published in Cincinnati, reflected the larger range of the movement.

We see the same scope in the formation of horticultural societies. The first such was the New York Horticultural Society, established in 1818. It was followed in the next decade by what quickly became the leading organizations of their kind in the nation, the Pennsylvania Horticultural Society, established in Philadelphia in 1827, and the Massachusetts Horticultural Society, established two years later in Boston. Over the next few decades, other societies were established until, by the eve of the Civil War, there were over forty horticultural societies in the United States. Not surprisingly, in line with their reformist function, they were located in areas that represented the cutting edge of social and economic change. Some, such as Baltimore's Maryland Horticultural Society, were established in the rapidly expanding cities of the eastern seaboard. Those in Albany, Rochester, and Buffalo lined the route of the Erie Canal, an important catalyst of national economic expansion. Still others—in Cincinnati, in Chicago, in St. Louis—appeared in the commercial and manufacturing centers of the American interior. Here the symptoms of the disease of modernization were the most acute; here the cure would have to be effected. That is why the horticultural movement never took firm root in the one region of the nation relatively untouched by these changes, the South.

Horticultural societies sponsored exhibitions, awarded premiums for prize entries, established libraries, and distributed seeds and cuttings solicited from domestic and overseas correspondents. But what is most interesting about these societies is the type of people they attracted into their ranks. Until after the Civil War, they were male organizations. Members tended to fall into two categories—nurserymen, seedsmen, and practical gardeners on the one hand and, on the other, wealthy and socially prominent merchants, manufacturers, financiers, and professionals. The first group dominated the exhibitions and often assumed responsibilities that required professional expertise, such as judging entries. But it was the second group that dominated the societies as a whole. They held the important offices; they speechified and toasted at the annual dinners; they set the tone. In Philadelphia, we find banker Nicholas Biddle; in New York, the eminent physician, David

The Massachusetts Horticultural Society's headquarters, Horticultural Hall, housed exhibition space, meeting rooms, and a library on the upper floor while accommodating related business enterprises at street level. The expertise provided by professional nurserymen and seedsmen lay at the foundation of horticultural society activities, but the elevated status of the society's merchants, industrialists, and professionals guaranteed their dominance.

Hosack; in Boston, blueblood lawyer John Lowell; in Albany, Judge Jesse Buell; in Cincinnati, lawyer and real estate magnate Nicholas Longworth.

Nor was theirs a superficial interest in horticulture. Take, for example, Thomas Handasyd Perkins, a wealthy Boston China merchant. He invested ten thousand dollars a year—a princely sum—in laying out and improving the gardens of his Brookline estate. Perkins maintained an impressive horticultural library, imported fruits, flowers, and trees from abroad, and built several huge steam-heated greenhouses for his pineapples, peaches, nectarines, and camellias. Among his horticultural delicacies were the *Enkianthus quinqueflorus,* a rare Chinese shrub, the only one of its sort in America, and a variety of grape presented to him by no less than Sir Joseph Paxton, gardener to the Duke of Devonshire (and later, designer of the Crystal Palace). Abroad on business trips, Perkins visited private estates, commercial nurseries, and botanical gardens; at home, he appended requests for cantaloupe seeds to his letters to foreign business agents.

Even more tireless in his horticultural efforts was fellow Bostonian Marshall Pinckney Wilder, a wealthy commission merchant. On his Dorchester estate, Hawthorn Grove, Wilder cultivated fruits and flowers on an almost commercial scale. His fruit trees numbered in the thousands, producing at one point an astounding nine hundred varieties of the pear alone. Three hundred varieties of the camellia grew under glass. To carry out this enormous enterprise, Wilder maintained an extensive staff of gardeners, but he personally spent several hours every morning supervising operations and even on occasion getting his hands dirty. "After breakfast and family duties," wrote one horticultural editor, "he goes forth to see that each man is at his post, to drop a word of encouragement to the industrious and the faithful, and by his own example to encourage and instruct them, now training a vine, or giving a finishing touch to a boquet [*sic*], then wielding the spade or the pruning knife, hybridizing a Camellia, planting a tree, inserting a bud, sketching a flower, or gathering the first fruit of a new variety of Pear for subsequent study, delineation, and description."[8] Perkins and Wilder were by no means unique in their zeal for horticulture. Many of the nation's wealthiest men of business and the professions purchased country estates and actively pursued a horticultural program after hours, on weekends, and in the summertime.

Why the elite should dominate the horticultural movement is one of the key issues in understanding the role of horticulture in nineteenth-century America. As we have seen, horticulture as presented by such men as Andrew Jackson Downing was a cure for the moral ailments of America as a whole. Elite horticulturists went along with that interpretation and

added something new that served their own purposes—horticulture as an antidote to the moral diseases endemic among America's upper classes, the afflictions of greed and ambition. These ills were hardly unique to the upper classes, but while others might engage in an unrestrained scramble for wealth and power, only these men had been fatally successful at it, and so the stigma of materialism and boorishness pressed most heavily on them. Thus, in much horticultural propaganda, those people in desperate need of the horticultural cure are clearly upper class.

These characters are truly pathetic men. Here is one "panting and stirring in the ranks of Fashion," another engaged in a "feverish" race for wealth, a third "the man of the world, panting with the gold-fever."[9] Their single-minded worship of Mammon threatens spiritual and physical health alike, torturing their consciences, infecting their bodies. "Let him who is engaged in the racking cares of commerce, say in what frame of mind *his* eyes close in sleep," wrote one horticulturist in 1837, "and what are the anxieties of his waking hours. Let the manufacturer tell of his feverish dreams by night, and his dyspetic symptoms by day. . . . Look at all this—follow these men—look at their daily walks and occupations—and then turn to the horticulturist." He alone sleeps in peace, dreaming of his fields and orchards, awakening refreshed. "His dreams," unlike those of the merchant, "are not harassed by thieves that rob the vaults, the keys of which are tied to the wrists of the cashier for safety." And unlike the manufacturer, he has no nightmare of a "villanous [*sic*] hook [that] catches him by the waistband, and drags him through intricate machinery" to his death, much as it may have done to his factory operatives that very day. No, the horticulturist need not suffer "the fears of the deep curse which rests on him who has injured the widow and the fatherless." His sleep is sweet, his conscience clear, and all because, in the garden, he "can commune with higher powers," year by year, until "his nature will approximate more to the simplicity and purity of innocence."[10]

As the horticultural vogue caught on among upper-class Americans, the new taste for gardening was touted as proof that America's millionaires had

By the late antebellum period, increasingly elaborate horticultural displays, such as this one of the 1850s at the Horatio Hollis Hunnewell estate, Wellesley, Massachusetts, had become the vogue. In their preference for ornamental gardens, elite horticulturists hoped to demonstrate their rejection of a philistine concern for utility and their embrace of a more aristocratic ethos of beauty.

in fact risen above the drive for riches. Indeed the new popularity of horticulture was seen as the climax of a moral drama of epic proportions. For Henry Dearborn, an insurance executive and the first president of the Massachusetts Horticultural Society, the entire history of the human race was best understood as a procession from "the wild and erratic pursuits of the savage" to the "quiet avocations of the husbandman" to the "triumphant labors" of the horticulturist. Significantly, Dearborn acknowledged that in between the moral simplicity of the agricultural stage of human progress and the moral sublimity of the horticultural climax, there existed an age of commerce characterized by greed and materialism. Drawing on

biblical authority, Dearborn noted that only after Solomon had enriched his kingdom with foreign commerce and his people had been rebuked for their extravagant ways of living, were the legendary gardens of ancient Israel created. [11] Among those listening to Dearborn's address were many a nineteenth-century Solomon, but in their very participation in horticultural activities, these men could convince themselves that greed was a thing of their past as well. "Ladies and Gentleman," announced the textile millionaire Abbott Lawrence to the audience at Boston's 1842 horticultural festival, "the exhibition here to-night, altogether, is the best proof that can be presented of a high state of civilization and refine-

At annual dinners like this one, in 1848, held by the Massachusetts Horticultural Society in Boston's Faneuil Hall, society members indulged in a feast of self- congratulation. Speeches and toasts celebrating the unselfish beneficence of the well-heeled members highlighted the festivities.

ment." Elaborated Caleb Cushing, who had just extracted a commercial treaty from the Chinese: "We have got beyond mere utility."[12]

Horticultural gatherings thus became orgies of self-congratulation, at which participants toasted each other on their mutual achievement of moral purity and cultural refinement. A favorite theme was the wealthy horticulturist as unselfish benefactor of the human race. One proper Bostonian raised his glass to *Our Merchant Princes,*—Their ships have ploughed the sea, and furrowed the ocean; their enterprise garners up rich crops, which their liberality now dispenses with an unsparing hand."[13] Another toasted horticultural societies, associations "not like many others, founded on *selfishness,*"—could he have meant business partnerships?—"but conferring *essential benefits* on the whole human race."[14] And the 1832 dinner of the Massachusetts Horticultural Society wrapped up with an *Ode* written for the occasion:

Yet, not for ourselves would we draw from the soil
  The beauty that Heaven in its vitals has hidden;
For, thus to lock up the fair fruits of our toil,
  Were bliss half-possessed, and a sin all-forbidden,
    Like morning's first ray,
    When it spreads into day,
Our hearts must flow out, until self fades away.[15]

An even more popular theme was the horticulturist himself as a product of "cultivation." The very practice of gardening would ennoble the gardener, much as his efforts improved plant species. Jacob Lorillard expressed this sentiment at a New York Horticultural Society dinner, when he toasted "the Horticulturist, who unites the cultivation of the moral sense with the cultivation of the vegetable tribes." At a similar gathering of Boston's elite horticulturists, the toast was to "Horticulture and Mental Culture,—the one the *cause,* the other, the *effect.*"[16]

Far more than just a play on words was involved. The wealthy men of America were in search of some criterion that would justify their near monopoly on wealth and power in the land of opportunity and equality. Lineage would not do in a nation that had quite explicitly rejected hereditary aristocracies. Obviously, neither would superior greed and ambition. But cultivation—what must be earned, what deserves merit—that might serve very well as a characteristic that could legitimately distinguish some men from others, much as one would sort out the unblemished, well-formed fruit from the bruised and stunted. Thus it was no mere clever pun when Boston horticulturists toasted one of their own as "a noble specimen of the fruits of New England culture."[17]

We see now why it is that women were not accepted as members of horticultural societies until after the Civil War. As long as the major purpose of horticulture was to cure its practitioners of those decidedly male vices—greed and ambition—women, excluded from the worlds of business and politics, would be excluded from horticultural societies as well. This is not to say that women played no role in these societies or that they were discouraged from gardening. In fact, the antebellum rage for horticulture did make room for the female sex, although as with men, in ways defined and delimited by gender stereotypes. If horticulture was to purify money-grasping, power-hungry men, it was also to complement women's "natural" refinement, delicacy, and purity.

In line with their image as moral innocents and with the role of horticulture as moral purifier, women were allowed into the annual dinners of at least some horticultural societies—once liquor was banned from these extravaganzas. Participants took note of the improved moral tone. "Woman, with her bright smiles and cheerful looks, has come up to participate with us," noted M. P. Wilder at the Massachusetts Horticultural Society's 1842 dinner, "and to chasten and refine this Feast of Fruits and Flowers." Other participants recalled an earlier day "when groups of our own sex only were collected, with bottles and decanters circulating among us" and praised the exchange of "the intoxicating cup for the more elegant

and refining gratification realized by the presence and smiles of woman."[18]

Women rarely submitted entries to horticultural exhibitions—perhaps it was believed that women were ill-suited to competition of any sort—with the exception of floral displays. Many of these displays were simple bouquets, but others were bizarre, even grotesque, creations. Visitors to the Pennsylvania Horticultural Society's exhibitions might view Chinese pagodas, Greek temples, and even a model of the Bridgewater Canal Monument, all made out of flowers. The footsore might be tempted to rest on a rustic settee covered with greenery inscribed with the words "Sit Down!," a triumph in white gomphrenas. Up north in Boston, one Miss Russell seems to have outdone even these productions. Her submission was a Newfoundland dog executed in black hollyhocks and, "to imitate spots," greyish moss. "This was a very capital design," reported the transactions of the Massachusetts Horticultural Society, "and 'Tray' seemed to have stalked into the room alive."[19]

If women played only the most marginal role in horticultural societies, they were nevertheless encouraged to take up gardening as a form of recreation. Of course no dirty work was to be involved. "It is not recommended to a young lady to dig up the earth," read one advice book, "study the modes of manuring it, or prepare compost."[20] But women's work in the garden was no mere passive amusement. Women were encouraged to undertake such light tasks as weeding and raking. Indeed gardening was recommended as a recreation suitable for females precisely because it involved some labor and exposure to the elements. Victorian women had a reputation for physical frailty, and while delicacy might be appropriately feminine, sickliness was quite another matter. Such weakness of constitution, it was believed, might affect a woman's fertility and therefore, in an age in which the maternal role was considered the essence of woman, her very identity. (By the end of the century, some Americans also feared that native-born women of "Anglo-Saxon stock" would be "outbred" by more robust but genetically undesirable immigrant women—a form of "race suicide.") A. J. Downing was among those who advocated gardening for the improvement of female

Middle-class women were urged to garden for their health, although any real physical exertion was seen as dangerous in light of feminine frailty. In this illustration, *Springtime in the Country*, a gloved and corseted lady gardener dares not stray from the garden path.

health. He published an American edition of the English *Gardening for Ladies* in the hope "that the dissemination in this country of works like the present volume, may increase, among our own fair country-women, the taste for these delightful occupations in the open air."[21] No undue risks were to be taken, however. In her *Treatise on Domestic Economy,* Catharine Beecher endorsed gardening to promote physical vigor but warned that "any risk of health, in this pursuit, is sinful." She advised lady gardeners to wear "flannel drawers and India-rubber shoes, and a warm shawl" as a precautionary measure. [22]

While women were not discouraged from culti-vating fruits and vegetables, it was expected that their true love would be for flowers. "I take it for granted," wrote the author of *The Young Lady's Book,* that any young woman "feels all that delight in them which seems so naturally to belong to her age and sex. A love of the beauties of nature . . . is always amiable; and there is something peculiarly adapted to feminine tenderness in the care of flowers."[23] Women gravi-tated to flowers, then, because of their innate sensi-tivity to beauty and instinct for nurturing. But women were also expected to like flowers because, to Victorian Americans, women in a sense *were* flowers —beautiful, ornamental, and essentially useless, del-icate, frail, and evanescent. One women's magazine explicitly stated that the cultivation of flowers was best suited to women because of their mutual "fragility, beauty, and perishable nature."[24] In fact women were often compared to flowers in this era's literature. In 1847, for example, there appeared a curious work titled *The Flowers Personified,* in which flowers assumed the characters of young women to spin moral tales of vice and virtue. A major theme of sentimental fiction and poetry was the tragic death of the young woman, like the flower petal, at her most beautiful before the inevitable wilting and decay. Most widespread of all was the notion of a secret language of flowers. Popularized in such works as Catherine Waterman's *Flora's Lexicon,* this notion held that each type of flower represented a unique emotion or thought. Thus an exchange of flowers was a conversation, a well-chosen bouquet a declaration of sentiments. While men might participate in these floral communications, women, with their keen sensitivity to emotional life, were the ones expected to master this parallel, symbolic language of feeling.

WAS THERE NO ONE in America with a bad word for the horticultural movement? Evidently there were some objections. To the extent that horticulture conjured up visions of extravagant English aristocrats lavishing ill-gotten wealth on their country estates, it seemed inappropriate for the simple and virtuous American republic. Admitting that some Americans felt "a secret recoil" at the whole notion of gardening as a national pastime, horticultural advocates marshalled a defense, carefully distinguishing the morally questionable brand of gardening found in Europe from the pure, republican one found in America.[25] In England, stated one horticulturist, "a few of the rich and great . . . wallow in the enjoyment" of such exotic and expensive luxuries as tropical fruits grown under glass, but in America, all "enjoy in one universal festival" of "the most choice and delicious fruits and vegetables of the temperate zone."[26] Elaborating on this point in a speech to the New York Horticultural Society, Abraham Halsey explained that in a practical country such as America, where there was little room for the "elegancies and embellishments of life," horticulture, like other national institutions, "must be useful in its objects and must apply itself to the wants and demands of a sober

minded and laborious people."[27] Thus while the orangeries and orchid houses of aristocratic England had no place in America, the useful and universally available products cultivated by American gardeners were morally consistent with a republican agenda. Horticulture was "a Republican Fine Art," its products, "cheap but splendid ornaments."[28]

There was of course a paradox here. On the one hand, only by cultivating what had no market value could Americans prove their moral victory over materialism and boorishness. Seen from this light, the more ornamental and useless—one thinks of Miss Russell's floral Newfoundland—the better. On the other hand, only by restricting horticultural pursuits to those with some apparent utility could Americans avoid the charges of aristocratic decadence. Best then to focus on, perhaps, fruit cultivation, with its obvious practical, even commercial, applications. The paradox was a real one, reflecting a larger cultural ambivalence about national identity and national character. Should we aspire to European refinement or should we dismiss it as moral corruption and take a brash pride in our rustic practicality?

After the Civil War, prosperous Americans appear to have come to terms with their changed society and to have embraced a new set of brazenly acquisitive values. Horticulture, no longer a counterweight to greed and ambition, was free to take on new associations and functions. The signs are many. Perhaps most tellingly, women entered the ranks of horticultural societies. Here was a clear indication that horticulture was no longer thought of as an antidote to the "gold-fever" of antebellum days. At the same time, horticultural societies became more unabashedly elitist, a development particularly noticable in their fascination with breeding as a horticultural concept applicable to human beings. Take, for example, the horticultural writings of a man better known as one of America's first historians, Boston Brahmin Francis Parkman. "Like all things living, in the world of mind or matter," wrote Parkman in his *Book of Roses,* "the rose is beautified, enlarged, and strengthened by a course of judicious and persevering culture, continued through successive generations." Such efforts, of necessity, include "rigid systems of selection and rejection." Thus, continued Parkman in increasingly suggestive language, the successful breeder "chooses those marked out by conspicuous merit; protects them from the pollen of inferior sorts, intermarries them, perhaps, with other varieties of equal vigor and beauty; saves their seed, and raises from it another generation."[29] By the 1890s, Parkman's fellow Brahmins would be lobbying Congress to restrict foreign immigration lest inferior "stock" from southern and eastern Europe taint the superior native American "variety." We are not reading too much into Parkman's *Book of Roses* when we see in it a new fascination with scientific breeding that by the early twentieth century had developed into a dangerous flirtation with eugenics.

Parkman's convictions were certainly a long way from the antebellum notion that the practice of gardening could heal upper-class Americans of their moral ills. But the horticultural cure was not altogether a thing of the past; it simply targeted new patients. This time around, horticulture was to function as an antidote to the moral failures of the *lower* classes. Thus, in 1878, society women of the Massachusetts Horticultural Society organized a window-gardening movement, hoping to counter temptations to vice among "children of the laboring classes."[30] In the early twentieth century, social reformers appropriated this horticultural approach to controlling the behavior of the poor. They established gardens in urban public schools, claiming that giving immigrant children their own individual garden plots was an effective lesson in the virtue of hard work and the sanctity of private property. Thus could the social dynamite of the slums be defused. "Our armies of tramps and hordes of hoodlums," wrote one advocate of school gardens in 1902, "are among the first fruits of an educational system that slights such a matter."[31]

Yet other reformers included horticulture as part of their prescription for middle-class Americans. The disease was "neurasthenia," a debilitating mental condition brought on by the complexities of modern— that is, early-twentieth-century—life. The cure was the simple life, in which direct contact with nature —including, of course, gardening—figured promi-

nently. Some went so far as to recommend rural homesteading, but most took their programs no further than the cultivation of a backyard vegetable garden. In fact, long before the Victory Garden movement of World War Two, many middle-class Americans, hoping to reap spiritual and economic rewards alike, found sustenance in growing their own produce. In our day, similar desires—for economy and simplicity, household self-sufficiency and spiritual harmony—lie behind the organic garden movement.

If horticulture never completely lost its reformist agenda, it is nonetheless true that it increasingly took on the character of a pastime rather than a movement. Horticulture had found a new base—middle-class suburbanites. By the end of the nineteenth century, an entire industry had developed in response to the new mass popularity of horticulture. Such books as Frank J. Scott's *The Art of Beautifying Suburban Home Grounds of Small Extent* catered to this growing middle-class audience. Seed houses broadcast their ever more comprehensive catalogues through the mails. And factories mass-produced newly invented lawn mowers, outdoor furniture, and garden ornaments. As horticulture developed in the twentieth century, it underwent further changes. Increasingly, the suburban garden, a place for quiet contemplation of nature's treasures, became the suburban lawn, an outdoor space suitable for sports and recreation, and

OPPOSITE:
Early-twentieth-century proponents of public school gardens argued that the moral influences of a gardening regimen could prevent slum-dwelling immigrant children from turning to lives of crime and vice. In seeking to mold character through environment, they shared much in common with other reformers of the era who sought to build playgrounds and parks in —and to eliminate saloons and brothels from—poor urban neighborhoods.

After the Civil War, middle-class domestic bliss became firmly identified with the newly created suburbs. The new generation of suburbanites, such as those addressed by Frank J. Scott in his *Art of Beautifying Suburban Home Grounds*, strove to emulate models of taste in both home and garden.

finally the fenced-in backyard, an outward extension of private, domestic space. Once a locus of moral regeneration, the garden has become so much square footage to be maintained.

Few gardening enthusiasts today would recognize the practice of horticulture as it was represented in the nineteenth century. We have long since ceased to think of the cultivation of geraniums as a solution to poverty. Any links between genetic engineering in the horticultural and the human worlds are unthinkable. And the even older claim made for the practice of horticulture—that it could make a pure and high-minded nation of a boorish and materialistic people —are dismissed as downright laughable. But we should probably not dismiss the notion of a horticultural cure as altogether outdated. If horticulturists of the nineteenth century celebrated apples as republican luxuries, perhaps we laud them for their role in the anticancer diet made necessary by a lifetime of fast food. If our forebears regarded gardening as a moral antidote to the "restlessness and din of the rail-road principle," perhaps we regard it as a medical antidote to heart disease brought on by the stress of the "free-way principle." In both centuries, horticulture has been recommended as a way of transcending the ills associated with "modern" life, and in so doing, it has proved that we have not yet learned to transcend ourselves. ✦

NOTES

1. A. J. Downing, "On the Improvement of Country Villages," *The Horticulturist* 3 (June 1849): 549; Report of the Massachusetts Horticultural Society exhibition of 1845, *Transactions . . . 1843-4-5-6*, p. 10; "Rural Ornamentation Has a Good Moral Tendency," *Genesee Farmer* 6 (25 June 1836): 208.

2. "Horticultural Pursuits," *Horticultural Register* 1 (November 1835): 107.

3. A. J. Downing, *The Horticulturist* 3 (July 1848): 9.

4. Report on the Fourth Annual Exhibition of the Pennsylvania Horticultural Society, *American Farmer* 14 (7 December 1832): 309; *The Horticulturist* 3 (July 1848): 9; Sigourney, "Horticulture," p. 179; *New York Farmer* 2 (September 1829): 203.

5. A. J. Downing, *The Horticulturist* 2 (July 1847): 9–10, 11.

6. J. E. Teschemacher, Address to the Massachusetts Horticultural Society, *Transactions . . . 1842–1843*, pp. 5–6.

7. John C. Gray, review, p. 449.

8. "Biographical Sketches of Distinguished American Horticulturists: Marshall Pinckney Wilder, of Dorchester, Mass.," *The Horticulturist*, n.s., 5 (March 1855): 114.

9. Unattributed excerpt from *Godey's Lady's Book*, in *Horticultural Register* 3 (1 January 1838): 33; Gray, "Review," p. 448; Sigourney, "Horticulture," p. 179.

10. Review of Quintinye's *The Complete Gardener*, pp. 366–68.

11. H. A. S. Dearborn, *Address*, pp. 3, 4–7.

12. Description of the Massachusetts Horticultural Society festival of 1842, in *Transactions . . . 1842–43*, p. 30; Description of the Massachusetts Horticultural Society festival of 1845, in *Transactions . . . 1843-4-5-6*, p. 111.

13. Description of the Massachusetts Horticultural Society festival of 1845, p. 112.

14. Description of the Massachusetts Horticultural Society festival of 1832, in Harris, *A Discourse*, p. 58.

15. Ibid., p. 59.

16. *New York Farmer* 6 (October 1833): 302; Description of the Massachusetts Horticultural Society festival of 1845, p. 125.

17. Ibid., p. 99.

18. Description of the Massachusetts Horticultural Society festival of 1842, pp. 22–23, 27, 40.

19. Description of the Massachusetts Horticultural Society exhibition of 1845, p. 86.

20. *The Young Lady's Book: A Manual of Elegant Recreations, Exercises, and Pursuits*, 2d ed. (Boston: Carter, Hendee and Babcock, n.d.), p. 36.

21. Loudon, *Gardening for Ladies and Ladies' Companion to the Flower Garden*, introduction.

22. Beecher, *A Treatise on Domestic Economy* p. 385. Only middle- and upper-class women—not slave, immigrant, or working-class women—were regarded as delicate and therefore in need of horticultural therapy in cautious doses. "Many young ladies," wrote Catharine Beecher and her sister Harriet Beecher Stowe, regarding gardening for women, "whose habits are now so formed that they can never be induced to a course of active domestic exercise so long as their parents are able to hire domestic service, may yet be led to an employment which will tend to secure health and vigor of constitution." *The American Woman's Home* (reprint ed. 1869; Watkins Glen, N.Y.: Library of Victorian Culture, 1979), p. 294.

23. *The Young Lady's Book*, p. 35.

24. Unattributed excerpt from *Godey's Lady's Book*, in *Horticultural Register* 3 (1 January 1838): 33.

25. *Horticultural Register* 3 (1 April 1837): 121.

26. William Wilson, "A Sketch of the Different Kinds of Gardens in the United States," *New York Farmer* 1 (September 1828): 201.

27. Abraham Halsey, Address to the New York Horticultural Society, 7 September 1830, in *New York Farmer* 3 (October 1830): 219.

28. *Report of the Twentieth Annual Exhibition of the Massachusetts Horticultural Society, and Third Triennial Festival, Held at Faneuil Hall, September 19, 20, 21, 22, 1848* (Boston: Tuttle and Dennett, 1848), p. 36; Description of the Massachusetts Horticultural Society festival of 1829, in Dearborn, *Address*, p. 27.

29. Parkman, *The Book of Roses* pp. 95–96.

30. Within a decade, with the project foundering, one organizer explained that "garden work was pretty hard" and that the "children had all they could do with going to school," whereupon one Miss Smith, with a sensitivity to working-class realities probably typical of her social stratum, "asked if garden work was any harder than playing lawn tennis." Albert Emerson Benson, *History of the Massachusetts Horticultural Society* (Boston: Massachusetts Horticultural Society, 1929), pp. 201–2, 267–68.

31. Clifton F. Hodge, *Nature Study and Life* (Boston: Ginn, 1902), p. 10.

BIBLIOGRAPHY

The American Gardener's Magazine, and Register of Useful Arts.

Beecher, Catharine E. *A Treatise on Domestic Economy.* Boston: Marsh, Capen, Lyon, and Webb, 1841.

Beecher, Catharine E., and Harriet Beecher Stowe. *The American Woman's Home.* Reprint ed. 1869; Watkins Glen, New York: Library of Victorian Culture, 1979.

Benson, Albert Emerson Benson. *History of the Massachusetts*

Horticultural Society. Boston: Massachusetts Horticultural Society, 1929.

Boyd, James. *A History of the Pennsylvania Horticultural Society, 1827–1927.* Philadelphia: Pennsylvania Horticultural Society, 1929.

Cook, Zebedee, Jr. *An Address Pronounced before the Massachusetts Horticultural Society, in Commemoration of Its Second Annual Festival, the 10th of September, 1830.* Boston: Isaac R. Butts, 1830.

Dearborn, H. A. S. *An Address Delivered before the Massachusetts Horticultural Society, on the Celebration of Their First Anniversary, September 19, 1829.* 2d ed. Boston: T. Buckingham, 1833.

Downing, A. J. *Rural Essays.* New York: Leavitt & Allen, 1854.

The Genesee Farmer and Gardener's Journal.

Grandville, Jean Ignace Isidore Gerard. *The Flowers Personified, Being a Translation of Grandville's "Les Fleurs Animées" by N. Cleaveland.* New York: Martin, 1847–49.

Gray, John C. *An Address Delivered before the Massachusetts Horticultural Society, at Their Sixth Anniversary, September 17, 1834.* Boston: J. T. Buckingham, 1834.

Gray, John C. Review of "Kenrick's *American Orchardist,*" *North American Review* 47 (October 1838): 444–51.

Hand Book of the Sentiment and Poetry of Flowers. 2d ed. Boston: Saxton and Kelt, 1845.

Harris, Thaddeus William. *A Discourse Delivered before the Massachusetts Horticultural Society, on the Celebration of Its Fourth Anniversary, October 3, 1832.* Cambridge: E. W. Metcalf, 1832.

Hedrick, U. P. *A History of Horticulture in America to 1860.* New York: Oxford University Press, 1950.

Horticultural Register and Gardener's Magazine.

"Horticulture." *New England Magazine* 1 (August 1831): 144–49.

The Horticulturist and Journal of Rural Art and Rural Taste.

The Language of Flowers Poetically Expressed. New York: Leavitt and Allen, 1847.

Leighton, Ann. *American Gardens of the Nineteenth Century: "For Comfort and Affluence."* Amherst: University of Massachusetts Press, 1987.

Loudon, Mrs. [Jane]. *Gardening for Ladies and Ladies' Companion to the Flower Garden,* ed. A. J. Downing. New York: Wiley and Putnam, 1843.

Magazine of Horticulture, Botany, and All Useful Discoveries, and Improvements of Rural Affairs.

Manning, Robert. *History of the Massachusetts Horticultural Society, 1829–1878.* Boston: Massachusetts Horticultural Society, 1880.

The New England Farmer, and Horticultural Journal.

The New York Farmer, and Horticultural Repository.

Parkman, Francis. *The Book of Roses.* Boston: J. E. Tilton, 186.

Proceedings on the Establishment of the Massachusetts Horticultural Society (Boston: Isaac R. Butts, 1829).

Review of "Quintinye's *The Complete Gardener.*" *American Quarterly Review* 21 (June 1837): 364–98.

Report of the Transactions of the Massachusetts Horticultural Society, for the Year 1837–38 (Boston: Tuttle, Dennett and Chisolm, 1839).

Report of the Twentieth Annual Exhibition of the Massachusetts Horticultural Society, and Third Triennial Festival, Held at Faneuil Hall, September 19, 20, 21, 22, 1848 (Boston: Tuttle and Dennett, 1848).

Schmitt, Peter J. *Back to Nature: The Arcadian Myth in Urban America* (1969; Baltimore: Johns Hopkins University Press, 1990).

Shi, David E. *The Simple Life: Plain Living and High Thinking in American Culture* (New York: Oxford University Press, 1985).

Sigourney, Lydia H. "Horticulture," *Godey's Lady's Book* 21 (October 1840): 179.

Stilgoe, John R. *Borderland: Origins of the American Suburb, 1820–1939* (New Haven: Yale University Press, 1988).

———. "Suburbanites Forever: The American Dream Endures," *Landscape Architecture* 72 (May 1982): 89–93.

Thornton, Tamara Plakins. *Cultivating Gentlemen: The Meaning of Country Life among the Boston Elite, 1785–1860* (New Haven: Yale University Press, 1989).

Tice, Patricia M. *Gardening in America, 1830–1910* (Rochester: The Margaret Woodbury Strong Museum, 1984).

Transactions of the Massachusetts Horticultural Society 1 (Boston: Wm. D. Ticknor, 1847–51).

Transactions of the Massachusetts Horticultural Society for the Year 1842–43 (Boston: Dutton and Wentworth, 1843).

Transactions of the Massachusetts Horticultural Society for the Years 1843-4-5-6 (Boston: Dutton and Wentworth, 1847).

Traub, Hamilton. "Tendencies in the Development of American Horticultural Associations." *National Horticultural Magazine* 9 (January 1930): 18–26.

Waterman, Catherine H. *Flora's Lexicon: An Interpretation of the Language and Sentiment of Flowers* (Philadelphia: Hooker and Claxton, 1839).

The Young Lady's Book; a Manual of Elegant Recreations, Exercises, and Pursuits. 2d ed. (Boston: Carter, Hendee and Babcock, n.d.).

Gardening Under Glass

Tovah Martin

It has long been a temptation for gardeners to wish in Faustian fashion that their gardens would stay just as they are, suspended throughout the year in some perfect, glorious moment. For so many gardeners in America the climatic factors simply do not allow anything of the kind. The acceptance of this impossibility has led to many and varied ventures. The earliest and simplest was to pot up a few, usually medicinal, herbs and bring them into the house and onto the windowsill. At the other extreme are the elegant and glorious greenhouses and conservatories described by Walter Punch in "The Garden Organized."

During the eigtheenth and nineteenth centuries such factors as the common practice of forcing bulbs, improvement in the manufacturing and distribution of glass, the growth in scientific horticulture, the spread of the nursery business, and various social considerations for horticulture and plant exploration and trading all led to the increased use of plants indoors for residences as well as commercial establishments. Eventually the scope and design of indoor gardening led to huge commercial nurseries under glass that accommodated both climate and the new exotic plants. Also, with the ability to grow a large number of plants yearround, the desire to design the greenhouse led to elaborate conservatories that were truly garden rooms, extensions of the house.

As with many things horticultural, indoor gardening is subject to trends and taste, and in recent years the indoor gardening so popular among Victorians and into the early twentieth century has waned. (Tamara Plakins Thornton, in "Horticulture and American Character," suggests reasons for such intense indoor plant cultivation.) Perhaps the increased number of people living in large cities and the busy schedules of so many will cause a revival in popularity for the tray of houseplants. It is a long and lovely tradition that can satisfy our need for beauty and nature throughout the year. ❧

A YEAR FILLED with uninterrupted blossoms has always been a glimmer in the eye of the gardener. The tragedy of gardening outdoors is its transience, especially in upper latitudes of North America. Although a flower bed might provide a great deal of pleasure while it is growing, it tantalizes your senses for a brief season or two, leaving half the year bereft of botanicals. A long, dull winter stands between the last rose of summer and the first crocus of spring.

If modern gardeners find winter long and dull, it was doubly difficult for the early settlers in North America to endure the seemingly endless months of dearth. Not only were they strangers in a strange New World, but their adopted home provided only a bleak, frozen landscape for a goodly portion of each year. The strong lure of necessity coaxed gardeners to bring botanicals indoors. At the time, plants served some important life-sustaining functions. Herbs, for example, furnished indispensable medicines, cleaning fluids, moth and insect repellents. Not least among their virtues, herbs also added a little culinary spice to the settlers' bland lives.

Some essential herbs, such as thyme, sage, and wormwood, were sufficiently hardy to endure winter outdoors in northern American gardens, but Mediterranean herbs and other tender species had to be sheltered inside. In addition, it was also pleasant to have the companionship of a pot of rosemary, a scented pelargonium or two, and maybe a myrtle or sweet bay flowering, flourishing, and helping to maintain the family's good health throughout the year. Even during this country's unadorned Puritan days, gardeners desired the company of plants indoors.

At first, houseplants remained a wish rather than a reality. The average home was pathetically inappropriate for nurturing plant life. Most crucially, Colonial homes lacked light. Windows were small and glass was expensive. In the 1700s, a square foot of glass cost half a day's wage. Despite the cost, the panes were thick and full of imperfections. In sunny

weather, a pockmark in the pane acted like a magnifier that could burn thin objects (such as plant foliage) inside the house. An improved process for pressing glass originated in the United States in 1826 but, even then, the technology was not immediately put into use in this country. Quality did not improve in the United States until after the Civil War, which caused the need to import glass of good quality from France.

To further confound the issue, there was the problem of heat. Throughout the first half of the nineteenth century, the family's living quarters froze every chilly winter's evening, with indoor temperatures being colder around a room's periphery and close to the windows. Even after central heating became widespread, it was considered a wasteful extravagance to keep furnaces fired during the night.

So throughout the eighteenth century, herbs were shocked into dormancy by allowing the pots to go dry while subjecting them to very cold, nearly freezing, temperatures before they were brought indoors. In that somniferous state, the plants were unceremoniously hung upside down in the attic or bedded in flats in the root cellar. When spring arrived, they were watered, revived, and replanted outdoors. The plants usually survived to see another growing season, but they certainly did not add to the interior decor in the meantime.

By the 1830s, things began to change for the better, botanically speaking. Gardeners began forcing bulbs such as tulips, lily-of-the-valley, paperwhites, and hyacinths indoors. Bulbs, especially tulips, already had an aura of aristocracy. In the sixteenth century, bulbs from Turkey fetched incredible prices on the European market and were invested in and speculated upon by wealthy financiers. The phenomenon became known as Tulipomania, and it gathered fervor throughout the 1500s before peaking in the 1630s. Not long afterward, growers in Holland found that bulbs native to the Levant grew fruitful and multiplied in their climate, and Dutch growers began mass-producing them, selling the bulbs to eager collectors in Europe.

Eventually Dutch bulbs traveled to this country. John Bartram (1699–1777) was responsible for shar-

Gardening under glass makes it possible for bulbs such as amaryllis and hyacinths to provide colorful relief from winter's doldrums.

ing many North American plants with European correspondents and in exchange he imported many European novelties. Among the fruits of Bartram's exchange was a generous shipment of crocus, narcissus martagons, lilies, gladiolus, ornithogalums, iris, and alliums sent by his most ardent British pen pal, Peter Collinson. By the 1830s, Dutch bulbs were no longer expensive rarities and a bevy of hybrids were available to most home gardeners, their price decreasing as the era progressed. Bulbs were within everyone's reach.

Bulb forcing was a feat that could be accomplished quite easily without altering the existing con-

ditions in the average home. After all, bulbs produce blossoms almost magically with scant light and little heat, although additional light certainly adds color to the blossoms. Tulips, hyacinths, crocus, lily-of-the-valley, and narcissus were among the most popular botanical pioneers to be adopted into American homes. America's first attempt at indoor gardening was a resounding success.

By the 1840s, when glass was more prevalent and light levels had increased, gardeners had broadened their interior horizons to include perennial garden plants. Every autumn, gardeners lifted primroses, cinnamon pinks, roses, and whatever else they could lay hands on, and brought the transplants indoors. To everyone's delight, those perennials continued to

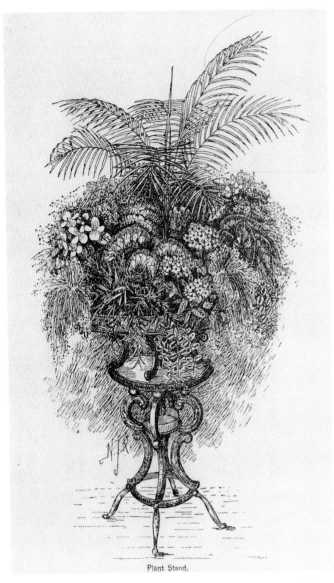

Plant Stand,

With typical Victorian superfluity, urns were crowded with tropicals.

completely alien environment. For the most part, it was Europeans who went on collecting expeditions, sponsored by kings and queens who had their sights on the expansion of their geographic realms, as well as on multiplying the number of plants over which they reigned. The exotics that somehow survived the ocean voyage from tropical jungles to Europe were immediately sequestered in hothouses. They were coddled by highly experienced growers, and were studied, classified, and named by the world's most renowned botanists. Then they were propagated and shared with other, equally avid, gardeners. Eventually, the most hale and hardy of those plants came to North America and, once here, were primarily entertained on windowsills. By the 1880s, the average American windowsill had definitely become a brighter affair.

Meanwhile, bay windows had crept into vogue. Introduced by Alexander Jackson Davis, the architect who popularized the Gothic Revival style, bay windows were everywhere. City flats as well as suburban cottages sported these recessed alcoves built specifically to catch the sun's rays from several exposures. Window-lined verandas were also popular. Bright, cheerful rooms ruled the day, making the home more conducive to raising the new flora that was quickly infiltrating American homes.

Before long, in fact, plants became an essential ingredient of Home Sweet Home. Quite literally, they won our hearts. Nineteenth-century gardeners felt strongly that plants lent people moral support. In the words of the American Victorian periodical, *Vick's Monthly,* "The person who habitually cultivates plants and flowers is by this practice constantly, if insensibly, refining his thoughts and sensibilities." Tasteful people grew plants close by, and crude folks lived in homes bereft of blossoms; it was as simple as that.

If one plant provided moral salvation, imagine what a dozen plants could do to uplift the character of one's family. Windows were crammed with living things; their casements disappeared as vines wended their way on trellises that trained them around the window frame; trailing plants cascaded green arms and legs down to the floor. Greenery groped, spilled,

flourish and flower. In fact, they enjoyed the frigid nighttime temperatures indoors. Depending upon the light available, they lived for a few days or a few weeks or—if conditions were favorable—for several months.

In the meantime, while Americans were searching for ways to bring their old favorites inside, explorers were wandering around the globe in search of new plants to broaden their botanical horizons. By the end of the seventeenth century, they began successfully to bring live plants and seeds home to cultivate in a

In the mid-nineteenth century, the windowsill developed into a lush indoor garden complete with festooned vines.

Perfectly adapted to nurturing plant life, the bay window supplied light from three exposures.

and intertwined everywhere. Inspirational statuary, ornate urns, and classically styled jardinieres were incorporated into the scene. A bird cage holding its captive canary added music, and an aquarium with a few fish navigating around an aquatic calla lily or umbrella plant completed the mood. Compared to Victorian windowsills, twentieth-century indoor gardens are rather tame affairs.

By the 1890s, the home had evolved into an environment suitable for nurturing nature. Light was no longer a problem, and the home was enjoying the benefits of improved furnaces. However, humidity was rapidly becoming a major issue. As furnaces forced temperatures higher, the relative humidity simultaneously took a nosedive. And, of course, tropical plants demand abundant moisture in the air. Nineteenth-century gardeners were forced to find a solution or forfeit the family's source of inspiration. Terrariums were seen as the answer.

They began with Nathaniel Ward, a surgeon and amateur naturalist who practiced medicine in London and spent his spare time in the nearby countryside collecting entomological and botanical souvenirs. Ferns were his primary passion, and he spent his holidays and weekends scouring woodlands around London for interesting pteridophytes to take home. But unfortunately, as soon as he brought a fern into town, it perished without further adieux. The polluted air in the city poisoned his plants.

Ward's efforts continued in the same disappointing manner until 1830, when he collected a hawk moth pupa and stored it in a sealed glass bottle to await metamorphosis. Six months later, while checking his cocoon, Ward noticed that a fern had sprouted and was growing more salubriously than any other fern had fared in his city garden. That small sporeling literally changed the gardening world.

Following his discovery, Ward began to experi-

Sealing plants into a crystal world, Wardian cases were designed like miniature landscapes locked in glass.

ment with other ferns in glass cases. In 1842, he published his findings in a paper entitled "On the Growth of Plants in Closely Glazed Cases." The treatise created quite a stir, turning Ward into a celebrity.

The ingenious Victorians found all sorts of applications for Ward's case. Sturdy, heavy Wardian cases went along with plant explorers on their expeditions, providing minigreenhouses to give humidity-loving jungle plants safe conduct throughout their ocean trips back to Britain. While they traveled, those tropical introductions no longer had to share the precious fresh water supply of the ship's crew; they were self-contained. Wardian cases sat on the ship's deck and enjoyed sunshine throughout the voyage without fear of being doused with sea spray. The influx of new botanicals increased drastically, thanks to Wardian cases.

Glass cases eventually became available to the general public, and the fad crossed the Atlantic to titillate gardeners on this side of the ocean. Wardian cases came in all sizes and shapes, ranging from relatively modest bell jars that would hold a single fern to immense and elaborate glazed cases shaped to look like Oriental pagodas or miniature versions of Kew

Gardens. Those prototypical terrariums boasted all sorts of gimmicks, including attached bird cages and steeples that could be converted into toad quarters for those who required the services of a captive amphibian to keep the resident plants free of insect pests. And true to their origins, Wardian cases usually held a collection of ferns sheltered from the dry atmosphere of the average home.

MEANWHILE, THE PLANTS on windowsills had increased and multiplied. It was not long before gardeners began craving more light, more space, and improved growing conditions for their plant collections. They wanted the relative humidity of an Amazon jungle combined with the sun of the Mediterranean and the warmth of Africa. They yearned to see how tropical plants would perform if given free rein. They wanted to walk among those plants as if they were wandering on a safari. Only a greenhouse could deliver a reasonable facsimile of a jungle habitat in the midst of the North American climate.

Greenhouses had been in use since antiquity. The Romans created transparent structures known as *specularia* to shelter tender fruit such as grapes and peaches for the table of Caesar, his family, and friends. Those buildings were glazed with thin sheets of mica and talc and were warmed by stoves hooked into flue systems that sent heat throughout the expanse.

Through the centuries, kings and the nobility— primarily in Italy and the Orient—exercised their power and wealth to produce fruit where it could not grow unprotected. By 1619, Europe had caught the contagion, and its first greenhouse was built by Salomon de Caus to house orange trees in Heidelberg for the king and queen of Bohemia. Orangeries, as they were later called, held their crops of glistening, juicy fruit to satisfy the privileged palates of wealthy estate owners and their guests. Although the quality of the crop might be questionable, the yields of the trees were impressive: a gardener at the Beddington estate in Britain recorded that no fewer than 10,000 oranges were harvested in 1691.

The influx of tropical plants flooding Europe provided a strong impetus to develop greenhouse technology. An orangerie had large windows on three vertical sides but the structure was usually a two-story affair covered by a shingled roof, with a gardener's residence and storeroom on the second floor. By 1717, the first glazed roofs were added to allow housed citrus trees to stretch their branches toward the light. And by the early 1800s, engineers were beginning to experiment with different slopes to catch maximal sun rays. In 1815, in a letter to the London Horticultural Society, Sir George McKenzie suggested the use of curvilinear glazing. From that moment onward, it seemed obvious to many builders that the curve of a greenhouse should follow "the plane of the sun's orbit," in Sir George's words. Later, J. C. Loudon devised the ridge-and-furrow system, which would become the most common greenhouse style in this country.

While all this was going on in Europe, North Americans assumed the role of spectators. Greenhouse technology was not moving briskly on this side of the ocean. Of what use was a greenhouse if its contents continually froze in cold weather? Efficient furnaces capable of heating an expanse of glass in the inclement colonies had yet to be perfected.

And yet, there were those who wanted glasshouses nonetheless. American greenhouse firsts are not as well documented as their British counterparts. To completely confuse the issue, in its February 15, 1887 issue, *The American Florist* pictured James Beekman's greenhouse built in New York City in 1764 and labeled the illustration "The First American Greenhouse." Since then, several historians have echoed the magazine's claim, citing Beekman's glasshouse as the first in the colonies. Although it was an important structure, fashioned in the orangerie style, Beekman's greenhouse was certainly not the first in this country.

In their book *Glasshouses,* Arete Swartz Warren and May Woods established a more accurate record of the chronology of glass structures in North America. The first greenhouse in North America probably appeared on Tremont Street in Boston, where Andrew Faneuil built a house in 1710, to which he added a greenhouse sometime before his death in 1738. Following his lead, a neighbor, Gardiner Greene, built another greenhouse in Boston shortly after 1738.

A mixture of the greenhouse bench style and conservatory planting is found at Logee's Greenhouses.

Gradually other greenhouses appeared, scattered throughout the wealthier regions of the East Coast. In Virginia, Colonel John Tayloe II built a sizable greenhouse between 1748 and 1758 to complement his estate at Mount Airy. Mount Clare, the Baltimore home of the Carroll family, had a greenhouse in place by 1768. That greenhouse eventually provided citrus and herbs to fill George Washington's glasshouse at Mount Vernon, completed in 1789. Farther south,

In 1797, Theodore Lyman began adding greenhouses to The Vale, his estate in Waltham, Massachusetts.

John Gibbes built a noteworthy greenhouse in 1755 in Charleston, South Carolina, that was destroyed two decades later in the Revolutionary War.

In 1799, Henry Pratt, of Philadelphia, converted a villa in what today is Fairmount Park into a greenhouse and named it Lemon Hill. As the name implied, it housed a noteworthy collection of citrus.

Similarly, Theodore Lyman (who later won fame for his camellia collection) added a greenhouse to his estate, The Vale, in 1797 and stocked it with citrus. Situated in the Boston suburb of Waltham, it is believed to be the oldest greenhouse still standing in this country and in use, maintained by the Society for the Preservation of New England Antiquities.

Obviously, the lure of out-of-season fruits was overwhelming, especially for early American gardeners. However, not everyone hearkened to its call. John Bartram was among those who wanted to devote his greenhouse simply to satiating his horticultural appetite in the midst of Philadelphia winters. He wrote, in 1760:

> I am going to build a greenhouse. Stone is got; and I hope as soon as harvest is over to begin to build it—to put some pretty flowering winter shrubs, and plants for winter's diversion, not to be crowded with orange trees, or those natural to the Torrid Zone, but such as will do, being protected from frost. [1]

Undoubtedly it was more than merely a matter of personal taste that kept Bartram from growing plants native to the torrid zone in his greenhouse. Had he wished to grow tropicals, his hopes would have been dashed. At the time, furnaces could not reliably support tropicals in the colder regions of this country.

Although the exact sequence of North American firsts is still a conundrum, one issue remains undisputed: before 1850, there were very few greenhouses in this country. The problem lay partly in availability, as Robert Leuchars complained in 1851:

> "There appears to be a great want of practical knowledge on these subjects, and though much information can be gleaned from various English works, they are either unobtainable or the information is inapplicable to the wants of this country." [2]

That situation began to improve in 1855 when Frederic A. Lord built his first greenhouse, in Buffalo, New York. The location was impressive. After all,

Buffalo is notorious for its bitter-cold winter nights and heavy snowfall. If Lord could successfully design a greenhouse and fit it with a furnace system that would remain reliable through a Buffalo winter, he could certainly construct one that might protect the most fragile plants in other parts of the country.

Gardeners quickly grasped at that ray of hope. Lord received so many requests for similar glass structures that, in 1872, he took his son-in-law, W. A. Burnham, into partnership. By 1883, the firm of Lord and Burnham was incorporated. Others also saw a chance to break into the new market and specialize in building glasshouses. Apparently there was plenty of work to go around. In 1888, Hitchings & Company (who later constructed the Enid A. Haupt Conservatory for the New York Botanical Garden) and Thomas W. Weathered's Sons, of New York, both devoted departments of their business specifically to the task of greenhouse construction.

Although British greenhouse researchers spent a great deal of time pondering slopes, heat was the main issue in North America. The earliest greenhouses were heated by manure piles lying under the benches where they simmered and were raked to stir up the heat during the night. This was a gradual but not intense form of heat, but the system wasn't ideal for a hobby greenhouse. After all, the fumes did not render the place particularly pleasant for human visitors, although the plants did not seem to find the fumes noxious.

Next, small movable stoves were utilized and by all accounts were a slight improvement. However, they had their quirks. Not only was such a stove subject to fits and starts, it could not heat a large expanse. Gardeners complained that their greenhouses were either frigid or baking, not to mention the smoke that came billowing out, filling the greenhouse whenever fuel was added. Only the most enduring plants could survive the early stoves.

Neither the manure pile nor the stove could successfully support tropicals in this country's colder regions. The first sizable American greenhouses had huge boilers in the cellar that sent heat circulating through flues, a system that originated in 1822. Although more efficient than a stove, it had one major

Sonnenberg Gardens in Canandaigua, New York, incorporates this Victorian dome-shaped Lord and Burnham greenhouse.

hitch: On cold nights, caretakers had to build raging fires in the furnaces, which frequently led to flames escaping into the flues and igniting adjacent woodwork. Plant collections that did not fall victim to frost often met their doom in a greenhouse blaze.

Finally, hot-water heat was successfully put into

The Newport Preservation Society, in Newport, Rhode Island, still operates a large Victorian estate greenhouse to propagate annuals for their bedding displays.

use in 1826, and this became the system of choice throughout the nineteenth century, especially for professionals. The system required hefty four-inch pipes that sent heated water running underneath benches throughout the glass range. No noxious smoke escaped into the growing area, and the heat could easily be regulated by opening and shutting water pipes. The only problems were the expense of fitting a greenhouse with the oversized pipes and the inconvenience of manipulating those bulky fittings for plumbing repairs.

By the mid-1890s, steam heat had won supremacy. Although the system was originally invented by Joseph Hayward in 1820, it could not compete with the reign of hot-water heat until greenhouses became popular with casual hobbyists in addition to professionals and wealthy dabblers. Steam systems required

relatively dainty two-inch pipe. When cost was a factor, steam heat was usually installed.

Even so, greenhouses were considered a luxury item until late in the century. According to Robert Morris Copeland's *Country Life,* an 18 by 30-foot freestanding wood-frame greenhouse built in the vicinity of Boston in 1860 cost $600; a greenhouse of brick construction could be had for $800 to $1,000. He commented, "Such things are out of the question for men whose every moment is spent struggling for freedom from debt."[3] Obviously, the average American could not afford such an expense, especially when operating costs were added in.

OPPOSITE:
At Longwood Gardens an early-nineteenth-century greenhouse is planted in the conservatory style that developed in the Victorian era. It is meant to appear like an indoor park with winding paths roaming through beds of blossoms.

And yet, where there is a will, gardeners find a way. The answer lay in utilizing the dwelling's heating system. In America, the attached lean-to conservatory was the most common type of glasshouse, especially in suburban settings where house lots were meager. By throwing open a door or window, the greenhouse gained the benefit of the house's heating system. When the greenhouse stood in such intimate proximity to the house, the chances of a freeze-up were greatly diminished, lessening the fear of finding the miserable remains of a collection of frozen plants one frigid winter's morning.

There were also aesthetic benefits to consider. By simply walking through a door, members of the family could wander into an enclosed garden despite inclement weather. For a generation of incurable romantics, the vision of a winter garden so close at hand was irresistibly tempting. Then, too, there were spiritual benefits to be weighed. If a few plants in the parlor uplifted the family, a full-fledged garden growing throughout the year would shower proportionately greater Beauty and Goodness on the home's residents. A greenhouse filled to brimming with nature would undoubtedly also nurture virtuous children. As William Cobbett explained in *The English Gardener,* published in 1829:

> It is the moral effects naturally attending a greenhouse that I set most value upon. There must be amusement in every family. Children observe and follow their parents in almost everything. How much better during the long and dreary winter for daughters and even sons to assist their mother in a greenhouse than to be seated with her at cards or in the blubberings over a stupid novel.

Distinctions were made between a greenhouse and a conservatory. With a garden scene as the goal, the greenhouse was designed accordingly. It played home to a botanical collection of potted plants staged neatly on benches, the focus of interest being on their diversity or rarity. In a conservatory, on the other hand, design was the main attraction. Although conservatories may have been patterned after parks, a much wilder approach to nature was followed. Plants were bedded in the ground and encouraged to attain their natural form and stature. Rather than being pruned into tidy little specimens, they were persuaded to reach toward the roof. Vines were given leave to wend their way around energetically. Ground covers carpeted the floor and gravel paths wound between the beds. Sitting benches were placed here and there to encourage lingering in the parklike setting.

Exotics ruled the conservatory realm—palms, citrus, brugmansia (angel's trumpet), and camellias were popular tree forms. Tendrils of ficus, tender ivies, cissus, allamandas, and clerodendrums wove the scene together in a multicolored web. Underneath crept ferns and selaginellas as groundcovers. Conservatories attempted to distill a jungle scene into a few square feet of growing space. It was hoped that they would provide all of the ecstasies and none of the agonies of the tropics, as an 1880s *Ladies Floral Cabinet* described in an article entitled "An Hour in the Tropics":

> To the lovers of tropic wealth in plants and flowers, the prospect of a trip through their own natural domain is most alluring, and doubly so when we can step from our own brisk autumn air into the heavy perfume-laden atmosphere of Borneo or Ceylon. . . . We have only to enter the portals of some great hothouse and . . . the tropic world is before us. Palms and orchids are as an East Indian jungle in miniature, without the decided disadvantage of the innumerable creeping things, more or less noxious, that are apt to make a tropic ramble anything but desirable.

Although most creeping, crawling things were not welcome in the home conservatory, certain four-legged, finned, and feathered creatures were instrumental in creating the mood. After all, if the conservatory was to be a place for interaction with nature, it must harbor representatives not only from the plant kingdom, but from the animal world as well. Fountains featured glistening fish and perhaps a toad or salamander as well. Birds flitted around cages dangling from tall trees, and industrious bees as well as an occasional butterfly were also invited to share the bounty.

The scene might be more or less fantastical, depending upon the family's budget. And by the turn of the century attached greenhouses could be found gracing the homes of citizens at all levels of society. As *The Household* put it in the 1870s, "Here not lords and merchant princes alone revel in this cheap and refining luxury, but the carpenter's wife, the mechanic's daughter, and the hard-worked city clerk meet their families in their own cozy little glass-covered greenhouses." A world encased in crystal was within everyone's grasp.

After their initial novelty had worn thin, greenhouses slipped from the forefront of horticulture. During the first years of the twentieth century, commercial glasshouses and estate greenhouses were speckled here and there throughout the country, but greenhouses were no longer a common sight in upper-middle-class neighborhoods. When the world wars intervened and turned the nation's horticultural energy toward victory vegetable gardening outdoors, many existing greenhouses slipped into disuse.

The downswing continued into the 1940s and 1950s, when a token philodendron or African violet might reside in the kitchen, but that was the extent of the average indoor garden. It was not until the arrival of the "flower children" in the 1960s that indoor horticulture began to gain momentum again.

Suddenly, herbs again spilled from kitchen windowsills and exotic plants blossomed in living rooms. Glass became an important element of architecture. Geodesic domes sprouted beside suburban and rural homes while postmodern walls of windows dominated urban architecture. Later still, atriums and solariums were incorporated into homes of various price ranges. Glass had come of age in North America, allowing gardeners in all regions of the country to extend summer throughout the year.

The universal love of nature fueled the desire to grow under glass. But the harshness of the climate in much of North America made greenhouses all the more popular on this side of the ocean. The marked contrast between the crystal kingdom and inhospitable weather outside made the greenhouse a place suspended in time. To the English poet William Cowper, it seemed a natural extension of the gardener's year. He wrote, in "The Garden," his poem of 1784:

> Who loves a garden, loves a green-house too
> Where blooms exotic beauty, warm and snug
> While winds whistle and the snows descend.

If year-round blooms were a gardener's most fervent prayer, then greenhouses became a grower's paradise. The ultimate garden knows no season. ❧

NOTES

1. Taylor, Kathryn S., *Winterflowers in the Sun Heated Pit* (New York: Charles Scribner's Sons, 1941), p. 10.
2. Leuchars, *Practical Treatise on the Construction, Heating and Ventilation of Hot-houses.*
3. Copeland, *Country Life.*

BIBLIOGRAPHY

Copeland, Robert Morris. *Country Life: A Handbook of Agriculture, Horticulture and Landscape Gardening.* Boston: John P. Jewett, 1860.

Fawkes, F. A. *Horticultural Buildings.* London: Swan Sonnenschein, 1886.

Field, F. E. *The Green-House as a Winter Garden.* New York: G. P. Putnam's Sons, 1870.

Hix, John. *The Glass House.* Cambridge, Mass.: MIT Press, 1974.

Kohlmaier, Georg, and Barna Van Sartory. *Houses of Glass.* Cambridge, Mass: MIT Press, 1986.

Koppelkamm, Stefan. *Glasshouses and Wintergardens of the Nineteenth Century.* New York: Rizzoli International Publications, 1981.

Leuchars, Robert B. *A Practical Treatise on the Construction, Heating and Ventilation of Hot-houses.* Boston: John P. Jewett, 1851.

Loudon, J. C. *The Greenhouse Companion.* London: Harding, Triphook, & Lepard, 1825.

Martin, Tovah. *Once Upon a Windowsill.* Portland, Oreg.: Timber Press, 1988.

McIntosh, Charles. *The Greenhouse, Hothouse and Stove.* London: Wm. S. Orr, 1838.

Taft, L. R. *Greenhouse Construction.* New York: Orange Judd, 1894.

Woods, May, and Warren, Arete Swartz. *Glasshouses.* New York: Rizzoli International Publications, 1988.

The Garden Organized

The Public Face of Horticulture

❧❦

Walter T. Punch

❧ *There is more than strength in numbers—enjoyment, sharing, knowledge, and progress can all be derived from groups. In gardening and horticultural circles the inclination to form associations, institutions, and societies has been widespread and enthusiastic. The many aspects of horticulture—scientific, artistic, social, historical—have been institutionalized for their improvement and promotion and for the benefit of those concerned with such issues.*

Botanic gardens, horticultural societies, garden clubs, and other organizations have advanced gardening in all its dimensions on an enormous scale. Whether devoted to plant importation, civic beautification, scientific research, historical scholarship, or floral exhibition, these institutions put before the public the essential part that plants play in our physical and spiritual lives.

Many of these organizations date from the earliest years of the republic (a few even earlier), while some are quite recent. In all cases the intent has been to be actively involved with the plant world for knowledge and delight. In "Horticulture and American Character," Tamara Plakins Thornton deals with the motivations and cultural context of some of the founders and supporters of various horticultural associations; Elisabeth Woodburn, in "American Horticultural Books," and Phyllis Andersen, in "The City and the Garden," both mention the important contributions of such organizations in specific circumstances. Keith Morgan describes in "Garden and Forest" the cultural context for the beginnings of many of the organizations discussed in this chapter.

The thousands of American horticultural, botanical, and gardening organizations daily touch the lives of millions of people and reach out beyond geopolitical borders, joining together this single ecosystem that we all inhabit. ❧

GARDENING IS USUALLY CONSIDERED A private act, a solitary occupation. And so it is. But few activities have generated so many organizations, societies, clubs, and associations. These institutions are themselves also of many kinds—scientific, artistic, social, and cultural. The proliferation of various organizations is indicative of the sundry expressions and dimensions of the plant world and of gardening. All of these, though differing in aspect of consideration, are complementary and, together, represent a magnificent demonstration of the diversity and virtually limitless phases of gardening.

Botanic Gardens and Arboreta

AN ENORMOUSLY IMPORTANT and effective institution that has played an essential role in the history of American gardening is the botanic garden/arboretum.* These institutions have had a threefold part to play: scientific, educational, and demonstrative. Throughout the early history of this country, from the early Quaker gardens around Philadelphia to the very sophisticated establishments at Eastern universities, the role played by these institutions has generally been a scientific one. Although this role was also practical, there are enough instances even in the early years to indicate the need of the mind for instruction and the soul for beauty. When the country had reached a sufficient sophistication and economic level, these great institutional gardens were established and have since set the tone and offered creative direction on an international scale.

The first American botanic garden, as we under-

* An arboretum is a botanic garden for trees, and some botanic gardens include arboreta.

OPENING ILLUSTRATION:
A lovely part of the New York Botanical Garden is the Jane Watson Irwin Garden. Adjacent to the Haupt Conservatory, this perennial garden was designed by Lynden B. Miller. As a showcase for ornamental shrubs, grasses, and flowering plants, this collection suggests possibilities for the home gardener in search of inspiration.

stand the term today—a place that fosters education, beauty of display and, in many cases, scientific research—was the Missouri Botanical Garden, founded in St. Louis. Just a few decades before this garden's inception, its home city had been described as a "dingy little settlement."[1] Surely it was such in 1819 when the young Englishman Henry Shaw arrived by way of Canada and New Orleans. Shaw had been sent to North America by his father to branch out the family's wholesale crockery and cutlery business into the growing states. An astute businessman and in the right place at the right time, Shaw became an outfitter for trappers and Indians as well as for westward-moving settlers for whom St. Louis was one of the last outposts of "civilization." He did very well, expanding his investments into real estate and exportation of the staples of cotton and tobacco and receiving a number of army contracts, all of which made him a wealthy man. So much so that at the relatively young age of forty, in 1840, he retired. For the next several years he traveled and oversaw the construction of two homes—city and country—and his gardens.

In 1849 Shaw returned to England, and in 1851, while at Chatsworth, he decided that he, too, would have such a country estate and open it to the public. Back in St. Louis, Shaw had thousands of trees and shrubs planted in eighty of his eight hundred acres some miles outside the city. Shaw's personal physician and friend George Engelmann, an eminent botanist in his own right, suggested that Shaw should add a greenhouse, herbarium, and other research facilities in order to create an important institution. Shaw began to work at once and continued for another ten years before opening the garden to the public. The opening was delayed until 1859 when the museum and library were completed.

The garden proved very popular with the people of St. Louis, who found it not only a botanical marvel but a respite from their labors. In the American Midwest, working-class people were able to walk through a garden reminiscent of an English estate and view such new and exotic plants as palms. They took great pleasure in the magnificent rose gardens and the wide variety of trees, especially chestnuts, magnolias, and English yews. Shaw became a very fine

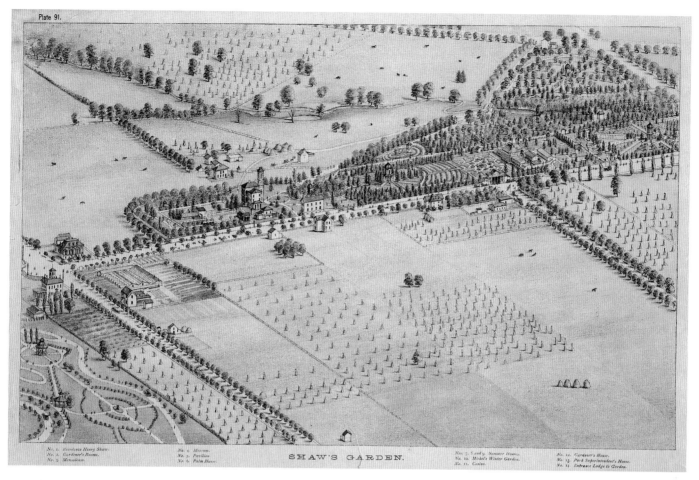

An 1875 topographical survey shows several of the buildings that had already been constructed in "Shaw's Garden," later to become the Missouri Botanical Garden. Included in this view is the Palm House as well as the mausoleum Shaw had built for himself.

amateur botanist and developed a friendly association with Sir William Hooker, director of the Royal Botanic Garden at Kew. Hooker visited Shaw on his way West and encouraged him, as had Engelmann, to turn this beautiful garden into a true botanic garden. This was something to which Shaw was committed and he devoted the rest of his life to the improvement and perfection of that garden, which took almost half of his years. Shaw died in 1899, leaving the major portion of his estate, more than two million dollars, to be an endowment for his beloved garden, still called "Shaw's Garden" in St. Louis.

Since that time the Missouri Botanical Garden has become one of the leading scientific research centers in the world, especially in the area of tropical botany. The seventy-nine acres of gardens, greenhouses, pools, fountains, and special collections include a number of internationally known landmarks. Perhaps most renowned is the Climatron, built in 1969. This geodesic-dome conservatory, covering half an acre, is built on two levels. Four separate climatic situations are maintained technologically. In one section is a waterfall surrounded by orchids, bromeliads, tropical and exotic trees, and various carnivorous plants. A magnificent Japanese garden, built around a lake, contains the traditional teahouse and numerous authentic ornaments; it is known for its exquisite moon bridge. Two areas constructed especially for the blind are the English woodland garden and the scented garden, both of which place an emphasis on intensity

of plant fragrances. There are two formal rose gardens and several display gardens with exhibits throughout the year.

A Tree Museum

THE ARNOLD ARBORETUM in Boston is the culmination of a fortuitous series of events that started in a garden. In 1805, the founding of the Cambridge Botanic Garden began to set the stage for Harvard University to be involved with horticulture in some fashion. In time, a Boston merchant and gentleman farmer, Benjamin Bussey, left a large property in Boston to Harvard for use as a school of horticulture or agriculture. In 1869 another gift, this time of money—$100,000—was left by wealthy New Bedford merchant James Arnold. The money, given to the care of three trustees, was "for the pro-

motion of Agriculture and Horticulture improvements or other Philosophical or Philanthropic purposes at their [the trustees'] discretion." Happily, one of the trustees was George B. Emerson, author of *A Report on the Trees and Shrubs Growing Naturally in the Forests of Massachusetts* (1846). Emerson was a friend of Asa Gray, director of the Cambridge Botanic Garden, and wanted an aboretum, which inspired him to suggest an amalgamation of the Bussey land and the Arnold money. Chosen to head the Arnold Arboretum was Charles Sprague Sargent, a wealthy Brahmin and Harvard alumnus. Sargent was young, energetic, and well-connected—all qualities that would be needed if the fledgling arboretum was to thrive.

At the time of his appointment, Sargent was perhaps not as confident as the Harvard officials who put him into office, for years later he wrote:

OPPOSITE:
Today, the Climatron—
the world's first geodesic-
domed greenhouse—is the
centerpiece of the Missouri
Botanical Garden.

The natural appearance of
the Arnold Arboretum
disguises the scientific
planting of trees by genus,
an approach that combines
beauty with instruction.

I was appointed Director of the new Arboretum by the President and Fellows of the College on November 24, 1873. The prospect of
being able to establish a useful institution
would not have been encouraging if the men
interested in it had had at that time as much
knowledge as hope and enthusiasm. For it is
safe to say that not one of them had an idea
of what an Arboretum might be, or what it
was going to cost in time and money to carry
out the provisions of the indenture between
the Trustees under Mr. Arnold's will and the
President and Fellows of Harvard College; and
certainly not one of them was more ignorant
of the subject than the man selected to carry
out the provisions of the agreement. He found
himself with a worn-out farm, partly covered
with natural plantations of native trees nearly
ruined by excessive pasturage, to be developed
into a scientific garden with less than three
thousand dollars a year available for the
purpose. [2]

Two of the visionaries who created the Arnold Arboretum—Charles Sprague Sargent (right) and Ernest Henry "Chinese" Wilson—stand before a *Prunus* *subhirtella*. The two people most responsible for the great growth of the Arboretum, their combined service to it amounted to nearly seventy years.

Sargent's remarks, whether the result of expected Brahmin modesty or a true assessment of the situation in 1873 certainly do not give any indication of the magnificent work he had performed at this "worn-out farm." One very important step Sargent took toward establishing the Arnold was hiring the man who was then working on the planning and construction of a park system for the city of Boston, Frederick Law Olmsted. Sargent and Olmsted wanted somehow to link the nascent park system and the arboretum in a mutually beneficial relationship. The only two supporters of this idea were its originators, and it took almost a decade for Sargent to convince both the college and the park commissioners that this would work to their mutual good.

In that decade Sargent and Olmsted worked out many details; Olmsted did almost twenty studies for the distribution and planting of trees and shrubs. Sargent set the tone for the nature of the arboretum, writing in 1878:

In such a [tree] museum, everything should be subservient to the collections, and the ease with which these can be reached and studied; and none of those considerations of mere landscape effect, which properly govern the laying out of ordinary public parks, should be allowed to interfere with these essential requirements of a scientific garden, however desirable such effects undoubtedly are.[3]

Over the next several years, other events occurred that added to the success of the forming institution, including a federal commission for Sargent to study the nation's forests, which enabled him to send specimens back to Boston. In 1882, the Arnold Arboretum was finally approved as part of the city greening plan—the Emerald Necklace—and Harvard and the city of Boston entered into an agreement that called for, among other things, the arboretum to be a free and open space for all. The next year, Olmsted's plan for the design of the Arnold was put into effect. Soon an herbarium collection and a library, the latter chiefly funded by Sargent himself, were established. Sargent continued the constant improvement of his "tree museum," sending specimens back from virtually all over the world during his plant exploration trips. This was carried on from 1906 until about 1920 by Ernest Henry "Chinese" Wilson, whom Sargent had brought from England to explore and retrieve specimens for the arboretum. During his years of service, Wilson was responsible for sending back thousands of species and varieties, mostly from Asia, and introduced to gardens many plants of particular note, including the primrose jasmine (*Jasminum Mesnyi*), the beautybush (*Kolkwitzia amabilis*), the tea crab (*Malus hupehensis*), several cotoneasters, the regal lily (*Lilium regale*), the dovetree (*Davidia involucrata*), and *Magnolia Wilsonii*.

The pace at which the Arnold collected and introduced plants during the Sargent and Wilson years was phenomenal and resulted in the arboretum's becoming one of the greatest horticultural/botanical institutions in the world. Currently the collections, numbering more than seven thousand types of trees and shrubs, are especially known for crab apples, lilacs, conifers (standard and dwarf), maples, honeysuckles, viburnums, dogwood, and rhododendrons. One of the most fascinating introductions has been the *Metasequoia glyptostroboides* (dawn redwood). Brought back from China in 1948, it had been believed to be extinct for millions of years.

The 265-acre arboretum has been responsible for the introduction of more than five hundred ornamental tree and shrub varieties into American gardens. Today it maintains a vigorous education program, performs scientific research in woody plants, plant exploration, and continues to be part of the Boston parks system, fulfilling its original intent to be a tree museum and a cultural institution free and open to all.

New York Botanical Garden: The Next Generation

NEW YORK CITY is the only city in the country which can boast of two internationally acclaimed botanical gardens. Each of these is quite different in intent and in tone. The older is the New York Botanical Garden, often called the Bronx Botanic Garden because of its location.

The idea of having such a garden had been discussed for quite some time but it was not acted upon until a rather well-to-do couple, fresh from a honeymoon in England, raised the subject at a meeting of the Torrey Botanic Club, an association of men and women who were passionately and intelligently concerned with the plant world. Nathaniel Lord Britton, a professor of botany at Columbia College, and his wife, Elizabeth, the country's leading bryologist, had recently toured the Royal Botanic Gardens at Kew and suggested at an 1891 meeting of the Torrey Club that such an institution be established in New York —an American Kew! The idea was enthusiastically received and plans were made for raising funds and involving people of means and motivation. The Brittons were able to utilize their positions of influence to get the City of New York to set aside two hundred acres of the recently formed Bronx Park for the site and to commit $500,000 over the next four years if the Brittons and their companions could raise an additional $250,000. Fortunately the Brittons were well connected and supported by friends and colleagues who gave teas and luncheons to raise money. At these functions clergy spoke of the morally uplifting benefits, especially to the poor, of horticulture and gardening. The most prominent men of the time

were called upon to support this endeavor, which would be of enormous scientific and social benefit, and within the four years the money was raised. Among the most ardent and generous benefactors were Andrew Carnegie, Cornelius Vanderbilt II, and J. Pierpont Morgan. Columbia College also donated the generous sum of $25,000. Once the money was raised, although more would be needed, Britton was appointed director.

Construction of buildings and laying out of the grounds began in earnest. A survey showed that more than a thousand different kinds of plants were already on the property. To these Britton added more than fifteen hundred trees and shrubs in order to form several types of gardens, including a fruiticetum, a pinetum, and an arboretum. A marsh was drained to form two lakes. Plantings of rhododendrons and azaleas were put in many parts of the property.

Perhaps the biggest attraction, however, was the conservatory system built by Lord and Burnham.

These glasshouses were modeled after the Palm House at Kew and the Crystal Palace at Hyde Park. The conservatory, finished in 1902, held about nine thousand plants, especially those too tender to withstand New York winters, and consequently plants were included that few people in New York had ever seen in person. This array of exotics became an important learning opportunity in itself. About this time a museum building was also completed in which were housed offices, a herbarium, and exhibition halls, one of the first museums in this country devoted exclusively to botany.

So popular had the Garden become by 1915 that the City of New York added an additional one hundred and forty acres. The crowds were getting larger, too—thousands on a weekend. Such success brought more benefactors, and in 1918 the Guggenheim family contributed $100,000 for the construction of more conservatories. These, unfortunately, were later torn down in the name of progress when

OPPOSITE:
The conservatories of the New York Botanical Garden provided a place to exhibit many exotic plants, which were enjoyed by an urban, frequently poor, population at the turn of the nineteenth century.

New York's other internationally acclaimed botanic garden, the Brooklyn Botanic Garden, founded in 1910 by concerned citizens, is in many respects the ideal botanical garden—one that offers rest and contemplation as well as intensive educational programs and an active publications department. The exquisite beauty of the fifty-acre garden, situated in a densely populated urban area, provides the kind of reflection and focus that have inspired gardeners the world over with impetus and imagination. The Japanese Gardens, seen here, are among the most serene and delightful of the garden's offerings, attracting visitors from all over the world.

some of the land was retaken by the city's park commissioner Robert Moses.

The scientific aspects of the New York Botanical Garden were not neglected. Research, especially in the tropical regions, has been a hallmark of the institution since the early years. In 1898 Cornelius Vanderbilt financed an expedition to Puerto Rico that resulted in eight thousand plants being brought back to be housed and displayed in the greenhouses. Shortly thereafter the Brittons set out for the West Indies on a plant-collecting trip. These early trips would multiply into more than five hundred expeditions on the part of the research staff over the years to virtually every continent and climate in the world.

When Nathaniel Lord Britton retired in 1929 after thirty years as director, the Garden could boast one of the finest research facilities in the world, with an herbarium of almost two million specimens, a library of more than forty-three thousand volumes, and a diverse educational program for all levels of expertise.

Over the years since the Britton regime, the New York Botanical Garden has continued to grow and to increase its programs and research. One specialty of the garden is taxonomy, the naming and classification of plants. In 1981 the garden began its Institute of Economic Botany, which finds and develops plants for new sources of fuel and food, especially in tropical countries.

The display gardens have been augmented over the years as well. These include the refurbished conservatories now named for their benefactor Enid A. Haupt, in which are displayed desert garden plants, a fern forest, a palm grove, and a learning center for children. The rose garden contains two hundred varieties; the rock garden, which includes a re-created alpine scene, has magnificent species of these hybrid plants.

The native plants garden offers a view of plants native to the northeastern United States. It is organized in four parts, according to habitat: a deciduous woodland, a limestone outcropping, a pine barren, and a meadow. One particularly wonderful area of the garden is its forest, a forty-acre stand of trees that constitutes the only uncut woodland in the City of New York.

For almost one hundred years, the New York Botanical Garden has been offering courses to all levels of students and now offers a Ph.D. program in botany, in conjunction with the City University of New York, as well as several certificate programs from the garden's school of horticulture. As the New York Botanical Garden begins its second century, New Yorkers can look back at the original intent of creating an American Kew and feel that it has been achieved.

Library, Museum, and Garden: The Huntington

IN 1906, THE RAILROAD and real estate tycoon Henry Edward Huntington retired from his family's business and devoted himself to collecting books and works of art and to designing his San Marino estate, in the San Gabriel Valley near Los Angeles. Huntington engaged botanist William Hertrich to travel throughout Mexico and the southwestern United States to collect plants suitable for the two-hundred-acre property.

Among the difficulties encountered by Huntington, or H. E., as he came to be known, was a hillside area of the property that was barren, seemingly infertile, and sun drenched. Hertrich thought at once of establishing desert plants there, but his employer did not like cactus, probably as a result of having backed into one years before while supervising railroad construction. However, he let Hertrich have a half acre with which to experiment. What a surprise it must have been for Huntington when Hertrich returned with several train cars full of cactus and other desert plants for that small space. Either Huntington became accustomed to cactus or Hertrich was an eloquent and persuasive man, for, by 1912, the half acre had become five acres, expanding to twelve after H. E.'s death in 1927. It has become one of the leading gardens at the Huntington and one for which it is well known.

When not creating the fabulous grounds of his estate, Huntington collected works of art and scholarly books. Indeed, it is hard to speak of the Huntington without mentioning all three aspects—garden, library, and museum—of this remarkable place.

The North Vista of the Huntington Botanical Garden is flanked by seventeenth-century stone statues depicting mythical and allegorical figures.

Each has been developed with the same principle of focused attention. In the garden this has meant a concentration of certain flowers, with five acres devoted to camellias alone. The desert garden now has more than five thousand species, making it the largest outdoor garden of its kind in the world. Among the dozen other display gardens are to be found a great greensward of lawn lined with azaleas, camellias, and palms as well as antique Italian statues. This elegant strolling area is in keeping with the mansion, which now houses the library. The acre devoted to the Shakespeare garden contains English plants that were in cultivation in the Bard's time. Upward of one thousand varieties of roses, arranged in historical order and representing a thousand years of rose culture, compose the elegant rose garden. The delightful five-acre Japanese garden, with its authentic nineteenth-century house, bonsai grove, temple bell, Zen garden,

and famous moon bridge, is internationally recognized. Camellias figure prominently at the Huntington, which fosters more than fifteen hundred types. Palms, too, are of major importance, the palm garden featuring more than two hundred mature specimens. Due to the similarity of climate to that of the continent down under, the Huntington also has an Australian garden that boasts more than one hundred varieties of eucalyptus and other plants native to that country.

The Huntington has one of the finest research libraries in the world, with special collections in English and American literature that include well over six hundred thousand items, among them reference works, manuscripts, and thousands of incunabula as well as rare books and manuscripts. H. E. married his uncle's widow, Arabella Huntington, in 1913, and it was largely through her promptings that he began his art museum, although at first it was, like the library and grounds, simply for the family's own edification. Among the better-known paintings are

Gainsborough's *Blue Boy* and its companion piece, *Pinkie*, by Sir Thomas Lawrence. The tripartite experience of the Huntington allows one a more dramatic view of one of the strengths of a botanic garden—that of being a cultural institution much like a museum, opera house, theater, library, or symphony hall. In no other botanic garden in this country is this acknowledgment of the broad-based human need for beauty and delight so evident.

Longwood: Elegance and Theater

WHEN PIERRE S. DuPONT FIRST SAW the property he was to make into Longwood Gardens, it had already been considered a historic site for many years. In 1906, while out for a Sunday drive, DuPont, who was later to become the financial head of the DuPont empire and the chairman of General Motors, noticed a sawmill being constructed near Kennett Square, Pennsylvania. Upon investigation, he found that the property to be cleared was none other than that owned by the descendants of Joshua and Samuel Peirce, whose grandfather had received the property from the land distributors of William Penn himself. The twin Quaker brothers had begun an arboretum on the property and planted in it many then-exotic trees including the bald cypress (*Taxodium distichum*). DuPont could not accept the destruction of the trees and bought the property in order to save them. In addition he was looking for a site on which to build his summer house, and the location of Kennett Square suited him very well. Since the Peirce family was selling the trees for timber in order to meet financial obligations, the sale to DuPont was fortuitous.

As a child DuPont had been fascinated by fountains, and he would indulge his fancy in a grand manner as an adult. On one of his trips to Europe, he traveled through England, France, and Italy, touring the gardens of the nobility and finding inspiration for design at Longwood, especially in the fountains and other water elements. In 1918 construction began on the magnificent conservatories, and as early as 1921 the public was permitted in to see the first one built, which served as an orangerie. A few years later,

following another tour of Europe, Longwood's Italian water garden was begun. Shortly thereafter, the main fountain garden with its exuberant jets and sculptured stonework was embarked upon.

This garden is built on two levels and presents a complex array of fountains, with canals, basins, and 229 water jets. It is one of the most opulent gardens anywhere. To further extend the water theme, DuPont built a water lily pool which contains lotus and water hyacinths as well as the royal water lily *Victoria amazonica*. The culmination of the water gardens is found in two large natural lakes and a waterfall sided by dogwoods and evergreens.

DuPont died in 1954 and left his estate in trust, but not before forming the Longwood Foundation. From his purchase of the land until his death, the enormously wealthy tycoon spent more than $25 million of his own money on Longwood to make it the most magnificent garden in the country. In addition to the water features, there are several other display gardens of note, comprising 350 of Longwood's 1,000 acres (the other 650 are field and woods). The conservatories cover about three and a half acres and host permanent collections, as well as changing displays such as elegant seasonal attractions of spring bulbs and lilies for Easter, poinsettias, paperwhite narcissus, and cyclamen at Christmas, and a variety of chrysanthemums in the autumn.

The theater garden is reminiscent of its counterparts in Italian villa gardens of the Renaissance and features many Mediterranean plants that are hardy in Pennsylvania. The theater, patterned after the one at Villa Gori, near Sienna, seats 2,100 people and has dressing rooms under the stage and lawn. The stage itself is flanked by clipped arborvitae (*Thuja occidentalis*), and its backdrop consists of hemlocks (*Tsuga canadensis*) and Kentucky coffee trees (*Gymnocladus dioica*). The "curtain" is actually water from jets.

The Flower Garden Walk, designed by Pierre DuPont himself, was begun shortly after he moved into the old Peirce residence, in 1907. It is a fine example of Victorian formality, with its brick wall, central fountain, and bench at one end. Other period styles are represented as well. The Italian Renaissance garden is square, enclosed by clipped walls of arbor-

Spectacular displays of dramatically shooting fountains are the hallmark of Longwood Gardens. Those in this view are part of the Italian Gardens.

vitae, and contains a fountain. A wonderfully pastoral scene has been created in the gardens derived from those of eighteenth-century England, especially in the style of Capability Brown and Humphry Repton.

Allées are in abundance, including one of copper beech (*Fagus sylvatica* 'Atropurpurea') and another of Empress trees (*Paulownia tomentosa*), which set out exquisite lavender flowers that bloom before the tree puts out leaves. The conservatories form a world unto themselves, housing a virtually unrivaled collection of orchids, for example. Also cultivated under glass are several types of American desert plants, mature specimens of citrus trees, and many "common" plants (e.g., azaleas, rhododendrons, tulips, and geraniums) that are always on display for the benefit of home gardeners. As might be expected, many exotic, even bizarre, plants are on display, such as the carnivorous *Nepenthes maxima*. A palm house allows one to view its denizens as though from above. Economic plants are also shown, such as the climbing vanilla orchid (*Vanilla planifolia*), the chocolate tree (*Theobroma Cacao*), and banana trees (*Musa spp.*).

While the display aspect of botanic gardens is obviously the one emphasized at Longwood, there is also work being done on developing new varieties of plants for public green spaces and on taxonomic improvement. Equally important is the program sponsored jointly with the University of Delaware—a master's program that trains students to take on administrative posts in the various public institutions devoted to horticulture and landscape beauty. In this way Longwood Gardens reaches far beyond its own elegant and inspiring acres.

Fun Out of Paying a Debt:
The Fairchild Tropical Garden

IN THE INTRODUCTION to his book *Exploring for Plants* (1930), Dr. David Fairchild wrote:

> I am modest in my ambition with regard to its success, however, for I shall be content if a perusal of its pages shall convert a single person to the romantic life a deep study of plants can give. It makes no difference whether he or she should remain in one spot on the surface of the globe, exploring the inexhaustible resources of that particular place, or float about over its mountains and deserts searching from the air for forms which man shall in the years to come draw about his dooryard and make a part of the more beautiful environment of his life.

Such a person was Colonel Robert H. Montgomery of Florida and Connecticut. Though perhaps not in need of conversion, Montgomery was admittedly greatly inspired by Fairchild's work. The owner of one of the world's largest pinetums (on his summer estate in Cos Cob, Connecticut, since given to the New York Botanical Garden, Montgomery had already begun another garden in Florida when he decided to establish a public garden to honor Fairchild and collect "in one spot on the surface of the globe" as many of the plants introduced by Fairchild as possible. This, thought Montgomery, would be a fitting and lasting tribute to Fairchild, under whose direction fifty-four plant explorations were carried out. Fairchild was quite enthusiastic about the project and was consulted from the beginning, even choosing the place where the garden would be built. A site between Miami and Cutler was chosen, chiefly for climatic reasons.

Montgomery, a former attorney and federal tax authority, was a wealthy man; he purchased a parcel of about eighty-three acres in 1934 and incorporated the Fairchild Tropical Garden Association, which was composed of subscribers, to administer it. He then "split" the garden administration, asking Dade County to take title and responsibility for fifty-eight

acres. The remaining twenty-five acres remained with the association, as did the duties of maintaining plant records, research, and general administration. The smaller area would become the palmetum, a collection of a favorite plant of Montgomery's, which suggests that Montgomery wanted to keep closer control on this section of the estate. A couple of years later Montgomery could write to a friend that there were three hundred members in the association, chiefly his friends and colleagues. He needed more—about one thousand—to make the garden a success. To show his own devotion, over the course of the rest of his life Montgomery spent most if not all of his time, as well as $350,000 of his own money, establishing and improving the garden.

William Lyman Phillips was chosen to design the garden. Phillips had studied with the great F. L. Olmsted as well as at Harvard's School of Landscape Architecture. It was perhaps his knowledge of the Arnold Arboretum that assisted him in laying out the grounds in a horticulturally pleasing way, at the same time keeping plant families together for scientific observation, much as Olmsted had done at the Arnold. The Fairchild, in fact, is known for the beauty of its display, which in no way compromises the integrity of its scientific mission.

At the dedication ceremony in 1938, Colonel Montgomery spoke of the debt that the country owed to Fairchild, who was Supervisor of Plant Introductions for the USDA from 1897 until 1927 in which role he had been responsible for more than 65,000 plant introductions, personally going on several expeditions himself even after retirement. This debt, Montgomery said, could be paid in only one way: "to make this garden, which has been named and founded in his honor, a worthy tribute to his unselfish efforts. It is a debt which will be a pleasure to pay. Think of getting fun out of paying a debt."

Since its foundation, the Fairchild has certainly been a worthy tribute and has grown into the world's largest and finest collection of palms and cycads, with well over five hundred species combined. In the Palm Garden, one may see the Palmyra palm (*Borassus flabellifer*) with its fan-shaped leaves that grow up to seven feet in length and width and its fruit weighing

The Rare Plant House of the Fairchild Tropical Garden includes tree ferns, bromeliads, and orchids among its collections. Even in Florida's subtropical climate, some plants need extra housing and care, and this two-level structure houses the garden's nonhardy rare plants.

eight to ten pounds; the Talipot palm (*Corypha umbraculifera*), which blooms once in its lifetime in beautiful cascading flowers; or lovely and very rare species such as the *Nephrosperma*. Equally fascinating are the cycads, which are among the oldest plants extant. The ornamental types include the *Cycas circinalis*; but one of the exotics is the very rare—and dreadfully named—*Encephalartos horridus*.

The scientific aspects of the garden have not been overlooked. Through a grant from the Michaux fund of the American Philosophical Society, the garden was able to save many Bahamian plants from extinc-tion by obtaining several species and removing them to Fairchild before the encroachments of real estate development obliterated them forever. The research division collects the works of nineteenth-century botanists for historic documentation of plants, and the herbarium is part of the research component. On a more general level are courses that include the study of the various plants in the garden, including the River Front Section and the glasshouses. It is these plants and (in the case of the River Front Section) their layout that are for many the most spectacular part of this garden. The design is worked around eight major lakes and includes examples of the techniques of extended chiaroscuro as well as contrasting plantings in masses with open spaces. Magnificent vistas and winding paths are incorporated, making the whole experience of strolling and viewing one that offers a delightful and surprising sight wherever the visitor turns.

Horticultural Societies

HORTICULTURAL SOCIETIES have long been in the vanguard of the most effective organizations promoting, encouraging, and improving gardening in America. This is due in part to the scope of their interests and endeavors and the commitment they traditionally have made to a full public educational program.

Horticultural societies were first developed out of a progressive refinement of earlier organizations devoted to natural history and agriculture, and which included some horticultural components that were later adopted, enlarged, and perfected by the horticultural societies. Associations like the American Philosophical Society (Philadelphia, 1769) and the American Academy of Sciences (Boston, 1780) issued learned papers and offered lectures on "useful knowledge," which included information on botany, entomology, soils, pomology, and native and foreign plants.

Agricultural societies abounded. In South Carolina, Virginia, New York, Massachusetts, and several other states, such organizations attracted the most prominent men in the social, political, and agricultural arenas. These associations, with their emphasis on problem solving, information gathering and sharing, and a social element (few "dirt" farmers would have been found among their ranks), rapidly proliferated during the late eighteenth century and first three decades of the nineteenth century and became the enthusiastic promoters of improvement and "useful knowledge." The importance of these organizations in a country that was almost wholly agricultural and agrarian cannot be overstated.

The first intentional horticultural society, per se, was founded in 1818. The New York Horticultural Society was begun by some of the leading botanists, nurserymen, and plantsmen of the time. Among them was Dr. David Hosack, who established the Elgin Botanic Garden in New York in 1801. He also maintained a seven-hundred-acre estate that was a premier place for horticultural research and design. Grant Thorburn, whose seed and nursery establishments had great influence on the development of gardening, was much involved with the New York Horticultural Society. William Prince's family had begun a nursery on Long Island in 1737, which they split with his brother; William founded his Linnaean Botanic Garden and Nursery, and his book *A Short Treatise on Horticulture* (1828) enjoyed great popularity. He was an active and influential member of this important but short-lived society, as was André Parmentier, who arrived in America in 1824 and established a garden in Brooklyn, where he cultivated hundreds of species of ornamental trees. His influence in American garden design was quite strong and wide due both to this nursery and to his designs for estate gardens, especially along the Hudson.

All of these men and others of their ilk gave great impetus to the horticultural society as a unique institution. The New York Horticultural Society also set the tone for future horticultural societies in its intentions, albeit unrealized, of establishing a garden, a library, a lecture hall, and a professorship of botany and horticulture. While these did not come to fruition, the very start of an organization devoted to horticulture acted as a catalyst: over the next nineteen years ten more such organizations were begun. Such a rapid rate was significant. As Robert Emerson Benson writes, "the establishment of all these societies at practically the same period makes it evident that the time was ripe for concerted systematized effort in horticultural science and for the organization it implied."[4] This effort found its most enduring and influential expression in two sister organizations: the Pennsylvania Horticultural Society (1827) and the Massachusetts Horticultural Society (1829).

Philadephia had long been considered a center of horticultural activity. Downing recognized this in 1837 when he wrote of Philadelphia's primacy as a garden and horticultural capital: "This is owing in some degree to the early settlement of the town, but in a great measure to its having been, at any early period, the residence of a few devoted botanists and amateurs, whose zeal infused a corresponding taste among their fellow-citizens."[5]

The enormous depth of horticultural activity, the splendid gardens, the garden history already well established in 1827, the plethora of expert nurserymen—all made it a very natural place for a horticultural society, and on November 24, 1827, the Pennsylvania Horticultural Society was founded. By June 1829 the society held its first public exhibition, which was the first flower show of any importance in the country. Again Downing commented: "The Horticultural Society of Philadelphia [the Pennsylvania Horticultural Society] occupies a large sphere of usefulness, and, through the means of its annual exhibitions, which are thronged with spectators, disseminates a knowledge of the progress of horticulture, and a taste for gardening pursuits through the whole mass of citizens."[6]

During the same month, in Boston, another group was incorporated, having been founded four months earlier. The Massachusetts Horticultural Society began its life in the insurance office of Zebedee Cook, in Boston's financial district. This fact is significant, for the founders and early members were men of great means and they did not hesitate to use those means—financial and personal—to pursue the ends of the society. "Asked to name the horticultural organization in North America that has had the greatest influence on horticulture," U. P. Hedrick notes, "few would hesitate to name the Massachusetts Horticultural Society [whose] charter members were among the most distinguished men in Massachusetts."[7] These gentlemen farmers and estate owners were not so concerned with flowers and ornamental plants as their counterparts in Philadelphia were. Rather, the New Englanders concerned themselves with the growing of fruits. In this and other matters, the society was much influenced by the Horticultural Society of London (later the Royal Horticultural Society) and other European horticultural societies.

The education and research emphases of the Boston society were present from its inception. Indeed, into the capable hands of John B. Russell, general agent for the society and proprietor of the *New England Farmer*, the society consigned all "donations of seeds, scions, roots, drawings of fruits, models of implements of use in horticulture, or donations to the Library."[8] It was clear from the start that the society would be involved in horticulture in all its aspects. From its chief concern with fruit, the society, like its counterpart in Philadelphia, became the sponsor of an annual show of both flowers and fruit. Both of these organizations reached thousands with these major exhibitions—as well as smaller, more specialized ones presented throughout the year—where plants of all kinds were introduced to the public for the first time. Perhaps the most well-known plant to be brought to the attention of people, one that was widely in use, was Ephraim Wales Bull's Concord grape, which was exhibited at the Massachusetts Horticultural Society's show in September 1853.

From the beginning competition has played a large role in the perpetuation of agricultural and horticultural societies. Both the Pennsylvania and Massachusetts societies awarded medals and premiums to promote amelioration in horticultural practices and successful cultivation. The inclination to compete and win was strongly affirmed by these prestigious awards and cash benefits. They were used not only to encourage improvement in fruits and flowers but also to recognize achievement, thus facilitating many advances in horticulture. In addition, public lectures, publications, and the encouragement of scientific improvement in horticulture occupied the work of the two groups. The Massachusetts society undertook a

The Pennsylvania Horticultural Society's Philadelphia Green project inspires civic pride by means of its beautification endeavors and through the care the society devotes to the many local neighborhood gardens it sponsors.

bold work in 1831 with the establishment of Mount Auburn Cemetery, which was to double as an experimental garden. Differences over matters of governance eventually severed the society's ties with Mount Auburn, but not before it had become a model for other gardens of its kind in the country.

Neither of these societies has been content to rest on history or reputation, but both have maintained programs that fulfill their statements of mission in a creative and useful fashion. The Pennsylvania Horticultural Society continues to produce the largest flower show in the country. At present, the proceeds directly benefit two programs in the greater Philadelphia area: Center City Green and Philadelphia

The Massachusetts Horticultural Society conducts its educational and community outreach programs on many levels. Here a group of children congregate by the society's artfully painted plantmobile for a lesson on bulbs as they prepare to plant several hundred daffodils along Olmsted's Muddy River section of the Emerald Necklace in Boston.

Green. Both of these outreach and community-service programs sponsor activities that improve life in the urban setting. The Society also maintains a fine library of about fourteen thousand items and an education department that offers classes at all levels of expertise.

Currently the Massachusetts Horticultural Society carries out its mission—now more than 160 years old—in contemporary and responsive ways. The New England Spring Flower Show attracts more than 150,000 people each March and is the largest public exhibit in New England. The education department sponsors courses, tours, lectures, and demonstrations to learners of all ages, providing a wide scope of useful and sophisticated information about virtually every aspect of horticulture and gardening and extends into the fields of design and ecology as well. The department conducts a hot line for specific plant questions of a practical and remedial type.

Through its community services office, the society also reaches out to the underserved in urban areas and assists community and public groups with innovative beautification and greening projects. The children's educational office works with parents, teachers, and children in several areas of plant instruction. Grade-school students benefit immensely from the Massachusetts Horticultural Society plantmobile. This ubiquitous and highly regarded program instructs young minds in a pleasurable learning situation that introduces them to the wonders and excitement of plants, often in areas where no plant science has been offered. The society also issues occasional publications on relevant and practical gardening procedures for the home gardener in suburb and city.

The library of the Massachusetts Horticultural Society, established in 1829, holds more than eighty-five thousand items and serves the informational needs not only of the society's ten thousand members but the general gardening public, scholars, researchers, historians, writers, and artists. Currently the society is taking active steps to create a botanical garden in Boston, a dream that should come to fruition in a few years.

Looking to the Past for the Future

THE INTEREST IN AMERICAN GARDEN HISTORY has been approached by means of many disciplines. Art historians, architects, preservationists, and others have added their own focus and insights, creating a multifaceted approach that is itself indicative of the richness and diversity that contribute to the contemporary study of garden history.

The American South has a long and lovely garden history and a splendid sense of its own regional history. For several years, beginning in 1979, a series of conferences on restoring Southern gardens and landscapes was sponsored by Old Salem, Inc., the Reynoldia Gardens of Wake Forest University, and the Stagville Center of the North Carolina Department of Cultural Resources. So effective and well received were these conferences that a more structured and ongoing vehicle was needed to sustain the interest sparked by the symposia. In 1982 the Southern Garden History Society was formed to promote interest in Southern garden and landscape history and to disseminate information on historic horticulture and the restoration of gardens and landscapes in the South. To accomplish this the society—whose domain includes fourteen states and the District of Columbia, with an international membership—holds an annual meeting each spring, in a different part of the South, to study and tour the history, gardens, and landscape of that area with the hope that such meetings will result in continued investigation and preservation.

The exchange of information among the more than five hundred members is facilitated by the Society's quarterly bulletin, *Magnolia*. A publications committee was recently formed to investigate material that the Society could publish on its subject areas. The Southern Garden History Society also collects books, manuscripts, and other documents, which it houses at the Cherokee Garden Library of the Atlanta Historical Society. As this first regional garden history society in the United States enters its second decade it looks back on an impressive list of accomplishments and forward to many fascinating future challenges and programs.

Another regional garden history society was founded in October 1989 when several garden historians, landscape architects, preservationists, and librarians met in the library of the Massachusetts Horticultural Society to determine whether a garden history society in New England was warranted. The decidedly affirmative conclusion led to the formation of the New England Garden History Society. It was felt that this society should take a wide view of gardens and include in its province parks, cityscapes, farms, and the "unbothered" landscape as well as the more usually studied estate and cottage gardens. Horticulture would also play a prominent role, especially

in its historical aspects. The society believes that the garden is best appreciated when understood in all its complexity and cultural accretions. To this end the New England Garden History Society sponsors tours and trips for its members. In addition, lectures and symposia are offered on a wide range of subjects. Appropriate archival material is being collected and the society has an extensive publications program that includes a newsletter (*Labyrinth*), a register of research, bibliographies, and a scholarly journal. The New England Garden History Society of the Massachusetts Horticultural Society seeks to preserve a fascinating and vital history in all its dimensions, giving life to its motto: "Our cultural history is written on the landscape just as surely as on the printed page."

Both of these organizations promote lively involvement in the experience and study of gardens, as well as enjoyment of the vitality and elegance, the meaning and place, that they have in our lives.

Garden Clubs and Societies

UNTIL THE LATE NINETEENTH CENTURY the role of women in gardening was, with some wonderful exceptions, limited to the area surrounding the house, especially the kitchen garden. This role was indicative of the general tenor of society regarding the "place" of women. In some respects it took a war to change things. Women played a significant part, on both sides, during the Civil War, acting as nurses, farmers, organizers, and bureaucrats, and in a myriad of other functions previously considered the domain of men. Following the war the suffrage movement gave additional impetus to the changing status of women in America. During the 1870s and 1880s women organized into various kinds of clubs and associations, chiefly social, cultural, and civic. Regional amalgamations were formed for mutual support and sharing of information. Julia Ward Howe and a few other ladies formed the New England Women's Clubs, a consortium of local reform-minded, social organizations. By 1890 there was such a number of similar groups in the country that the General Federation of Women's Clubs was formed. At about this same time the garden city movement was taking hold in some areas, with its attendant reaction to the horrible urban conditions brought on by industrialization, political corruption, and the crowded, squalid conditions resulting from waves of immigrants being forced into limited areas of the country's main cities.

This organizing tendency in the last few decades of the nineteenth and first few decades of the twentieth century was not without repercussions for gardening. Several individual attempts, many successful, were made to organize women into clubs. In 1876 the Lexington Field and Garden Club was formed to maintain existing trees in that Massachusetts town, to sponsor the planting of new trees, shrubs, and flowers for local beautification, and for the study of botany, geology, horticulture, and related areas. This organization continues today with its civic improvement and study groups. The year 1889 saw a southern garden club attempt but it was shortly disbanded. That same year, however, another Massachusetts garden organization—the Cambridge Plant Club—was founded by Miss Caroline Hays, who had been "besieged" by numerous requests for her method of cultivating a passion flower. She met with twenty ladies at her mother's home on January 20, and the club was formed to exchange experiences and to discuss plant culture.

A few years later a dozen ladies of Athens, Georgia, with the assistance of Professor C. C. Newton, a botanist, began the Ladies Garden Club of Athens. These ladies devised rules for governing the clubs and criteria for awarding premiums by judges; these rules were later sent to friends in other cities and towns in Georgia, and thus was established the Garden Club of Georgia in 1928. A year later thirty-five clubs in the state had become federated.

Another local group, the Garden Club of Philadelphia, was begun in 1904 in Andalusia, Pennsylvania. At about this time, similar clubs, like the Gardeners of Montgomery and Delaware Counties, and the Weeders, were also founded. In 1913 there were eleven such clubs nationwide, generally made up of wealthy women who were in a position to implement change more effectively and quickly than most. Invitations were sent out to representatives of these clubs, and the Garden Guild of America—soon thereafter the Garden Club of America—was born.

After spreading into the whole state of Georgia, the group from Athens expanded into other states, always with the same purpose. More than three hundred clubs had been formed in 1925 and in nineteen states the clubs joined forces to form federations of state garden clubs, with New York as the first, in 1924, founded by Mrs. John W. Paris. At the International Flower Fair in New York City, in 1929, Mrs. Paris invited the presidents of the garden clubs present, as well as other interested women, to form a national club. Two months later, at a meeting in Washington, D.C., thirteen of the nineteen state clubs were represented, while the other six federations sent reports and the National Council of State Garden Clubs was formed.

The Garden Club of America and the National Council of State Garden Clubs have a similar focus, and each has been highly effective in several areas of gardening, from horticultural-therapy programs for the elderly and handicapped to environmental education. Indeed, as early as 1944 one objective of the National Council read: "To aid in the protection and conservation of our natural resources." The Garden Club of America's policies mirror this concern. In its stated objectives one reads that it was founded "to aid in the protection of native plants and birds and to encourage civic planting." Such succinct statements have blossomed over time into national and international concern and global thinking. Both groups have assisted with such pressing issues as preservation of the rainforests, educational scholarships, and land conservation.

The Garden Conservancy

CONSERVATION OF VARIOUS WILDERNESS areas, open spaces, and places of stunning natural beauty is the responsibility of a number of environmental and trust organizations. Some of these also maintain fine old estates and their gardens, but until recently there was no organization devoted solely to the conservation of America's premier gardens. In 1989 New Yorker Francis H. Cabot, who himself maintains two splendid gardens, founded the Garden Conservancy with the support of the Tides Foundation of San Francisco. The Garden Conservancy is dedicated to identifying truly special private gardens of national importance and arranging their passage from private hands into independent nonprofit ownership to be operated for the benefit of the public. It accomplishes this by acting as consultant and facilitator in providing the proper legal, managerial, and development expertise. In this way the Garden Conservancy, quite literally, keeps alive some of the finest examples of American gardens (gardening). As part of a larger national movement toward preservation, the Conservancy hopes that its gardens will act as catalysts for promoting this interest.

To date the Conservancy has been involved with some unique properties, including the Hay estate at Lake Sunapee, New Hampshire, summer home of John Hay, biographer of Lincoln and secretary of state under William McKinley and Theodore Roosevelt.

The work of the almost two-thousand-member organization is an effective and unique vehicle for focusing attention on nationally significant gardens for public enjoyment, cultural inspiration, and, in the larger view, preservation of a special part of the country's artistic and natural heritage.

It is clear from this review that gardening has been organized into virtually every possible kind of association for information, improvement, enjoyment, and study. This is proof that the garden and gardening are an integral and vital part of our history and our lives. ✍

NOTES

1. Hedrick, p. 327.

2. Quoted in *The Arnold Arboretum*, S. B. Sutton, Boston: Nimrod Press, 1971, p. 15.

3. Sargent, Charles Sprague, *Annual Report* of the President and Fellows of Harvard College for the Year Ending August 31, 1878.

4. Benson, p. 21.

5. Downing, A. J., "Notes on the State and Progress of Horticulture in the United States," in *The Magazine of Horticulture, Botany, and All Useful Discoveries, Improvements and Rural Affairs*, vol. 3, 1837, Boston, p. 3.

6. Ibid., p. 4.

7. Hedrick, p. 506.

8. From "A Notice" found in the *Transactions* of the Massachusetts Horticultural Society, 1829, Boston, Press of Isaac R. Butts, p. 52.

BIBLIOGRAPHY

Benson, Albert Emerson, *History of the Massachusetts Horticultural Society*. Norwood, Mass.: Plimpton Press, 1929.

Boyd, James. *A History of the Pennsylvania Horticultural Society*. Philadelphia: Edward Stern, 1929.

Bry, Charlene, Marshall R. Crosby, and Peter Loewer. *A World of Plants: The Missouri Botanical Garden*. New York: Harry N. Abrams, 1989.

Garrard, Jeanne. *Fairchild Tropical Garden*. Miami: Argos, 1980.

Hedrick, U. P. *A History of Horticulture in America to 1860. With an Addendum of Books Published from 1861–1920*, by Elisabeth Woodburn. Portland, Ore.: Timber Press, 1988.

Hyams, Edward. *Botanical Gardens of the World*. London: Bloomsbury Books, 1969.

Lawrence, George H. M., ed. *America's Garden Legacy: A Taste for Pleasure*. Philadelphia: Pennsylvania Horticultural Society, 1978.

Leighton, Ann. *American Gardens in the Eighteenth Century: "For Use or for Delight."* Amherst: University of Massachusetts Press, 1986.

———. *American Gardens of the Nineteenth Century: "For Comfort and Affluence."* Amherst: University of Massachusetts Press, 1987.

———. *Early American Gardens: "For Meate or Medicine."* Amherst: University of Massachusetts Press, 1986.

Manning, Robert, ed. *History of the Massachusetts Horticultural Society*. Boston: Rand, Avery, 1880.

Sargent, Charles S. *A Guide to the Arnold Arboretum*. 2nd ed. Cambridge, Mass.: Riverside Press, 1925.

Tanner, Ogden, and Adele Auchincloss. *The New York Botanical Garden: An Illustrated Chronicle of Plants and People*. New York: Walker, 1991.

Thornton, Tamara Plakins. *Cultivating Gentlemen: The Meaning of Country Life among the Boston Elite 1785–1860*. New Haven: Yale University Press, 1989.

Tice, Patricia M. *Gardening in America 1830–1910*. Rochester: Strong Museum, 1984.

Van Ravenswaay, Charles. *A Nineteenth-Century Garden*. New York: Universe Books, 1977.

Wilson, E. H. *America's Greatest Garden: The Arnold Arboretum*. Boston: Stratford Company, 1925.

THE PRACTICAL
FLOWER GARDEN

HELENA·RUTHERFURD·ELY

American Horticultural Books

Elisabeth Woodburn

ؤ The role that books have played in advancing and improving gardening in America cannot be overstated. A cursory look at virtually all the chapters in this book will give some indication of how useful and essential horticultural books have been in every aspect of American gardening.

The first such books appeared shortly after Independence and over the years have reflected the social, technological, and cultural conditions of the country and an increasing awareness of the necessity to address the particular needs of specific environmental factors. In the beginning, books were often imported and the climatic conditions they described were unlike those found in America. The influential Bernard M'Mahon addressed this problem in 1806, which suggests one reason, no doubt, that his book "The American Gardener's Calendar Adapted to the Seasons of the U.S." went through eleven editions. The attempt to establish a truly American corpus of garden literature has resulted in a magnificent variety of approaches to gardening. A widening view of the purpose and function of gardens, which mirrors social and economic conditions, has emerged. In the beginning the basic approach was survival gardening: vegetables, fruits, and herbs. Later, in a more prosperous society, an emphasis on flowers emerged and, most recently, with increasingly sophisticated taste being encouraged by these books, the landscape has come to be seen as available for design. These and related issues have continued to be the focuses of American garden books, changing to reflect the times and emphases. This is amply demonstrated by the bibliographies accompanying each of the preceding chapters as well as by the discussions of books and their authors' contributions to American gardening found within many of these essays.

The written record of gardening in America goes beyond documentation. It provides a comprehensive understanding of how, over more than two centuries, gardeners have transformed the land and been, in turn, transformed by it. ؤ

THE HISTORY OF GARDENING in the United States is clearly recorded. It was not until after winning independence from Great Britain that Americans began to create a garden literature of their own. The emphasis of the earliest books was on food, naturally enough. In time, thanks to changes in social, economic, and technological conditions, time was found for beauty, too. The appearance of books on flowers provided a means by which a garden could host more than fruits and vegetables exclusively. The books we shall consider, in chronological order within subject areas, will reveal not only the gardening interests of Americans over the years, but also the increasing awareness of a need for books appropriate to American cultural conditions.

Newspaper notices in South Carolina record that Mrs. Martha Logan wrote *The Gardener's Kalendar,* which was published in 1779. This tantalizing piece of information has yet to be verified. No copy of this book has survived to substantiate this honor for Mrs. Logan as the first U.S. garden writer. Reprints of her earlier calendar appeared in South Carolina papers in 1756 and 1798 and were reprinted again in a small pamphlet by the National Society of Colonial Dames of America in the State of South Carolina.

Charleston, South Carolina, also bears the distinction of being the place where the first-known horticultural book indigenous to America was published. Robert Squibb's *The Gardener's Kalendar for South Carolina and North Carolina* was published in 1787. As was the case with many other American garden writers, Squibb was born and trained in Great Britain. He immigrated to Charleston and became interested in plants of the South. As a nurseryman he found that in order to have his customers grow plants successfully he needed to give them instructions. There is little doubt that his book filled a real need. The enlarged edition of 1807 added *Georgia* to the title, and additional material to the text. Reprinted in 1813, it was further enlarged in 1827 and was

adorned with a frontispiece showing two views of a greenhouse, another first.

Squibb's book established a pattern followed by most of the books published in the United States before the Civil War. With very few exceptions our horticultural publications were written by nurserymen, not only as notices of the seeds and plants they offered, but also to instruct potential customers in the best way to grow them. Most of the books were small and concise. They were not distinguished for their appearance because bookmaking arts were still in their infancy in America. While contemporary Europe was turning out some of the most beautiful books on botany and horticulture that have ever been published, our publications were created for a New World with a different set of priorities. Their very appearance provides a graphic picture of the tenor of society at the time.

General Gardening

IN 1806 BERNARD M'MAHON issued *The American Gardener's Calendar Adapted to the Seasons of the U.S.* This work of more than 650 pages is the key to every garden operation at the time. It ran through eleven editions, the last (1857) having a memoir of the author. It followed the calendar approach to gardening, taking up the work to be done "in the kitchen-garden, fruit-garden, orchard, vineyard, nursery, pleasure grounds, flower-garden, green-house, hot-house and forcing frames" month by month. Directions are clear; lists of suitable plants show what was grown. This was the work of a man who was also British trained and who had a successful seed store in Philadelphia that was the gathering place for men interested in new crops and new plants. M'Mahon was the recipient of some of the seeds and plants brought back by the Lewis and Clark expedition for propagation.

M'Mahon's book is basic for studying horticulture

OPENING ILLUSTRATION:
In *The Practical Flower Garden*, Helena Rutherfurd Ely offered practical information and used photographs of her own garden.

in the first half of the nineteenth century. His own reasons for writing the volume echo the early desire of many people to help their new country:

> [In] a country which has not yet made that rapid progress in Gardening, ornamental planting, and fanciful rural designs which might naturally be expected from an intelligent, happy and independent people, possessed so universally of landed property, unoppressed by taxation or tithes and blest with consequent comfort and affluence . . . the neglect in these respects is, no doubt, to be attributed to various causes, among the most prominent of which, is the necessity of having reference for information on those subjects, to works published in foreign countries, and adapted to climates, by no means according with ours, either in the temperature or course of the seasons, and in numerous instances differing materially in modes of culture, from those rendered necessary here, by the peculiarities of our climates, soils and situations. [1]

M'Mahon's plea for American books for American gardeners, written at the beginning of the nineteenth century, is still apt as the twenty-first century nears.

The general gardening book covering all aspects of gardens was a format that was successfully repeated by other writers. In New York, Thomas Bridgeman first published *The Young Gardener's Assistant* in 1829. The first edition was largely devoted to vegetables. It expanded to include fruits and flowers through twelve numbered new editions, finally appearing in 1871 as *The American Gardener's Assistant*. The various ways the publisher presented this work point to the fact that "marketing a product" is not exclusively a twentieth-century idea. The practical advice given, Mr. Bridgeman states, is "to enable our respectable seedmen to afford instructions . . . at a trifling expense to such of their customers as may not have a regular gardener, and thereby save themselves the blame of those who may not give their seeds a fair trial, for want of knowing how to dispose of them in the ground." [2] To give full measure to his book, Mr. Bridgeman lists culinary vegetables and herbs in both

English and French as well as Latin and adds some recipes to tempt customers to grow vegetables.

In Boston in 1828, Thomas G. Fessenden's *The New American Gardener* came out, offering "practical directions on the culture of fruits and vegetables, including landscape and ornamental gardening grapevines, silk, strawberries." He was aware that adding some words on flower gardening was frivolous but notes that there were comparatively few of "the fair daughters of America" who did not take an interest in flowers. Fessenden, editor and writer for the periodical *The Horticultural Register and Gardener's Magazine* also wrote on agriculture. His interest in horticulture was evident in his support for the development of the Massachusetts Horticultural Society.

Another later general work that was long popular was William N. White's *Gardening for the South*, published in New York in 1857. This, too, covered fruits, vegetables, landscape, and flower gardens but was aimed at a kinder climate than that of the North. It was reprinted several times and for many years was the principal guide to southern gardening. General gardening books have continued to appear but few have had such a long printing life as these early works.

Flower Gardens

THE MAN WHO HAD the courage to write the first book devoted solely to flowers was Roland Green. *A Treatise on the Cultivation of Ornamental Flowers*, published in Boston in 1828, also has a list of "Dutch Bulbous Roots" for sale at G. Thorburn & Son, New York, and John B. Russell of Boston, two of the leading nurserymen of the day. Mr. Green seems to have left no record of himself. Speculation on the identity of the author is still to be answered. However, the fifty-nine-page book gives directions on sowing, transplanting, general management, treatment of bulbous roots, and greenhouse plants, which seems to indicate there was an audience to appreciate this "appropriate amusement for young ladies." It may be due to a still-felt Puritan disapproval of the frivolity of flowers that the author preferred to use a pseudonym when promoting such pleasures.

In Philadelphia in 1832 no apology was made

Camellia fimbriata.
Brown Lith.

Camellia ferribriala, the frontispiece for *The American Flower Garden Directory*, by Hibbert and Buist, one of the first books printed before 1869 to be devoted solely to flowers.

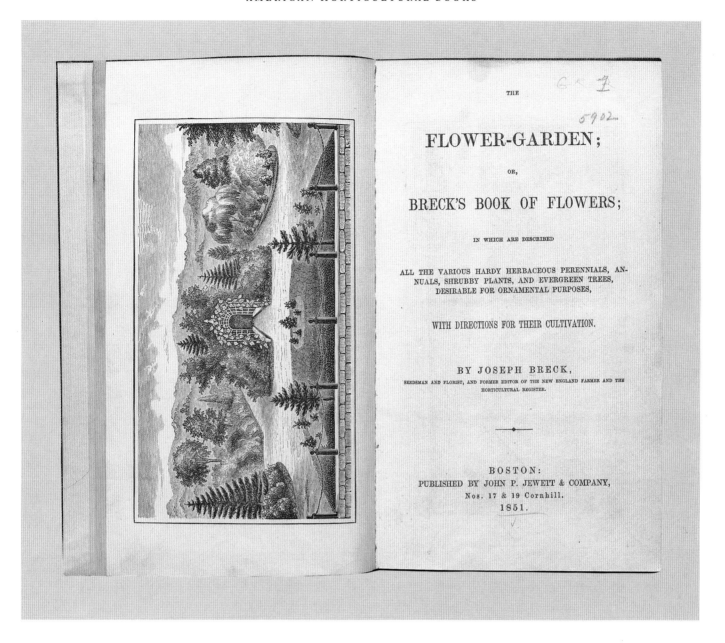

THE

FLOWER-GARDEN;

OR,

BRECK'S BOOK OF FLOWERS;

IN WHICH ARE DESCRIBED

ALL THE VARIOUS HARDY HERBACEOUS PERENNIALS, AN-
NUALS, SHRUBBY PLANTS, AND EVERGREEN TREES,
DESIRABLE FOR ORNAMENTAL PURPOSES,

WITH DIRECTIONS FOR THEIR CULTIVATION.

BY JOSEPH BRECK,

SEEDSMAN AND FLORIST, AND FORMER EDITOR OF THE NEW ENGLAND FARMER AND THE
HORTICULTURAL REGISTER.

BOSTON:
PUBLISHED BY JOHN P. JEWETT & COMPANY,
Nos. 17 & 19 Cornhill.
1851.

when *The American Flower Garden Directory* by Thomas Hibbert and Robert Buist was attractively published. The color-lithograph frontispiece of a *Camellia japonicu 'fimbriata'* is proof of the early popularity of this flower. The text covers the culture of plants "in the hot-house, garden-house, flower garden and rooms or parlours, for every month of the year." A note of interest at the end of the first edition states that Buist had purchased the nursery of the late Bernard M'Mahon.

Joseph Breck, another Boston seedsman and strong supporter of the Massachusetts Horticultural Society, wrote *The Flower Garden,* which was published in Boston in 1851. Its delightful garden frontispiece appeared only in this edition. A revised edition (1866) was called *A New Book of Flowers.* While Mr. Breck made his living selling seeds, he must also be credited with encouraging the use of native plants. He says "It was thought desirable to bring to notice many of our beautiful indigenous plants and shrubs, as worthy of cultivation. A handsome flower-garden may be made of these alone; many of them are within

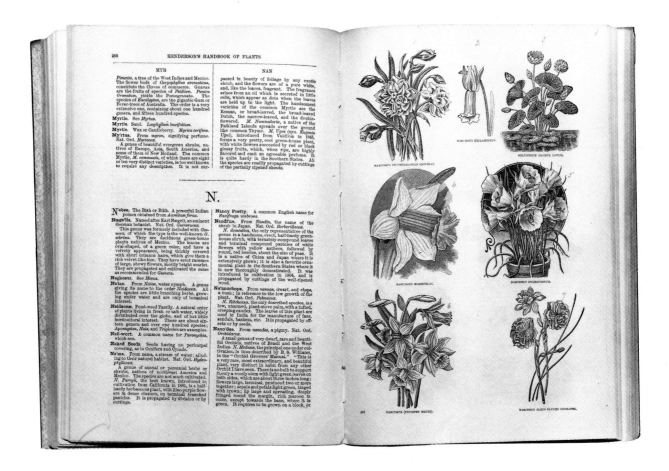

the reach of every one, and may be obtained without money and without price. The care and trouble is all the outlay, and this may be offset by the pleasure derived in collecting them from the fields, woods, or meadows."[3]

From the 1875 first edition of Peter Henderson's *Gardening for Pleasure,* on into the twentieth-century printings of later editions, this work was extremely popular, undoubtedly due to Mr. Henderson's thorough knowledge of the subject gained in maintaining his very large nursery in northern New Jersey. He wrote three other widely used books: *Gardening for Profit* (1867) was the key to the successful market garden business which started after the Civil War and is often given credit for starting many veterans of that war on their way to becoming truck gardeners.

Practical Floriculture (1869) was also enlarged and reprinted many times. Another book of lasting value is his garden dictionary—*Henderson's Handbook of Plants and General Horticulture*—which was issued in dictionary form in 1881. A new edition of 1890, much enlarged, was popular into the 1900s. Few writers had more influence on popular gardening practices.

The most knowledgeable—and influential—horticulturalist yet to write a book in this country was Liberty Hyde Bailey. His *Garden-making,* issued in 1898, is a characteristic example of the thoroughness he practiced in all he wrote. For many years dean of Cornell's College of Agriculture, he was in a fine position to share such observations as: "A patch of lusty pigweeds, growing and crowding in luxurious abandon, may be a better and more worthy object of

OPPOSITE:

Peter Henderson, one of the most knowledgeable plantsmen of his century, wrote *Handbook of Plants and General Horticulture*, one of the earliest authentically American plant dictionaries and an excellent reference for identification of plants of the time.

PETER HENDERSON & CO., NEW YORK.—BOOKS.

BOOKS ON HORTICULTURE AND AGRICULTURE BY *Peter Henderson*

THE ACKNOWLEDGED AUTHORITIES FOR GARDEN, GREENHOUSE AND FARM.

Henderson's New Handbook of Plants and General Horticulture

Gives a short history of the different genera, and concise instructions for their propagation and culture, and embraces the botanical name (accentuated according to the latest authorities), derivation, natural order, etc. A valuable feature of the book is the leading local or common English names, together with a comprehensive glossary of Botanical and Technical terms. Instructions are also given for the cultivation of the principal vegetables, fruits and flowers, with very full instructions on forcing Tomatoes, Grapes, Cucumbers, Mushrooms, Strawberries, etc., together with comprehensive practical directions about soils, manures, roads, lawns, draining, implements, greenhouse buildings, heating by steam and hot water, propagation by seeds and cuttings, window gardening, shrubs, trees, etc. In short, everything relating to general horticulture is given in alphabetical order to make it a complete book of reference. 526 pages, 800 illustrations. **Price, $4.00,** postpaid, *or given free as premium on an order. See 2d page cover.*

GARDENING FOR PLEASURE.

NEW EDITION. Tells how to grow Flowers, Vegetables and Small Fruits in the Garden and Greenhouse; also treats fully on Window and House Plants, the Lawn, Bulbs, Aquatic Plants, Modes of Heating, Small Fruits, Insects, the Grapery, Monthly Calendar of Operations. 404 pages; fully illustrated. Price, $2.00, postpaid, *or given free as premium on an order. See 2d page cover.*

GARDENING FOR PROFIT.

NEW EDITION. A new, revised and greatly enlarged edition of this popular work. This book gives in detail our 25 years' experience in *Market Gardening*, and a revised list of varieties in vegetables recommended for market culture. Written particularly for the Market Gardener, but is equally as valuable for the Private Gardener. 375 pages; fully illustrated. Price, $2.00, postpaid, *or given free as premium on an order. See 2d page cover.*

GARDEN AND FARM TOPICS.

Contains essays on some special Greenhouse, Vegetable and Bulb, Fruit and Farm Crops. 244 pages; fully illustrated. Price, $1.00, postpaid, *or given free as premium on an order. See 2d page cover.*

CULTURE OF WATER LILIES.

42 pages; illustrated. Price, postpaid, 25 cents, *or given free as premium on an order. See 2d page cover.*

PRACTICAL FLORICULTURE.

NEW EDITION. Written particularly for the Commercial Florist, but equally as valuable for the Amateur. This work teaches how flowers and plants can best be "grown for profit." It is admitted to be the leading authority on the subject. 325 pages; fully illustrated. Price, $1.50, postpaid, *or given free as premium on an order. See 2d page cover.*

HOW THE FARM PAYS.

By Messrs. Henderson and Crozier. An acknowledged authority for Farmers. Gives all of the Latest Methods of growing Grass, Grain, Root Crops, Fruits, etc.; and all about Stock, Farm Machinery, etc., etc. 400 pages; fully illustrated. Price, $2.50, postpaid, *or given free as premium on an order. See 2d page cover.*

CONDENSED VEGETABLE AND FLOWER SEED CULTURE.

An eight-page pamphlet, containing, in a condensed form, instructions for the cultivation of Garden Vegetables and Flowers from seeds. Also, full directions for making Hotbeds and Cold Frames. Price, 10c., *or given free as premium on an order. See 2d page cover.*

INJURIOUS INSECTS AND PLANT DISEASES, WITH REMEDIES.

76 pages; illustrated. Price, 25 cents, postpaid, *or given free as premium on an order. See 2d page cover.*

...HENDERSON'S BULB CULTURE...

Tells how to grow bulbs for winter flowering in the house or greenhouse, and for spring flowering in the garden. It also treats on summer flowering bulbs; in fact, gives full instructions when and how to plant, and after-management. It also tells how to "force" bulbs.

It tells how to grow bulbs in glasses, crocus pots, moss and other novel ways. It gives designs for beds of bulbs and tells what to put in them. It gives a list of common names; tells what bulbs are suitable for naturalization, for bedding, for winter flowering, for summer flowering, etc., etc., and much other valuable information. 24 pages; illustrated. **Price, postpaid, 25 cents,** *or given free as premium on an order. See 2d page cover.*

Special Offer: If ordered at one time, we will supply the full set of ten books, described above, carriage prepaid, for $10.00. (Separately, they would cost $13.85.) This set of books form A COMPLETE LIBRARY OF THE GARDEN, GREENHOUSE AND FARM. **For $10.00**

Advertisement from the 1897 catalog of Peter Henderson & Co. of New York, which sold not only seeds and bulbs but also a wide array of equipment and books written by Henderson himself.

affection than a bed of coleuses in which every spark of life and spirit and individuality has been sheared out and suppressed."[4] Much else he had to say carried this type of forthright opinion concerning what he felt to be poor practices. Bailey wrote books on a large number of horticultural subjects. The greatest source of nineteenth-century horticultural information left to us is his *Cyclopedia of American Horticulture,* issued in six thick volumes from 1900 to 1902. In later editions the name was changed to *Standard Cyclopedia of Horticulture,* which was issued in different numbers of volumes, ending up in three volumes on thin paper.

Women played a very important role in the creation of gardening literature. Not only was the genre initiated in this country by a woman, Martha Logan, as we have seen, but women were instrumental in its perpetuation in a grand manner. In addition, women have frequently been in the vanguard of gardening and landscape design.

Alice Morse Earle was one of the first people to realize the record of our early gardens was fast disappearing. In 1901 her *Old Time Gardens* described gardens of earlier times which were then extant. Her book included a number of photographs of some of these gardens and their old-time flowers which helped readers visualize them.

The American Flower Garden (1909), by Neltje Blanchan, was a major work on the subject, beautifully published in a large, attractively decorated volume with color plates. It was published by the author's husband, Nelson Doubleday.

From the 1918 appearance of Louise Beebe Wilder's *Colour in My Garden,* with Anna Winegar's excellent color paintings of Mrs. Wilder's garden, it is evident that Mr. Doubleday found publishing attractive garden books to be worthwhile. Mrs. Wilder's contribution to our garden literature is so knowledgeable, in addition to being well written, that her books on rock gardens, on fragrant gardens, and on hardy bulbs are all classic contributions in their subject areas.

Louise Shelton is another writer whose books are interesting to read. *Beautiful Gardens in America* was first published in 1915 and enlarged in 1924. The descriptions and photographs of the gardens, whose owners are named, reveal the richness of the gardens at this time when it was still possible to find trained gardeners.

Elsa Rehman's *Garden Making* was published in 1926. She was among a growing group of women landscape architects with vision and knowledge. This book, with a supplementary text and photographs by Antoinette Perrett, again presents a number of good examples of the gardens on the East Coast, with identification of place and owner. In addition, the landscape architect who designed the garden is frequently given. Another important work on which Professor Rehman, who taught at Vassar, collaborated, was *American Plants for American Gardens,* which was written with Edith Roberts in 1929. Its subtitle, *Plant Ecology—the Study of Plants in Relation to Their Environment,* makes it a pioneer work on the subject in our garden literature.

The interest in books on gardens encouraged further specialization. In 1927 Leonard Johnson produced *Foundation Planting.* The photographs in this book show plants and planting methods later assessed as difficult to maintain. *Patio Gardens* (1929), by Helen Morgenthau Fox, was an incentive to try this Spanish style of garden, especially in warmer areas. Good drawings illustrated emphasis and details. Mrs. Fox also wrote books on her herb garden, translated a work by the French landscape architect, J. C. N. Forestier, as well as writing a book on Le Nôtre, all of which contributed richly to our garden literature.

Gardens of Colony and State, edited by Alice Lockwood for the Garden Club of America, is a very large, two-volume work celebrating the past of American gardens, many of which were known only through photographs and illustrations. The value of this work cannot be overestimated for its scholarly yet accessible account of gardens and gardening in America.

OPPOSITE:
First published in limited edition in large format, with many color photographs, *The American Flower Garden* is the work of Neltje Blanchan.

AN ABANDONED STONE QUARRY, TRANSFORMED BY THE SUBTLE ART OF THE GARDENER, WHICH ALMOST DEFIES DETECTION, INTO A NATURALISTIC ROCK GARDEN

The
American Flower Garden

By
NELTJE BLANCHAN [Doubleday]

Planting Lists by LEONARD BARRON

ILLUSTRATED
WITH NINETY TWO FULL-PAGE
PHOTOGRAPHS

London
William Heinemann
1909

Examples of regional interest include John Mc-Laren's *Gardening in California,* first published in San Francisco in 1908, with two further enlarged editions in 1914 and 1924. *Portraits of Philadelphia Gardens,* by James and Louise Bush-Brown, published in 1919, also provided illustrations of our evolving landscape and garden changes.

Further concentration on gardens includes the single garden or estate. A good example of this genre is *The Gardens of Kijkuit* (1919), photographs of the Rockefeller estate by the great photographer Arnold Genthe, with brief text by the architect Welles Bosworth. Frances Kinsly Hutchison's *Wychwood* (1928) is the history of an estate in Wisconsin that became a wildlife sanctuary, and Harriet Hammond McCormick's *Landscape Art* (1923), with its introduction by Mrs. Francis King, foreword by Cyrus Hall McCormick, the author's husband, plus fifty-six plates, is devoted to classic gardens, including Walden, the author's Lake Forest, Illinois, home. All were published in limited editions.

Flowers

WITH THE ADVENT of books on flower gardens it was logical that flower monographs would follow. A translation of a French work, *Monography of the Genus Camellia,* by Abbé Berlese, was issued by Joseph Breck and Sons in Boston in 1838. The translation was by the first president of the Massachusetts Horticultural Society, General Henry A. S. Dearborn. Its color chart of classified camellia colors was a landmark in garden-book publishing. The camellia made another, later, appearance in the nineteenth century. Robert Halliday's *Practical Camellia Culture* was a little book with a colored frontispiece and four color lithographs. The author, a florist, published this in Baltimore in 1880.

A Treatise on the Culture of the Dahlia and Cactus, by Edward Sayers, was the first flower monograph written entirely by an American. Published in 1839, in Boston, it was devoted largely to the dahlia—the flower of the period—but the addition of the information and description of cactus is another first. The previous year Sayers had published *The American Flower Garden Companion, Adapted to the Northern States.* It had five pages of Boston nursery trade ads, which says much for the flourishing state of horticulture. A second edition added *and Middle States* to the subtitle. By the third edition Mr. Sayers was living in Cincinnati, where the book was published with ads that included one offering the services of the author as landscape gardener.

It is interesting to note that both the camellia and the dahlia preceded the rose in popularity in this country. The first American book on roses was by Robert Buist, whose *Rose Manual* was published in 1844 in Philadelphia, becoming so popular that a fourth edition had come out by 1854. William Prince's *Manual of Roses,* published in 1846, in New York, contained a few remarks by Mr. Prince that seemed to indicate that, by virtue of his background of three generations in the nursery business, he was better qualified to write about roses than others.

A third important monograph on this flower is Samuel B. Parson's *The Rose: Its History, Poetry, Culture and Classification.* The first edition (1847), published in New York, had two beautiful color lithographs of roses by Cheirat. Like Hibbert and Buist's *American Flower Garden Directory,* mentioned previously, this book was published in subsequent editions without color plates, in smaller format, and renamed *Parsons on the Rose.* Its popularity continued into the twentieth century. All three rose books are made particularly interesting to collectors of old roses today by their descriptive lists of varieties.

Other flower monographs that highlight the interest and popularity of specific plants include two by Edward Sprague Rand, Jr. In 1871, *The Rhododendron and American Plants* was the first book on this plant. The fourth edition (1876) describes H. H. Hunnewell's first U.S. exhibit of rhododendrons, which was held in Boston in 1873. Sponsored by the Massachusetts Horticultural Society, this event was attended by forty thousand people.

Rand's second monograph—*Orchids: A Description of the Species and Varieties Grown at Glen Ridge,* was published in New York in 1876. It had text illustrations in its 476 pages and also contained a list of the illustrated books to which the author referred in the

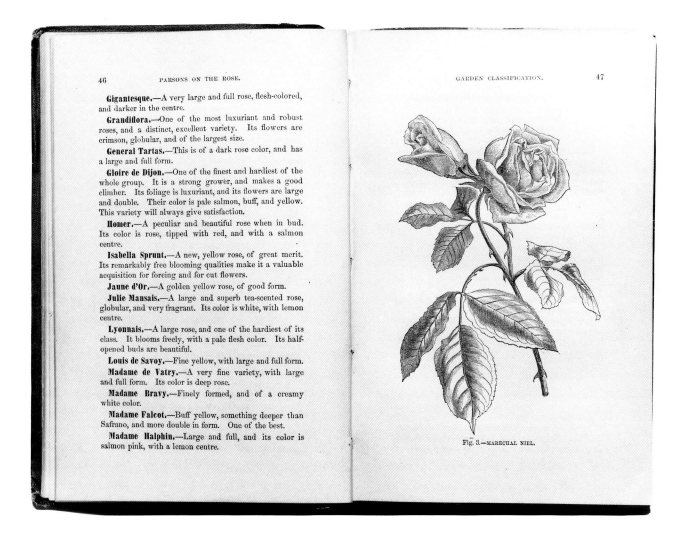

Gigantesque.—A very large and full rose, flesh-colored, and darker in the centre.

Grandiflora.—One of the most luxuriant and robust roses, and a distinct, excellent variety. Its flowers are crimson, globular, and of the largest size.

General Tartas.—This is of a dark rose color, and has a large and full form.

Gloire de Dijon.—One of the finest and hardiest of the whole group. It is a strong grower, and makes a good climber. Its foliage is luxuriant, and its flowers are large and double. Their color is pale salmon, buff, and yellow. This variety will always give satisfaction.

Homer.—A peculiar and beautiful rose when in bud. Its color is rose, tipped with red, and with a salmon centre.

Isabella Sprunt.—A new, yellow rose, of great merit. Its remarkably free blooming qualities make it a valuable acquisition for forcing and for cut flowers.

Jaune d'Or.—A golden yellow rose, of good form.

Julie Mansais.—A large and superb tea-scented rose, globular, and very fragrant. Its color is white, with lemon centre.

Lyonnais.—A large rose, and one of the hardiest of its class. It blooms freely, with a pale flesh color. Its half-opened buds are beautiful.

Louis de Savoy.—Fine yellow, with large and full form.

Madame de Vatry.—A very fine variety, with large and full form. Its color is deep rose.

Madame Bravy.—Finely formed, and of a creamy white color.

Madame Falcot.—Buff yellow, something deeper than Safrano, and more double in form. One of the best.

Madame Halphin.—Large and full, and its color is salmon pink, with a lemon centre.

Fig. 3.—MARECHAL NIEL.

Originally published as *The Rose* in 1847, the title was changed to *Parsons on the Rose* to reflect the importance of Samuel Parsons's name in horticultural circles and his prowess as a nurseryman.

text. It appeared again in 1888. Both books also came out in a limited issue with a few color plates. All editions are scarce.

Practical Azalea Culture was another Robert Halliday book issued in Baltimore in 1880. The first American azalea monograph, it had thirty-four illustrations from drawings, largely in the text.

Other nineteenth-century flower monographs that recall the enthusiasm for certain flowers include those on the carnation and the chrysanthemum. Levi Leslie

Lamborn, M.D., wrote *Carnation Culture* in 1887, and Lora L. Lamborn of Alliance, Ohio, is cited as its publisher. Dr. Lamborn's work, a careful history of the development of *Dianthus Caryophyllus semperflorens,* discusses the plant's species, its culture, the people involved in growing it, and so on. The book went through four different editions by 1904.

Chrysanthemum Culture for America, by James Morton, was published in New York in 1891. Mr. Morton, who also wrote *Southern Floriculture,* gives considerable attention to the history of the chrysanthemum, devoting a chapter to its Oriental and European history and another to its American history. The book contains some engraved illustrations.

Landscape

THE INCREASING PROSPERITY of the United States as the nineteenth century wore on brought wider horticultural interest. In 1841, Andrew Jackson Downing published *A Treatise on the Theory and Practice of Landscape Gardening.* This work influenced the way American landscapes were planned for the rest of the nineteenth century and on into the twentieth. Downing was a man of remarkable vision, not only regarding landscape, but on the development of fruit, and planning of houses. This vision was also made evident in his editorials for *The Horticulturist,* an influential periodical. His early death did not end the interest in his books, which were reprinted and enlarged by others. His brother Charles revised his work on fruits and Henry Winthrop Sargent revised his landscape work. The *Treatise* was introduced to the twentieth century with a tenth edition, revised by Frank A. Waugh, which was followed in 1967 by publication of a facsimile of the 1859 edition.

A few excerpts from Mr. Downing's preface to his *Treatise* suggest reasons for the book's interest:

> A taste for rural improvements of every description is advancing silently, but with great rapidity in this country. While yet, in the far west the pioneer constructs his rude hut of logs for a dwelling, and sweeps away with his axe the lofty forest trees that encumber the ground, in the older portion of the Union bordering the Atlantic, we are surrounded by all the luxuries and refinements that belong to an old and long cultivated country. Within the last ten years especially, the evidences of the growing wealth and prosperity of our citizens have become apparent in the great increase of elegant cottage and villa residences on banks of our noble rivers, throughout our rich valleys, and wherever nature seems to invite us by her rich and varied charms. . . . Professional talent is seldom employed, in Architecture or Landscape Gardening, but almost every man fancies himself an amateur, and endeavors to plan and arrange his own residence. With but little practical knowledge, and few correct principles for his guidance, it is not surprising that we witness much incongruity and great waste of time and money. . . . While we have treatises in abundance on the various departments of the arts and sciences, there has not appeared even a single essay on the elegant art of Landscape Gardening. [5]

The move westward was addressed by Maximilian G. Kern in *Practical Landscape Gardening* (1855), published in Cincinnati, Ohio. The author stated that our continued prosperity is "nowhere more so than in our great Mississippi Valley." A German immigrant, Kern also wrote *Rural Taste in Western Towns and Country Districts, In Its Relation to the Principles of the Art of Landscape Gardening,* which was published in Columbia, Missouri, in 1884.

Another "western" book is H. W. S. Cleveland's *Landscape Architecture as Applied to the Wants of the West; with an Essay on Forest Planting on the Great Plains,* published in Chicago in 1873. The author contended rather gloomily that the West needed a vast amount of preliminary preparation before it would be ready for landscaping. His work designing parks around the country gave him extensive experience in planning, as well as in city problems.

Robert Morris Copeland's *Country Life: A Handbook of Agriculture, Horticulture and Landscape Gardening,* published in Boston in 1859, presents a view of estate planning and life in calendar form. The book has a folding frontispiece showing "A Plan for Laying Out a Country Place of 60 Acres" as well as a number of woodcuts, which add to the text of over eight hundred pages covering much more than the laying out of grounds. It sets the scene for what country living was like during the Civil War years. Several printings were issued between 1859 and 1866.

A landscape work of great influence during the last quarter of the nineteenth century is Frank J. Scott's *The Art of Beautifying Suburban Home Grounds of Small Extent,* published in New York in 1870. Scott wrote: "There comes an increasing need of practical works to epitomize and Americanize the prin-

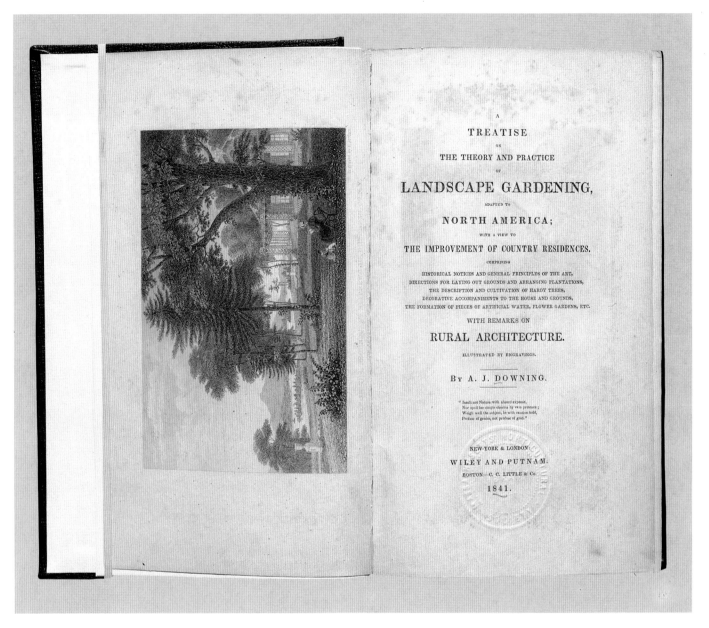

A

TREATISE

ON

THE THEORY AND PRACTICE

OF

LANDSCAPE GARDENING,

ADAPTED TO

NORTH AMERICA;

WITH A VIEW TO

THE IMPROVEMENT OF COUNTRY RESIDENCES.

COMPRISING

HISTORICAL NOTICES AND GENERAL PRINCIPLES OF THE ART,
DIRECTIONS FOR LAYING OUT GROUNDS AND ARRANGING PLANTATIONS,
THE DESCRIPTION AND CULTIVATION OF HARDY TREES,
DECORATIVE ACCOMPANIMENTS TO THE HOUSE AND GROUNDS,
THE FORMATION OF PIECES OF ARTIFICIAL WATER, FLOWER GARDENS, ETC.

WITH REMARKS ON

RURAL ARCHITECTURE.

ILLUSTRATED BY ENGRAVINGS.

BY A. J. DOWNING.

" Insult not Nature with absurd expense,
Nor spoil her simple charms by vain pretence ;
Weigh well the subject, be with caution bold,
Profuse of genius, not profuse of gold."

NEW-YORK & LONDON:

WILEY AND PUTNAM.

BOSTON—C. C. LITTLE & Co.

1841.

One of the most influential books in American horticulture, *A Treatise on the Theory and Practice of Landscape Gardening*, by Andrew Jackson Downing, went through five editions during the author's relatively short life.

ciples of decorative gardening, to illustrate their application to small grounds and to effect in miniature, and around ordinary homes some of their loveliest results."[6] The book is well illustrated with engraved scenes and vignettes. It is divided into two parts— the first on landscape and the second a descriptive listing of suitable trees and shrubs. A large-format work of 618 pages, its popularity is witness to the rush at the time to take up suburban living. A number of reprints kept the book in print until 1886. A 1982 reprint published as *Victorian Gardens* left out the section on the trees and shrubs that Scott recommended.

Franklin Reuben Elliott also saw the need for suburban designs. His *Hand Book of Practical Landscape Gardening* was published in Rochester, New York, in 1877, with a chromolithograph frontispiece of a *Betula alba* plus fourteen plans and text illustra-

HAND BOOK

OF PRACTICAL

LANDSCAPE GARDENING

DESIGNED FOR

CITY AND SUBURBAN RESIDENCES,

AND COUNTRY SCHOOL-HOUSES,

CONTAINING

DESIGNS FOR LOTS AND GROUNDS,

From a lot 30 x 100 feet to a 40 acre plot.

Each plan is drawn to a scale, with schedule to each, showing where each Tree,
Shrub, etc., should be planted. Also, Condensed Instructions of how to form
Lawns, and the care thereof; the Building of Roads, Turfing,
Protection of Trees, Pruning and care of, making Cuttings,
Evergreens, Hedges, Screens, etc.; Perennials, Herbaceous
Plants, etc. Also, Condensed Descriptions of all the
leading Trees and Shrubs, with remarks as to soil
and position in which they should be grown.
Illustrations not only of the Ground Plans
and Elevations are given, but Illustra-
tions of various Trees, Shrubs,
Winter Gardening, etc.

BY F. R. ELLIOTT.

LANDSCAPE GARDENER AND POMOLOGIST.

SECOND EDITION—ENLARGED AND IMPROVED.

D. M. DEWEY,
HORTICULTURAL BOOKS, ARCADE HALL, ROCHESTER, N. Y.
1881.

COPYRIGHT SECURED

AMPELOPSIS VEITCHII.

JAPANESE CLIMBER.

This new, elegant climbing plant resembles the Virginia Creeper, but is much richer in color, and
clings more perfectly to the wall; does not require training or fastening. Has full, dense
foliage, a glossy green in spring and summer, turning to a mottled green and red,
and in the fall a brilliant crimson scarlet. It is thoroughly hardy,
and requires no care. It originated in Japan.

D. M. DEWEY.

tions. The 1881 second edition has sixteen color plates of trees in addition to the plans. Rochester was a leading city in the development of chromolithography plates for the nursery trade; this is a typical example of their publications.

Elias A. Long wrote *Ornamental Gardening for Americans: A Treatise on Beautifying Homes, Rural Districts, Towns and Cemeteries,* which was first published in 1885. Since it addressed the problems of increasing urbanization as they affected people of limited finances, this title was still being reprinted as late as the 1920s. It has a lengthy description of desirable trees and shrubs and also offers good planting suggestions. The illustrations provide a number of designs for carpet bedding and other garden features.

Samuel Parsons, Jr., as superintendent of parks in New York City, had a good location in which to display his ideas. His *Landscape Gardening,* published in New York in 1891, made some interesting points denoting changes in times and techniques from the nineteenth to the twentieth century. While the text has an authoritative tone in discussing the new viewpoints, one is struck by the difference in the book's appearance. It is published on good paper, nicely bound and—strongly marking a transition—illustrated by photographs as well as the standard engravings. It was not the first horticultural book to use photographs, but its composition emphasized that photography had become part of new horticultural publishing.

It is to be regretted that such influential landscape architects as Olmsted, Vaux, and Eliot did not publish books for the layman. Their professional reports on their landscape work are not easy to find. However, they are historic sources for land use and planning ideas, often having before-and-after photographs.

Frank A. Waugh was ready for the new century with *Landscape Gardening* (1899), a work developed in his landscape courses, which was quite influential

OPPOSITE:
Frontispiece of the *Hand Book of Practical Landscape Gardening* (second edition), by F. R. Elliott, the work of Rochester lithographer D. M. Dewey, a leader in the use of color lithography for horticultural books.

despite its small size. In *The Landscape Beautiful* (1910) he pleaded for natural landscapes, while his *Rural Improvement* (1914) contained "the Principles of Civic Art Applied to Rural Conditions including Village Improvement and the Betterment of the Open Country." A further example of his grasp of the subject can be found in his 1927 book *Formal Design in Landscape Architecture.*

The beginning of the twentieth century saw the publication of folio estate books that described and showed photographs of the enormous show places popular with the very wealthy. These tomes present a who's who of the times in such volumes as Oliver Bronson Capen's *Country Homes of Famous Americans* and Guy Lowell's *American Gardens,* both published in 1902, Barr Ferree's *American Estates and Gardens* of 1904 and Louis V. Le Moyne's *Country Residences in Europe and America* of 1908. Mercifully for those compelled to keep up with the Joneses in planning their estates, the period of publication for these titles was brief.

Early-twentieth-century landscape books reflect the increased wealth, improved transportation and social changes that were shaping the American perception of landscape. Landscape architecture as a profession was encouraged by the widespread interest in home building in the expanding suburbs and country estates, and, in fact, the American Society of Landscape Architects was founded in 1899. While not everyone could have a Vanderbilt estate, in a free country anyone could copy ideas from it.

Many books from the beginning of this century may be found in local libraries. A few mentioned here not only discuss the newer planting ideas but were also illustrated. The rapid change in illustration from engraving to photography explains the sharp difference in these books' appearance at the cusp of the two centuries. It creates the sense of "this was yesterday" as opposed to "here we are."

Besides the books of Parsons and Waugh, Samuel T. Maynard's *Landscape Gardening As Applied to Home Decoration,* first published in 1899, with 167 text figures, was important. The second edition, "rewritten and enlarged" in 1915, was largely illustrated with photographs. Included are chapters on renovat-

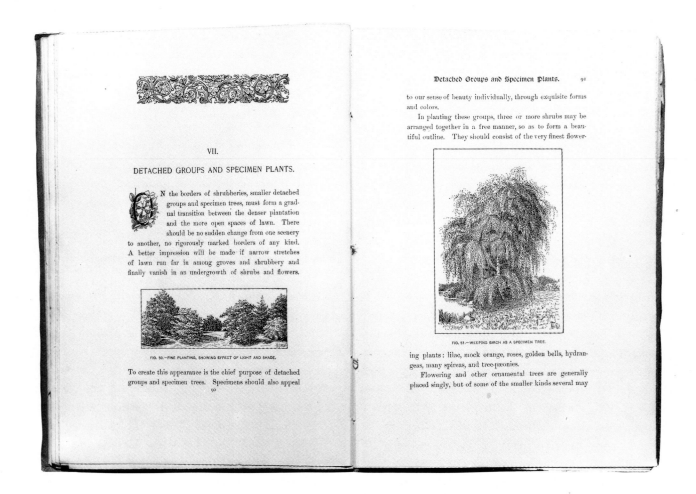

VII.

DETACHED GROUPS AND SPECIMEN PLANTS.

N the borders of shrubberies, smaller detached groups and specimen trees, must form a gradual transition between the denser plantation and the more open spaces of lawn. There should be no sudden change from one scenery to another, no rigorously marked borders of any kind. A better impression will be made if narrow stretches of lawn run far in among groves and shrubbery and finally vanish in an undergrowth of shrubs and flowers.

FIG. 50.—FINE PLANTING, SHOWING EFFECT OF LIGHT AND SHADE.

To create this appearance is the chief purpose of detached groups and specimen trees. Specimens should also appeal

90

to our sense of beauty individually, through exquisite forms and colors.

In planting these groups, three or more shrubs may be arranged together in a free manner, so as to form a beautiful outline. They should consist of the very finest flower-

FIG. 51.—WEEPING BIRCH AS A SPECIMEN TREE.

ing plants: lilac, mock orange, roses, golden bells, hydrangeas, many spireas, and tree-pæonies.

Flowering and other ornamental trees are generally placed singly, but of some of the smaller kinds several may

ing old houses, parks, public squares, and schoolhouses in addition to general ideas on planning grounds, and selection of suitable trees and shrubs. Herbert J. Kellaway's *How to Lay Out Suburban Home Grounds* (1907) was enlarged in a 1915 second edition that had fifteen plans and maps. Grace Tabor's *Landscape Gardening Book* (1911) was well illustrated, with practical suggestions. In 1914 the Chicago-based Ralph Rodney Root, with Charles Fabiens Kelley, wrote *Design in Landscape Gardening.* Mr. Root taught in Chicago, so his ideas were disseminated through the Midwest. Robert B. Cridland's *Practical Landscape Gardening* was written for the homeowner to try in 1916. It included full-page plans for suburban lots with photographs of the finished products.

Lawn and Gardens, by N. Jonsson-Rose, was one of the first books to emphasize lawns once lawnmowers had gained popularity.

OPPOSITE:
American Landscape Architecture, edited by P. H. Elwood, Jr., in 1924, was one of the earliest books intended to show the scope and interests of the relatively new profession of landscape architecture and to illustrate some of the most magnificent gardens in America.

In 1917 a book of wide and continuing influence appeared. *An Introduction to the Study of Landscape Design*, by Henry Vincent Hubbard and Theodora Kimball, included forty pen-and-ink drawings and thirty-six photographic plates in its more than four hundred pages. A revised edition was issued in 1929 that was still being reprinted in the 1960s. It would not be

ESTATE OF JOHN D. ROCKEFELLER ESQ., POCANTICO HILLS, NEW YORK
THE TERRACE STAIRWAY WITH BAY TREES

ESTATE OF JOHN D. ROCKEFELLER ESQ., POCANTICO HILLS, NEW YORK
A FOUNTAIN

possible to estimate the number of landscape architects who were trained with this comprehensive text, which was adopted by numerous design schools for their curricula.

Although the roster of landscape names from this century is too long to include, the following brief selection of authors and titles of their works published before 1940 is included as a selected guide to the literature. A book devoted to the landscape architects of the twentieth century would be welcome for a look at the influence their ideas has had on our immediate surroundings and our landscapes.

After World War I, Waugh's *Textbook of Landscape Gardening* (1922) provided a link with prewar years. In addition, P. H. Elwood, Jr., was editor of the very large *American Landscape Architecture* (1924), which was filled with photographs. Two other works published that year were Arthur J. Jennings and Leonard H. Johnson's *The Complete Home Landscape,* another "how-to" work; and Fletcher Steele's *Design in the Little Garden.* Due to Steele's creative approach this book, issued in "The Little Garden Series" edited by Mrs. Francis King, has had a long life on its own.

Stephen Child's *Landscape Architecture* (1927) consists of a series of letters by the author on the solution of landscape problems. A short bibliography is an interesting addition to this thoughtful work published in Stanford, California. Marjorie S. Cautley's innovative *Garden Design* (1935) combined the landscape and the garden in an interesting fashion, and, three years later, Louis Van de Boe's *Planning and Planting Your Own Place* (1938) was to be one of the last works on landscape issued before World War II.

Horticultural Diversions

INDOOR GARDENING has also long been a suitable subject for gardening literature whether of the greenhouse, parlor, or window variety. The subject is addressed as early as M'Mahon's sections on the hothouse in *The American Gardener's Calendar* right up to today's solar-heated houses.

James Norman Eley's little *The American Florist; Or, A Guide to the Management and Cultivation of Plants in Conservatories, Greenhouses, Rooms and Gardens* was enhanced with attractive text ornaments when it was published in Hartford, Connecticut, in 1845.

A delightful little volume is Cornelia J. Randolph's *The Parlor Gardener: A Treatise on the House Culture of Ornamental Plants* (Boston, 1861). The author, Thomas Jefferson's granddaughter, claims this was translated from the French and adapted to American use. It seems "adapted" so well one wonders about its French "origin." The eleven engraved plates supply a first-hand look at "parlor adornment" of the period and enhance the first-person narration of the text.

E. S. Rand, Jr., wrote *Flowers for the Parlor and Garden* in 1863, and excerpted *The Window Gardener* from it in 1872. Mr. Shirley Hibberd accused Rand of having plagiarized from his work, *Rustic Adornments.* Elias Long's *The Home Florist,* first published in 1874, is particularly useful for its extensive lists of plants popular at the time, along with the methods of growing them.

The increased use of engraved text "cuts" to illustrate books is exemplified in Henry T. Williams' *Window Gardening.* With a total of 199 text engravings in its 300 pages, it is not surprising that it is still sought today even though it was first published in 1872. The ornate decorations must have required a lot of feather dusters to keep them clean. Edwin A. Johnson's *Winter Greeneries at Home* is also nicely illustrated with a frontispiece and eighteen engravings, which include five plates showing the use of plants as decorations in Victorian rooms of 1878.

Proof of the continued popularity of house plants at the beginning of the century is shown by several publications. The engraved illustrations have been superseded by photographs. In the 1908 *Window Gardening,* by Herman B. Dorner, the title page includes "with illustrations from photographs" to indicate that it is up to date. The same year, Parker Barnes's *House Plants and How to Grow Them* proved to be a popular book. It was still being published more than twenty years later. In 1910, *Indoor Gardening,* by Eben Rexford, continued the flow of these titles "devoted mainly to the care of indoor flowers and plants." F. E. Palmer's *Milady's House Plants* (1917) was not only full of black-and-white photographs, it featured one in color on the front cover. The book also includes "a Remarkable Chapter on the Ideal Sun Parlor," taking us a step closer to present ideas.

As time passed and prosperity increased, women had more leisure for gardens, and gardening books reflect this increasing focus on the woman gardener. Women were motivated to write about gardening as well as to practice it. Mrs. S. O. Johnson ("Daisy Eyebright") wrote *Every Woman Her Own Flower Gardener: A Handy Manual of Flower Gardening for Ladies* (1871). It was published by the *Ladies Floral Cabinet,* a New York magazine. Some of Mrs. Johnson's remarks are revealing of the attitudes of the times and could be quoted at length. A brief excerpt will set the tone:

> Of course, flounces, puffs, and furbelows, with their accompanying upper skirts are not suitable for such occupations. A dark chintz dress is the best, for it can go into the wash-tub when it is in need of cleansing. A woolen bathing dress makes an excellent garden costume—for skirts are always in the way. If it is admissible on the beach, where wealth and fashion do congregate, why not in the garden surrounding one's house. A large shade hat and a pair of old kid gloves are indispensable. . . .[7]

The roll of names of women who began to write at the very beginning of the twentieth century is impressive. They wrote under their own names— Mabel Osgood Wright (*Flowers and Ferns in Their Native Haunts,* 1901)—and under pseudonyms: "Barbara" (*The Garden, You, and I,* 1906), and "The Gardener" (*The Garden of a Commuter's Wife,* 1901). Practical manuals, such as Ida D. Bennett's *The Flower Garden* (1904), were reprinted for more than twenty years, and Helena Rutherfurd Ely's *A Woman's Hardy Garden* (1903), *Another Hardy Garden* (1905), and *The*

Practical Flower Garden (1911) were frequently reprinted. Their books provide good reading not only for practical advice but for the glimpse they give of social attitudes toward gardening. It is invidious, but necessary, to leave out so many of the gardeners who continued—and continue—to share their gardens and ideas. For gardeners, the search for kindred souls can be found as much in the past as in the present.

This brief look at the richness and variety developed in American horticultural literature is meant to encourage present-day gardeners to discover how much they can learn from their forebears. It is also a challenge to their successors to add their ideas to this long list of happy gardeners who shared and passed on their knowledge, for our horticultural history is indicative not only of changes in the landscape or in the way we perceive our earth, but of how we see ourselves and our own place in it. ✤

NOTES

1. Bernard M'Mahon, *The American Gardener's Calendar Adapted to the Seasons of the U.S.* (Philadelphia: B. Graves, 1806).

2. Thomas Bridgeman, *The Young Gardener's Assistant* (Brooklyn: Nichols and Matthews, 1829), preface.

3. Joseph Breck, *The Flower Garden; or Breck's Book of Flowers* (Boston: John P. Jewett, 1851, p. iv; Guilford, Conn.: Opus Publications, 1988).

4. Liberty Hyde Bailey, *Garden-Making: Suggestions for the Utilizing of Home Grounds* (New York: Macmillan, 1898), p. 2.

5. A. J. Downing. *A Treatise on the Theory and Practice of Landscape Gardening Adapted to North America* (New York: Wiley and Putnam, 1841), pp. i–ii.

6. Frank J. Scott, *The Art of Beautifying Suburban Home Grounds of Small Extent* (New York: D. Appleton, 1870), pp. 13–14.

7. Mrs. S. O. Johnson, *Every Woman Her Own Flower Gardener: A Handy Manual of Flower Gardening for Ladies* (New York: Ladies Floral Cabinet, 1871), pp. 7–8.

Ansel Adams, *Tenaya Creek, Dogwood, Rain, Yosemite National Park,* 1948

Afterword:
The Garden's Prospects in America

❧❧

Michael Pollan

WHAT CAN YOU SAY about a country whose two most important contributions to the history of landscape consist of the front lawn and the wilderness park? One safe conclusion would be that this is a culture whose thinking on the subject of nature is somewhat schizophrenic—that it is unsure whether it wants to dominate nature in the name of civilization or to worship it, untouched, as a means of escape from civilization. It has been more than a century now since the invention of the front lawn and the wilderness park (both, interestingly, date from the same period: the decade following the Civil War), yet these two very different and equally original institutions continue to shape and reflect American thinking about nature—and, in turn, our attitudes toward the idea of a garden.

It might be possible to stretch and twist the definition of a garden in such a way as to encompass a place like Yosemite or an American lawn, but it is doubtful how much force or precision the concept would still retain. I would argue that both the American front lawn and the wilderness park, as brilliant in their ways as these two creations are, represent the antitheses of gardens, and their hold on our imaginations and yards has done much to retard the development of the American garden. Its prospects cannot be considered without reference to their own.

As the improbable coexistence of two such different landscape ideals suggests, we seem to have acquired a habit of regarding nature and culture as distant, even antagonistic, terms. It is one of the unexamined assumptions of the American mind that nature and culture are engaged in a kind of zero-sum game, such that the gain of one necessarily entails the loss of the other. Certainly we've made an American landscape that accurately reflects this sort of either/or thinking: some 8 percent of the country's land has been carefully preserved as wilderness, while the remaining 92 percent has been deeded unconditionally to civilization—to the realm of the highway, the commercial strip, suburban development, the parking lot, and, of course, the lawn. The idea of a middle landscape—a place that might partake equally of nature and culture, that might seek to strike some sort of compromise or balance between the two realms—has received short shrift, with the result that, even after some five hundred years, the American garden has yet to come into its own.

This assertion may strike some readers as unfairly dismissive. And surely there are many beautiful gardens in America, as well as a great many Americans who garden well and take garden making seriously. But I don't think anyone would argue that American garden design is on a par with American music or painting or literature or, even now, American cooking. Indeed, even to venture such comparisons would probably strike many Americans as absurd, since we do not generally think of gardening as an art at all. Historically, our motives in the garden have usually been more utilitarian than aesthetic or sensual. As a result, the United States has produced remarkably few landscape architects who can claim an international reputation. In a century in which Americans made large contributions to virtually all the arts, landscape architecture has lagged far behind. Virtually the only American landscape artists with international reputations today are our golf course designers. On the links, it seems, we have made a significant mark, which perhaps makes sense given our long infatuation with lawn. But why isn't there a single American garden designer with the international reputation of a Robert Trent Jones? Or, for that matter, a Roberto Burle Marx?

Whether it is the wilderness ideal or the convention of front lawns that is more to blame is debatable. But the question is worth exploring because the future of the American garden is so closely bound up with it. Certainly from an intellectual standpoint, it is our romance of untouched land that has done the most to keep our gardens from attaining the distinctiveness and status of the other arts in this country.

The problem begins with the transcendentalists, who believed that the American landscape was sacred—nature, Emerson held, was the symbol of Spirit. Once you have come to regard the landscape as a moral or spiritual space, altering it in any way—even gardening it—becomes problematic. This is what Thoreau discovered very soon after he planted his bean field at Walden. He was actually racked with guilt about pulling weeds, of all things, and he failed to see why he had any more right to his beans than the resident woodchucks or moles. Thoreau ends up having to forsake his garden, declaring that he would rather live hard by the most dismal swamp than the most beautiful garden. With that (somewhat obnoxious) declaration, the garden was all but banished from American writing about nature. I think it is fair to say that a culture whose literature takes the moral superiority of wilderness as an article of faith is going to have a hard time making great gardens.

But of course the romance of wilderness was not the only landscape idea to come along in America—if it had been, we'd still be eating bark and living in huts. In general we tend to indulge our worship of wilderness only in books or while on vacation. The rest of the time, we have historically indulged a very different idea about nature—the idea that the land is ours to dominate, whether in the name of God, at the start, or, later, in the name of Progress. This notion, which is rather more evident in the actual American landscape than in our writings about it, does not bode well for the making of gardens, either. It is far more likely to give us parking lots and shopping centers and lawns.

Anyone who has ever mowed a lawn can understand the undeniable pleasure that comes from bringing a heedless landscape under control, however temporarily. But this is not quite the same thing as gardening, except perhaps in America. For when we hear that gardening is the "number one leisure activity" in this country—that some ninety million Americans consider themselves gardeners, according to *Time* magazine—the statistics have made room for all those people for whom "gardening" is limited to the pushing or driving of an internal combustion engine over a monoculture of imported grass species.

It is too simple to reduce the ideology of lawns to the drive to dominate nature, though certainly that is one element of it. The love of closely cropped grass may well be universal, as Thorstein Veblen speculated in *The Theory of the Leisure Class*; it is a reminder of our pastoral roots, and perhaps also of our evolutionary origins on the grassy savannas of East Africa. America's unique contribution to humankind's ancient love of grass has been, specifically, the large, unfenced patches of lawn *in front of* our houses—the decidedly odd custom "of uniting the front lawns of however many houses there may be on both sides of a street to present an untroubled aspect of expansive green to the passerby." This definition of the American front lawn was set forth by Ann Leighton, who concluded after a career studying the history of American gardens that the front lawn was our principal contribution to world garden design. It is one contribution that this American, at least, is not particularly proud of.

The aspirations behind the front lawn are not the problem. On paper at least, the front lawn is an admirable institution, a noble statement of our sense of community and equality. With our open-faced front lawns we declare our like-mindedness to our neighbors. In fact lawns are one of the minor institutions of democracy, symbolizing as they do the common landscape in which we all take part. And since there are no fences around the American lawn (for we have traditionally looked on these as feudal, old-world, exclusive, selfish, and antidemocratic), upkeep becomes nothing less than a civic obligation. Indeed, the failure to maintain one's portion of the national lawn (for that is what it is, every single lawn in American being contiguous with every other) is in many communities punishable by fine.

Our lawns exist to unite us. It makes sense that in a country whose people are unified by no single race, religion or ethnic background the land itself —our one true common denominator—should emerge as a crucial vehicle of consensus. So across a continent of almost unimaginable geographic variety, from the glacial terrain of Maine to the desert of California, we have laid down a single green carpet of lawn.

A noble project, to be sure, but one that is ultimately at cross purposes with the idea of a garden. In practical terms, the custom of the front lawn has done even more than the wilderness ideal to retard the development of gardening in America. (That is probably because we have no trouble ignoring the wilderness ideal whenever it suits us; ignoring the convention of the front lawn is much harder to do, as anyone who has neglected to mow his lawn for a few weeks well knows.) In fact, it is doubtful that the promise of the American garden will ever be realized as long as the lawn continues to rule our yards and minds. The future of the American garden and the future of the American lawn are inextricably bound up with one another; a lively future for the former hinges on the decline of the latter.

It's important to note that it is not lawns, per se, that are inimical to gardens; indeed, some patch of grass is essential to many kinds of gardens—the English landscape garden is inconceivable without great passages of lawn. The problem is specifically the unfenced front lawn, and that problem has both practical and theoretical dimensions:

1. By ceding our front yards to lawn, we immediately sacrifice the greater part (and, often, the best part) of the acreage available to our gardens. It is as though this space has been condemned by eminent domain, handed over to the community. (A few years ago, a writer for *Landscape* magazine polled a group of California homeowners and found that most thought of their front yards as "belonging" to the community, their backyards to themselves.)

2. Because the front lawn convention calls for the elimination of fences, we have rendered our land unfit for anything but exhibition; our front yards are simply too public a place to spend time in. As a rule, Americans don't venture into their front yards except for the purpose of maintenance. As the American landscape designer Grace Tabor noted in the 1920s, our lawns are designed "for the admiration of the street." For most of history, gardens have been thought of as enclosed places—the notion is embedded in the word's etymology. And though there have certainly been great unenclosed gardens (think of Le Nôtre's, or those of the English landscape school), these have invariably been so vast in scale that privacy was not an issue. Our lawns descend from the English Picturesque, in which the establishment of unimpeded views takes precedence over the creation of habitable space. But on the small scale of a suburban development, you cannot have a "prospect" without destroying the idea of habitable individual spaces—of meaningful gardens. The most beautiful of suburban developments is a garden only from the perspective of the motorist.

3. The very idea of lawn shreds the fundamental principle of gardening as expressed by Alexander Pope: "Consult the genius of the place in all." (The idea is hardly Pope's alone: Virgil said the same thing, as does the *Sukuteiki*, an eleventh-century Japanese manual of garden design.) The lawn is imposed on the American landscape with no regard for local geography or climate or history. No true gardener, consulting the genius of the Nevada landscape, or the Florida landscape, or the Kansas landscape, would ever in a million years propose putting in a lawn in any of these places—and yet there and there and there lawns are found. If gardening is a process of give and take between the gardener and a piece of land, putting in a lawn represents instead a process of conquest and obliteration, an imposition—except in a few places—of an alien idea and even a set of alien species (for the grasses in our lawns are all imported).

4. The culture of the lawn discourages the very habits of mind needed to make good gardens: besides a sensitivity to site and willingness to compromise with nature, the gardener needs to be able to approach his or her land not as a vehicle of social consensus but as an arena for self-expression.

For all these reasons, it will probably take a declaration of independence from the American Lawn before the American Garden can be fully realized.

THE FRONT LAWN and the wilderness ideal still divide and rule the American landscape and probably neither will readily be overthrown. But there do seem to be important changes taking place in our attitudes toward nature and, looked at from one perspective at least, these give some reasons for optimism. One of the few things we can say with any certainty about the next five hundred years of American landscape history is that they will be shaped by a much more acute environmental consciousness—the pressing awareness that nature is in serious trouble, and that it will take our active intervention to save it. (The reason we can be reasonably certain about this prediction is very simple: if a heightened sense of environmental concern does not come to pass, there probably will not *be* another five hundred years of human history.) How will the American garden fare in an age dominated by such an awareness? What about the wilderness ideal? And the front lawn?

It might seem axiomatic that the greater our concern for the environment, the greater will be our regard for wilderness. And yet most of us now realize that attention to wilderness no longer constitutes a sufficient response to the crisis of the environment. True, there are now radical environmentalists who believe our salvation lies in redrawing the borders between nature and culture—in blowing up dams and power lines so that the realm of wilderness might expand by so many acres and the realm of lawn shrink. But an environmentalism dominated by love of wilderness has been around since the time of John Muir, and while it has done much to help protect the sacred 8 percent of the American landscape, it has done little to help us manage with any sanity the remaining 92 percent, where most of us spend most of our time.

We need to continue to defend wilderness—that goes without saying—yet adding to the wilderness is not going to solve our problems. And, even more important, neither will an environmental ethic based on the ideal of wilderness—which is in fact the only one we've ever had in this country. About any particular piece of land, the wilderness ethic says leave it alone; do nothing; nature knows best. That's fine in some places, but the wilderness ethic has nothing to say about those places we cannot help but alter, those that it is no longer possible to "give back to nature"—and today that is *most* places. It is too late to follow Thoreau back into the woods. There are simply too many of us and not enough woods.

And yet if we can no longer hope to find salvation in wilderness, we are also gradually waking up to the fact that the lawn—as a landscape practice as well as a synecdoche for a whole approach to nature—may be insupportable in an age of environmental concern. Remarkably, the lawn itself has emerged as an environmental issue in recent years. More and more Americans are asking whether the price of a perfect lawn—in terms of pesticide, water, and energy use—can be justified any longer. Congress is for the first time considering regulating the lawn-care industry. Municipal lawn-mowing ordinances have come under legal challenge in many places.

The lawn may well not survive a long period of environmental activism—and no other single development would do more for the American garden. For as soon as someone decides to rip out a lawn, he or she becomes, perforce, a gardener, someone who must ask the gardener's questions: What is right for this place? What do I want here? How can I go about creating a pleasing outdoor space on this site? How can I use nature here without abusing it?

The answers to these questions will probably be as different as the people posing them and the places where they are posed. For as soon as homeowners start thinking like gardeners, they start coming up with individual and local answers. In all likelihood, the landscape of post-lawn America would not have a single national style—if only because we are too heterogeneous a people, and our geography and climate are too various, to support a single national garden idea. That, after all, was the lesson of the American lawn—imposing the same front yard in Tampa and Bangor and Omaha and Santa Rosa exacts too steep an environmental price. There will undoubtedly be places where lawns will survive (the genius of the cool, damp Northwest may well accommodate them), but the American front yard will be an entirely different affair in Marin County and Westchester County, in Charleston and Fort Worth. Some people may judge this a loss, to give up the idea of a single national landscape style. But while the value of unifying national institutions is undeniable, nature is not the right place to try to establish them. Whatever one thinks about multiculturalism, multi*horti*culturalism is probably an environmental necessity.

But even if an age of environmentalism doesn't attack the lawn head-on, it would still bode well for the garden in America. The decline of the lawn may turn out to be gradual and piecemeal and even inadvertent, as the garden gradually expands into its realm, a square foot at a time. For a family thinking environmentally will find many reasons to garden. At the most basic level, growing one's own food is the only way to assure its purity. Composting, which should be numbered among the acts of gardening, is an easy way to lighten a household's burden on the local landfill. Any garden has the potential to lessen our dependence on distant sources not only of food, but also of energy, technology, and even entertainment. If Americans still require a moral and utilitarian reason before they feel justified putting hoe to ground, the next several years are certain to supply plenty of unassailable, even righteous, ones.

So I am optimistic about the American garden—or at least about the proliferation of gardens in America. As the environment takes its necessary and inevitable place in our attention, the reasons to garden will become more and more compelling—and the reasons to maintain lawns progressively less so. Whether there will be a flowering of distinctive, beautiful gardens in America is another question, but here too there is a reason to be optimistic, one that may seem at first off the point: Almost overnight, Americans have invented a distinctive and impressive cuisine. It was only a few years ago that American

cooking was no better than Britain's or Germany's—heavy, unimaginative, relentlessly utilitarian. Our culinary revolution suggests that an area of culture formerly ignored or disdained may suddenly become the beneficiary of the sort of sustained attention and support that makes genuine, original achievement possible. Still more encouraging, though, is the fact that the preconditions for a brilliant cuisine and a brilliant garden are so similar: both to be successful require the artful intermingling of nature and culture. "Cookery," the poet Frederick Turner has written, "transforms raw nature into the substance of human communion, routinely and without fuss transubstantiating matter into mind." Can't we say much the same thing about gardening? Perhaps the Puritan American opposition of nature and culture is at last relaxing its hold on us. If we are finally willing to sanction the mingling of these long-warring terms on our dinner plates, then why not also in our yards?

That would be good news for the quality of our gardens, and also, in turn, for the quality of our thinking about the environment. For if environmentalism is likely to be a boon to the American garden, gardening could turn out to be a boon to environmentalism, which, as I've tried to suggest, stands in need of some fresh ways of thinking about nature. The garden is as good a place to look as any. Gardens by themselves obviously cannot right our relationship to nature, but the habits of thought they foster can take us a long way in that direction—and can even suggest the lineaments of a new environmental ethic that might help us out in all those situations where the wilderness ethic is silent or unhelpful. Gardening tutors us in nature's ways, fostering an ethic of give and take with respect to the land. Gardens instruct us in the particularities of place. Gardens also teach the necessary if still rather un-American lesson that nature and culture can be compromised, that we might be able to find some middle ground between the wilderness and the lawn. That, finally, is the best reason to be optimistic about the garden's prospects in America: we need the garden—and the garden's ethic—too much today for it *not* to flourish. ✜

General Bibliography

Although you may cull from the bibliographies for the various chapters books and periodicals that address specific interests, the following are recommended as representative of the writings on the history of gardening, landscape design, and horticulture in America. Some also appear in the contributors' individual bibliographies and some will be new.

Alcosser, Murray. *America in Bloom: Gardens Open to the Public*. New York: Rizzoli, 1991.

Favretti, Rudy J., and Gordon P. De Wolf. *Colonial Gardens*. Barre, Mass.: Barre Publishers, 1972.

Fogle, David P., Catherine Mahan, and Christopher Weeks. *Clues to American Garden Styles*. Washington, D.C.: Starrhill Press, 1987.

Haley, Jacquetta, M., ed. *Pleasure Grounds: Andrew Jackson Downing and Montgomery Place*. Tarrytown, N.Y.: Sleepy Hollow, 1988.

Hedrick, U. P. *A History of Horticulture in America to 1860*, "With an Addendum of Books Published from 1861–1920," by Elisabeth Woodburn. Portland, Oreg.: Timber Press, 1988.

Lacy, Allen, ed. *The American Gardener: A Sampler*. New York: Farrar, Straus, Giroux, 1988.

Leighton, Ann. *Early American Gardens: "For Meate or Medicine."* Amherst: University of Massachusetts Press, 1986.

———. *American Gardens of the Eighteenth Century: "For Use or For Delight."* Amherst: University of Massachusetts Press, 1986.

———. *American Gardens of the Nineteenth Century: "For Comfort and Affluence."* Amherst: University of Massachusetts Press, 1987.

Lockwood, Alice G. B., ed. *Gardens of Colony and State: Gardens and Gardeners of the American Colonies and of the Republic Before 1840*. New York: Scribner, 1931–1934.

Loewer, Peter. *American Gardens: A Tour of the Nation's Finest Private Gardens*. New York: Simon & Schuster, 1988.

Martin, Tovah. *Once Upon a Windowsill: A History of Indoor Plants*. Portland, Oreg.: Timber Press, 1988.

McGuire, Diane Kostial. *Gardens of America: Three Centuries of Design*. Charlottesville, Va.: Thomasson-Grant, 1989.

Newcomb, Peggy Cornett. *Popular Annuals of Eastern North America, 1865–1914*. Washington, D.C.: Dumbarton Oaks, 1985.

Tanner, Ogden. *Gardening America: Regional and Historical Influences in the Contemporary Garden*. New York: Viking Penguin, 1990.

Tice, Patricia M. *Gardening in America, 1830–1910*. Rochester, N.Y.: Strong Museum, 1984.

Tishler, William H., ed. *American Landscape Architecture: Designers and Places*. Washington, D.C.: Preservation Press, 1988.

Van Ravenswaay, Charles. *A Nineteenth-Century Garden*. New York: Universe Books, 1977.

For Further Information

The organizations listed below are devoted solely or in part to landscape preservation or historic horticulture.

Alliance for Historic Landscape Preservation
82 Wall Street, Suite 1105
New York, NY 10005

America the Beautiful Fund
219 Shoreham Building
Washington, DC 20005

American Association of Botanical Gardens
and Arboreta
786 Church Road
Wayne, PA 19087

American Horticultural Society
7931 E. Boulevard Drive
Alexandria, VA 22308

American Society of Landscape Architects
Historic Preservation Open Committee
4401 Connecticut Avenue
Washington, DC 20008

Association for Living Historical Farms
and Agricultural Museums
Smithsonian Institution
Washington, DC 20560

Council on Botanical and Horticultural Libraries
New York Botanical Garden
Bronx, NY 10458

Forest History Society
701 Vickers Avenue
Durham, NC 27701

Garden Club of America
518 Madison Avenue
New York, NY 10022

The Garden Conservancy
P.O. Box 219
Cold Spring, NY 10516

Massachusetts Horticultural Society
300 Massachusetts Avenue
Boston, MA 02115

National Association for Olmsted Parks
175 Fifth Avenue
New York, NY 10010

National Council of State Garden Clubs
401 Magnolia Avenue
St. Louis, MO 63110

National Parks and Conservation Association
1701 18th Street, NW
Washington, DC 20009

National Trust for Historic Preservation
1785 Massachusetts Avenue
Washington, DC 20036

New England Garden History Society
Massachusetts Horticultural Society
300 Massachusetts Avenue
Boston, MA 02115

Pennsylvania Horticultural Society
325 Walnut Street
Philadelphia, PA 19106

Southern Garden History Society
Old Salem, Inc.
Box F Salem Station
Winston-Salem, NC 27101

About the Contributors

WILLIAM HOWARD ADAMS is a noted garden historian with many books to his credit, including *The French Garden 1500–1800*, *Jefferson's Monticello* and, most recently, *Nature Perfected: Gardens Through History*. His instigation and curatorship of "Roberto Burle Marx: The Unnatural Art of the Garden," in 1991, marked the first time in its history that New York's Museum of Modern Art presented a solo exhibition devoted to the work of a landscape architect.

PHYLLIS ANDERSEN is a landscape design consultant specializing in urban issues. She teaches at the Radcliffe Seminars in Landscape Design and at Yale and has published several guides to urban plants. She is a past president of the Massachusetts Horticultural Society.

Along with being Publisher of the American Botanist Press, D. KEITH CROTZ is an antiquarian bookseller who specializes in books on horticulture and American agriculture. He is the author of a number of articles on historic agriculture and gardening.

RICHARD H. DALEY is Executive Director of the Denver Botanic Gardens and former Executive Director of the Massachusetts Horticultural Society. He also held administrative positions at the Missouri Botanic Garden for several years, and is the author of

many books and articles on botany and management.

Formerly Head Horticulturist at Boston's Arnold Arboretum, DR. GORDON DE WOLF was also series editor for the Taylor Guides to plants and gardening, three of which he authored. In addition, he has written a number of books on horticulture and botany and is a consultant to *Horticulture* magazine.

MAC GRISWOLD is the author of *Pleasures of the Garden: Images from the Metropolitan Museum of Art* and, with Eleanor Weller, *The Golden Age of American Gardens: Proud Owners, Private Estates 1890–1940*. She is a frequent contributor to *HG* and has written for other publications such as the *New York Times*, *Hortus*, *Southern Accents*, and *Garden Design*. She lectures on gardens and garden history in the United States and England.

University of Georgia Professor of Landscape Architecture CATHERINE M. HOWETT is a historian with a specialization in nineteenth- and twentieth-century landscape architecture in America. She has added many valuable contributions to the study of garden history and the meaning of gardens through articles she has written and books to which she has contributed, which include *The Meaning of Gardens: Idea, Place and Action* and *The Architecture of Western Gardens: A Design History from the Renaissance to the Present Day*.

TOVAH MARTIN is a well-known writer on indoor gardening. Drawing on her extensive experience at Logee's Greenhouses in Connecticut, she has written many articles and books, including *Once Upon a Windowsill: A History of Indoor Plants* and, most recently, *The Essence of Paradise: Fragrant Plants for Indoor Gardens*.

A landscape architect and garden historian, DIANE KOSTIAL McGUIRE is a founder of the Radcliffe Seminars in Landscape Design, for which she continues to teach. She has held fellowships at the Bunting Institute at Radcliffe and at Dumbarton Oaks. Her most recent book is *Gardens of America: Three Centuries of Design*.

KEITH N. MORGAN is Chairman of the Department of Art History at Boston University. His area of specialization, the architecture and landscape architecture of the nineteenth and early twentieth centuries, resulted in his book *Charles A. Platt: The Artist as Architect*. His most recent book, co-written with Naomi Miller, is *Boston Architecture, 1975–1990*.

PEGGY CORNETT NEWCOMB, Assistant Director of Gardens and Grounds at Monticello, has made the history of plants her specialty. She is the author of *Popular Annuals of North America, 1865–1914* as well as many articles on historic plants and gardens.

Author of *Second Nature: A Gardener's Education*, MICHAEL POLLAN has distinguished himself as an outspoken advocate of environmentally conscientious gardening practices. He is the Executive Editor of *Harper's* magazine and author of several articles on gardening and other subjects.

Head Librarian of the Massachusetts Horticultural Society and General Editor of *Keeping Eden*, WALTER T. PUNCH is also on the faculty of the Radcliffe Seminars in Landscape Design. He is the founder of the New England Garden History Society and is editor of the Bibliography Series for the Council on Botanical and Horticultural Libraries. Currently he is editing a reference companion to American gardens and writing a history of horticulture.

MELANIE L. SIMO, author of *Loudon and the Landscape*, has published essays on the work of such seminal twentieth-century landscape architects as Garrett Eckbo, Dan Kiley, Hideo Sasaki, and Peter Walker. She is currently collaborating with Walker in writing a book on twentieth-century landscape architecture, particularly from the period after World War II.

DAVID C. STREATFIELD is Professor of Landscape Architecture at the University of Washington at Seattle, where he specializes in the history of garden design in California. He is the author of several articles on garden design history.

Author of *Cultivating Gentlemen: The Meaning of Country Life Among the Boston Elite, 1785–1860*, TAMARA PLAKINS THORNTON is Professor of History at the State University of New York at Fredonia. Her interest in the intersections between social history and garden history is also attested to by her frequent articles.

ELISABETH WOODBURN was recognized as doyenne of antiquarian book collectors before her death in 1990. She was a founding member of the Antiquarian Booksellers Association of America and the Council on Botanical and Horticultural Libraries. Her writings include the important "Addendum" to U. P. Hedrick's seminal *History of Horticulture in America to 1860* as well as several articles on horticultural history and rare books.

Acknowledgments

Many people have added to this book and it is truly the work of many hands. Betty Childs, former Senior Editor at Bulfinch Press, and Rick Daley, former Executive Director of the Massachusetts Horticultural Society, were the first people with whom I discussed this idea and both have been supportive of it over the many months it evolved. Betty got things going at Bulfinch and continued, even after retirement, to make suggestions and offer guidance and always good practical advice culled from her many years in publishing. Rick was generous in his support while the book was being done in and around the duties I perform at the Massachusetts Horticultural Society and had the insight to encourage such an undertaking. Brian Hotchkiss, who became Senior Editor upon the retirement of Betty Childs, has worked with me on much of the book. In fact it must be said that he is a partner in this project. His help, patience and understanding have been paramount in putting this book together.

For her work in gathering, organizing and maintaining a web of documents I must thank Ann Wierda of Bulfinch Press. She has been consistently helpful and has made all the transitions smooth. Tina Schwinder, Picture Editor on this project, has been a bastion of efficiency and a resource in herself and the book owes much to her. Susan Marsh, the book's designer, has quietly made a lot of words and images into a work of beauty and joy that reflects the essence of garden history. Finally, Betty Power's tireless and careful copyediting was invaluable.

My colleagues at the Massachusetts Horticultural Society have been only supportive of this work and their support and enthusiastic interest in it is much appreciated. I am especially grateful to Catherine Montagne of the Education Department for active support and to my former assistant Hugh Wilburn, now of the Loeb Library of the Harvard Graduate School of Design, who stepped into the breach more often than can be mentioned. In addition, it goes without saying that many people at various other garden-oriented organizations gave me great assistance. While they are too numerous to name individually, I do thank them all.

I should like to say a word of thanks to my mother, who was ever supportive and proud and to a wonderful little girl, Devon Elizabeth Punch, who had to do without many hours of avuncular play so that this book could be finished. I dedicate my own small part in this book to them.

Finally I must thank my co-contributors for their efforts in sharing their knowledge and time. All of them are enormously busy people and worked hard on their chapters for less than princely recompense. They gave much of themselves to this work because they believed in its importance and what it will, we all hope, inspire in others to investigate and celebrate.

WALTER T. PUNCH

Index

Picture Credits

Page ii, viii: © Richard W. Brown

P. x: reproduced courtesy the Trustees of the British Museum

P. 12: courtesy James River Garden Club

P. 15: © Mick Hales

Pp. 16, 17: courtesy James River Garden Club

P. 18: © Ron Colbroth

P. 20, 23: courtesy James River Garden Club

P. 24: © Robert Llewellyn

P. 27: © Hickey-Robertson

P. 35: Maurice Prendergast, *Central Park, 1900*. Watercolor on paper, 14⅜ × 21½ inches (36.5 × 54.6 cm). Collection of Whitney Museum of American Art, New York, purchase 32.41

P. 39: from *An Island Garden*, by Celia Thaxter. Houghton Mifflin, Boston, 1894, reprinted 1988

Pp. 40, 41: courtesy National Park Service, Frederick Law Olmsted National Historic Site

Pp. 44, 46, 47: © Melanie Simo

P. 48 (top): © Robert Fine

P. 49: © The Frank Lloyd Wright Foundation, 1963

P. 50: *American Landscape Architect*, courtesy Christopher Vernon

P. 51: courtesy Freer Gallery of Art, Smithsonian Institution, Washington, D.C., 17.182 American painting; by John Singer Sargent (1856–1925), *Breakfast in the Loggia*; oil on canvas: 51.5 × 71.0 cm

P. 53: © Melanie Simo

P. 56: © Filoli Center, "The Darkroom"

Pp. 57, 58 (top): courtesy Garrett Eckbo

P. 58 (bottom): © Melanie Simo

P. 59: © Melanie Simo

P. 62: © Kevin Schafer / Martha Hill

P. 66: courtesy Natalie P. Davenport

P. 67: College of Environmental Design Documents Collection, University of California, Berkeley

P. 68: courtesy Biltmore Estate, Asheville, N.C.

P. 69: © Richard Cheek for Old Westbury Inc.

P. 70: © John Neubauer

P. 71: © Richard W. Brown

P. 73: © Everett Scott

P. 75: © University Art Museum, Architectural Drawing Collection, University of California, Santa Barbara

P. 76: © Harold Corsini, Western Pennsylvania Conservancy

P. 77: © Julius Shulman

P. 80: The Gibbes Museum of Art / Carolina Art Association

P. 83: © Catherine Howett

P. 84: © David King Gleason

P. 85: The Gibbes Museum of Art / Carolina Art Association

P. 86: photograph by Van Jones Martin from *Gardens of Georgia*, page 14, co-published by The Garden Club of Georgia, Inc., and Peachtree Publishers, Atlanta, Georgia; reprinted with permission

P. 87: Southern Historical Collection, University of North Carolina at Chapel Hill

P. 89: Belmont Mansion Association

P. 90: Bellingrath Gardens and Home

P. 92: McClung Historical Collection

P. 93: © Michael Carlebach

P. 96: © Charles Mann

P. 99: courtesy Charles Francis Saunders

P. 101 (top): American Friends of the Canadian Centre for Architecture, New York; Collection Centre Canadien d'Architecture / Canadian Centre for Architecture, Montreal; (bottom): courtesy Special Collections Department, Stanford University Libraries

Pp. 102, 104, 105, 106: © David Streatfield

P. 107: © Saxon Holt

Pp. 108, 109: © David Streatfield

P. 110: © Saxon Holt

P. 111: courtesy College of Architectural and Urban Planning, University of Washington

P. 113 (top): © David Streatfield

P. 113 (bottom): © Saxon Holt

P. 114: © Charles Mann

P. 121 (top): from *The Book of the Tulip*, by Sir Alfred Daniel Hall. London: M. Hopkinson Ltd., 1929

P. 124: from *Standard Cyclopedia of Horticulture*, by Liberty Hyde Bailey. New York: Macmillan, 1939

P. 127: from *Sweet Peas: Their History, Development, Culture*. Charles Unwin,

W. Heffer, Publishers, Cambridge, England, 1926

P. 129: © Saxon Holt

P. 143: from *The Harvest of the Years*, by Luther Burbank with Wilbur Hall. Houghton Mifflin, Boston, 1927

P. 144: © Dan Guravich

P. 146: © Alex MacLean

Pp. 149, 150, 151: print collection, Miriam and Ira D. Wallach Division of Art, Prints and Photographs, The New York Public Library, Astor, Lenox and Tilden Foundations

P. 153: photograph courtesy Concord Museum, Concord, Mass

P. 154 (top): James Smillie, *Union Park, 1849*; Lithographers: Sarony and Major; Museum of the City of New York, 29.100.2097; The J. Clarence Davies Collection; (bottom): The Historic New Orleans Collection, Museum/Research Center, Acc. No. 1979.61.7

P. 156: Chicago Historical Society, neg no. DN 8220

P. 158: courtesy National Park Service, Frederick Law Olmsted National Historic Site

P. 159: courtesy Bostonian Society / Old State House

P. 162: © Mick Hales

P. 163: photograph by Southie Burgin; reprinted with permission of the Beacon Hill Garden Club

P. 164: © Felice Frankel

P. 165: © Richard W. Brown

P. 166: Barbara Stauffacher Solomon, *2 Fields + 3 Houses = A Landscape*

P. 169: The Pierpont Morgan Library, New York. MA 3900, f.121

P. 170: *The South Wall Prospect of the Seat of Colonel George Boyd*, anonymous, 1774, oil on canvas. The Lamont Gallery, Phillips Exeter Academy, Exeter, New Hampshire (gift of Thomas W. Lamont, Class of 1888)

P. 171: indefinite loan from The Peabody Institute. Maryland Historical Society

P. 172: Historical Society of Pennsylvania

P. 173: Metropolitan Museum of Art, gift of Edgar William and Bernice Chrysler Garbisch, 1963 (63.201.3)

Library of Congress Cataloging-in-Publication Data

Keeping Eden: a history of gardening in America / Walter T.
Punch, general editor, with essays by Walter T. Punch . . . [et al.].
— 1st ed.
p.   cm.
Includes bibliographical references and index.
ISBN 0-8212-1818-2
1. Gardening—United States—History.   2. Gardens—United States—
History.   3. Gardening—United States—History—Pictorial works.
4. Gardens—United States—History—Pictorial works.   I. Punch,
Walter T., 1947–
SB451.3.K44   1992
635'.0973—dc20   91-16495

DESIGNED BY SUSAN MARSH

COMPOSITION BY DEKR CORPORATION IN GARAMOND OLD STYLE

PRINTED AND BOUND BY TIEN WAH PRESS